T0319420

THE MOSCOW BUSINESS ELITE: A SOCIAL AND CULTURAL PORTRAIT OF TWO GENERATIONS, 1840–1905

THE MOSCOW BUSINESS ELITE: A SOCIAL AND CULTURAL PORTRAIT OF TWO GENERATIONS, 1840–1905

JO ANN RUCKMAN

NORTHERN ILLINOIS UNIVERSITY PRESS • 1984

Library of Congress Cataloging in Publication Data

Ruckman, Jo Ann, 1938–
  The Moscow business elite.
Bibliography: p.
  Includes index.
    1. Merchants–Russian S.F.S.R.–Moscow–History–
19th century.   2. Businessmen–Russian S.F.S.R.–Moscow
–History–19th century.   3. Elite (Social Sciences)–
Russian S.F.S.R.–Moscow–History–19th century.
4. Moscow (R.S.F.S.R.)–Social conditions.   I. Title.
HF3624,5.R83   1984   305.5'54   83-23732
ISBN 0–87580–096–3

Design by Joan Westerdale

TO MY PARENTS
FRANCES N. SCHRAMPFER
WILLIAM H. SCHRAMPFER

CONTENTS

PREFACE

THE purpose of this study is to present a social and cultural profile of one section of the Russian business community focusing on the 1890s and the early years of the twentieth century. Russian businessmen constituted a singularly interesting and not unimportant group in the social, economic, and even political life of Imperial Russia, yet they have until recently attracted little attention from historians. They have suffered from the neglect that befalls many of history's "losers," a neglect much intensified in their case by the general hostility of educated Russian society toward them before 1917, by the total victory of their sworn enemies in 1917, and by their complete annihilation as a social group after 1917. Only in recent years have Soviet historians sought to continue the investigation of the Russian "bourgeoisie" begun by P. A. Berlin with the publication of his *Russkaia burzhuaziia v staroe i novoe vremia* in 1922. At the same time, a number of American and European students of Russian history have begun to take an interest in Imperial Russia's business community, and much valuable work has been done in the past decade. Nonetheless, much further research remains to be done before we will be in a position to draw a complete picture of the Russian businessman and his activities.

The present study attempts, entirely on the basis of published sources, to describe one particular section of the Russian business community at one particular point in time. Attention is given to several different aspects of the Moscow business elite, that small group of business families, or "dynasties," which constituted the upper stratum of the Moscow *kupechestvo* (merchantry). The introduction considers the general climate of opinion within which Russian businessmen, including those of Moscow, were forced to live and work, while the first chapter defines the membership of the elite and clarifies the position of that group, and the position of the *kupechestvo* as a whole, within the social structure of Imperial Russia. The second chapter, a brief summary of the economic status and business activities of the leading Moscow business families, presents a general indication of the economic foundations of the Moscow elite. In the following chapters, attention is directed toward the fields outside business in which these families excelled: philanthropy, patronage, collecting, the arts and sciences, public affairs, and leadership of the business community, particularly in its relations with the tsarist government. My point of view throughout is that of the social historian, interested in investigating the inner life and development of a particular social group and its interaction with other social groups and with the state.

Within the Moscow business elite in the 1890s, a clearly recognizable line of demarcation existed between the two generations that in this period represented the city's leading business families. The above-mentioned topics are therefore approached in terms of a generational dichotomy, contrasting the activities and attitudes of the two age groups. The contrast between the two generations rested primarily on their vastly different education and upbringing and was a measure of both the great cultural progress made by the Moscow *kupechestvo* during the course of the nineteenth century and of changes occurring in Russian society as a whole. Generally speaking, the older generation, born in the 1830s, 1840s, and 1850s, included the individuals who had established the reputation of their families not only through successful business activity but through philanthropy, patronage of the arts and sciences, creation of artistic or scientific collections, and participation in public affairs. In most cases, members of the younger generation, born in the 1860s, 1870s, and 1880s, inherited from their elders a secure position at the top of the business world's social hierarchy. Not unexpectedly, this younger generation tended to strike off in new directions. While frequently continuing the philanthropy, patronage, and public activity so typical of their fathers, as well as their contributions to business, the younger generation gave a new tone to all these activities and, above all, showed a greater interest in the display of their own unique talents and abilities. While the older generation helped and patronized others and tended to play a passive role in public affairs, leaving the initiative to better-qualified members of the bureaucracy, the nobility, and the intelligentsia, the members of the younger generation were more interested in developing their own talents, not the talents of others, and were prepared to take a much more active and independent role in public life.

In order to give a many-sided picture of these two generations of the Moscow business elite, I have kept the structure and organization of this book loose and flexible, and the chronological boundaries of the study are also deliberately fluid. While concentrating on the Moscow elite in the

1890s and early 1900s, up to and including 1905, I have attempted also to give some indication of the previous historical evolution of the Moscow *kupechestvo*, particularly of those historical events in the life of the Moscow business community that had an important influence in shaping the older generation of the 1890s. Consideration of the nature of the Moscow business community in earlier times helps to bring out in clear relief the areas in which the younger generation of the 1890s strongly resembled their predecessors, while at the same time indicating the innumerable ways in which this generation departed from the traditions of their forefathers and attempted to turn the Russian *kupechestvo* onto a new path.

A brief note on Russian terms is essential here, since I have retained a number of Russian terms throughout the text in preference to seeking what could be only rough English equivalents. Words influence our perceptions, and the use of Russian terms often seems to me to bring us at least a hair's breadth closer to the Russian realities that those words attempt to convey. Thus, I prefer *soslovie* to the only available English renderings, "estate" or "order." As Chapter 1 explains, Russian *sosloviia* (plural of *soslovie*) differed in some substantial respects from the social orders or estates of Western societies. Similarly, the usual translation of the Russian term *kupechestvo* as "merchantry" (*kupets* and *kuptsy* as merchant and merchants) can be misleading. As will become apparent, the Russian *kupechestvo* comprised a wide variety of both merchants and industrialists, as well as financiers. Common usage of the term *kupechestvo* changed during the course of the nineteenth century, accommodating itself to changing social and economic realities. In the earlier part of the century, *kupechestvo* connoted a caste-like group that was indeed composed largely of merchants, in a literal sense (accordingly, I have had no qualms about using the term "merchants" in speaking of the businessmen of the early nineteenth century). But in the later decades of the century, *kupechestvo* was used to refer to the business community as a whole, substantial businessmen above the level of the *meshchanstvo* who were engaged in a wide variety of business undertakings—and many of whom were not, in legal terms, actually members of the *soslovie* known as the *kupechestvo*. Therefore, the preferable translation, following popular usage in this period, is "business community" or simply "businessmen."

The term *meshchanstvo*, referring to the *soslovie* comprised chiefly of small businessmen of various sorts, is essentially untranslatable. The nearest English equivalent would be "petty bourgeoisie," but since few students of Russian history would argue that a bourgeoisie existed in Russia in the nineteenth century, such a translation would be inappropriate. The usual translation of the Russian term *dvorianstvo* as "nobility" might also be questioned, but by now this has become an accepted convention and so *dvorianstvo* and "nobility" (*dvorianin* and nobleman) are used interchangeably in the text.

Many persons have contributed generously of their time, criticism, and sympathy in the preparation of this book. My major thanks must go to W. Bruce Lincoln of Northern Illinois University; his comments and advice have always been valuable, but his chief virtue as an advisor is his willingness to allow students a considerable freedom and independence in the pursuit of their own interests. Also deserving of special mention are Albert Resis, whose close reading and critical insights have proved to be extremely helpful, and Elaine Glovka Spencer, who did much to develop my blossoming interest in social history and who encouraged me in the preparation of this book, not only by her specific advice but by sharing my interest in businessmen. I would also like to take this opportunity to state my gratitude to the late Jacob B. Hoptner, whose wit and sense of humor so often lightened the burdens of graduate study and helped to keep things in a proper perspective, and to J. Patrick White, who smoothed my path in many ways. Leopold H. Haimson, whose guidance during the first stage of my graduate career was invaluable, has also come to my rescue in the preparation of this book; his advice has helped to strengthen it considerably.

My work on this book was largely completed before the publication of two recent works also dealing with Russian businessmen, Thomas C. Owen's *Capitalism and Politics in Russia* and Alfred J. Rieber's *Merchants and Entrepreneurs in Imperial Russia*. I have been able to consult their books only in doing the last-minute revisions on my manuscript, but I owe a debt of gratitude to both of these scholars: to Professor Owen for his comments and criticisms and to Professor Rieber for kindly allowing me to see his work while it was still in manuscript form. While there are broad areas of agreement in our respective interpretations of the historical evidence concerning Russian businessmen, there are also some important divergencies which should give rise to fruitful historiographical controversy in the future.

A number of persons who read my manuscript suggested using methods of quantification. To this suggestion, which will no doubt occur to other readers, I can only reply that, in my judgment, the data at my disposal were too incomplete to provide reliable quantitative answers to most of the questions I sought to investigate. Even in the single case where I ventured into a very rudimentary sort of quantification, I felt so little confidence in the completeness and reliability of my data that I relegated it to a footnote and surrounded it with reservations (chap. 2, n. 2).

Northern Illinois University provided the financial assistance that made possible my initial research in Finland and the Soviet Union. A research grant from Idaho State University and a summer research associateship from the Russian and East European Center at the University of Illinois permitted further research in the University of Illinois Library's excellent Slavic collection. A fellowship from the Russian Institute of Columbia University provided me with the time and access to materials necessary in making final revisions.

A very personal word of thanks is due to Peter Machotka and to Betty and Donald Azar, whose moral support, advice, and patience with my absorption in the preparation of this work were freely given and greatly appreciated. I also want to thank Aune Koskenmäki, who contributed in so many ways to the success of my stay in Finland. Finally, no words can express my gratitude to my parents, to whom this work is dedicated and who have been constant pillars of support and understanding.

Jo Ann Ruckman
Pocatello, Idaho
December 1982

INTRODUCTION

IN the last decades of the nineteenth century, the Russian economy entered a period of rapid industrial and commercial development which saw the predominantly agrarian Russian Empire begin to take on the trappings of a modern industrial society. In the years immediately following 1861 this development for the most part had been unplanned and dependent chiefly upon the scattered efforts of private enterprise, but in the 1890s the Russian state, under the forceful leadership of Minister of Finance S. Iu. Witte, undertook a concerted program to encourage industrial expansion. The results were striking, with all statistical evidence indicating that the decade of the 1890s was a period of rapid industrial advance in Russia, only temporarily brought to a halt by the recession beginning in 1899–1900. Between 1893 and 1902 new private investment in industry and transport totalled some four billion rubles. The number of joint-stock companies rose from 648 in 1893 to 1,369 in 1900, and almost two-fifths of the industrial enterprises existing in 1900 had been founded between 1891 and 1900. If one sets total industrial production for 1913 at 100, then in 1892 it stood at 31, and by 1903 had risen to 64.[1]

Much of the advance of these years came in heavy industry and transportation, two fields whose development the government considered of special importance. Between 1889 and 1899 there was an eightfold increase in the capital invested in metallurgical industries, a fivefold increase in the capital of the chemical industry, and more than a threefold increase of capital in mining.[2] Light industry, though it was the recipient of less attention and fewer favors from the government, nonetheless benefited from the generally expansive state of the economy in the 1890s, and production figures rose substantially, if not so dramatically as in the various fields of heavy industry. The production of cotton textile goods nearly doubled during the 1890s, as did capital investment in light industry in general.[3] In Moscow province, one of the major centers of light industry, the number of workers employed in textiles rose between 1890 and 1900 by 19.3 percent (from 140,581 to 167,750), in spite of an 18.5 percent decline (from 671 to 547) in the number of textile enterprises during the same period. The total annual production of textiles in Moscow province increased in value by 43.7 percent during the decade (from 156,639,000 rubles to 225,014,000 rubles).[4]

If the 1890s represented an especially important era in the economic development of Russia, they were also a crucial period in the social and political development of Russia's business community. Although agriculture still reigned as the field of paramount importance in the Russian economy,[5] and the *kupechestvo* still constituted only 1 percent of the population of the Empire,[6] big businessmen (and especially industrialists), basking in the attention now showered upon them by the government and glorying in constantly rising production figures, came to see themselves in a new light and to feel a new sense of self-esteem. Aware of their growing economic weight in the country, they gradually moved toward a realization that their political and social influence was hardly commensurate with their economic importance, and they more and more resented the continuing political and social supremacy of the economically decadent nobility. Experiencing, in addition, increasing impatience over obstacles to further rapid commercial and industrial development which the tsarist bureaucracy either created or failed to remove, businessmen finally began to question their traditional passive acceptance of the status quo, and in 1905 many took up a position in the ranks of the opposition to the autocracy. In the forefront of these important changes within the Russian business community was the business elite of Moscow.

At the end of the nineteenth century, Moscow was perhaps the single most important commercial and industrial center of the Russian Empire. For many centuries of great importance in Russian trade because of its central geographical position, Moscow in more recent times had also become the center of an industrial region concentrating chiefly on light industry, particularly textiles; it was, as well, the railroad hub of the Empire. In 1900, when the total turnover of all industrial enterprises in European Russia was valued at 3,669,000,000 rubles, enterprises located in the Moscow region accounted for 961,000,000 rubles, or approximately 23 percent, of the total. In the textile industry, the enterprises of the Moscow region accounted for 557,000,000 rubles, or almost 58 percent, of the total turnover of 1,001,000,000 rubles. Stimulated by the development of industry and by the new modes of transport and communication, the commerce of the Moscow region underwent a steady expansion. In 1900, trade firms located in the Moscow region handled goods valued at 1,181,000,000 rubles, representing almost 18 percent of the total turnover in trade in all of European Russia. In textiles alone the comparable figure was nearly 30 percent.[7]

The importance of Moscow as a commercial and industrial center was reflected in the special position occupied by Moscow's businessmen within the Russian business community as a whole. Long recognized as the cultural and spiritual "heart" of Russia, Moscow in the nineteenth century had also become the heart of the country's slowly modernizing economy, and Moscow businessmen were regarded by many of their colleagues in the provinces as standing at the head of the diffuse Russian business community. St. Petersburg might indeed have shown signs of overshadowing Moscow in economic significance, but St. Petersburg evoked few stirrings of empathy in the average Russian trader or industrialist. Moscow, the center of light industry, the hub of a vast network of internal trade, the major point of concentration of native Russian capital, never experienced any real challenge from Petersburg for the emotional allegiance of most Russian businessmen. To many of them, Petersburg, with its emphasis on international trade and heavy industry and its considerable foreign investment, was a different and unfamiliar world, not only in the nature of its economic activities but also because it was a bureaucratic center and Russia's "window to the West." In Moscow the provincial businessman felt more at home. Here one could do business with men who understood the Russian market, who showed genuine understanding of the problems and the mores of the provincial *kupets*, and who were, above all, "real Russians."[8]

Thus, Moscow's business leaders came to find themselves at the head of an amorphous grouping which affected the title of the "all-Russian *kupechestvo*." In fact, this grouping was hardly "all-Russian" but consisted chiefly of *kuptsy* who did their business in Moscow and at the Nizhnii Novgorod fair, which in the later nineteenth century was completely dominated by Moscow business interests. The businessmen of Petersburg itself, the mineowners of the Urals, the sugar magnates of southern Russia, the textile industrialists of Lodz, and numerous other businessmen who had few dealings with Moscow did not constitute a part of this self-proclaimed "all-Russian *kupechestvo*," nor did they share its tendency to look to Moscow for leadership. Above all, it was the businessmen of the Central Industrial Region—the heartland of Russian commercial and industrial activity—who found their spokesmen in Moscow, though businessmen from southern and eastern Russia and from Siberia also had, not infrequently, close economic ties with Moscow and followed the leadership of Moscow's business community.[9]

Because of their economic weight and the respect accorded them by other businessmen, Moscow's big business leaders, most of them textile industrialists, frequently served as spokesmen for at least a large section of the Russian business community. The Moscow Exchange Committee, which was in effect the executive committee of Moscow's business elite, gave voice to the views of the city's leading businessmen on all matters relating to trade and industry. The government often sought the advice of businessmen, both by soliciting opinions from the Exchange Committee and by inviting individual representatives of the Moscow business elite to Petersburg for conferences and consultations. If their advice frequently went unheeded, they at least had some opportunity to influence government policies affecting trade and industry.

Because of its position at the heart of the Russian economy and at the head of a considerable section of the Russian business community, Moscow's business elite constitutes a subject requiring investigation by historians interested in the economic and social development of the Russian Empire. As a result of past neglect, we have at the present time only a meager understanding of this important sector of Russia's business community (or, indeed, of the Russian business community as a whole). We know almost nothing about these men who made important economic decisions, concentrated an increasing amount of wealth in their hands, and attempted to influence state policies. The historical literature provides little information about what sort of men they were, about the forces that shaped them, about their achievements and ambitions, about their place in Russian society.

The search for answers to such questions regarding Russian businessmen might well concentrate on any number of particular sectors of the Russian business community, but besides its general economic and political importance, the business elite of Moscow exercises strong fascination for one further reason. Besides giving rise to many of the Empire's most adept and powerful merchants and industrialists, the families who made up the business elite of Moscow produced, first of all, the most outstanding businessmen-politicians to emerge in Russia after 1905. The names of A. I. Guchkov and A. I. Konovalov, both ministers in the Provisional Government of 1917, are familiar to all students of Russian history, though the names of other skillful Moscow businessmen-politicians, such as N. A. Naidenov and P. P. Riabushinskii, are, somewhat undeservedly, less well known. Furthermore, in addition to the outstanding individuals it gave to Russian politics, the Moscow business elite also produced an unusual number of individuals who made major contributions to the development of Russian culture. Again, the names of P. M. Tretiakov, the creator of the famous Gallery of Russian Art, and of K. S. Alekseev-Stanislavsky, the great actor and theatrical director, are known to many. But Tretiakov and Stanislavsky were merely the most outstanding of a very large number of representatives of Moscow's elite business families who performed brilliantly either as philanthropists, patrons, and collectors or as creative individuals in their own right—painters and sculptors, actors and producers, writers and scientists. Any student of this group can hardly fail to be impressed by their generous contributions of time, money, and talent to the development of Russian culture. It would be difficult not to agree with P. A. Buryshkin, himself a marginal member of this elite, when he wrote in his memoirs that it was quite incredible that such a brilliant group of individuals had not yet found their historian.[10]

The student of Moscow's business elite in the later nineteenth and early twentieth centuries is fortunate in having at his disposal a relatively large amount of material compiled by Moscow businessmen themselves. There exists in published form considerably more material dealing with the Moscow business elite than with any other group of the Russian *kupechestvo*. Most of these publications, including in particular memoirs and works combining the history of individual families and their businesses, resulted directly from the efforts of Moscow businessmen to publicize their own activities and to preserve their memories to posterity. In their desire to ensure their own recognition and immortality, they were considerably in advance of their colleagues in other localities, who produced little literature of a comparable nature. Earlier than other Russian businessmen, Moscow's business leaders began to develop real pride in their profession and confidence in their future, a pride and confidence reflected in the publications they sponsored.

This precocious development resulted perhaps in part from the fact that by the end of the nineteenth century trade and industry had long been extremely important components of Moscow life and by the end of the century were beginning to overshadow in importance all other sectors of the city's life. In many provincial towns, by contrast, significant commercial and industrial activity was likely to be of more recent origin and, in any case, frequently remained secondary to agriculture as the town's major economic concern. In St. Petersburg, however important trade and industry were to the life of the city, businessmen were overshadowed by bureaucrats and by the court nobility, and the tone was set by government and court activities. But in Moscow, trade and industry held a more dominant position, and businessmen were better able to hold their own against the less numerous bureaucrats and the economically declining Moscow nobility. Indeed, because of their great significance in the city's life, Moscow businessmen perhaps developed a somewhat exaggerated idea of the importance of their *soslovie* (order or estate), the Russian *kupechestvo*, in the life of the nation as a whole. They occasionally seemed to forget that the Empire remained basically agricultural and that the bureaucracy and the nobility were still the preeminent forces in the life of most of the country.

Another major factor in the early development of a sense of self-esteem among the Moscow business elite was undoubtedly the fact that Moscow's leading business families were relatively old families, with a strong sense of continuity and personal pride in family achievements that in some cases spanned a century. In St. Petersburg and certain other commercial and industrial centers, there were few such business dynasties. Here, impersonal forms of business organization predominated over the family firm that typified Moscow's major enterprises, and the personnel of the business community tended to be fluid and unstable.[11] At the same time, in many other centers of business life, the leading strata of the local *kupechestvo* were composed of families who, had entered upon business activity in their developing communities only recently and who therefore had no strong sense of the past achievements of their *soslovie* and only gradually began to perceive what the future might hold in store for it. The Moscow business elite was perhaps much more aware of how far the *kupechestvo* had come in a century and, as a result, was more convinced of its glorious future.

While Moscow businessmen were becoming increasingly convinced of their own importance, as indicated in their publications, there were evidently few other educated Russians who shared in this conviction. Contemporary Russian journalists, publicists, and scholars continued to ignore businessmen in the present as they had in the past; as a result, outside the works sponsored by Moscow businessmen themselves, contemporary publications offer only meager information on the activities of Moscow's business community—or, indeed, on the activities of the Russian business community as a whole. While contemporary publications gave increasing attention to questions of economic development, their concern was focused on the role played by the state in that development, and they avoided consideration of the role taken by those private individuals who, in the last analysis, bore the major responsibility for the growth of Russian industry and trade. Thus overshadowed by the state, businessmen were neglected as an object of serious study and concern.

As far as Russia's major journals were concerned, it is no exaggeration to say that they completely ignored the economic activities of private entrepreneurs as well as the political and social development of the business community.[12] In the field of scholarship, no serious studies of Russia's business community appeared before 1905. The numerous biographical dictionaries published in the late 1890s and early 1900s tended to slight, if not completely ignore, businessmen. Only five members of the Moscow elite were included in the *Biograficheskii slovar*, and at least four of those earned mention because of their philanthropical and cultural contributions rather than because of their business activities. The country's leading newspapers rarely commented on events within the business world. An economic crisis of major proportions, such as the tariff war with Germany in 1893, might produce a sudden outpouring of articles on Russia's businessmen—articles which are extremely valuable for their indication of public attitudes toward the *kuptsy*. But such crises were infrequent; once they had run their course, the newspapers returned to their habitual silence on the subject of the Russian *kupechestvo*.

In Moscow, the two leading local papers, the conservative *Moskovskie vedomosti* and the liberal *Russkie vedomosti*, gave considerable attention to state economic policies, at the same time ignoring local economic life and businessmen. As early as the 1840s Baron August von Haxthausen, in his *Studies on the Interior of Russia*, had noted that Moscow was losing its former aristocratic character and becoming primarily an industrial and commercial city,[13] but the realization that Moscow, whatever its past traditions, had during the course of the nineteenth century been transformed into a center of trade and industry seemingly escaped the city's leading papers. Anyone reading *Moskovskie vedomosti* and *Russkie vedomosti* in the 1890s and early 1900s would have come away with a very distorted picture of Moscow life, a picture totally devoid of any indication of the commercial and industrial importance of the city or of the increasingly important place in its social structure of the merchant and the industrialist. If a Moscow businessman occupied an important position in some philanthropical or artistic society, or if he left a considerable sum to charity in his will, he might receive fleeting mention on the pages of these newspapers. Otherwise the papers showed no interest in his activities and hardly recognized his existence. Ironically, anyone interested in the nature of Moscow's economic life and its business community could find more information on these subjects in a number of Petersburg papers (especially *Novosti i birzhevye vedomosti* and, to a lesser degree, *Novoe vremia* and *Birzhevye vedomosti*) than in the major Moscow papers, as the Petersburg press generally gave more attention to the business community and its activities. In fact, the *Novosti* feuilletonist N. O. Rakshanin, who wrote under the names of N. Rok and N. Osipov, was probably the most acute outside observer of the Moscow *kupechestvo* to be found in Russia in the 1890s, and his occasional feuilletons constituted a unique exception to the general neglect of the business milieu.

If this neglect stemmed in part from an unspoken assumption that the role of the state in economic development was far more crucial than the role of private businessmen (who, indeed, were sometimes seen simply as executors of the government's will), another and perhaps more fundamental reason for it was the traditional and deep-seated contempt felt at every level of Russian society toward the Russian *kupets*. As Alexander Gerschenkron observed,

> there is no doubt that throughout most of the 19th century a grave opprobrium attached to entrepreneurial activities in Russia. Di-

vorced from the peasantry, the entrepreneur remained despised by the nobility and the intelligentsia. The good life which God intended man to lead implied tilling the land, which belongs to God, and receiving the divine blessings of its fruit. Good life did not mean craving for riches, laying up treasures on earth "where moth and rust doth corrupt." In innumerable adages, fairy tales, and songs, the wisdom of folklore insisted upon the unrighteous origin of wealth. Still entrepreneurial activities went on unchecked.[14]

While the origins of the general contempt felt toward the businessman in Russia related to an earlier period and were undoubtedly complex, there can be no doubt of the existence of a generally negative and hostile attitude toward Russian *kuptsy* in the later nineteenth and early twentieth centuries. Far from unknown among the peasantry, it was perhaps especially strong in those social groups that continued to mold public opinion, namely, the nobility, the intelligentsia, and the higher levels of officialdom. It was the views of these groups that found expression in the press (in Moscow, for instance, *Russkie vedomosti* expressed the viewpoint of the liberal intelligentsia, while *Moskovskie vedomosti* was still oriented toward the nobility), and press comments tended to reflect their hostility toward the Russian *kupechestvo*.

As expressed in newspapers and journals, the hostility and contempt of Russia's socially dominant groups toward the businessman tended to assume the form of two stereotypes, which dominated what little public discussion occurred on the subject of the Russian *kupechestvo*. The older and more enduring of these stereotypes was that of "Kit Kitych," or "Tit Titych," an image of the Russian *kupets* which had been popularized by the comedies of A. N. Ostrovskii.[15] Although it had originated much earlier in the century, the image of Kit Kitych continued to shape public discussion of the *kupechestvo* and was almost inevitably dragged into press comments on Russian businessmen even as late as the early twentieth century.

The most prominent characteristics of this supposedly typical Russian *kupets* were thus familiar to the entire literate Russian public. According to the stereotype, Kit Kitych, as a businessman, was above all dishonest and prepared to employ any sort of trickery in order to turn a profit. His methods of doing business were summed up by the supposed motto of the Russian businessman, "If you don't deceive, you won't sell," a motto exemplified in these instructions which one of Ostrovskii's businessmen was in the habit of giving to his clerks:

> "Now, my boys," I say, "look sharp, now. Maybe there's a chance for a sale; some idiot of a purchaser may turn up, or a colored pattern may catch some young lady's eye, and click!" I say, "you add a ruble or two to the price per yard."

Furthermore, he added,

> "you must measure," I say, "more naturally: pull and stretch
> ju-u-ust enough, God save us, not to tear the cloth: you see," I say,
> "we don't have to wear it afterwards. Well, and if they look the
> other way, nobody's to blame if you should happen to measure one
> yard of cloth twice."[16]

And if he deceived his customers in such a fashion, Kit Kitych was also
famed for his fraudulent bankruptcies, designed to cheat his creditors of
their due. Moreover, Kit Kitych was considered an *arshinnik*, a businessman of extremely narrow horizons who seldom thought beyond the *arshin*
of cloth in his hands at the moment and who was totally incapable of
showing real imagination and initiative in business.

As both businessman and private individual, the stereotypical Kit
Kitych was regarded as a *samodur*, a petty despot who ruthlessly exercised
his modicum of power over his employees, his family, and any other
persons unfortunate enough to fall within his grasp. His tyranny was
combined with ignorance and boorishness, and any attempts on his part,
or on the part of his family, to imitate the cultural attainments of their
betters only made them seem more comical. Thus, the daughter of one of
Ostrovskii's merchants, who regarded herself as a generally superior and
highly cultivated person, evoked this lament from a matchmaker charged
with trying to find her a husband:

> God knows what kind of bringing-up she's had: she walks like an
> elephant crawls on his belly; whether French or the piano, it's a bit
> here and a bit there, and there's nothing to it; and when she starts
> to dance—I have to stuff a handkerchief in my mouth.[17]

Finally, in addition to their other sins, Kit Kitych and his family were
held to be incapable of extending their horizons beyond business and the
family circle and guilty of total lack of concern for their town, their
country, or their fellow citizens.

Even in the 1890s, most journalists who wrote about the Russian businessman referred frequently to Kit Kitych as the prototypical *kupets* and
to Ostrovskii as the still-reigning authority on the manners and mores of
the Russian business community. At the same time, however, a few writers were beginning to express doubt as to whether the image of Kit Kitych
was still widely applicable, and many journalistic observers agreed that
however few or many Kit Kityches still existed in the Russian *kupechestvo*,
the type was destined to future oblivion as the forces of economic and
cultural change increasingly affected the business community.[18] Indeed,
in tacit recognition of the progress of the past half-century, the image of

Kit Kitych now began to be supplemented, though hardly displaced, by a more modern image of the Russian businessman, an image which applied particularly to an increasingly common social phenomenon resulting from Russian economic development—the big industrialist.

According to this later stereotype of the Russian *kupets*, as expounded in the press, the typical Russian businessman was generally shortsighted, unenterprising, incapable of solving his own problems, and accustomed to state intervention to rescue him from any sort of difficulty. If Russia's generally inept businessmen had in the past achieved some modest degree of success, it was only because of considerable measures of support by the government—above all, because of a high protective tariff. In their interminable demands for state assistance, it was said, Russian businessmen were always totally selfish, unable to think in terms of what was good for the economy or the country as a whole, chiefly concerned with maintaining their own ridiculously high level of profits. Because of their shortsightedness, their "egotistical" absorption in the development of their businesses, often at the expense of other areas of national life, Russian businessmen were almost unanimously deemed unworthy of assuming a leading role in public life beyond the economic sphere. Even the younger generation of businessmen, who, it was admitted, now had some education and social and cultural polish, in no way differed from their elders in their acceptance of the doctrine that all Russia could perish, if only Russian industry should survive, and they were therefore no more worthy of public confidence than their predecessors.

To a certain degree, this newer stereotype also stressed an image of the Russian businessman as an "exploiter," not only of the consumer and the worker but also, at least indirectly, of the farmer. The protective tariff that shielded Russian businessmen from the threat of foreign competition was seen as enabling them to exploit the Russian consumer, the captive purchaser of the high-priced and shoddy goods of Russian industry. In addition, Russian businessmen offered to their employees, whether shop clerks or factory workers, only low wages, long hours, and wretched working and living conditions. Such exploitation of both consumers and workers, it was held, was in large part responsible for the "super-profits" enjoyed especially by many industrialists. Businessmen were also seen as profiting at the expense of Russian agriculture, still regarded by most educated Russians as the nation's major "industry." Businessmen appeared to show no understanding of agricultural problems, and their insatiable demands on the resources of the state, it was argued, caused diversion of those resources from agriculture to industry, with the result that little attempt was made to give relief to Russia's blighted rural areas. The chief blame for this sad situation was generally seen as resting with the government, but as the beneficiaries of state blessings that many felt would have been better directed toward the salvation of agriculture, businessmen were seen as symbols of the government's badly misguided policy of favoring industrial development at the expense of the sector of the economy on which the well-being of the vast majority of the country's population depended.[19]

Any comparison of these two images—the Kit Kitych of early years and the industrialist of the later part of the century—immediately suggests the sharpening of economic and social tensions that occurred along with increasing industrialization in the years after 1861. If the image of Kit Kitych contained a large measure of contempt and hostility, the contempt, which focused chiefly on the general cultural backwardness of the Russian *kupets*, was not without humor, and the hostility arose in large measure from resentment over the merchant's grasping for kopeks. But the newer image, propounded in the press in the later nineteenth and early twentieth centuries, reflected the appearance of a new breed of businessmen, whose growing economic power was no laughing matter and whose decisions, often made in concert with the government, involved not kopeks but millions of rubles, to say nothing of the well-being of millions of their fellow citizens. If Kit Kitych had been a deplorable businessman and a hopelessly uncouth person, he had never been regarded as a major threat to other social groups. But the newer magnates of industry, in particular, tended to be regarded as a hostile force in the life of the nation, threatening the well-being of other groups. If the remaining Kit Kityches, now largely to be found in the middle and lower strata of the business community, still could evoke humorous reactions in the educated public, the new captains of industry were regarded with apprehension and even fear.

In a sense, this new image of the Russian businessman was simply a refurbished Kit Kitych—a Kit Kitych updated to take into account the growing wealth and power of the business community and the economic changes and dislocations accompanying Russia's rapid industrial growth, but still retaining many of his earlier characteristics. Like the older image, the newer one was, at the most fundamental level, a vehicle for the expression of the age-old hostility Russians felt toward the *kupets*, but this hostility was now reinforced by certain new elements, such as the nobility's increasing fear of losing their position at the top of Russian society to the newly wealthy and powerful businessmen and the intelligentsia's sympathy for those social groups in the lower strata of the population who appeared to be the victims of Russia's developing industrial capitalism. Interestingly enough, insofar as this image represented the views of the educated Russian public, it would be impossible to say that the public in general, unlike certain radical intellectuals, questioned the advisability of promoting the growth of industrial capitalism in Russia. On the contrary, press discussions of Russian businessmen contained an implicit acceptance of capitalism, combined with a conviction that somehow Russia was experiencing all the evils of capitalistic development without enjoying many of its benefits. While Russian capitalists, like capitalists elsewhere, exploited their workers, at the same time they relied on the government to protect them from the competition that in other countries seemed to stimulate the production of high-quality goods, which were made available to consumers at relatively low prices. If the government's plans envisaged reaping the benefits of capitalism in the future, that future seemed a long way off. In the meantime, expressions of public opinion reflected the impatience and anger with which the educated public reacted to the economic realities of the present. In their frustration, the public found a scapegoat in the form of the traditionally despised Russian businessman, who was blamed for most economic evils, while whatever credit was allotted for economic achievements generally was given to the state.

Although the new image of the Russian businessman stemmed basically from the old dislike of the *kuptsy* and the newer frustrations created by a period of rapid economic change, it seems likely that Russian literature played a certain role in its formation. Just as the older image of Kit Kitych had owed something to Ostrovskii, the newer stereotype of the Russian businessman was also perhaps partially derived from Russian fiction. In the absence of much press or scholarly discussion of the business community, it seems probable that the educated Russian public derived a good deal of its information about the *kupechestvo* from *belles-lettres* and formed its conceptions of the business world partly on the basis of fictional works. Though no later author exerted such an enduring influence on the educated public's view of the Russian businessman as had Ostrovskii, the writers of the 1880s and 1890s, while in part simply reflecting changing views of the Russian *kupets*, also perhaps helped to clarify and to shape the newly emerging stereotype.

Indeed, in the later decades of the nineteenth century, the businessman became a somewhat more common figure in Russian fiction.[20] Many writers, struck by the increasing prominence and economic importance of the *kuptsy*, devoted at least a play or a few short stories to this group. The tone of such works ranged from the quietly stated distaste for business and businessmen of Anton Chekhov's story "Tri goda" to the virulent denunciation of the immorality and ruthlessness inherent in the business milieu found in V. I. Nemirovich-Danchenko's novel *Tsari birzhi*. Almost without exception, the writers continued to express hostility and contempt toward the *kupechestvo*, at the same time giving apprehensive attention to the growing wealth and power of the business community. Further, the fiction of the period, reflecting to some extent debates raging among radical intellectuals over the evils of capitalism, showed increased concern with questions of morality and values raised by business conducted within a capitalistic framework.

During the 1880s and 1890s, one of the most talented of those authors who wrote about businessmen was P. D. Boborykin. Though largely forgotten today, Boborykin, a very popular novelist in his time, focused on the upper levels of the Moscow *kupechestvo* and modeled many of his characters after well-known Moscow businessmen and businesswomen. Attempting to achieve objectivity, he nonetheless tended to look at businessmen through the eyes of the nobility and the intelligentsia—a viewpoint common among the writers of his day. In his *Kitai-gorod*, Boborykin drew a contrast between the *dvorianin* (nobleman) and the *kupets*, with the latter getting by far the worst of it. The point of his novel was, in effect, that even the most honorable and well-intentioned nobleman who enters business will in the end be dragged down into the moral gutter inhabited by his fellow businessmen. In another novel, *Pereval*, Boborykin seemed to be arguing that no true Russian *intelligent* could possibly adapt to the standards and practices of the business world without sacrificing the very ideals that had created the Russian intelligentsia.

While Boborykin's view of business and businessmen was generally negative, his novels about Moscow businessmen nonetheless clearly brought to light some of the changes that had taken place in recent decades. For one thing, in contrast to the silence of Moscow's leading newspapers on the subject, Boborykin emphasized the increasing importance of the upper strata of the business community in Moscow's social, cultural, and economic life. As one of his noblemen in *Kitai-gorod* lamented, "the *kupets* is everywhere and into everything"; for this nobleman "the '*kupets*' was simply becoming a sort of nightmare. Nowhere was it possible to escape him."[21] Moreover, Boborykin in his novels stressed the considerable social and cultural change that had occurred over the past decades, at least among the upper strata of Moscow's *kupechestvo*. Most of Boborykin's businessmen were well educated and enjoyed a life-style similar to that of the nobility, at least in its external manifestations. If the characteristics of Kit Kitych had by no means entirely vanished from Boborykin's *kuptsy*, nonetheless his novels made it clear that a new Russian businessman had emerged.

Thus, the literature of the period, as exemplified by Boborykin's works, presented a derogatory picture of the Russian businessman but at the same time emphasized the ways in which he had changed since the time of Ostrovskii. In doing so, it undoubtedly contributed to the formation of the new stereotype—a stereotype which in 1905 constituted essentially the entire sum of Russian wisdom regarding the nature of Russia's business community. Even though the new stereotype, like the older image of Kit Kitych, did indeed reflect many actual characteristics of Russian businessmen, it failed to include other equally characteristic features of the Russian *kupets*. It also ignored the rather sizable number of exceptions to the general rules. And, of course, neither of the stereotypes formed as they were against the background of the persistent hostility felt toward the *kupechestvo* by other social groups, reflected any attempt to take into consideration the businessman's point of view. By no means can either stereotype be accepted as the final word on the Russian business community.

THE MOSCOW BUSINESS ELITE AND ITS
POSITION IN THE SOCIAL STRUCTURE
OF RUSSIA AND MOSCOW

A T the end of the nineteenth century, the Moscow *kupechestvo* constituted a kaleidoscopic panorama of widely differing types, of
which the prevalent stereotypes of Russian businessmen were but
pale reflections. While public attention had come to focus chiefly on the
large industrialist who, however great his "egotism," was often European-
educated, acquainted with European business methods and technology,
and conversant with art and literature, such industrialists still represented
a small minority within the business community. Alongside them continued to exist many businessmen not far removed from the old Kit Kitych,
barely literate *kuptsy* who still possessed a large bag of shady tricks to pull
on their customers, still dressed in old-fashioned styles, with long beards
and high boots, and still indulged in drinking orgies which frequently
ended in brawls and destruction of property. Between these two extremes
was a wide variety of men in transition, who found themselves at various
way stations along the *kupechestvo*'s path of economic and cultural progress. One could find, for instance, in many Moscow warehouses old traders who, though still dressed in the fashion of Kit Kitych and perpetuating
the old methods of doing business, dedicated considerable effort to a
process of self-education, reading, for example, Belinskii and Chernyshevskii and while still not quite comprehending the meaning of the essays,
feeling awareness of the power of the printed page and determination that
their sons should have every educational opportunity. The offspring of
these men, beneficiaries of secondary education, were likely to dress in
what they imagined to be the latest Parisian styles, to immerse themselves
in dime novels and in the comic operettas and light drama offered by
Moscow theaters, and to copy their business methods from local German
traders.

In addition to such representatives of the old *kupechestvo*, the Moscow business milieu had also come to include increasing numbers of individuals who came to business from other *sosloviia* and who, even after entering the business world, largely retained the manners and mores of their original social group. Thus, to the array of types within the business community could be added the scion of an old noble family, turned to business to salvage the failing family fortune, the *raznochinets* or *intelligent* with a technical education who either started his own business or found employment as the manager of an already established concern, the peasant who made a fortune in the grain trade and invested it in various commercial and industrial undertakings. And to round out the picture one should also add the foreign businessman. In Russia to make his fortune, he entered into the everyday commercial life of his new homeland but at the same time preserved a strong non-Russian cultural identity. Every one of these businessmen was to some degree typical of the Moscow business world, and each represented a particular dimension of the Moscow *kupechestvo*.

At the head of this variegated *soslovie* stood a small social grouping recognized by contemporaries as the social elite of the Moscow business world. This elite consisted of a small number of old families—business "dynasties," as Boborykin dubbed them—whose origins dated back to the late eighteenth or early nineteenth centuries, but who, for the most part, had emerged to social prominence only after 1861. In the early 1800s, while a few families still prominent at the end of the century already then constituted a part of the *kupechestvo*'s elite, for example, the Alekseevs and Guchkovs, that earlier elite had consisted mostly of other names and other faces. Usachevs, Kumanins, Dolgovs, Moskvins—such had been the leading families of the Moscow *kupechestvo* in the earlier nineteenth century. Most had now passed from the business scene, whether because of failure to produce male heirs, elevation into the nobility, or abandonment of business activity for some other reason. Primarily commercial in nature, this earlier elite had begun by mid-century to give way to an elite which was being drawn upward from the middle and lower strata of the *kupechestvo*, chiefly as a result of successful industrial activity, particularly in the textile field. Once formed, this new elite remained fairly stable before 1905, the lack of new candidates for membership perhaps explained by the fact that no major new enterprises appeared in the all-important textile industry of the Moscow region during the later nineteenth century.[1]

Even though the dynasties which emerged to prominence after mid-century represented the business elite of Moscow, it is impossible to identify them in purely economic terms. Unquestionably, all these families comprised a part of the economic elite of the Moscow business community, defined in terms of the assets they controlled. But if wealth was a basic requirement for admission into the business elite, wealth alone did not suffice. Much more than an economic elite, the upper stratum of the *kupechestvo* comprised a social elite, membership in which depended not only on wealth but on cultural attainments and brought with it positions of leadership within the business community. The place of these families at the top of the business world's hierarchy in effect rested on two equally important foundations: business success, with its concomitant of considerable financial means, and a high level of cultural and social development, as evidenced chiefly by patronage of or participation in various fields of art and science, enlightened philanthropy, and broad participation in public affairs, involving both the community as a whole and the business community in particular.

Buryshkin, in attempting to identify the leading families of the Moscow *kupechestvo*, put great stress on the relative unimportance of wealth, as compared with cultural development and social conscience, as a requirement for inclusion within the elite. He wrote that

in the genealogy of the Moscow *kupechestvo* there was a very complicated hierarchy and a very distinctive *mestnichestvo* [i.e., system of ranking]. There were families who were considered by everyone to be at the top of the Moscow *kupechestvo;* there were other families who considered themselves such, but others did not always agree with this; there were those who pretended to primacy, thanks to their wealth or the large income of their enterprises. But again I must repeat: however strange, in old Moscow wealth did not play a decisive role. Almost all the families who must be put in the first place in the sense of their significance and influence were not from among those who would be celebrated for their wealth. Sometimes there was a correspondence, but only in those cases where wealth served as the source of broad philanthropical undertakings.[2]

Thus dismissing wealth as more or less irrelevant, Buryshkin characterized the business elite as "people who occupied an honorable position in popular economic life and remembered their fellow men: they helped the suffering and the needy and responded to the needs of culture and enlightenment."[3]

Buryshkin somewhat exaggerated the relative unimportance of wealth as a prerequisite for membership in the elite. It is true that the possession of a huge fortune alone never brought general recognition as members of the elite to any family, but without considerable financial resources, it would have been impossible for these families to engage in the broad philanthropical and cultural activities on which their reputation was in large part based. Nonetheless, Buryshkin's de-emphasis of wealth is an interesting feature in the self-definition of the Moscow business elite.

Buryshkin noted elsewhere in his memoirs that "in Russia there was not that 'cult' of rich people which is seen in western countries."[4] He implicitly attributed the failure of Russians to admire wealth per se to the predominance in Russian educated society of values stemming not from Russia's "bourgeoisie" but from the nobility and, especially, the intelligentsia. "Not only in the revolutionary milieu," Buryshkin explained, "but in the urban intelligentsia there was a somewhat hostile attitude" toward wealth and wealthy people.[5] From his comments it is clear that businessmen were unable to achieve social prestige by flaunting their wealth and that, in seeking to rise from obscurity to a respected position in society, they were forced to accommodate to the values of the dominant social groups—the nobility and the intelligentsia. As a result, they claimed and were accorded social respect on the basis of their service to society, their level of cultural development, and other factors that reflected the values of the dominant groups.

It is not difficult to discover individuals who were not a part of this Moscow business elite in spite of their great fortunes. Moscow abounded in new millionaires, many from the peasantry, who did not acquire culture as rapidly as they acquired wealth and thus had no hope of being numbered among the *kupechestvo*'s leading families.[6] One example of this phenomenon was P. A. Smirnov, of vodka fame. Born a peasant, Smirnov started his liquor business in the 1850s and soon accumulated a massive fortune. Although he took on some of the external trappings of culture, building for himself a magnificent mansion in Moscow, he used none of his wealth for cultural or philanthropic purposes, and neither he nor his heirs participated actively in public affairs. When Smirnov died, note was duly taken of the fact he left none of his money to charity.[7] If someone like Smirnov, who had acquired at least some external polish, could not gain admission to the elite, it was even more obvious that new peasant millionaires who continued to dress in peasant fashion and retained the manners and mores of the village could hardly be considered a part of the true business elite.

The Smirnov wealth was of fairly recent origin, but it seems unlikely that the newness of his wealth in itself would have barred Smirnov from the charmed circle. The peasant forebear of the Ushkovs, one of Moscow's most prominent business families by the turn of the century, had begun the family chemical business only in the 1850s,[8] the same decade in which Smirnov went into the liquor business. If most of the families which composed the elite were indeed old business families, age in itself was not necessarily a requirement for admission. The fact is that while fortunes could be made quickly, it took a considerably longer period for most business families, coming from the peasantry or the lower ranks of the urban population, to acquire the cultural polish and social conscience that were required for recognition as part of the business elite.

Since membership in the elite was based on such vague criteria as the level of social and cultural development of a family, it is not always possible to say exactly which families formed a part of it. The elite was amorphous at its outer boundaries, and it is not possible to determine exactly where those outer boundaries lay. There is, however, no difficulty in identifying the top twenty families of the Moscow *kupechestvo*. This small group of dynasties dominated business participation in the various fields of Moscow cultural, social, and public life and at the same time provided leadership to the business community. These same names recur again and again—as big contributors to charity and leaders of various philanthropical institutions, as patrons of the arts and companions of certain circles of the artistic intelligentsia, as artists and scientists, as members of the city council, as trustees of municipal schools, as justices of the peace, and, finally, as leading members of the Exchange Committee, the Nizhnii Novgorod Fair Committee, various government commissions, and political groupings formed in 1905. Few families excelled in all these fields (perhaps with the single exception of the large Morozov clan), but most made their mark in a number of these areas. These twenty families were the families who, as Buryshkin put it, "were considered by everyone to be at the top of the Moscow *kupechestvo*," whose membership in the elite cannot possibly be open to question. Included within this crème de la crème were the following families: Abrikosov, Alekseev, Bakhrushin, Botkin, Guchkov, Iakunchikov, Khludov, Konovalov, Krestovnikov, Mamontov, Morozov, Naidenov, Prokhorov, Riabushinskii, Rukavishnikov, Shchukin, Soldatenkov, Tretiakov, Ushkov, and Vishniakov.[9]

Beyond this small inner circle, one begins to run into arguable cases, and a variety of problems in determining membership in the elite arises. For one thing, there is in some cases a problem of primary geographical identification. Some families, like the Bardygins and Baranovs, who had very close connections with the social and business worlds of Moscow, nonetheless were primarily identified with other localities within the Central Industrial Region and frequently had their main residences in other towns. If they were easily recognizable as part of the business elite of Kostroma or Egorevsk, their position as part of the Moscow business elite was more questionable.[10] And yet, such families often played an important role in Moscow, and to rule them out entirely as members of Moscow's elite would probably be misleading. For example, the Iasiuninskiis were primarily identified with the textile industry of Ivanovo-Voznesensk, but the family had long maintained close business and social ties with Moscow and finally established its main office in Moscow in the early 1890s. One of the Iasiuninskii brothers, who evidently established his residence in Moscow at that time, was soon chosen president of the Nizhnii Novgorod Fair Committee,[11] a body dominated by the Moscow elite in the 1890s, and thereafter played an important leadership role within the Moscow business community. A similar case was that of the Konovalovs, who had much stronger ties with Kostroma province, the site of their textile factories, than with Moscow. Yet there can be little question of the Konovalovs' membership in the Moscow elite, particularly after 1905, when A. I. Konovalov began his political activity and emerged as one of the leading political spokesmen for the Moscow business community. Thus, although some important business families—and especially the Bardygins, Baranovs, and Iasiuninskiis—were primarily identified with other localities, they should still be recognized as at least marginal members of the Moscow elite. And in the case of the Konovalovs, their right to inclusion in the elite is unchallengeable.

In many cases it is difficult to know whether to include a family within the elite because it is difficult to define just how much culture, how much philanthropy, how much public service sufficed to merit inclusion. Such categories are not quantifiable, and it is impossible to draw any hard-and-fast line and say that only families with just so much culture were part of the elite. A considerable number of wealthy business families made a name for themselves as philanthropists and the like, but their activities hardly approached the impressive scale characteristic of the leading families. In addition, some families were generally undistinguished except for perhaps one outstanding individual whose activities did much to establish a family claim to preeminence. A number of other families were in effect "satellites" of the leading dynasties, rising to prominence because of marital or other ties with these top families. Families in these categories should probably be recognized as constituting a second layer within the elite. The achievements of families at this level were not so noteworthy as those of Moscow's leading dynasties, but the families nonetheless distinguished themselves in one way or another. Families included within this second layer would be: Chetverikov, Karetnikov, Karzinkin, Krasilshchikov, Lepeshkin, Liamin, Maliutin, Mazurin, Perlov, Protopopov, Sapozhnikov, Shelaputin, Tarasov, Vostriakov, and perhaps a dozen or so additional families, about whom very little information is available.

Other individual cases raise particular problems. The Perlovs, for instance, although not members of the inner circle, were undoubtedly a part of the elite before 1887, but in that year they were elevated to the nobility.[12] They nonetheless continued their tea business on the same scale as before and continued to be a highly respected mercantile family. They found themselves in the not uncommon situation where, while not legally full-fledged members of the *kupechestvo* as defined by law, they nonetheless were engaged in business activity and were identifiable primarily as businessmen. To regard a noble family as part of the elite of the *kupechestvo* perhaps seems a contradiction in terms, but Russia's social structure was full of such contradictions, created chiefly by the gap between social realities and the legal definition of social structure. In any case, because of their long standing as part of the business elite and the continuation of their business activity even after elevation into the nobility, it would seem reasonable to continue to regard them even after 1887 as part of the business elite. This rule even more obviously would apply to the Prokhorovs, long one of the most respected business families in Moscow, who received nobility in 1911 but who could hardly be ejected from their position within the elite solely on that basis.[13]

If the families mentioned were more or less obviously included within the Moscow business elite, certain other commercial and industrial families, while lacking neither wealth nor culture, nonetheless cannot be considered a part of that group. This applies, first of all, to "foreign" businessmen based in Moscow. One definite requirement for inclusion within the elite was Russian nationality, and the exceptions to this rule were extremely few in number.[14] This is not to say that businessmen of foreign origin did not play an important role in the economic life of Moscow. While Moscow and light industry in general were much less penetrated by foreign capital and foreign capitalists than other geographical regions and other fields of industry (notably, St. Petersburg and most fields of heavy industry), a small handful of foreigners nonetheless played a significant role in the development of the industry and trade of the Moscow region. Among the largest textile factories in Moscow itself were the Hübner and Zündel factories, both founded by natives of Alsace.[15] A number of Frenchmen occupied leading positions in silk production.[16] The metallurgical and machine-building industries in Moscow, small though they were, were almost entirely in the hands of foreigners—the Goujon, List, Bromley, and other families.[17] Undoubtedly the most remarkable businessman of Moscow's foreign colony was Ludwig Knoop, a German who had come to Russia in the 1840s and had served as an intermediary between the textile industrialists of the Central Region and foreign suppliers of textile machinery. Knoop had played an instrumental role in the mechanization of most of the large textile factories in the Central Region, and in the process he had managed to acquire an interest in many of these same factories, at the same time taking the lead in the creation of the Kränholm cotton textile factory, one of Russia's largest. Knoop and his heirs also went into the cotton trade and supplied a good share of the raw cotton used by textile factories in the Central Region.[18]

Like Knoop, some of Moscow's prominent "foreign" businessmen had lived in Russia for many decades. Some, like Knoop's sons, were actually born on Russian soil and were Russian citizens. But however long they had been in Russia, whatever their official citizenship, they still remained foreigners in the eyes of their Russian colleagues; and indeed, many of them, even if they were Russian citizens, regarded themselves primarily as Frenchmen or Germans. Historians have continued the practice of regarding such individuals as "foreigners." As William Blackwell has noted,

Andrew Carnegie, born and raised in Scotland, is not considered a foreign entrepreneur by historians of the United States. Ludwig Knoop, on the other hand, who came to Russia before he was twenty, who became a Russian subject and a baron, and who remained in the adopted land that had enriched him for over half a century until his death, is considered a foreigner by most historians of Russian industry.[19]

Though Blackwell seems justified in arguing that historians ought to reconsider their classification of enterprises as "foreign" and "native" in many cases, nonetheless, the fact remains that not only historians but contemporary Russians regarded such persons as Knoop as foreigners.

Indeed, many of these individuals, however long they remained in Russia, did not become particularly Russified. Most of Moscow's "foreign" businessmen appear to have maintained strong ties with their homelands, frequently returning for prolonged visits and sending their sons "home" for their education. Some retained their foreign citizenship.[20] And the foreign colony—or colonies—for the most part maintained a separate social and cultural existence in Moscow. They had their own churches, their own clubs and schools, their own philanthropical societies. The Germans, by far the largest group, regularly celebrated the birthday of the German emperor and even raised a statue to him in the heart of the German colony.[21]

Whether the separation between themselves and their Russian colleagues was self-imposed or the result of Russian prejudice against foreigners is difficult to determine, but most likely both factors played their part. Some foreign businessmen undoubtedly felt that they had been transported from a higher to a lower culture and had no desire to adapt themselves to Russian ways. Vladimir Polunin, son of an unsuccessful Moscow trader, recalled the German businessmen who frequented a neighboring dacha during the 1880s:

> Quite shamelessly these Russo-Germans drank to their German Kaiser, railed against Russia's backwardness and prophesied her speedy downfall. For notwithstanding the fact that the majority of them were German only in name and had been born and bred in Russia, the force of gravitation drew them to the land of their origin with such attraction as to make them avowed traitors to the country of their birth.[22]

Russian prejudices against foreigners also existed, although they appear to have broken down somewhat in the business community in the later decades of the nineteenth century, a process encouraged by the increasing number of joint business ventures between "foreigners" and Russian businessmen.[23] In the 1880s, at a time when few marriages occurred between the native business elite and foreign business families, P. M. Tretiakov threatened his wife that he would "bury her alive" if she permitted a marriage between their daughter and the son of a prominent German businessman.[24] But the attitude exhibited by Tretiakov, who was generally more conservative in such matters than many of his fellow businessmen, would appear to have been increasingly on the wane. A survey of genealogies of some of Moscow's elite business families reveals an increasing number of marriages with foreigners in the last decades of the nineteenth century, a trend which continued in the early twentieth century. Something of a rarity in earlier times, marriages with foreigners could now be found in families such as the Morozovs, Shchukins, Prokhorovs, Alekseevs—and even the Tretiakovs.

Moreover, the "foreigners" were gradually beginning to assume a greater leadership role within the business community and to provide spokesmen for Moscow business. Jules Goujon in particular emerged as one of the leading spokesmen for the Moscow business community in the early twentieth century. When G. A. Krestovnikov became president of the Exchange Committee in 1905, he supported the admission of foreign businessmen to that prestigious body and was prepared to permit them a greater role within the leadership of the Moscow business world despite numerous protests which indicated that old prejudices had not yet entirely disappeared.[25] Thus, it seems that particularly after 1905 the more outstanding "foreigners" of the Moscow business community, at least those whose families had been in Russia for many decades, were moving closer to their Russian colleagues and were perhaps on the verge of integration into the elite of the Moscow *kupechestvo*.[26] But in the years before 1905, there can be no question that the foreigners were excluded from the true business elite.

Another group—Moscow's leading Jewish business families—was even more firmly excluded from the recognized elite of the *kupechestvo*, in spite of their wealth, their large industrial and financial enterprises, and their philanthropy. The Moscow Jewish colony had been much reduced in 1891, when most Jews were forced to leave the city by order of the imperial government, but a number of the wealthier Jewish families managed to remain. Most notable of these were the Poliakovs, a large family with vast interests in diverse fields of industry and finance and in various parts of the Empire. The Moscow Poliakovs were most closely associated with railroads and banking, and one of their number, the head of the Moscow Land Bank, had been taken into the nobility.[27] In spite of the Poliakovs' wealth and high level of cultural development, Moscow's leading business families had little to do with them. The generally low status of Jews in the Empire and the undoubted if mild anti-Semitism of the Moscow *kupechestvo* combined to prevent the intermingling of wealthy Jewish business families with the city's business elite.

Although Jews were barred by their religion from social acceptance, the same fate did not befall the Old Believers in the business community, despite continuing governmental disapproval and sporadic persecution of this schismatic sect. As has been often observed, many of Moscow's most prestigious business dynasties emerged from the Moscow communities of Old Believers.[28] Morozovs, Riabushinskiis, Konovalovs, Guchkovs, Soldatenkovs, Khludovs, and others were all originally Old Believers, though many of them abandoned the Old Belief at some point during the nineteenth century for the compromise between Orthodoxy and the Old Belief represented by *edinoverie*.[29] During the reign of Nicholas I, the Old Believers of Moscow were subject to sporadic persecution by the government, a persecution which frequently sought to undermine the obvious economic prosperity of Moscow Old Believers and thus persuaded many businessmen to compromise on their religion for the sake of preserving their businesses and fortunes. In the 1850s, for instance, it was suddenly forbidden for Old Believers to register as members of the *kupechestvo*. This ruling, which was in effect only a few years, seems to have promoted a mass exodus from the Old Belief, since loss of membership in the *kupechestvo* would have meant loss of the right to carry on trade and industry. It was during this period of persecution that the Guchkovs converted to *edinoverie*,[30] a step also taken by the Khludovs and some of the Morozovs at some time during the century. But other Morozovs, as well as the Riabushinskiis, Konovalovs, and Soldatenkovs, clung to their religion, despite all persecutions and difficulties.[31]

Adherence to either the Old Belief or *edinoverie* had no adverse effect on a family's standing in the eyes of fellow *kuptsy*. By the end of the century, the business elite harbored no prejudice against the Old Believers in their midst, and there was little apparent difference between Old Believer or *edinoverie* families and Orthodox families in any important respect. Perhaps with the single exception of the Vikula Morozov family,[32] the Old Believer and *edinoverie* families among the elite had long given up the special dress and customs typically associated with the Old Belief. The process of cultural change seems to have affected them at much the same rate and in much the same manner as the more numerous Orthodox families, so that the chief difference between them came down to a matter of church affiliation. As P. I. Shchukin observed, K. T. Soldatenkov's strict observance of the religious rituals of the Old Belief did not prevent Soldatenkov from having a French mistress.[33]

Thus, in the last analysis, religion played no important role in determining the membership of the elite except in the case of the Jews. Whether adhering to the Old Belief, *edinoverie*, or Orthodoxy, a family found that its social position rested chiefly on its wealth, its cultural attainments, and the evidence it gave of social conscience. These were the most significant factors in determining its position at the top of the Moscow *kupechestvo*.

BEFORE discussing the activities of this Moscow business elite in various fields of endeavor, it seems appropriate to give some indication of the position they occupied in the social structure of Russia and, in particular, of their native town. A definition of their social position can best be approached by considering the workings of Russia's system of *sosloviia* and, within that context, the business elite's relationship with other urban social groups.

As specified by law, the official social structure of Russia consisted of a number of *sosloviia*, social categories in one of which each individual was expected to find his place.[34] Often likened to the estates or orders of Western societies, Russian *sosloviia* actually differed from them in a number of ways. Membership in a *soslovie* was not necessarily hereditary. Membership in the *soslovie* known as the *kupechestvo*, for instance, was dependent upon annual payment of a guild fee, and failure to pay the requisite fee meant, in most cases, that one automatically descended from the *kupechestvo* into the *meshchanstvo*, the *soslovie* composed of generally small traders. In addition, some *sosloviia*, such as the personal nobility and the individuals bearing the title of "honored citizen" *(pochetnyi grazhdanin)*, had no corporate organization of any type.

The system as originally spelled out in the law code (Ulozhenie) of 1649 was so rigid and simplistic—recognizing only four social groups: nobility, townspeople, peasantry, and clergy—that later modifications were inevitable. The ramifications of the system became gradually more complex as a result of successive attempts by lawmakers either to force the social structure into molds of their own imagining or to create a greater correspondence between law and reality. The townspeople *(posadskie liudi)*, for instance, were divided into three groups, the *meshchanstvo*, the artisanate, and the *kupechestvo*, while members of the *kupechestvo* were distributed among three, and later two, guilds. But in theory, at least, the basic principles on which the *soslovie* system was founded remained the same: society was to be divided into social categories on the basis of functions performed by the various groupings, and the state was then to assign each group certain rights and duties related to its basic function. According to this rather mechanistic conception of the workings of society, all would go well if only each *soslovie* would carry out its functions and obligations. Overseeing the system was, of course, the tsar, who stood above and outside the *sosloviia* and who was expected to determine the obligations and rights of each in a fair and even-handed manner.

One of the most long-lasting effects of this system was the creation of what might be conveniently termed a *"soslovie* mentality," which persisted even after the *soslovie* system itself, in the later nineteenth century, began to seem more and more of an abstraction only tenuously related to social realities. Encapsulated within their separate categories, the members of the various *sosloviia* were in effect forbidden to concern themselves with matters not directly pertinent to the complex of functions, duties, and rights peculiar to their own *sosloviia*. Only the tsar was expected to see the "whole picture." It was his function to determine and preserve the best interests of the state and of the country as a whole. Each *soslovie* could offer opinions to the tsar in the form of petitions or of advice when requested, but only on matters affecting its own interests. Even within this narrow sphere, spokesmen for the *soslovie* were neither expected nor permitted to couch their views in terms of what might be the best policy to adopt from the point of view of the general welfare. Their only concern was, in effect, to defend the interests of their own particular *soslovie*. The tsar would decide what policy or resolution of a problem would be in the best interests of all. This characteristic of the Russian system of governing had its origins in pre-Petrine Russia and evoked comment especially from observers of seventeenth-century Muscovy, including the Englishman Giles Fletcher. Having watched representatives of the various *sosloviia* at work in a *zemskii sobor* (assembly of the land) called to advise the tsar, he remarked: "to propound bils what every man thinketh good for the pub-like benefite (as the manner is in England), the Russe parliament knoweth no such custome nor libertie to subjects."[35] Such proposals could come only from the tsar and his direct agents.

The best-known display of the *sosloviia* in action in the eighteenth century came during the Legislative Commission established by Catherine the Great in 1767.[36] The empress presented to the commission a plan for legal reform (her famous Nakaz, or Instruction) based on the principles of the Enlightenment and motivated by a concern for the common good. The members of the commission, representing the various social groups, showed little interest in Catherine's enlightened principles and demonstrated an almost total inability to transcend their particular *soslovie* interests and to respond to her concern for the welfare of the nation. Instead, their proposals sought in almost every case only to defend and expand the legal rights and privileges granted to their own *sosloviia*, often at the expense of other social groups. That Catherine was somewhat taken aback by this response demonstrated only her own lack of familiarity with the relationship between the Russian state and society. The delegates well understood that they might attempt to influence the ruler to expand their rights or reduce their obligations—so that, as they argued, they could perform their functions more effectively—but that their responsibility for public affairs extended no further. The mutual hostility among the commission delegates also served to highlight one other long-lasting result of the *soslovie* system. In practice, the system put each *soslovie* into competition with all others for benefits from the throne. Most often, a boon granted to one group would affect others adversely. These two important components of the *soslovie* mentality—a narrow focus on the interests of one's own *soslovie*, accompanied by lack of any feeling of responsibility for the nation as a whole, and competitiveness and mutual hostility among *sosloviia*—lingered on despite all change and continued to exert an effect in shaping relations between the members of various *sosloviia*, as well as their relationships with the government, even as late as the twentieth century.

During the first part of the nineteenth century, the government made a determined effort to preserve what one Moscow businessman, N. P. Vishniakov, called in his memoirs "the division of society into compartments." As an illustration of this policy, Vishniakov recalled a visit made by Emperor Nicholas I in 1846 to a Moscow school for children of *meshchane* that was maintained by the Merchants' Society. During the course of the visit, Nicholas remarked to one of the trustees: "Try to inspire in your pupils the goal toward which their education is directed, so that they should remember their calling and not think about anything higher."[37] Nicholas's remark accurately reflected his government's educational policy, which sought to keep separate the different *sosloviia* and to provide members of each with the sort of education appropriate to their particular "calling" or function.

Another interesting illustration of this policy on the local level can be found in the history of the Moscow Merchants' Club. Founded in 1786, the Merchants' Club had by the early nineteenth century become well known for its balls and "literary evenings" (as well as for its card games, at which large sums of money often changed hands). It attracted to these functions guests from other *sosloviia*, and this intermingling of social groups evidently gave rise to some concern. In any case, in 1839 some of the Moscow nobility decided to seek permission from the government to form a *soslovie* club of their own, and in support of their request the Moscow governor-general pointed out to the Minister of the Interior that, as things stood, many nobles went to the Merchants' Club in search of companionship and that this social mixing was bound to cause trouble.

Moreover, when it was first founded, the Merchants' Club's charter permitted it to accept as members both *kuptsy* and those persons known as *uchenye*, who were members of the professions—professors and teachers, doctors, artists, and the like. If Catherine's government had originally permitted this departure from the *soslovie* principle in pursuit of Catherine's hope that a true middle class might somehow be forced into existence in Russia, her successors eventually rectified the situation, at least in part. When the Merchants' Club applied for a new charter in 1859, Governor-General A. A. Zakrevskii demanded that only *kuptsy* and honored citizens be accepted as members while individuals from other *sosloviia* could become only visiting members without full voting privileges. Visiting memberships could be granted to members of the nobility, officials, and representatives of the professions; *meshchane* and artisans would not be accepted as visiting members—indeed, they would not even be allowed onto the club's premises as guests. Visiting members complained about their status several times during the 1870s, and in 1879 the club's charter was again changed to state that "people of all callings and conditions" could now become full members.[38]

This bit of Moscow history illustrates both the government's determination to maintain *soslovie* distinctions before 1861 and the changing attitudes that began to appear in the 1860s and 1870s regarding intermingling of *sosloviia* in various institutions, both public and private. Such changing attitudes were in part responsible for and in part the result of the Great Reforms enacted by Alexander II in the 1860s and 1870s, so many of which transcended the *soslovie* principle and created for the first time what were referred to as "all-*sosloviia* institutions." Members of the various social groups might now come together in the new juries and zemstvos, in the reformed schools and city councils, in the barracks of the reformed army. The impact of this attack on the *soslovie* principle was very far-reaching, perhaps especially in urban areas. In Moscow, the municipal reform of 1862, replacing the old municipal institutions dominated by the *kupechestvo* with a new duma (city council) made up of representatives of all urban *sosloviia*, played an important role in ending the relative isolation of the each *soslovie*. One Moscow municipal activist, Prince V. M. Golitsyn, in a passage worth quoting at length, vividly recalled the pre- and post-reform *sosloviia* relationships in his city:

The great service of such an organization [the reformed duma] was a new phenomenon, formerly completely unknown in the social structure of Moscow: I call it the merging of *sosloviia*. The fact is that in the pre-reform era people belonging to one or another *soslovie* lived in isolation, . . . nothing tied them together with people of another *soslovie*, there was no solidarity among them. Some nobles lived as landowners, others as civil servants, while the merchants were occupied with trade, and the points of fortuitous contact between them were interests arising out of these positions, or professions. But at the same time both for the nobles and for the merchants the other two *sosloviia*—the *meshchane* and artisans—were secondary, beneath them, people with whom they were forced to associate again only because of some sort of professional needs. This professionalism was so deeply rooted in the conceptions of that time that when the name of a merchant was mentioned in a circle of nobles, it was immediately followed by the question: "What does he trade in?" Nothing tied together these *sosloviia*, neither interests common to the inhabitants of the same town, nor association in any sort of organizations, such as philanthropical organizations, whose members looked on the merchants only as contributors of money, nor public life, while on the other hand there was much which divided them—mutual distrust, diffidence, a certain envy of one another, and fear of compromising oneself by familiar relations with people of another *soslovie*. It went so far that many were openly distressed by the fact that one notable merchant became a member of the English Club.

When the duma of *sosloviia* was formed, the scene suddenly changed, intercourse began among these varied elements, originally in common municipal tasks, and later it went even further—into the field of intellectual life, artistic and social interests.[39]

Even before the enactment of the reforms of the 1860s and 1870s, the *soslovie* system had entered upon a gradual process of decay and dissolution, and as the century progressed, the system increasingly failed to reflect social and economic realities. One sign of the process of dissolution was the appearance of the group known as *raznochintsy* (literally, people of various ranks). The term was coined in recognition of the fact that social and economic change was creating opportunities for more and more urban inhabitants to take up new occupations unknown to the old *soslovie* system. Journalism, for example, was one of a number of new professions whose practitioners could not easily be classified according to any of the existing functional categories. In addition, the proliferation of bureaucracy in the nineteenth century produced an army of petty bureaucrats who defied classification. Some of these *raznochintsy* attached themselves to the intelligentsia—another new unofficial social category to appear in the nineteenth century. Originally recruited chiefly from members of the nobility who, if they retained their standing as *dvoriane* in law, ceased to feel any personal identification with their *soslovie* of origin, the intelligentsia drew into itself increasing numbers of educated persons from various urban social groups, including many from the *raznochintsy*. Neither of these groups received legal recognition, but they were nonetheless real and important parts of the Russian social structure.

In general terms, Russia found itself by the end of the nineteenth century in a transitional phase between the old system of *sosloviia* and the formation of a modern class system. During this transitional period, the *soslovie* system, even though some were already pronouncing its demise, nonetheless continued to affect Russian social and political relations in many ways. Increased intermingling of members of various *sosloviia* did not immediately erase the sense of differences or the prejudices cherished by the different groups toward one another, nor did it quickly overcome the *soslovie* mentality inculcated over past centuries. The corporate organizations of the various *sosloviia* continued to function right down to 1917 and helped to keep alive old identifications while making more difficult a new conceptualization of society. In Moscow, as elsewhere, the nobility continued to hold their periodic assemblies, both local and provincial, to discuss matters of particular interest to their *soslovie*, and continued to elect marshals of the nobility to look after their interests in the interim. The local *soslovie* organizations of both the Moscow *kupechestvo* and the Moscow *meshchanstvo* (the Merchants' Society and the Meshchanskoe Society) remained in existence and still commanded the loyal support of many members of their respective constituencies.

In point of fact, however, the functions of these *soslovie* organizations were undergoing a gradual, but drastic, reduction as more and more of the duties of the *sosloviia* were taken over by the new institutions created during the period of the Great Reforms. The experience of the Moscow Merchants' Society is particularly instructive in this respect. In 1866, when it was still in flourishing condition, the Merchants' Society for the first time made a systematic inventory of its assets and discovered that the society owned property worth some 2,300,000 rubles and controlled some 3,000,000 rubles in capital. Much of the society's property generated income; it included, for example, many shops that were rented out to small merchants as well as a warehouse and a stockyard and slaughterhouse. These properties had been acquired in various ways. Some were gifts from members of the society, while the stockyard and slaughterhouse had originally belonged to the government, which in 1764 had required the *kupechestvo* to take over their management. The society at that time had also acquired the right to collect a tax on cattle brought to its yards, the income from which went to the support of the Merchants' Society. The non–income-producing property belonging to the society consisted chiefly of various charitable institutions, including several schools and almshouses intended for the use of individuals from the *kupechestvo* and the *meshchanstvo*. Much of the capital for the support of these institutions had been contributed by wealthy *kuptsy*. Such charitable contributions were still substantial in the 1860s and 1870s. In 1866 the society received gifts of more than 1,600,000 rubles for charitable purposes, and in 1871 the annual total had risen to more than 3 million rubles.[40]

The Merchants' Society continued to administer both income-producing properties and charitable institutions until 1917, but in the 1880s the municipal government began to attend to many of the needs served by these enterprises. For instance, the city duma created a municipal stockyard and slaughterhouse in 1888, largely for sanitary reasons, despite considerable opposition from the Merchants' Society. In 1892, when Moscow was threatened by a cholera epidemic, the governor of Moscow province ordered the closing of all stockyards except the one owned by the city, and so the yard operated by the Merchants' Society closed its doors. Also, in the 1890s the duma set up a municipal system for the administration of charity to the poor, and this system began to attract contributions which previously might have gone to the various *soslovie* organizations.[41] The trend was clearly in favor of the transfer of various necessary public functions to the municipal government, taking such concerns out of the hands of the *soslovie* societies and offering services to all citizens alike, regardless of their *soslovie* affiliations. All the same, in 1917 the Merchants' Society was still a going concern and its survival a testimony to the continuing existence of *soslovie* distinctions and a *soslovie* mentality at least in some sectors of the populace.

These corporate organizations of the *sosloviia* functioned for the most part as strictly local bodies. Only the nobility was allowed provincial assemblies, though no national gathering even of the nobility was permitted. Moreover, in the nineteenth century there were no occasions on which representatives of the various *sosloviia* came together to advise the throne. The lack of any national corporate organizations obviously hampered the effectiveness of the *sosloviia* both in generating any feeling of "*soslovie* solidarity" and in dealing with the central government. Petitions to the throne tended to dwell on matters of purely local concern and did not carry as much weight with the government as would petitions expressing the views of a united national group. Lacking any feeling of national solidarity, the mentality of the existing *soslovie* organizations therefore tended to be extremely particularistic, oriented around local needs. Certainly in the nineteenth century many Russians, especially those identifying themselves with the intelligentsia, began more and more to regard themselves as "citizens" rather than as members of a certain *soslovie* and thus to broaden their horizons, putting Russian problems in a national, rather than purely local, context. Nonetheless, it was for many quite as difficult to transcend their particularism as it was to overcome other confining aspects of the *soslovie* mentality. Quite simply, the legacy of the *soslovie* system was a society of competitive and mutually hostile castes, accustomed to perceiving issues only in their relation to the interests of their own respective *sosloviia*, largely on a local level. Even with the rapid economic and social change occurring in Russia in the nineteenth century, the passage of a considerable amount of time would have been required to break down entirely the habits of centuries, and in the early twentieth century that process was by no means complete.

THE position of the Moscow business elite with respect to the *kupechestvo* demonstrates both the lingering hold of the *soslovie* system and the beginnings of breakdown within the system. Even though they recognized themselves and were recognized by their contemporaries as being part of the *kupechestvo*, many representatives of the Moscow elite were not actually registered as members of either of the two guilds that made up this *soslovie*. In 1832 the government had created the status of honored citizen and made it readily available to successful *kuptsy;* the title carried with it the same personal rights (in particular, freedom from corporal punishment and from the poll tax) and the same rights needed to conduct any business beyond a purely local, small-scale enterprise as were conferred by membership in the *kupechestvo,* without the payment of a guild fee. A new statute promulgated in 1863 and revised in 1865 required businessmen to acquire, by payment of a fee, either a guild certificate or a business *(promyslovoe)* certificate; the latter did not involve membership in the *kupechestvo* but bestowed the same rights in regard to the conduct of trade and industry. Finally, the law of 1898 on industrial taxation created a complicated scheme by which individuals and enterprises, through the payment of certain taxes, acquired the certificates and rights necessary to the conduct of business. Such individuals could request to be registered as members of the *kupechestvo,* but certainly for members of the business elite there was no compelling reason to desire such registration. Acquiring the status of a *kupets* was important chiefly to businessmen from the peasantry and the *meshchanstvo* who had accumulated the minimum capital required for entry into the guilds. Membership in the *kupechestvo* to them meant freedom from corporal punishment and the possibility of rising higher in the official social ladder by moving upward from the status of *kupets* to that of honored citizen.[42] While some big businessmen perhaps continued to register as *kuptsy* (Buryshkin, for example, related that he maintained his membership in the *kupechestvo* out of a sense of tradition), increasing numbers of businessmen were no longer, in the eyes of the law, members of the *kupechestvo,* even though they were constantly referred to in popular parlance as members of that *soslovie.*[43] In other words, there was a gap between public perception, which continued to label individuals with the old *soslovie* terms according to their social function and roles, and increasingly complex legislation that was forced to recognize increasingly complex social and economic differentiation.

Even if they were officially registered members of the *kupechestvo,* members of the Moscow business elite were able to write behind their names, instead of the simple *"kupets,"* a variety of titles granted to them by the government in acknowledgment of extraordinary achievement. Most possessed the title of honored citizen, created during the reign of Nicholas I for the purpose of bestowing special honor on successful businessmen in hopes of thereby elevating their miserably low social status. Achievement of the status of honored citizen was determined simply by longevity; in view of the high rate of business failure in Russia, sheer ability to survive was a not inappropriate measure of a businessman's competence and success. Any *kupets* who had been a member of the first guild for ten years was entitled to apply for the title of personal honored citizen. Ten years as a personal honored citizen or twenty years in the first guild permitted a *kupets* to request the status of hereditary honored citizen. This title had long ago become hereditary in most of the elite Moscow business families.

In addition to the title of honored citizen, various members of the elite identified themselves by other honorific titles. Many had been designated manufacturing councillors or commercial councillors, titles which conferred upon them the rights and privileges attached to the eighth civil rank in the Table of Ranks. These manufacturing and commercial councillors were quasi-governmental servants, responsible for advising the government on economic questions when so requested. Others were granted titles taken directly from the Table of Ranks, up to and including the title of active state councillor, designating the fourth civil service rank. Such distinctions were frequently awarded to businessmen not for their business achievements but for charitable contributions, the creation of private museums, or occupying some "service" position within a government department.[44] A few businessmen of the elite were awarded either personal or hereditary nobility (Perlovs, Iakunchikovs, Prokhorovs, and a few individual representatives of elite families, such as A. A. Bakhrushin), and at the same time some also acquired ranks of the three highest degrees in the Table of Ranks.

The granting by the government of all these various ranks and titles to representatives of the *kupechestvo* had the effect of creating a hierarchy of ranks within the business community, ranging from the few nobles, the active state councillors, and the commercial and manufacturing councillors down through the lower degrees of the Table of Ranks to the hereditary honored citizens, and progressing through personal honored citizens and first-guild *kuptsy* down to the second-guild *kuptsy*. Because the bestowal of titles and ranks was not always the result of excellence in business, this officially created hierarchy did not necessarily reflect actual economic and social divisions within the business community, though there was a rough correspondence. In any case, members of the Moscow elite were set apart from many of their fellow businessmen by possession of titles other than that of *kupets*.

Members of the Moscow elite also maintained a social distance between themselves and other lesser *kuptsy*. Though preserving some contact with the lower levels of the *kupechestvo* through their business activity and activity in the organs of municipal self-government, the elite families had almost no social contact with lesser businessmen, except in some cases where particularly close business or family ties existed. There is a striking contrast in this respect between the memoirs of N. P. Vishniakov, relating chiefly to the 1850s, and the memoirs of Vera Tretiakova and others dealing with the 1890s and early twentieth century. In the 1850s, the Vishniakovs, then only beginning to raise themselves above the mass of *kuptsy*, had extremely extensive ties—created by kinship, friendship, and business—with families at all levels of the business world. By the end of the century, however, the families of the elite consorted only with one another and with representatives of the nobility and the intelligentsia, having little or no social contact with the lower levels of the business world.[45] Both their wealth and their cultural attainments had come to constitute a barrier between themselves and other *kuptsy*, while on the other hand the elite's wealth and culture assisted in breaking down social barriers that before 1861 had prevented all *kuptsy* from cultivating social contacts outside their own *soslovie*.

The line dividing the elite from lesser businessmen was clearly indicated by a basic bifurcation of the business community that appeared in the later nineteenth century in the form of a division between the Merchants' Society and the newer Exchange Society, represented by its executive organ, the Exchange Committee. In Moscow, control of the *kupechestvo*'s corporate organization increasingly passed into the hands of businessmen who owned smaller and middle-sized enterprises. Until the 1870s, Moscow's leading businessmen had taken an active part in *soslovie* affairs and had provided leadership in the Merchants' Society. But in the later decades of the nineteenth century, they transferred their allegiance to the Moscow Exchange Society and its executive committee, which, in 1870, after a revision of the charter of the exchange, became the chief representative organ of the upper ranks of the Moscow business community before the government and the public at large. The very fact that members of the elite had sought to create their own representative organ indicated both some divergence of interests between themselves and lesser businessmen and a desire for an organ that they could control directly.[46]

While the membership of the Exchange Society transcended the business elite as defined in this book and included the major part of the economic elite of the Moscow business world (its membership in the early twentieth century was fewer than 500 persons),[47] leadership was provided almost exclusively by individuals representing families of the social and cultural elite. Membership in the Exchange Committee was almost entirely restricted to representatives of this smaller elite, and they retained control of the presidency of the committee. Through their leadership of the committee, representatives of this small group of families served as spokesmen for the entire upper stratum of the Moscow business world and were able to mobilize the support of the city's big businessmen for their political ventures—whether this meant dealing with the bureaucracy of the Ministry of Finance, or, during and after 1905, activities in a more open political arena.

The degree to which the elite, through the Exchange Committee, also spoke for the mass of *kuptsy* is difficult to determine. The evidence on this point is sparse and conflicting, but on the whole it seems to indicate that the lesser *kuptsy* accepted spokesmen from the business elite as their spokesmen and were generally willing to follow their lead. Early in 1905, some evidence of disagreement appeared, in that statements issued by the Merchants' Society tended to be more conservative than statements emanating from representatives of the business elite. But Moscow's smaller businessmen did not attempt to form a political party of their own in that year, as small businessmen in St. Peterburg had done; rather, they seemed content to support the parties formed by the elite and may well have been gradually won over to support these parties' more progressive stance.[48] In earlier years, *kuptsy* of all gradations had been able to function as a fairly solid bloc in the Moscow duma. The *kuptsy* were generally recognized as constituting a separate faction within the city council and were able to act together to fend off challenges to their dominance from representatives of the *meshchanstvo*. Certainly, members of the elite in the duma (particularly N. A. Naidenov, for many years president of the Exchange Committee) were zealous in the defense of all local business interests.[49]

Further evidence of the ability of the elite and lesser *kuptsy* to function as a group, not only on a local but on a regional level, comes from the Nizhnii Novgorod fair.[50] *Kuptsy* trading at the fair were permitted to select from among themselves members of a fair assembly—an interesting and important exception to the general rule of purely local *soslovie* organizations. In addition, a Nizhnii Novgorod Fair Committee was set up to administer fair business. The president of this committee oversaw the work of both the assembly and his committee and served as spokesman for the fair *kupechestvo*, frequently forwarding petitions in their name to government departments. These petitions are interesting in that they did tend to reflect the concerns of large numbers of *kuptsy* at various levels of the business world and from various regions of the Empire. A major concern in the 1890s, for example, was an innovation apparently first introduced by firms in Russian Poland, namely, the use of traveling salesmen. Regarding this practice as unfair competition for businessmen whose selling techniques were traditionally fair-oriented, the fair *kupechestvo* demanded regulation, if not abolition, of these traveling salesmen.[51] Such demands were typically voiced in the name of the "all-Russian *kupechestvo*," an obvious misnomer, but nonetheless the Nizhnii Novgorod fair was an important institution in bringing together *kuptsy* from various localities and giving them some experience in working together.

Moreover, the operation of the fair induced cooperation not only between *kuptsy* from different localities but between *kuptsy* at different levels of the business community. While the Moscow business elite certainly exerted a great deal of influence over fair policies, since the fair continued to be an extremely important event in their business calendar, the presidents of the Fair Committee during the latter decades of the nineteenth century came sometimes from the Moscow elite, sometimes from among lesser, though still distinguished, provincial *kuptsy*. The harmony exhibited by these various elements of the business community in the operation of the fair, especially in the process of making their wishes known to the government, would seem to indicate that the Moscow business elite's frequent claim to be speaking in the name of the "all-Russian *kupechestvo*" had some substance. If not actually representing a truly national group of businessmen, they probably could speak with some confidence for the *kupechestvo* not only of Moscow but of the Central Industrial Region and the few other areas represented at the Nizhnii Novgorod fair.

Some members of the Moscow business elite actually went out of their way to maintain good relations with lesser businessmen, chiefly by maintaining their connections with the Moscow *kupechestvo*'s *soslovie* institutions. While no member of the elite held any major executive position in the Merchants' Society or the Merchants' Club after 1860, some accepted nomination to less demanding offices, often honorary or supervisory in nature. The records of the Merchants' Club for 1888 through 1913 show that the major officers of the club—president, vice-president, and treasurer—were always chosen from among the lesser *kuptsy*. But during the period from 1888 to 1905, ten individuals from elite families served at one time or another as *starshina* (elder) of the club, among them V. S. Perlov, N. I. Shchukin, M. A. Morozov, and I. A. Morozov.[52] Some individuals from the elite, though in diminishing numbers, continued to sit as members of the representative assembly *(vybornye)* of the Merchants' Society. As late as 1913, three Naidenovs, two Riabushinskiis, a Krestovnikov, and a Sapozhnikov were listed as members of the assembly.[53] The elite thus accounted for only a small minority of the total of 100 representatives, but their token presence indicated a desire to maintain contact with the business community beyond the elite group.

However strong the evidence for solidarity among the Moscow *kupechestvo*, divisions within that group should not be minimized. Different levels of cultural development were one important factor splitting the *kupechestvo* along numerous fracture lines. If some millionaires had reached an advanced stage of cultural refinement, others were not far removed, culturally speaking, from the peasantry or the traditional merchants of earlier centuries. Communication under such circumstances could be difficult, and points of view were bound to differ.

In addition, the continuing existence of the *sosloviia* and the diverse *soslovie* membership of individuals making up the business community made any degree of unity problematical. To see the business community as a whole, one must step outside the *kupechestvo* and consider individuals from a variety of *sosloviia* who were engaged in business activity. Not a few businessmen continued to remain, in legal and often in cultural terms, members of the peasantry, even though their ties with the villages had often become extremely tenuous. An important minority of businessmen belonged to the nobility. Before 1898, nobles in business were required to register as "temporary" members of the *kupechestvo*, but then even this

requirement was removed and noble businessmen thereafter had no official connection, and usually felt no connection of any sort, with the *kupechestvo*. These businessmen from the nobility may have derived their
income largely from business pursuits and may have shared many of the
views of other businessmen on such matters as tariffs and labor policy.
But in their basic allegiance, in their style of life, in their whole mental
outlook, they remained in most cases noblemen first and foremost and
were not willing to give up their identity as members of the Empire's
highest social grouping for the sake of solidarity with businessmen who,
though they may have had many interests in common with noblemen in
business, represented a distinctly inferior social status.

Moreover, the maintenance of a division between the *kupechestvo* and
the *meshchanstvo* preserved what was in some respects an artificial barrier
between businessmen, particularly as some members of the *meshchanstvo*
were wealthy and successful businessmen who simply found it possible to
conduct their businesses without the specific rights conferred by membership in the guilds. In Moscow, even though it might have been expected
that similar economic interests would induce these two groups to cooper-
ate to some degree, in fact a strict division continued to be recognized
between *kupechestvo* and *meshchanstvo*, a division reinforced by lingering
feelings of envy and hostility on the part of the *meshchane* toward the more
privileged *kuptsy*. These attitudes were strongly expressed within the
arena of the Moscow city duma during the 1870s and early 1880s. During
those years, when the *meshchanstvo* had a substantial representation in the
duma (almost entirely eliminated by the more stringent qualifications for
voting imposed by the new municipal statute of 1892), conflict between
meshchane and *kuptsy* was a regular occurrence in the duma and seriously
interfered with the smooth operation of city government. That the dislike
was mutual was indicated not only by the *meshchane*'s attacks on *kuptsy* but
by the fact that the *kuptsy* had consciously chosen to ally themselves with
the representatives of the nobility and the intelligentsia rather than try to
forge an understanding with their fellow businessmen from the *meshchanstvo*. The fundamental causes of this conflict between *meshchane* and *kuptsy*
are impossible to discern from the public record of duma proceedings.[54]
It seems likely, however, that the heritage of competitiveness and mutual
hostility created by the workings of the *soslovie* system was an important
underlying factor.

Some confirmation of this supposition can be found in other sources.
One specific cause of tension between the two groups can be gleaned from
occasional newspaper articles reporting persistent complaints from the
Meshchanskoe Society over what seemed to its members an unfair and
burdensome aspect of the *soslovie* system. In accordance with the rules
specified by law, persons who failed to pay the annual fee required to
renew their membership in one of the guilds were transferred automati-

cally to the rolls of the Meshchanskoe Society. In the later decades of the nineteenth century, about 600 families each year became members of the *meshchanstvo* in this manner. Many of these persons were victims of bankruptcies or other misfortunes that had left them largely without means, and henceforth it was the Meshchanskoe Society rather than the Merchants' Society that became responsible for giving them aid. Even though the Merchants' Society helped out by contributing to the maintenance of schools and charitable institutions for persons from the *meshchanstvo*, still the Meshchanskoe Society was permanently aggrieved at having to assume responsibility for what were, in reality, indigent *kuptsy*.[55] In the 1890s the creation of a municipal welfare system, which gradually came to take the major share of the responsibility for poor persons of all *sosloviia*, no doubt mitigated this complaint. But for many years this peculiarity of the *soslovie* system perpetuated hostile feelings on the part of the *meshchanstvo* toward the *kupechestvo*.

On the basis of available evidence, it simply is not possible to assume that the Moscow business elite, when it spoke in the name of Moscow business, was speaking for the *meshchanstvo* as well as for the *kupechestvo*. There are numerous indications, including the independent behavior of members of the duma from the *meshchanstvo*, that the *meshchane* possessed their own points of view, differing from those of the *kuptsy*. On one memorable occasion in 1878 a band of small traders operating in the commercial area known as Okhotnyi Riad (Hunters' Row) physically attacked Moscow University students who were demonstrating to show their support for student revolutionaries recently arrested in Kiev.[56] Such incidents led to the branding of the *meshchanstvo* as politically reactionary and earned them their nickname of the "black hundreds" (a nickname applied regularly to the *meshchanstvo*'s representatives in the duma). However Moscow's more substantial businessmen may have felt about revolutionary students, it is difficult to imagine them participating in or even approving of such vulgar street brawling. And the fact that many of their own offspring were now attending universities would most likely have influenced their reaction to such manifestations among students.

Another indication of the differing attitudes of the *meshchanstvo* is the fact that they had in Moscow a newspaper catering specifically to the interests and prejudices of this lower urban social stratum. The paper was *Moskovskii listok*, which flourished from 1881 until 1918. Its publisher, N. I. Pastukhov, who came from the *meshchanstvo* of Smolensk province, had for a time operated a tavern in Moscow; after going bankrupt, he turned his hand to journalism and experienced instant success. *Moskovskii listok* quickly acquired the reputation of being something of a scandal sheet, but the "scandals" it retailed very often were attacks on *kuptsy*. The paper habitually attacked local businessmen who were thought to treat their employees badly or who were responsible for sanitary nuisances or who committed other offenses against the health and welfare of the lower strata of the city's populace.[57] The very existence of the paper indicated the existence of a gulf between the outlooks of the *meshchanstvo* and the *kupechestvo*, and the paper's constant attacks on *kuptsy* displayed the same strident (if somewhat unfocused) hostility against the *kupechestvo*, as did the verbal attacks by members of the duma from the *meshchanstvo*.

The continuing sharp division between *kupechestvo* and *meshchanstvo* is an important point in support of the argument of most Western historians that no such thing as a modern bourgeoisie or middle class existed in Russia in the nineteenth or even the early twentieth century. Russia had not yet experienced the creation of a bourgeois culture, set of values, and outlook that could unite even the various levels of the business community as a whole. But the major objection to applying the term "bourgeoisie" to Russian society in this period is that a bourgeoisie is usually considered to include not only persons engaged in commerce and industry but also members of the professions, many intellectuals, bureaucrats, and the like.[58] Parenthetically, when Soviet historians, following this conventional conceptualization of the bourgeoisie, employ the term to describe Imperial Russian society, they frequently do so in the most broadly inclusive manner; thus, in Soviet works we find petty shopkeepers and Mensheviks, liberal intellectuals and big industrialists, all thrown together as a single social grouping. Such a use of the term simply does not stem from Russian realities. There existed profound divisions between businessmen, on the one hand, and professional people, intellectuals, and bureaucrats, on the other, and it is impossible to see them as constituting any sort of cohesive social grouping.

The Russian intelligentsia, including most members of the liberal professions, not only harbored feelings of dislike for businessmen but showed the most determined hostility toward anything that smacked of *burzhauznost* ("bourgeoisness") and would have been morally outraged to find themselves included in the same social grouping with *kuptsy* and *meshchane* who, in their eyes, personified this *burzhuaznost*.[59] If an increasing number of intellectuals and professional people were beginning to find themselves either employed by businessmen or cooperating with them on various public projects, most were nonetheless consciously determined to maintain a certain distance between themselves and these bearers of "bourgeois" poisons. Ideologically, businessmen and the intelligentsia were poles apart, particularly before 1905. If during the revolution of 1905 they sometimes found themselves supporting similar programs, the basic assumptions on which the political and social views of these groups rested had little in common (see chap. 6). Economically, businessmen and intellectuals were united by few bonds, the one group basing its economic well-being on private commercial and industrial enterprise, the other chiefly on employment in various public institutions, such as the universities, the state bureaucracy, and the zemstvos, or an independent professional or artistic activity. Socially, businessmen and intellectuals found themselves increasingly thrown together, particularly in view of the broad cultural interests and patronage of many wealthy businessmen; but there remained a social gulf between the two groups that was never wholly bridged, no matter how increasingly frequent their social mixing.

In the case of bureaucrats, again, numerous obstacles to their integration into any sort of bourgeoisie existed. A scornful attitude toward *kuptsy* was hardly restricted to the intelligentsia but was rampant in bureaucratic circles as well. Even in the later nineteenth century, when the state had adopted a deliberate policy of promoting economic development, many officials maintained a contemptuous attitude toward businessmen, often seeming to regard them simply as tools to be used by the state in accomplishing its own purposes. Like the intelligentsia, higher officials took a stance "above classes" and were often irritated at the narrow self-interest that guided businessmen. Thus, state officials, drawn chiefly from the nobility, the intelligentsia, and the *raznochintsy*, had little in common with business people in terms of attitudes, life-styles, and economic employment. Like the intelligentsia, they would have resisted strenuously any attempt to include them in the same social grouping with businessmen. Russia was still a very long way from developing a bourgeoisie analogous to those of Western European countries.

ALTHOUGH the Russian government had made sporadic efforts to raise the low social status of the *kupechestvo*, such efforts had produced only meager results. The fact that a *kupets* assumed the title of hereditary honored citizen or even manufacturing councillor did not add greatly to his prestige, at least in the eyes of a nobleman or a high official. Much more effective in elevating the social standing of businessmen and their families were the growing wealth and increasing education and culture displayed by members of Russia's business elite. There is no question that in the years after 1861 Russia's wealthier business families gradually acquired greater social prestige and social acceptability. Nonetheless, they never succeeded in conquering the commanding heights of Russian society, a bastion still securely occupied by the *dvorianstvo* until 1917. However great their social advances, the leading families of the Russian *kupechestvo* repeatedly ran up against the determination of the *dvorianstvo* to retain its position at the top of Russian society and were never able to overcome this obstacle to their social ambitions. Economically in decline, deprived of many of the privileges which had buttressed its position in the past, the Russian nobility was all the more determined to cling to the lingering traces of its social influence.

The relationship that developed between the Russian business community and the Russian nobility in the last decades of the Empire was both complex and ambiguous and has so far been the object of only limited investigation. While an exhaustive investigation of the subject cannot be undertaken here, it seems worthwhile to dispose of certain myths regarding the businessman's attitude toward the nobility and to attempt to describe the relationship between the two groups at least as it existed in Moscow, in order to clarify further the position of the Moscow business elite in the city's social structure.

Prince S. A. Shcherbatov, a member of one of Moscow's most respected noble families as well as an artist and collector, noted in his recollections of Moscow in the early twentieth century that

> at that time the boundary between the merchant and the noble *sosloviia* was still rather strictly observed, not only because of tradition, but because of directives from above. One needs only recall, for example, that the *kupechestvo* was not invited to the large official balls of the Moscow Governor–General, Grand Duke Sergei Aleksandrovich.[60]

But Shcherbatov then went on to write about the businessmen-patrons of Moscow with whom he was well acquainted as a result of their mutual interest in art. In fact, he became a very close friend of I. S. Ostroukhov, son of a Moscow *kupets*, a painter and collector, a Botkin son-in-law and one of the principals in the Botkin tea firm.[61] His recollections sum up fairly well the relationship that existed between nobles and businessmen in Moscow at the turn of the century: if officially a firm line of social demarcation between the two groups was preserved, the line was frequently crossed.

The first breaches in the social barrier separating nobles and merchants would seem to have been effected at about mid-century. Before the 1850s there was almost no social mixing of the two *sosloviia*, but in that decade, as the noble memoirist D. Nikiforov recalled, some of the Moscow nobility's *jeunesse doré* had begun attending social functions given by wealthy business families.[62] Occasions on which representatives of the two groups were brought together increased substantially in the 1860s and 1870s as a result of the creation of "all-*sosloviia* institutions" by the Great Reforms. And not only did the new institutions encourage cooperation between members of the various *sosloviia* to realize common ends; they also assisted in promoting changes in attitude toward the mixing of different social groups. Impressed by the leveling effects of the reforms, certain nobles and intellectuals showed enthusiasm for the idea of abolishing all social privileges and distinctions and moving Russia in the direction of a "classless" society.[63] Evidence of the new attitude may be found in the memoirs of the period, including those of Prince E. N. Trubetskoi. Trubetskoi recalled that as long as his old grandfather lived, he and his brothers had not been permitted to play with the sons of a merchant who, much to the indignation of the elder Trubetskoi, had purchased a neighboring estate. But when his grandfather died, his parents, who had brought their children up to "believe in the equality of all before God," ignored the social distinction between themselves and their neighbor, and the merchant's sons soon became the inseparable companions of the young Trubetskois.[64] When Trubetskoi entered a Moscow gymnasium in 1874, he

> understood nothing about class distinctions. In school the boys loved to show off their democratic attitudes, and the word "prince" was somehow shameful. It was very painful for me, but this changed with time and we became great friends and comrades. Class distinctions, which seemed so important at first, disappeared with time. Here was an important and good influence of the all-*sosloviia* schools.[65]

But if representatives of the various *sosloviia* were increasingly brought together in the schools and other new institutions, the old prejudices never completely died out. Buryshkin recalled that during his school days at the prestigious Katkov Lyceum, while the students themselves ignored social distinctions, the administration was not so broad-minded. When Grand Duke Sergei was assassinated in 1904, the administration had to select a pupil to represent the school at the funeral ceremonies. All the students expected that the honor would go to Buryshkin, because of his standing at the top of the senior class. But the administration felt that the school should be represented by a scion of the nobility. Only reluctantly did they finally accept the merchant's son, after a Prince Golitsyn and the son of a provincial marshal of the nobility had both rejected the honor in indignation over the injustice being done to Buryshkin. The experience left Buryshkin with a very unpleasant memory and, he recalled, impressed upon him for the first time that he was a member of an "inferior" social group.[66]

The attitudes of Moscow's business elite toward mingling with the nobility were mixed and seem to have varied considerably from family to family and from individual to individual. This ambivalence within the elite had existed earlier in the century, when it still had required an almost superhuman effort for even the wealthiest business families to break into noble circles. There were at that time some families, like the Alekseevs, who made the effort. V. S. Alekseev, according to the memoirist N. P. Vishniakov, had a "policy" of trying to marry his daughters off to noblemen and indeed succeeded with three of them. And, as Vishniakov noted, "it is necessary to understand the conceit of the *dvorianstvo* of that time in order to appreciate for what it is worth the self-sacrifice of the Kislovskiis, Riumins and Kostomarovs who decided to become related to '*arshinniki*,' not fearing the poisonous reproaches of their own *soslovie*. Of course, the Alekseev money played the role of a mitigating circumstance."[67]

Ambitious business families earlier in the century could take advantage of the services of certain poor but noble ladies who, for a price, undertook to train merchant daughters in the social graces and to provide them with an entrée into Moscow's high society.[68] But while some families made use of this opportunity, many others scorned it. Vishniakov described the negative attitude that characterized the view of perhaps the majority of Moscow's *kuptsy* toward the nobility at mid-century. He wrote:

> Relations of the *kupechestvo* with the *dvorianstvo*, the ruling class, privileged, isolated within itself, and interested only in pursuing its narrow class goals, were naturally full of distrust, envy and hostility. To meet a *dvorianin* or *dvorianka* in the merchant milieu was as rare as finding a *kupets* or *kupchikha* in the noble milieu. If this happened, it aroused generally most lively and sarcastic curiosity about those who had violated the customs of their own caste. Usually this was explained by self-serving calculation. If a *kupets* received a nobleman, this meant: he will get a contract, order or medals, he wants to marry off his daughter to a "noble." And if, God forbid, a nobleman intended to marry a merchant daughter, the fate of the latter was mourned in advance: what else could the nobleman have in view except to fleece her and then leave her? The exception could only be a rich merchant family, possessing sufficient means so that they could "buy" a respectable nobleman, but this was a rarity. Also, if a *kupets* married a noblewoman, everyone felt sorry for him. It was not supposed that a noblewoman would marry a merchant except if she did not have a skirt to her name. And what good could be expected to come of such conditions?[69]

Indeed, the *kupechestvo* as a whole appears to have believed that little good could come of mixing nobles and merchants; if some wealthy business families lusted after sons-in-law from the nobility, most of their fellow *kuptsy* appear to have been extremely skeptical of such a practice.

In later decades the same division of attitudes seems to have persisted among Moscow's elite business families. On the one hand, some of the Alekseevs carried on the tradition of courting the nobility. K. S. Alekseev-Stanislavsky recalled the brilliant balls given by his aunt and uncle—balls to which many wealthy business families sought invitations because numerous aristocratic guests could be expected to be present.[70] On the other hand, P. M. Tretiakov exemplified the old suspicions. In spite of the fact that Tretiakov numbered many noblemen among his acquaintances, and his wife had tea with Countess Sollogub, their neighbor, Tretiakov tried sternly to limit his family's contacts with representatives of the nobility. His daughter Vera recalled that although the daughter of L. N. Tolstoi frequently came to paint at the Tretiakov Gallery and stayed to lunch with the family, further contacts between her and the Tretiakov girls were not so much explicitly discouraged by their father as implicitly understood to be undesirable.[71] When his daughters came of marriageable age, Tretiakov, who always showed a real pride in his *soslovie* and a firm sense of his own place in the social scheme of things, was determined that they must marry men of their own circle.[72] Vera's friendship with a young nobleman caused consternation in both their families, neither of which desired to see a marriage crossing social barriers.[73] When Vera finally announced her determination to marry another nobleman, the pianist A. I. Ziloti, her father successfully opposed the marriage for a number of years, partly out of fear that Ziloti was only after his money.[74] Similarly, when Vera's cousin Praskovia Konshina wished to marry A. I. Tchaikovsky, brother of the well-known composer, the elder Konshin reacted negatively, partly on the grounds that Tchaikovsky was a nobleman, partly on the grounds that the suitor was from St. Petersburg. Only the personal intervention of the highly respected N. A. Alekseev finally brought him round to accept the proposed marriage.[75]

In the last decades of the nineteenth century, when such members of the younger generation of the business elite as Vera Tretiakova were more and more setting the tone, a certain change in the attitude of Moscow's business elite toward the nobility was observable. While members of this generation, benefiting from the changes in institutions and attitudes effected in the era of the Great Reforms, mixed more freely with nobles than their fathers had done, they nonetheless at the same time began to show signs of increasing contempt and even hatred toward Russia's socially elite *soslovie*. Vladimir Nemirovich-Danchenko, a member of the Moscow intelligentsia, characterized the relationship existing between Moscow nobles and businessmen at the turn of the century as one of "external amiability and concealed hatred."[76] While attitudes among the business elite undoubtedly continued to vary a good deal, there is much to be said for this writer's characterization. If the attitude of the *kupechestvo* toward the nobility had always contained a good deal of dislike, expressions of this feeling had frequently been inhibited by a certain instinctive respect for the *dvorianstvo* and, perhaps, by fear of their power. But in the younger generation, such restraints were breaking down. Thus, Savva Morozov's reaction to a proposed visit from the Grand Duke Sergei, who wished personally to inspect Morozov's fabulous new home, openly indicated the contempt which he felt toward Moscow's social elite. Morozov willingly issued the requested invitation to the Grand Duke, but when Sergei arrived at the Morozov home, he was greeted only by servants: Morozov himself did not deign to be present.[77]

Such feelings of contempt toward the nobility were only infrequently expressed before 1905, but there are indications that they were mounting,

THE SOCIAL STRUCTURE OF RUSSIA AND MOSCOW · 45

especially among the more politically aware members of the younger generation. Imbued with a new sense of self-confidence, annoyed at the continuing social and political dominance of the nobility, certain members of this generation became increasingly irritated and impatient for a transfer of prestige and power into their own hands. This attitude, developing before 1905, would be expressed in the years after 1905 in P. P. Riabushinskii's newspaper, *Utro Rossii*. It was best summed up in a letter to the editor of this paper. Lamenting the poverty-stricken condition of the mass of the Russian people, the correspondent argued that

> it is impossible any longer for both the nobleman and the bourgeois to remain on the shoulders of the *narod* [the people] and one of them is going to have to get off. This is the circumstance which gives rise to the conflicts which, from time to time, arise between them. The sooner that the bourgeois becomes the sole master of the situation, the easier it will be for the whole *narod* to live.[78]

Riabushinskii himself, in both his newspaper and his speeches, argued strongly against businessmen's seeking elevation into the nobility, advising them to remain in the *kupechestvo* and thereby refrain from weakening their own class which, he was convinced, would control the future of Russia.[79] Riabushinskii's attitude was hardly new. In spite of the widespread belief that most heartfelt desire of every businessman was to become a *dvorianin*, the fact is that many wealthy businessmen, in the latter half of the nineteenth century, did not regard elevation into the nobility as a great boon.[80] When Boborykin portrayed his businessman-hero in *Pereval* as concentrating all his efforts on the achievement of noble status, *Novosti*'s Rakshanin rightly criticized him for it, noting that most of Moscow's business magnates had long ago ceased to covet the title of *dvorianin*.[81] Evidence of this attitude could be found in the writings of V. A. Kokorev, a well-known Moscow entrepreneur and for many years a leader of the Moscow business community, though he failed to found a dynasty. In the 1880s, Kokorev, foreshadowing the arguments of *Utro Rossii* in later years, insisted that elevation of businessmen into the nobility was a badly mistaken policy on the part of the government, since it tended to remove from the business community its most successful and able members. Because many businessmen who became nobles gave up business as a profession, Kokorev argued that their elevation both weakened the Russian economy and slowed down the development of a strong industrial and commercial class.[82]

Kokorev believed that even if a patent of nobility was offered to a businessman, he should turn it down in the interests of both his own business and his *soslovie* as a whole.[83] And, indeed, a number of leading Moscow families did refuse elevation to noble status or at least failed to pursue it actively even when they had a fair assurance of success. The Bakhrushins, according to Buryshkin, could have had nobility for the asking because of their extensive philanthropy, but most of the family did not wish it.[84] The Khludovs actually turned down an offer of ennoblement, as did N. A. Naidenov.[85] In Naidenov's case, it is indeed difficult to see what he might have gained by elevation into the nobility, except somewhat greater social prestige, though he certainly stood to lose a good deal. As chairman of Moscow's Exchange Committee for a quarter of a century, Naidenov had not only accumulated a good deal of power within the Moscow business community but enjoyed considerable influence in government chancelleries in both Moscow and St. Petersburg. Had he relinquished his standing as a *kupets*, his position as the chief spokesman for the Moscow business elite would have been adversely affected, with no corresponding gain from his new status. Thus, the fact that very few of Moscow's elite business families were elevated to the nobility in the later nineteenth and early twentieth centuries reflected not only the fact that the acquisition of noble status had, at the insistence of the nobility, been made more difficult by the government but also the fact that many wealthy businessmen no longer desired this supposed blessing. Certainly, the younger generation of the Moscow elite were no longer interested in entering the nobility but, rather, sought to replace it.

As at least one contemporary spokesman for the nobility pointed out, the declining enthusiasm of businessmen for entrance into the *dvorianstvo* was perhaps in part the result of the apparently declining economic and social status of that *soslovie*.[86] Indeed, in view of the numerous laments in these years over the decline of the nobility, it is possible that many businessmen sensed that by entering the *dvorianstvo* they would only be hitching their wagons to a falling star.

One other factor that diminished the desirability of noble status for Moscow businessmen was the increasing attraction they felt toward the intelligentsia. As will become apparent in later chapters, the younger generation in particular gloried in occasional mention of themselves as the "*kupecheskaia* intelligentsia" and showed considerably greater interest in achieving the informal designation of *intelligent* than in receiving the title of *dvorianin*. As their contempt for the nobility increased, their respect for the intelligentsia seemed to grow, partly because of the spread of education and cultural interests in the upper circles of the business milieu. Thus, the intelligentsia came to exercise increasing attraction for the members of Moscow's business elite, and this attraction undoubtedly helped to turn many of them away from seeking entrance into the nobility.[87]

The *dvorianstvo*, of course, showed no particular enthusiasm for taking businessmen into their midst. Not only had they put pressure on the government in the past to make it more difficult for members of the *kupechestvo* and other "inferior" social groups to achieve noble status, but certain circles of the nobility, consisting of many of the oldest and most illustrious noble families, continued to the end firmly to exclude businessmen from their company.[88] When the nobleman A. N. Naumov announced his intention to marry the daughter of a wealthy Moscow industrialist, one of his noble relatives, completely taken aback, requested that at least he would not bring his bride to the family estate.[89] Such prejudices were still strong in many noble families and worked to continue the general exclusion of businessmen from the highest circles of the nobility, particularly those close to the Imperial court or, in Moscow, to the court of the Grand Duke Sergei.

Indeed, if scorn and hatred for the nobility were increasing among Moscow's business elite toward the end of the nineteenth century, it seems likely that many nobles not only continued to regard businessmen with the traditional contempt but with a growing sense of hatred and fear. The contrast between innumerable noble families faced with economic decline and ruin and, on the other hand, the growing wealth and economic power of Moscow businessmen could, not inconceivably, have given rise to feelings of envy, tinged with the fear of increasingly being overtaken by wealthy businessmen. Certainly, evidence of the decline of the one group and the rise of the other was visible everywhere in Moscow. Innumerable mansions which had once belonged to noble families had fallen into the hands of businessmen. Elegant and fashionable streets such as Tverskaia, once entirely inhabited by the nobility, had long ago been invaded by representatives of the *kupechestvo*.[90] Even such once-sacred preserves of the nobility as the English Club and the Hermitage restaurant had been forced to admit businessmen, their rubles providing the money to keep these institutions going when the Moscow nobility alone could no longer do so. If the Hermitage's founder had given up his business and gone back to France rather than serve upstarts from the *kupechestvo*, Russian nobles had no such recourse and had to stand by and watch all their haunts being infiltrated by wealthy businessmen.[91] Faced with such a situation, many nobles undoubtedly reacted with the same feelings of intense irritation as beset one of Boborykin's *dvoriane* when he contemplated the fact that now "sons of fish merchants" were "writing monographs about the medieval guilds or about the teaching of Hugo Grotius," receiving higher degrees, and being given positions at the university.[92]

Moreover, some nobles increasingly found themselves in a position of financial dependence of one sort or another on representatives of the *kupechestvo*. The writer and nobleman Sergei Atava, in a frequently quoted description of the changing relationship of *dvorianin* to *kupets*, recalled the post-1861 transformation of that relationship, which had occurred largely because of the nobles' increasing need for money. Before 1861, if a *kupets* had business on the estate of a nobleman, he came not to the main house but "to an outbuilding, where the clerk lived, or where the horses were stabled," and he settled his business with the master's clerk. If momentarily admitted into the office of the estate owner, he conducted himself with respect, "constantly jumping up, smiling, sweating, wiping his brow." If he had to stay the night, he slept in the clerk's quarters. Inviting him to dinner with the master and his family was out of the question, because he "would blow his nose on the napkin." But with the emancipation of the nobles' serfs, "everything suddenly changed." "All of us at that time," Atava recalled, "were dreadfully in need of money. And the '*kupets*' had the money." As the nobles were forced to borrow more and more from the *kuptsy*, the relationship between them subtly changed. Now, when the *kupets* came to the estate, he came straight to the master's office. It was no longer possible to ask him to sleep with the clerk: he had to be given a divan in the main house. It became impossible to avoid asking him to dine with the master and his family, and stern warnings had to be given to the children not to laugh if he should use his napkin as a handkerchief.[93]

Atava found this new relationship distasteful and both resented and felt humiliated by the position which *kuptsy* had been able to assume vis-à-vis their noble debtors. Undoubtedly, many Moscow noblemen shared both his reliance on *kuptsy* for financial help and his resentment of the liberties taken by his new creditors. In Moscow, several leading businessmen made their fortunes largely by lending money to needy noble families.[94] One of them, the discounter and real estate magnate Firsanov, completed his humiliation of the defenders of noble purity by marrying his daughter to the son of a general.[95]

Thus, it seems likely that by the turn of the century, in spite of increasing social intercourse between the two groups, their attitude toward one another was often, indeed, one of "external amiability and concealed hatred." Faced with economic decline, forced to turn to businessmen to keep their estates going and their clubs open, Russian nobles would hardly have been human if they had not felt considerable hostility toward the traditionally despised social group which was now surpassing them in wealth and placing them in positions of economic dependence. Moreover, it did not take a visionary to point out that the increasing wealth and economic power of the *kupechestvo* constituted not only an economic but a political and social threat to the position of the *dvorianstvo*. Fear of being overtaken in all these respects by businessmen undoubtedly came to color the nobility's opinion of the Russian *kupets*, while at the same time the businessmen, secure in their wealth and ambitious for greater power, became increasingly determined to replace the *dvoriane* as the leading social group of the Empire.

THE ECONOMIC FOUNDATIONS OF THE
MOSCOW DYNASTIES

THE commercial and industrial activities of the Moscow business dynasties and the family fortunes which lay at the basis of their social position and ambitions had as their main foundation family enterprises founded in the late eighteenth or, more frequently, the early nineteenth century. As their capital gradually increased, almost all the dynasties expanded their business interests beyond the field of their original involvement and, either through investment or through entrepreneurial activity, acquired holdings in a variety of business undertakings. But however far-flung its assets, the mainstay of each family—and of its reputation in the Moscow business world—remained the original family-owned enterprise, founded in most cases by the same individual who was considered the founder of the dynasty.

The founding fathers of the Moscow dynasties were a remarkable group of men, most of whom started life as members of the peasantry or of the provincial merchantry and then through successful business activity achieved positions of respect in the Moscow *kupechestvo*. Very few were originally native to the city, but, like many other ambitious businessmen of Russia's central provinces, they were almost inevitably drawn to Moscow as the trade center not only for the central region but for Siberia and other outlying areas of the Empire as well. The Perlovs were perhaps the only family who could trace ancestors back to early eighteenth-century Moscow.[1] The founders of the other dynasties came, for the most part, from provinces within the Central Industrial Region, including Kaluga, Kostroma, Iaroslavl, Vladimir, and Moscow province itself. In most cases, they and their successors retained ties with their native provinces long after the move to Moscow had been made, usually by virtue of the fact that the family factories were located there although the head offices were in Moscow.

As for their social origins, almost all the founding fathers of the Moscow dynasties came from either the peasantry or the *kupechestvo*. The serf origins of many leading Moscow business families have received a good deal of emphasis from some historians, perhaps more than is merited. Many families did indeed have serf ancestors, including the Abrikosovs, Alekseevs, Guchkovs, Konovalovs, Morozovs, Naidenovs, and Ushkovs. Nonetheless, a surprising number of the Moscow dynasties originated in other social groups. A notable minority traced their origins back to the monastic peasants, who were freed from serfdom in the late eighteenth century. This group included such families as the Karzinkins, Khludovs, Krestovnikovs, Prokhorovs, and Riabushinskiis. A large number of families also came from various strata of the town population. The Botkins, Perlovs, Vishniakovs, and Karetnikovs traced their ancestors back to the *posadskie liudi*, the urban commercial and industrial population of the seventeenth and early eighteenth centuries, while the Bakhrushins, Shchukins, and Tretiakovs all claimed origin in the provincial *kupechestvo* of the eighteenth century. The founders of many other dynasties (including the Lepeshkins, Maliutins, Mazurins, Shelaputins, and others) were already registered in the merchant guilds of various provincial towns at the time that they moved to Moscow, but in some of these cases it is entirely possible that the family originally came from the peasantry and made the transition to the *kupechestvo* only shortly before arriving in Moscow.[2]

If the geographical and social origins of the dynastic founders were extremely varied, so were their business activities. They got their start in business in different ways, some beginning as small traders and then moving into industrial production, others moving from *kustar* (cottage industry) production or factory employment into independent business activity. Among those who started as traders were I. V. Chetverikov and M. P. Riabushinskii. Moving to Moscow from Kaluga province in the late eigthteenth century, Chetverikov first established a shop trading in textiles and later, in 1831, began factory production of woolen goods.[3] Riabushinskii worked for a time as a clerk in a Moscow shop trading in canvas, later purchased the shop from his employer, and expanded its trade to include cotton and woolen goods. At first he simply purchased textiles from peasant weavers, but later Riabushinskii went on to organize *kustar* production, distributing yarn to the weavers and collecting the finished cloth from them. Finally, in 1846, he established his first small weaving factory in Moscow and soon thereafter built cotton and woolen weaving factories in his native Kaluga province.[4]

Other dynastic founders went from factory employment or *kustar* production to the creation of their own factories, though sometimes passing through an intermediary stage of primarily commercial operations. The founder of the Morozov dynasty at first worked in a small silk factory in his native village of Zuevo, in Moscow province. Using knowledge gained at the factory, Morozov put his family to work producing silk ribbons, which he peddled in Moscow along with other goods. In 1797 he opened a small silk factory and soon thereafter added a woolens mill, later converting both factories to cotton textile production.[5] The founders of both the Naidenov and Guchkov enterprises were also originally serfs who worked in factories and then started their own woolen textile production on the basis of knowledge acquired in their factory employment.[6] The Khludov brothers were *kustar* weavers who began to trade in textile goods and soon had other peasant weavers working for them. In 1834 they opened two shops in Moscow and in 1842 established the family trade firm. Finally, in 1846, the Khludovs opened a cotton spinning factory.[7]

However their business careers began and whatever stages they passed through, by the end of the nineteenth century the vast majority of Moscow's business dynasties were identified chiefly with industrial production. Throughout the course of the century, most families combined extensive commercial operations with the ownership of factories, but as the decades passed, the commercial side of their businesses became relatively less important while industrial operations came to predominate. At the end of the century, many families continued to handle the wholesaling, and sometimes even the retailing, of their own products and occasionally the products of other factories. But if earlier in the century the majority of their profits had in many cases come from commercial operations, by the end of the century it was the industrial side of the businesses which had become by far the most profitable and which received the most attention.[8]

Although industrialists predominated among the elite, there were a few notable exceptions. The Botkins and the Perlovs both made their fortunes in the tea trade. The Shchukin wealth also came originally from trade, but in addition to their wholesale business in textile goods, by the end of the century the family had acquired interests in several of the largest textile factories in Moscow. In any case, these three families were practically the only commercial dynasties among the predominantly industrialist elite.

The explanation for the rarity of commercial dynasties among the elite would seem to lie chiefly in the backward organization of Russian trade. While factory production in many fields tended to be concentrated in huge undertakings, trade operations usually remained in the hands of hundreds of thousands of petty merchants.[9] Although the annual turnover of trade operations in the Moscow region was considerably greater than the annual turnover of goods produced in the factories of the region, there were few commercial enterprises in the Moscow region as large or as profitable as the leading industrial concerns; this was true even at the beginning of the twentieth century.[10] The tea trade, involving the importation of tea from China, was exceptional in this respect, and wholesale merchants in some fields such as textiles could build up good-sized businesses; but even in these fields the profits of most firms did not begin to approach the profits of the large industrial enterprises.[11] Thus, the accumulation of large fortunes was much more likely to occur in industry than in trade, dispersed as it was among so many small firms and petty traders.

Within the field of industry, the great family fortunes in the Moscow industrial region were made chiefly in textiles. Moscow was the capital of one of Russia's major textile-producing areas, and the city's major business interests centered around the textile industry. As a result, the vast majority of the elite business families were, not unexpectedly, involved in some field of textile production, most of them in cotton textiles. The Guchkovs, Alekseevs, Vishniakovs, Chetverikovs, Bakhrushins, and Naidenovs made their fortunes in the woolens industry, the Tretiakovs in linen, the Sapozhnikovs in silk, but these families were among the few exceptions to the general rule of involvement in cotton textile production.

A few industrial families within the elite had no connection with the textile industry. The Ushkovs owned a large chemical plant. The Abrikosovs were famous throughout Russia for their candies, jams, and other confections, though they made the larger share of their fortune through their interest in the Popov tea concern. The Mamontovs owned a factory in Moscow producing lacquer, varnish, and related products, and one branch of the family, whose progenitor originally accumulated a fortune as an *otkupshchik* (tax farmer), became involved in railroad construction and operation. The Rukavishnikovs, whose Moscow representatives constituted one branch of a family chiefly associated with Nizhnii Novgorod, were in the metals industry. But these few families were practically the only members of the elite not involved in some branch of the textile industry.

Whether they were primarily identified with the textiles or with some other field of industry or commerce, almost all the Moscow dynasties had subsidiary business interests of so far-flung a nature that it would now be extremely difficult to track them down. They were involved in a wide variety of industrial and commercial enterprises, as well as in banking, insurance, railroads, real estate, and even, to a small degree, agriculture. An exact delineation of the holdings of some of Moscow's leading business families would indeed make a fascinating study, but this is hardly possible on the basis of published sources. The best that can be done is to give a general indication of the nature of their varied business holdings.

In regard to industry, some families had much larger holdings even within the field of textiles than was immediately apparent. For example, the Khludov family was chiefly identified with its large factory at Egorevsk, but the Khludov brothers also held a major interest in the Kränholm textile plant, which they had founded in 1857 along with L. G. Knoop and K. T. Soldatenkov, and in the Zündel factory in Moscow.[12]

In addition, the Khludovs also owned the smaller Norskaia textile factory, and A. I. Khludov and his descendants controlled the Iartsevskaia factory until its purchase by the Prokhorovs in 1907.[13] Similarly, the Vladimir Alekseev Company owned two small factories in Moscow specializing in the production of gold braid and similar products,[14] but it was also involved in numerous other textile undertakings. The company held an interest in a small factory producing worsteds in Moscow and in a woolens plant in Pushkino and also owned cotton-producing land in Central Asia, several cotton-cleaning plants, a wool-cleaning plant, and even a small chemical plant.[15] Representatives of the company were also found among the directors of the Chetverikov firm, a connection that was created by both marital and financial ties: S. I. Chetverikov, married to an Alekseev, had borrowed a considerable amount of money from his wife's family to put his own woolens factory back on its feet, and the loan gave the Alekseevs a certain amount of control over the Chetverikov enterprise.[16]

Marriage between dynasties was not at all unusual but was indeed frequently responsible for a mutual expansion of business interests. The Chetverikov case is an extremely clear and interesting example of this recurrent situation. Married to an Alekseev, Chetverikov was also related through his sister's marriage to the Protopopov family, who controlled a large vodka business. Finding himself in business difficulties, Chetverikov was able to borrow money from both Alekseevs and Protopopovs and with that money to revitalize the family factory, which his father had badly neglected.[17] Understandably, representatives of both these families appeared among the directors of Chetverikov's enterprise, but Chetverikov himself, presumably after proving his business capabilities, also became a director of both the Vladimir Alekseev Company and the Protopopovs' vodka company.[18]

By the end of the nineteenth century, most enterprises belonging to the Moscow dynasties had been reorganized as stock companies, with exclusive control remaining in the hands of family members. The Riabushinskiis, for example, had converted their enterprise into a stock company in 1887, with the issuance of 1,000 shares, worth 2,000 rubles apiece, of which 787 shares went to P. M. Riabushinskii and 200 shares to his wife. The 13 remaining shares were distributed among five employees of the firm, all of whom later sold their holdings to Riabushinskii's sons.[19] Like the Riabushinskiis, most dynasties were determined to keep exclusive control of the shares of their companies in family hands and therefore preferred the form of the stock company known as the *tovarishchestvo* rather than the alternate *aktsionernoe obshchestvo*.[20] Although the law regarding stock companies made no real distinction between these two forms, in practice the *tovarishchestvo* was frequently a family-owned company which did not offer stock for sale to the public, while the *akstionernoe obshchestvo* in most cases had a larger number of unrelated stockholders and usually, though not always, sold its stock on the open market. In most *tovarish-chestva*, any shareholder who wished to sell his interest in the company was required to offer his shares first to other shareholders and could sell to outsiders only with their agreement.[21] In such a way, shares remained in family hands, and as a result all the officials of a company—its directors and candidate-directors, members of the auditing commission responsible for preparation of the annual report, and even the managing director—not infrequently bore the same family name. When outsiders appeared among the officers, they were more often than not sons-in-law or brothers-in-law, controlling the shares owned by their wives. In some cases, the non-family names represented the women themselves, as it was not unusual for female members of the family to hold official positions within the family firm and sometimes to take an active part in management of the company. In any case, marriage ties explain why one finds G. A. Krestovnikov as a director of the Morozovs' Nikolskaia enterprise, and A. A. Naidenov, P. G. Prokhorova, and D. R. Vostriakov as officers of the Khludov enterprises.[22]

While marriage ties helped to expand the business interests of various representatives of the Moscow dynasties, some families also expanded their business holdings by the simple expedient of buying into existing firms. Within the Moscow textile industry, this procedure was difficult, because of the determination of most families to retain control of their companies' stock, but opportunities occasionally presented themselves. When the male line of the Maliutin dynasty died out in 1892, the Maliutin descendants in the female line held onto the business for only a short time and finally sold it to M. N. Bardygin in 1906.[23] When the founder of the Zündel textile factory in Moscow died, his heirs were evidently not enthusiastic about carrying on the business and in 1874 sold shares in the company to I. A. Liamin, K. T. Soldatenkov, the Khludov brothers, L. G. Knoop, and other Moscow capitalists. The Zündel company in turn acquired full ownership of the Voskresenskaia textile factory in 1907, when its owners, the Iakunchikovs, decided to give up their industrial activity.[24] Similarly, the Danilovskaia cotton-printing factory in Moscow, after the death of its owner in 1880, was taken over by a group of leading textile magnates including Knoop, Soldatenkov, and the Shchukins.[25] The Prokhorovs were also active in buying up, or buying interests in, existing textile firms. In 1877, while their Trekhgornaia factory in Moscow was being rebuilt after a fire, they bought a small printing factory in Serpukhov. Later, in 1906, they acquired a one-third interest in the Karzinkins' Bolshaia Iaroslavskaia plant, and in 1907 they bought the Khludovs' Iartsevskaia factory.[26] Thus, expansion of business interests within the textile industry by the outright purchase of existing factories or by the purchase of large blocs of shares in existing companies was not impossible, although neither was a frequent occurrence among the Moscow dynasties.

Most families whose predominant interest was in textiles also became involved in other fields of industry and trade. Even in the earlier part of the nineteenth century, some textile dynasties had founded enterprises in other fields of industry which represented a major contribution to the family wealth. The Krestovnikovs, for example, in 1855 established a stearin plant, which later evolved into a good-sized chemical enterprise.[27] The Lepeshkins, Baranovs, and Maliutins all founded smaller chemical plants, while the Bakhrushins had a tannery in Moscow in addition to their woolens factory.[28]

This sort of entrepreneurial activity continued on a much broader scale in the later years of the nineteenth and early years of the twentieth century, but where the earlier creations had chiefly been the product of family enterprise, the companies founded in later years most frequently took the form of stock companies in which representatives of the dynasties participated along with other capitalists. Their participation in the creation of such enterprises led Moscow businessmen into a variety of fields of industry and trade, including chemicals, machine building, mining, oil, and the electrical industry. Among the more successful ventures of this type was the Moscow Trade-Industrial Company, which dealt in cotton, wool, silk, and furs, and which was founded by a group of leading Moscow capitalists. It included among its officers N. A. and V. A. Naidenov, P. M. Tretiakov, V. I. Iakunchikov, and V. G. Sapozhnikov.[29] Another noteworthy creation of Moscow capitalists was the first Russian plant to produce looms and other machinery for the textile industry, founded in 1882 by G. A. Krestovnikov, A. I. Baranov, and S. V. Lepeshkin.[30]

Besides creating new enterprises, some families also purchased already-existing firms in various fields of industry in order to expand their business holdings. S. I. Mamontov, one of the most imaginative of Moscow entrepreneurs, tried to ensure a supply of equipment for the railroad of which he was managing director by purchasing iron foundries in Siberia and a plant producing locomotives and steamships in St. Petersburg. Unfortunately, Mamontov's imagination outran his financial capabilities, and his railroad empire came crashing down in 1900.[31] In the period after 1905, the Riabushinskiis, partly through purchase of existing enterprises and partly through entrepreneurial activity, put together a conglomerate including the most diverse companies. While expanding their family cotton textile enterprise, the Riabushinskii brothers also bought a publishing company and several enterprises in the field of linen textiles, built a paper factory and a glass factory, founded a bank, entered the lumber trade, and in 1916 began building an automobile plant in Moscow.[32] Other representatives of Moscow dynasties were involved in the Riabushinskii enterprises. In particular, S. N. Tretiakov was closely associated with the Riabushinskii brothers, both in their business and their political activities, and among the founders of the Riabushinskii bank, besides Tretiakov, were several Morozovs and representatives of the Bardygin, Karzinkin, Konovalov, and Krestovnikov families.[33]

Involvement in banking was nothing new for the Moscow dynasties. In fact, they had established the three most important Moscow banks and continued to control them until 1917. The Merchant Bank, the largest bank in Moscow and second largest commercial bank in the Empire in 1900, was founded in 1866 by a small group of Moscow merchants and industrialists under the leadership of V. A. Kokorev, I. A. Liamin, T. S. Morozov, S. P. Maliutin, V. Rukavishnikov, and P. M. Tretiakov. Also included on the list of shareholders were names like Krestovnikov, Baranov, Bardygin, Bakhrushin, and Prokhorov. In 1876 the bank had seventy-seven shareholders, a number which increased to two hundred by 1885, much of the increase being accounted for by division of shares among the heirs of original shareholders. In 1876 only twenty-three families owned more than ten shares, and by 1885 that figure had increased to a mere twenty-five.[34] By 1917, with some 18 million rubles' worth of shares outstanding, fewer than forty families owned shares accounting for 16 million of the total. Still among the largest shareholders were the Maliutin heirs, the Morozovs, and Liamin, now joined by Vishniakovs, Khludovs, and Grachevs.[35] The other two major Moscow banks, the Moscow Discount Bank and the Moscow Trade Bank, both established in the 1870s, also drew their founders and stockholders chiefly from among the Moscow dynasties. In addition, the Moscow Merchants' Mutual Credit Society, founded in 1869, was the creation of the business elite and remained under its control.[36] Many families did not restrict their interest to a single financial institution but frequently held shares in two or more of them.

The dynasties' involvement in banking no doubt provided a substantial increment to their incomes, but it also brought other benefits. Above all, the members of the business elite were able to control the operations of these banks in such a way that they served chiefly as sources of credit for the big Moscow manufacturers and merchants, in particular for the textile manufacturers. While most large Moscow industrialists financed expansion and improvement of their own enterprises out of their profits, they nonetheless found the three major Moscow banks a useful source of credit for current operations or for meeting unexpected emergencies. Indeed, it became the primary function of these banks to provide Moscow's large industrial concerns with such credit. Contemporaries repeatedly accused the three major Moscow banks of serving only a small circle of big capitalists and denying credit to owners of small or medium-sized enterprises, and I. F. Gindin's study of the Moscow banks has largely confirmed the accuracy of these accusations. Thus, the industrialists' method of operating the banks contributed to the great difficulty smaller businessmen experienced in obtaining credit. Moreover, remaining firm in their commitment to service the well-established Moscow business firms at a time when other banks in Moscow and especially in St. Petersburg were increasingly involved in the financing of new enterprises, the Moscow banks came to seem slightly old-fashioned and conservative, lacking in vision.[37]

Perhaps one reason for the relative conservatism of the major Moscow banks was that the men who controlled them, mostly well-established industrialists, held a distinct prejudice against finance and financiers of any sort. Indeed, Moscow businessmen in general tended to look upon "high finance" of any kind with a jaundiced eye. Both P. A. Buryshkin and V. P. Riabushinskii agreed in their memoirs that in the business hierarchy of Moscow, industrialists held first place, with merchants placing a close second, and financiers coming in a poor third in regard to the general esteem in which they were held by the business community.[38] High finance was generally associated with speculation, which was, in theory at least, anathema to Moscow's business community. Muscovites frequently expressed horror at the extremely speculative financial operations that took place on the Petersburg Exchange and liked to think that the Moscow Exchange, which dealt chiefly in cotton and other raw materials, was uncontaminated by either speculation or financial manipulation.[39]

Some contemporaries contended that the Moscow Exchange was not so pure as it made itself out to be, but nonetheless there is no question that among many Moscow businessmen finance was regarded as a most dubious field of business activity. While they scorned the financial speculation and manipulation that accompanied the new era of economic development after 1861, they also regarded with contempt older forms of finance, and especially discounting, which frequently took the form of outright moneylending at usurious rates of interest. But even though discounting of commercial paper had long been held in low esteem among Muscovites, there is no doubt that many of Moscow's leading businessmen engaged in it. One knowledgeable journalist claimed that "all" of Moscow's leading business families owed at least part of their fortunes to discounting.[40] However that may be, there were certainly some families who were indeed heavily involved in discounting operations and made a good deal of money from them.

The Riabushinskiis, for example, put a considerable amount of their capital into discounting, originally moving into this field because of the conviction of one timid family member that industry was a very uncertain and risky form of business activity. The Riabushinskiis later went on to found a private banking house and then a commercial bank on the basis of their earlier discounting operations.[41] Another family of the elite, the Vishniakovs, had a somewhat dubious reputation as having made the major part of their fortune in discounting, but again they gradually moved into at least somewhat more respectable types of financial activity. One Vishniakov started a small private banking house, and another, the influential A. S. Vishniakov, became head of the Moscow Merchants' Mutual Credit Society, one of the town's major financial institutions.[42]

In addition to industry, trade, and finance, a number of families of the elite were also involved in insurance and real estate. One of Moscow's major insurance companies, the Northern Insurance Company, had been founded by V. A. Kokorev, a remarkable entrepreneur who made a fortune as a tax farmer, went on to build an empire that included railroads, banks, his insurance company, and a variety of other enterprises, but died in 1889 practically bankrupt.[43] After Kokorev's death, the Northern Insurance Company remained primarily in the hands of representatives of the elite families. The managing director of the company in the 1890s was D. I. Morozov. Among the officers of the company in the early 1900s were S. A. Protopopov, A. A. Naidenov, D. R. Vostriakov, N. I. Guchkov, and other notable Moscow capitalists.[44] Members of the elite also participated in the Rossiia Company and in several other large Moscow-based insurance enterprises.[45] As regards real estate, representatives of the elite invested in a wide variety of properties within Moscow. S. M. Tretiakov, for example, owned a group of shops known as the Tretiakov Arcade, while the Khludovs built one of Moscow's most elegant bathhouses, the Central Baths. Some businessmen joined together to form companies for the management of their properties in Moscow or for the purpose of real estate acquisition and development, one such company having been created by the Lepeshkins and A. I. Shamshin in 1896.[46]

In addition to ownership of property in Moscow, many families possessed landed estates, but the uses to which they put the land varied considerably. In many cases, their estates were used simply as country retreats, with little thought given to their cultivation. S. I. Mamontov, well-known dilettante and patron of the arts, purchased the estate of Abramtsevo from the Slavophile I. S. Aksakov in 1870 and used it chiefly as a gathering place for his circle of artist friends and as the site of the famous Mamontov *kustar* workshop.[47] Similarly, K. T. Soldatenkov purchased the estate of Kuntsevo from the Naryshkins and used the old Naryshkin manor house as his country retreat. Soldatenkov made a profit on this investment: he became the landlord of numerous families of the Moscow business elite who spent their summers in dachas built on land rented from Soldatenkov at Kuntsevo.[48]

Many other families made profitable use of the land they owned. Frequently, large tracts of land near the family factory were used to supply fuel or other products for the factory. The Morozovs' Tverskaia enterprise owned over 50,000 *desiatiny* of wooded land, used to provide the factory with fuel and lumber.[49] The Khludovs owned 22,000 *desiatiny* of forest land near their Egorevsk factory and another extensive tract of land containing a peat bog.[50] Many other factories similarly owned land supplying wood and peat, which continued to be used for various purposes even after the introduction of new forms of fuel such as oil.

A few families purchased land for use in the development of some field of industrial activity. The Botkins, for instance, bought a number of landed estates to serve as the basis for a small sugar business which they built up in addition to their tea business.[51] One of the Morozov families owned a huge estate in the Urals which they hoped could be used for profitable mining operations and as a source of raw materials for the new chemical plant that Savva Morozov was backing.[52] The Karzinkins owned 2,750 *desiatiny* of land in Central Asia, used for growing cotton and also as the site of the family's twelve cotton-cleaning plants.[53]

In a few cases, some businessmen purchased estates with the idea of exploiting them for purely agricultural purposes, unconnected with industry. I. F. Mamontov owned and cultivated an estate of 1,089 *desiatiny* in Tver province, though his heirs, who did not share his interest in agriculture, sold the estate shortly after his death.[54] V. S. Perlov, a dedicated agriculturalist, owned a small estate of 170 *desiatiny* near Moscow and tried to make it into a model farm, experimenting successfully with cattle breeding and growing different varieties of grain. When he died in 1900, he left the estate to the Moscow Agricultural Society to be used as the site of an agricultural institute.[55] K. K. Ushkov almost entirely gave up involvement in business to dedicate himself to the management of two estates inherited from his wife's father, a wealthy Kazan tea merchant.[56] But such cases were rare, and an interest in agriculture for its own sake was largely an idiosyncracy found in only a few individual members of the elite. Most of the landed estates owned by Moscow's leading business families were used either for purposes of recreation or as sources of materials needed by their factories or for other industrial purposes. None of the dynasties appears ever to have been continuously and seriously engaged in the cultivation of agricultural products for direct sale on the market.

Even if their involvement in agriculture was minimal, the foregoing discussion of the broad industrial, commercial, and financial activities of the Moscow business dynasties should make it clear that the usual description of Moscow's business elite as a textile elite hardly suffices to give an adequate idea of the extent of their business activity. Though textile production was the main concern of the majority of Moscow dynasties, their business interests in almost all cases also included diverse undertakings outside the textile industry. One cannot help but be impressed with the innumerable uses to which they put their capital and must greet with considerable skepticism the frequent accusations of their contemporaries that they were totally lacking in the entrepreneurial spirit. By the early twentieth century, Moscow's business elite no doubt seemed somewhat stuffy and old-fashioned to the freer capitalistic spirits of St. Petersburg. Continuing to believe in the virtues of the family firm and the personal management and financing of one's own business, Moscow's leading businessmen were somewhat skeptical of the newer stock companies *(aktsionerny obshchestva)* with their broad diffusion of shares, their hired managers, and their reliance on bank financing. They also took very slowly to the creation of syndicates or cartels, which appeared in the textile industry only after 1905 and even then were weakly developed.[57] Soviet historians are hard put to find any true examples of "finance capitalists" typical of the period of "monopoly capitalism" among the Moscow business elite, the Riabushinskiis being almost the only possible candidates.[58] Nonetheless, if they adapted slowly to newly developing forms of capitalism, contemporary accusations of total inertia and complete lack of entrepreneurial initiative seem clearly unjustified.

BESIDES their many investments in subsidiary lines of business, the Moscow dynasties were responsible for tremendous expansion of their basic family enterprises during the course of the nineteenth century. Starting from nothing, they built up enterprises that by 1900 were in many cases among the largest in the Empire. The greater part of this expansion typically occurred in the later part of the nineteenth century and in the early twentieth century and was stimulated both by rapid population growth and by the increasing purchasing power of the peasantry after 1861.[59] For example, an inventory of the Morozov family textile enterprises in 1852–1853 revealed that they employed a total of 2,572 workers, plus an unspecified number of peasants working at home, and had an annual production worth 1,943,000 rubles. By 1890, the Morozovs' Nikolskaia factory alone employed 17,252 workers and had an annual output valued at 13,302,000 rubles, making it the second largest single industrial enterprise in the Russian Empire. The Vikula Morozov company, controlled by another branch of the family, ranked as the sixth largest enterprise in the Empire in 1890, with an annual production worth 8,725,000 rubles and a staff of 9,500 workers. Still another Morozov enterprise (Bogorodsko-Glukhovskaia), operated by a third branch of the family, accounted for an annual output valued at 7,259,000 rubles in 1890, employed 8,136 workers, and was the Empire's tenth largest industrial enterprise. Finally, the Tverskaia factory, controlled by the fourth branch of the large Morozov clan, had an annual output valued at 5,877,000 rubles and was the sixteenth largest enterprise in the country in 1890. By 1913, the shares of all Morozov enterprises taken together were worth a total of 44 million rubles, almost all these shares remaining in family hands.[60]

The Morozovs' is undoubtedly the most dazzling success story to be found among the Moscow dynasties, and it would be misleading to consider them typical in any way, even though they have, in fact, been regarded as the "archetypical" Moscow capitalists by both their contemporaries and some later historians.[61] Most businesses owned by Moscow dynasties did undergo considerable expansion during the nineteenth century, but rarely on such a startling scale as the Morozov enerprises. Even the Prokhorovs' Trekhgornaia factory, which in 1890 was the nineteenth largest industrial enterprise in the Empire, developed at a much more moderate rate and grew to more modest dimensions. In 1842, the value of this factory's annual output was 450,000 silver rubles, a figure which by 1890 had climbed to 5 million rubles.[62]

Much of the growth of Moscow-based textile enterprises was accounted for by gradual expansion to include many or all of the various stages required for the production of the final textile product. In the beginning, most firms were restricted to one specific phase of the production process—spinning or weaving, dyeing or printing—but they gradually branched out to include other stages of production. For instance, what later became the Vikula Morozov company began as a small dyeing plant, established in 1837 by Elisei Savvich, the oldest son of the family founder. In 1847, Elisei added a weaving factory at the insistence of his son Vikula, and in 1872 Vikula himself built a spinning factory.[63] Similarly, the Prokhorovs were for many decades primarily occupied with cotton printing. Only in 1889 did they establish a weaving factory and in 1898 a spinning factory.[64]

While persistent expansion was the general rule for the main enterprises owned by the Moscow dynasties, a few families did not participate in this general trend but experienced instead a contraction of their businesses, or at least a very slow expansion. Within the textile industry, this generalization appears to apply especially to families in the woolens industry rather than in cotton. The Naidenovs, for example, experienced grave business difficulties beginning in the 1870s and gave up their woolens business entirely in 1885.[65] Thereafter, the family's leading representative, N. A. Naidenov, was chiefly preoccupied with the Moscow Trade Bank and with the Moscow Trade-Industrial Company, and other members of the family continued to participate in the textile industry only by virtue of their marriage ties with other textile families. Another family whose woolens business declined in the later years of the nineteenth century was the Guchkovs, who finally liquidated their factory in 1896.[66] Generally speaking, the woolens industry of the Moscow region had begun to experience difficulties as early as the 1860s, chiefly because of increasing competition from other and cheaper textile goods. As a result, the number of woolen mills had begun to decline in that decade, a trend which accelerated in the 1870s and 1880s.[67] Naidenov put the blame for the termination of his family's woolens business entirely on these changing conditions within the woolens industry,[68] but it would be difficult to say whether the Guchkovs' departure from this field was attributable primarily to unfavorable conditions or to increasing lack of interest in business on the part of the new generation of Guchkovs who came to the fore in the 1890s. In the case of the Abrikosovs, whose candy and jam business was not doing well at the end of the nineteenth century and was increasingly being overtaken by competitors, the family's business decline can clearly be traced to lack of interest in business on the part of the younger generations of Abrikosovs.[69] The same was true of the Iakunchikovs, whose withdrawal from the cotton textile industry in the early years of the twentieth century was also perhaps motivated in part by their elevation into the nobility.[70]

Thus, in regard to expansion of family enterprises there were widely separated extremes within the business elite, ranging from the Morozovs at the one end to families whose businesses were actually in decline at the other. The same large degree of variation can be found in regard to the size of the elite's family enterprises and the size of their profits. Here again, the Morozovs have all too often been taken as the typical example, with the same misleading results. In terms of number of workers employed, there was a wide gap between the huge Morozov factories at one end of the scale and the very small factories owned by some families at the other end. According to government figures for 1890, the Morozov Nikolskaia factory was the largest of the Moscow-based enterprises, with its 17,252 workers, while perhaps the smallest factory owned by members of the business elite was the Vishniakov-Shamshin factory, which employed 132 workers in its Moscow plant. Still very large, but smaller than the Morozov giants, were the Khludov factory in Egorevsk, with 3,673 workers, and the Danilovskaia factory in Moscow with 3,345 workers. At the low end of the scale, the Guchkov factory in Moscow employed a mere 340 workers, in contrast to the 1,850 workers employed there in 1853. The Sapozhnikov brocade and velvet factory in Moscow employed only 280.[71]

These figures for 1890 have been used because they are the most complete available, but figures on the number of workers employed some ten or fifteen years later would in the majority of cases be considerably larger and would indicate that the expansion of most enterprises belonging to the Moscow dynasties continued at a very rapid pace during the 1890s and the early years of the twentieth century. If the Prokhorovs had 1,230 workers in 1890, by 1900 the figure had increased considerably, to 5,046.[72] The number of workers employed in the Khludovs' Egorevsk factory went from 3,673 in 1890 to more than 6,000 in 1900.[73] The Konovalovs in 1890 employed 1,150 workers, but by 1913 they had 5,500 workers at their main factory and 1,000 at a nearby smaller plant.[74] Thus, most of these families, particularly those in the cotton textile industry, participated in the general and rapid economic expansion of the 1890s.

Merely citing the number of workers employed does not convey an adequate idea of the actual dimensions of the industrial establishments controlled by the Moscow dynasties. A "factory" in Imperial Russia was in many cases not simply a building containing production equipment. In the case of the larger establishments, the term referred in effect to a whole town, self-contained to a considerable degree. A typical factory belonging to a Moscow dynasty included not only buildings and equipment directly connected with production, but also a school, a hospital, often a church, living quarters for factory hands and other employees, and frequently an elegant residence for the factory owner. In the later nineteenth and early twentieth centuries, other amenities were often added: a library, a nursery, a maternity home, an old-age home, sometimes a theater or tearoom. Most large factories also had their own factory stores, where workers and employees purchased their basic supplies. Some factories had consumers' cooperatives for workers and employees, and a few had credit unions. Many had community dining rooms, run by workers' artels, that provided fairly cheap meals. In addition, most large factories maintained their own fire-fighting equipment and had to provide their own water supply and dispose of their own sewage. They maintained their own police, a practice that increased as factory disorders multiplied. All these institutions and activities were under the direct supervision of the management, who found themselves managing not simply a factory producing textiles or other goods, but, in effect, an entire town.[75]

The fact that most factories were located in areas where neither schools nor sewerage systems were provided by towns or zemstvos was no doubt chiefly responsible for the development of these extensive factory economies, though the factory owners were also spurred on by the pressure of public opinion, which was largely sympathetic to the idea of improving the working and living conditions of industrial workers; by strikes and other factory disturbances; and in some cases by government legislation. In any case, the industrialists' control of their workers' jobs, schools, living quarters, health care, and the like gave them tremendous power over the lives of factory personnel. F. Pavlov, a technician employed for many years at a large textile factory in the Central Region, described the situation existing in his factory as follows:

> Every step, every hour of the life of the worker and even of his family may be regulated by the administration of the factory, at the head of which stands one all-powerful individual, the manager of the factory—the director. The director is the sole legislator, judge, and executor of his own resolutions. He levies monetary fines on the worker without appeal, as long as he does not go beyond the legally established limits. At the end of the term of hire, i.e., not less than twice a year, he may legally deprive the worker of his living quarters, may stop his credit at the store, forbid his son to attend school,

and, finally, having refused him work, force him to seek a new place to live, perhaps to go hungry.[76]

With this considerable power at their disposal, the large factory owners, either personally or through hired factory directors, ruled their extensive domains in the manner of petty autocrats with little outside interference. Even the creation of the factory inspectorate in 1882, although greeted with cries of anguish and outrage by the factory owners of the Moscow region, did little to diminish the factory owners' autocratic powers. Subsequent factory legislation, though curbing some of the more arbitrary and oppressive practices of employers, still left them, as is obvious from Pavlov's account, with considerable room for the exercise of power over their workers. The spirit in which this power was wielded, and its effect on those who wielded it, were also described by Pavlov. Speaking of the director of the factory where he was employed, Pavlov wrote:

> How this omnipotence and the subordinate position of all around him have spoiled him! He tolerates with difficulty any sort of opposition, and any serious contradiction he considers a downright sin on the part of the objector. About the workers there is nothing to be said; not only impudence or coarseness, which in essence do not occur, but simply insufficient respectfulness of tone toward the director is considered practically a crime, evoking if not immediate removal from the factory, then a high monetary fine. The discipline reigning at our factory I could only compare with military discipline.[77]

No doubt many Moscow industrialists, who tended to regard themselves as the benefactors of their workers, would have regarded Pavlov's description of the factory regime as distorted and slanderous, but there seems little reason to doubt the truth of his observations. The tradition of a despotic paternalism was very strong in Russian industry (as in Russian society as a whole, which was permeated by the practice of a tyrannical paternalism from the structure of the peasant family at the bottom to the autocracy of the tsar at the top). In most factories, the despotism and the paternalism appear to have coexisted in equal parts. If many large factory owners were ready to introduce improvements for the benefit of their workers—and some were more ready than others—they nonetheless jealously guarded their traditional powers over the working force, maintaining that the right of what amounted to almost total control over the work and lives of their employees was necessary to keep the wheels of industry turning. Furthermore, they generally insisted that all changes for benefit of the workers must emanate from the factory management, acting in a spirit of enlightened paternalism. Any interference with their paternalistic care of their employees was deeply resented, whether it came from the government or, God forbid, from the workers themselves.[78]

In the later nineteenth century, the industrialists' treatment of their workers came in for a certain amount of criticism in the Russian press, but, partly because of the censorship imposed on press discussion of strikes and other signs of discontent among factory workers, an even more frequent subject of criticism was the large profits reaped by Russian industrialists in general, and by Moscow textile industrialists in particular. Again, both contemporaries and later historians critical of the industrialists' high profit levels have most frequently used the Morozovs as the typical example and have repeatedly singled out their Nikolskaia enterprise as supposedly indicative of Russian profit margins. While the rate of profit enjoyed by Moscow industrialists around the turn of the century was, generally speaking, most respectable and would probably be envied by many contemporary industrialists in any country, to cite the profits of the Nikolskaia factory as typical still creates a wrong impression. In the period from 1891 to 1893, when the Nikolskaia factory was reporting profits of almost 53 percent, the average profit for Russian cotton-spinning and weaving factories was 11.7 percent.[79] No doubt the existence of many small and marginal enterprises which barely managed to keep their heads above water pulled the average down considerably, but, in fact, many of the leading Moscow-based textile enterprises experienced rates of profit not far above the average. For instance, even the Vikula Morozov company reported a net profit of only 1,020,556 rubles for the operational year 1894–1895; on a basic capital of 5 million rubles, this gives roughly a 20 percent rate of profit. The same company's profit fell to 822,411 rubles (16 percent) in 1902–1903, a relatively bad period for the Russian economy. One of the smaller textile companies, the Alekseev-Vishniakov-Shamshin combine, in 1894–1895 had a net profit of 146,843 rubles on a basic capital of one million rubles, or about 15 percent, while in 1902–1903 its profit was 199,318 rubles, about 20 percent. At the same time, the Nikolskaia factory, with a basic capital of 5 million rubles, reported a net profit of 3,103,000 rubles for 1894–1895 and a profit of 3,060,000 rubles for 1902–1903, with its rate of profit thus holding steady in these years at more than 60 percent. There seems little doubt, on the basis of the published annual statements of Moscow companies, that the rates of profit reported by the Vikula Morozov and the Alekseev-Vishniakov-Shamshin companies were much more typical of Moscow-based industrial enterprises than the fantastic profits of the Nikolskaia factory. Leading Moscow industrialists perhaps had little to complain of in regard to their level of profits, but few, if any, enjoyed such phenomenal profits as did Nikolskaia.[80]

Considering the diversity among dynasties in rate of profit, size of enterprises, degree of expansion or decline of their businesses, and extent of involvement in subsidiary business undertakings, one could expect a considerable variation in the size of the fortunes possessed by families belonging to the Moscow business elite. This wide variation was confirmed by Buryshkin, who noted that some families whose membership in the elite was not open to question could not even have been considered as being among the very wealthiest families in Moscow (for instance, the Botkins and the Tretiakovs).[81] At the other end of the scale were, of course, the Morozovs. Taken together, the four branches of the Morozov dynasty represented the largest single concentration of family wealth in Moscow, and even separately each of the four branches would have placed very high in any financial ranking of Moscow business families.

It would now be extremely difficult, if not impossible, to arrive at any exact figures showing the total wealth of the Morozovs or of any of the other dynasties, especially considering the extensive and varied nature of their business operations and the great difficulty involved in tracking down all their business holdings. However, the contemporary press occasionally carried estimates of the wealth of various Moscow businessmen which, if not precisely accurate, at least given some indication of the size of these families' fortunes. The Morozov clan as a whole was reputed to be worth several hundred million rubles; when D. A. Morozov of the Borodsko-Glukhovskaia branch of the family died in 1893, his personal fortune was reported to stand at 10 million rubles.[82] Other published estimates of the personal fortunes of representatives of the business elite tended to fall within the range of 10 to 30 million rubles. G. I. Khludov, when he died in 1885, was said to be worth about 16 million rubles, while P. M. Riabushinskii was reputed to have left his eight sons over 20 million rubles when he died in 1899.[83] In any case, all these families controlled millions of rubles' worth of assets and represented an extreme of wealth in a society in which the extreme of poverty was far more typical.

WHATEVER the size of the elite's fortunes, there was little doubt in the minds of their contemporaries that these fortunes represented ill-gotten gains. As mentioned earlier, the Russian press around the turn of the century usually ascribed the wealth of merchants and industrialists to exploitation of workers and consumers and to the effects of the protective tariff and other government measures that encouraged the development of trade and industry while placing terrible burdens on Russian agriculture. It was extremely unusual to find any suggestion in the leading organs of the Russian press that the fortunes of Russia's successful businessmen might have been attributable to business abilities, entrepreneurial initiative, hard work, intelligence, or other such characteristics. In fact, the very idea that Russian merchants and industrialists might be considered good businessmen, capable of showing initiative and working hard, met with frequent and emphatic denials in the press. The educated public seems to have been convinced that the development of trade and industry in Russia resulted almost entirely from government measures which had the unfortunate side effect of enriching a small circle of businessmen at the expense of the consumer, the worker, and Russian agriculture.

On the other hand, Moscow's business elite seem rarely to have doubted that their fortunes represented the well-deserved fruits of exactly those characteristics that public opinion denied them: intelligence, ability, initiative, hard work. All the memoirs of members of the business elite and all the histories of business families and their enterprises stressed precisely such characteristics, while rarely mentioning such factors as the tariff as crucial to their success. And of all these virtues, hard work was the one most frequently singled out as the key to success. For instance, we read that the founder of the Konovalov family and business "gave all his strength to factory production and trade, putting his whole soul into them. The brilliant success of the enterprise which he founded was his fully deserved reward for all his cares and labor."[84] The success of the Prokhorov business was attributed to the "unceasing, energetic, and loving labor of four generations of the Prokhorov family."[85] One of the Krestovnikovs wrote that "our business lived through periods of difficult circumstances, fortune never smiled on us, and what has been achieved must be accounted for by persistence and industriousness."[86]

Such statements leave little doubt as to the development of a conscious work ethic among the Moscow business elite. I. F. Mamontov gave perhaps the most articulate formulation to this work ethic in letters he wrote in the late 1850s and early 1860s to his son Savva. The chief message of all his letters was that "idleness is the mother of all evils." In one letter Mamontov further explained to his son the reasons for his constant preaching of hard work, writing:

> Idleness is a vice, but work is not a virtue, but a simple immutable responsibility as the fulfillment of one's debt in life. Every citizen must toil spiritually or materially for his own sake, for the sake of his family, for the sake of society and his homeland. A man must work from childhood until old age, or otherwise turn into a parasite.[87]

If work was an obligation, Mamontov was of course not unaware of its possible financial rewards. When Savva was in Persia on business for his father, Mamontov wrote to his son: "I agree completely that it is dreary, difficult, and tedious to live there. But such a life will do you no harm, and will give you the practical experience of how difficult it is to amass that amount of money, through your own strength and toil, that is necessary for a comfortable life."[88] While others might have rationalized their belief in the value of hard work somewhat differently, many of Moscow's business elite would no doubt have accepted Mamontov's formulation.

If hard work was the basic virtue, the memoirs and histories also frequently mentioned as qualities leading to success other characteristics typical of what became known in Western Europe as the "Protestant ethic," or the "bourgeois ethic." Honesty in business dealings was often noted as a factor in business success.[89] Temperance was also mentioned as a necessary virtue in businessmen, with several memoirists noting that alcohol was used in moderation, if at all, in their families and observing that "dissipation" was the cause of business failure in all too many cases known to them.[90]

Many writers also set down thrift as a requisite for business success. N. A Naidenov's comment that his family "lived extremely modestly, avoiding any superfluous expenses," was fairly typical, at least for the earlier generations of the business elite.[91] A number of the histories of the elite's business enterprises noted the necessity of modest living in order to be able to plow profits back into the business. For instance, the history of the Khludovs' Egorevsk factory described an early agreement drawn up by the Khludov brothers, requiring that "in the interests of development and consolidation of the enterprise . . . half of the yearly net profit had to be left in the business." The author of the history noted that "in this wise rule lay the guarantee of the rapid growth of the factory."[92]

Even in later years, when the dynasties' wealth had increased considerably and their representatives could afford to live on a more lavish scale without causing harm to their businesses, the habit of careful money management continued. Nemirovich-Danchenko recalled that K. S. Alekseev-Stanislavsky was able to contribute only 10,000 rubles to the founding of the Art Theater. He noted that Stanislavsky's capital was all in his business and that his income from dividends and from his salary as a director of a family company "enabled him to live well, but did not allow him to indulge much in 'whims.' "[93] Similarly, Savva Morozov, who, as something of a maverick among the elite, had close connections with Moscow's Bolsheviks and contributed to their party's support, surprised his Bolshevik friends with the information that he was on a strict monthly allowance. While Morozov's allowance was generous by any standards, it was not large enough to permit him to contribute the millions of rubles to the party that the Bolsheviks had hoped for.[94]

The origins of a "bourgeois ethic" of hard work, honesty, temperance, and thrift among Russian businessmen have been thoroughly investigated only in the case of the Old Believers. The presence of so many Old Believers in the Russian business community has given rise to speculation that, as Max Weber proposed regarding the role of Calvinism in Western Europe, something in the nature of their religious beliefs might have served as a stimulus to capitalistic activity. But as Alexander Gerschenkron has so cogently argued, it is impossible to find anything in the mystical religious doctrines of the Old Belief that could have accounted for the Old Believers' unusual economic success. Rather, he concluded that "the social conditions of a penalized, persecuted group" provided the stimulus to make money—money that was necessary in order to support and ensure the survival of their persecuted cult (not a small part of this money being paid out in the form of bribes to state officials). Moreover, the unique communal organization of the Old Believers assisted in the accumulation of capital, making capital (and also a reliable labor force) available to the more enterprising members of the group. As for the development of a set of values that contributed to material success, Gerschenkron has stressed that "it stems with great clarity from the specific social position of the group." He noted that a persecuted group "in its defensive reaction against intolerance" tends to build up "a feeling of moral superiority to the outsider and then proceeds to bolster that feeling by developing habits that both evidence and vindicate it. Hence came the features of cleanliness, honesty, reliability, frugality, industry and thrift that were so generally observed to characterize Old Believers."[95]

Gerschenkron's explanation may help to account for the development of such values as hard work and thrift among the Old Believers, but it throws little light on a similar development among those Russian businessmen who did not adhere to the Old Belief. Given the general prejudice and contempt felt toward Russian businessmen, it may be that many of these men possessed something of the psychology of a persecuted group and therefore sought, like the Old Believers, to prove their own worthiness by espousing "superior" values. But if the Russian stereotype of Kit Kitych possessed some validity—as it undoubtedly did—then the typical Russian *kupets* placed little value on honesty or temperance, in particular. Perhaps such values began to take hold only after a certain level of ambition or success or pride in one's calling had been achieved by certain individuals. As for the source of these values, it seems impossible to isolate any facet of Russian culture that contained even the seeds of the values of a business society. The most reasonable supposition seems to be that such values develop out of practical experience with the necessities of the business world. Although lacking the glamour of Weber's theory, such a commonsense explanation seems the only one capable of accounting for the nearly universal development of "bourgeois" values in capitalistic societies (colored as those values may be by the indigenous culture).

Besides hard work, honesty, temperance, and thrift, the memoirs and histories also attributed business success to an emphasis on the quality of goods produced by the factory and, above all, constant attention to technological improvement. The factory histories in particular radiate an obvious pride in the quality of goods produced and in the level of technology existing in the factories. For instance, a brief history of the Mamontovs' lacquer and varnish plant noted that the chief reason for the success of the firm was "production and trade in goods exclusively of the highest quality. Thanks to this principle, the company won the confidence of the market throughout the whole Russian Empire and abroad."[96] The several histories of the Konovalov firm consistently stressed quality of goods and application of new technology. Assuming responsibility for the family business in 1858, A. P. Konovalov, we are told, was determined to apply the latest technological developments and was not afraid to break with tradition for this purpose. His son and successor, I. A. Konovalov, taking over management of the firm in 1889, merely followed in his father's footsteps in regard to application of new technology.[97] Similarly, the Prokhorov history noted that part of the family's business tradition was "keeping up with all improvements and discoveries in the technical field."[98] The history described the attitude and activities of S. I. Prokhorov, managing director of the factory in the later decades of the nineteenth century, as follows:

The fresh energy of S. I. and his deep confidence in the possibility of achieving his goals, his belief in the power of science—from the very first were noticeably reflected in the success of production: from almost purely empirical it gradually began to be established on a scientific basis. Knowing three foreign languages, he diligently kept up with successes in all fields of natural science: not one discovery in the field of theoretical and applied chemistry and physics escaped his earnest attention but immediately awakened in him the thought of practical application of this discovery.[99]

University-trained as a chemist, Prokhorov expanded the chemical laboratory at his factory and employed highly qualified chemists, with whose help he introduced a number of important innovations in his factory.[100]

The contrast between this self-evaluation of the Moscow industrialists and the evaluation of them by their contemporaries was almost complete. Russian industry in general was frequently criticized for its poor quality of goods and lack of concern for technical improvements, and the Moscow textile industrialists in particular were often subjected to such criticism. Journalists seemed to take it for granted that shoddy goods and backward technology were typical of the industry of the Moscow region, and they received support in this assumption from such noted contemporary students of Russian industry as M. I. Tugan-Baranovskii. But a few contemporaries and some later investigators have supported the claims of the industrialists rather than the opinions of their contemporary critics. In particular, the historians I. F. Gindin and Roger Portal have both given generally favorable ratings to the textile industry in regard to its level of technological development.[101]

Loath to admit that Moscow industrialists might be capable of keeping up with technological innovations, their contemporaries were even less ready to praise them for their display of bourgeois virtues. Part of the problem here was the fact that what Moscow businessmen regarded as virtues leading to success were simply not regarded as virtues of any kind by the rest of Russian society. Outside the business community, a work ethic did not exist in pre-revolutionary Russia. The Russian Orthodox church had never laid any particular stress on hard work as a virtue, and neither the nobility, nor the intelligentsia, nor any other stratum of the population was particularly impressed with the virtues of labor per se. If both nobles and intellectuals regarded "service" as a supreme value, neither had adopted an ethic elevating diligent labor to the same meritorious position that it had assumed in the Western bourgeois scheme of values.[102]

The virtue of thrift was equally foreign to existing value systems outside the business community. What businessmen regarded as thrift was most often seen as pure and simple stinginess by other groups of the population, and Russian businessmen came in for constant criticism on this account. They were also repeatedly accused of being extremely "calculating" (raschetlivyi) in regard to money, a characteristic not considered compatible with the "broad Russian soul." I. I. Ianzhul, a professor at Moscow University and one of the few intellectuals of his time who advocated the importation of certain Western bourgeois values into Russia, once wrote that Russians "not only do not like thrift, but even consider it harmful." To the Russian, the habit of saving, the habit of worrying about the future, seems "somehow strange, 'bourgeois,' typical of the German petty bourgeoisie, and not of the broad Russian nature!" By way of illustration, Ianzhul referred to an incident in Orel province in the early 1890s: incensed at the creation of savings funds in the primary schools, the provincial zemstvo petitioned for their abolition on the grounds that attempts to encourage the children to save would only inculcate in them an exaggerated idea of the importance of money and develop "egoism" and selfishness.[103]

However successful Moscow businessmen may have been, however hard-working, however enlightened in their entrepreneurship, they could expect little appreciation from contemporary Russian society. Educated public opinion refused to recognize the bourgeois virtues as virtues and was blind to the connection between the practice of these virtues by individual businessmen and the development of trade and industry. Accustomed to accepting government leadership in all fields of national life, the Russian public tended to give all credit for economic development to government policies, rather than to the efforts of individual entrepreneurs. When, however, it came time to distribute blame for social and economic dislocations caused by the policy of rapid industrial development, that same public, traditionally hostile toward the kupechestvo, was willing enough to allot a large share of the blame to Russian businessmen, as well as to the government. Frequently criticized and rarely praised, Russia's merchants and industrialists understood that if they wanted to achieve some measure of public respect and appreciation, they would have to seek it outside the field of industry and trade.

THE OLDER GENERATION OF THE 1890s:
CULTURAL CHANGE

A MOSCOW professor, recalling his friendship with Anna Ivanovna Volkova (born Vishniakova), an outstanding representative
of the older generation of Moscow's business elite in the 1890s,
once wrote of her:

> She was filled with a feeling of merchant pride [*kupecheskoe dostoin-
> stvo*], in the best sense of that expression. . . . She was always
> annoyed and displeased at meeting with a scornful attitude toward
> the "*kupechestvo*" . . . to her it seemed unjust to deny to the *kupechestvo*
> any significance other than purely commercial. And through her
> own literary activity she wished to prove that a "*kupchikha*" could
> also think, feel, understand and possess enlightened aspirations . . .
> when the stories of N. D. Teleshev appeared, she . . . expressed
> great pleasure that the author of such fine works was a *kupets*. She
> talked personally with me on this theme—and in our frequent con-
> versations she expressed her desire to prove the injustice of our
> notions about the *kupechestvo*.[1]

Volkova's feelings of pride and injustice were perhaps typical of the
members of her generation and go far to explain the fact that this generation of the business elite, while continuing to earn respect from their
colleagues as a result of their successful business activities, at the same
time sought to excel in other fields—particularly philanthropy, patronage,
collecting, and public affairs. Denied the respect of educated society for
their business success, they tried to show that the *kupechestvo* did indeed
possess some "significance other than purely commercial" and that it was
capable of contributing in other ways to Russian society and Russian
culture. The activities through which these men and women sought to
prove their own worth, as well as that of their *soslovie*, were activities

which could be counted on to attract the respectful attention of educated society. They were also activities for which the older generation of the elite possessed the requisite qualifications.

For the man or woman who wished to make some contribution as a philanthropist or patron, a collector or public figure, perhaps the most necessary attribute was simply wealth, a requirement easily met by representatives of the business elite. But beyond that, a further requirement for worthwhile activity in any of these fields was a certain degree of education and culture. If earlier in the century a philanthropist might have earned praise for the distribution of alms to the poor, by the end of the century Russian society expected its philanthropists to demonstrate a deeper understanding of social needs and more imagination in their attempts to respond to them. Likewise, patrons and collectors were expected to show some discrimination in their attempts to aid the development of Russian culture. As a result, the wealthy but uncultured individual rarely was able to achieve public acclaim in these fields. And men who sought positions of leadership in public work had to compete with nobles and intellectuals and to demonstrate talents and vision at least equal to theirs.

The level of education and culture required for successful participation in these various fields was not so high as that necessary for independent creative work in the arts and sciences; and, indeed, only a very few members of the older generation (in contrast to their offspring) possessed the requisite qualifications for independent literary, artistic, or scientific work. But even though they were unable to reach the educational and cultural heights later to be scaled by their sons and daughters, the older generation nonetheless accomplished what was the first and perhaps the most difficult step in the direction of cultural and intellectual development. Through a process of self-development which in most cases involved the exertion of considerable personal effort, they managed to expand their cultural horizons, to raise themselves above the traditional merchant culture into which they had been born, and to make a place for themselves in the world of educated society.

It was not easy. Most of the men and women of the older generation were the children of parents who, if not totally illiterate, had no formal education of any sort and who harbored grave doubts about the value of education for their own offspring. The fathers of this generation, who in most, though not all, cases were the founding fathers of their families and businesses, had succeeded in lifting themselves economically above the world of poverty into which they had been born.[2] But, dedicated to business and having no time (and in many cases still insufficient money) for other pursuits, they had given no thought to educational and cultural self-improvement. Typical in this respect was M. Ia. Riabushinskii, whose descendants later recalled that "subordination to the interests of *business* was always the most characteristic feature of M. Ia. Riabushinskii, and therefore he himself as an individual remained in the shade, not leaving any traces either in the public arena or in the recollections of his contemporaries. . . . Everything for the business—nothing for himself. Such was the motto of the life of M. Ia. Riabushinskii."[3]

Actually, a striking number of the dynastic founders were able to read and write, though there were illiterates among them too, such as old Fedor Alekseevich Guchkov, a millionaire from the peasantry who "could neither read nor write," who "was accustomed to sweeping his courtyard himself," who "collected old nails and straightened them out, went about in tatters and in a coachman's hat which was so greasy that it was frightful to look at."[4] And even those who, unlike Guchkov, had a passing acquaintance with the written language found literacy useful chiefly for business purposes, not for the purpose of expanding their horizons and acquiring knowledge in other fields. Thus, it remained for their descendants to improve themselves culturally as they had done economically. It was their sons and daughters—the men and women who constitued the older generation in the 1890s—who had to perform the frequently painful task of lifting themselves above the general ignorance and intellectual inertia of the merchants' world.

In one sense, the fathers of this generation should be given a certain amount of credit for setting in motion the process of cultural change in their families. They did this first by creating a financial security for their families which made possible the dedication of time and money to pursuits other than business and second by moving their families from the villages or slums where they themselves had been born into the distinctive merchant milieu of Zamoskvoreche or the Old Believer communities. The life in these merchant sectors of Moscow was certainly in many respects very primitive, distinguished above all by extremely narrow horizons, a great deal of ignorance of the world beyond Kitai-gorod, and a strong emphasis on religion. But in the early years of the nineteenth century, merchant life was beginning to be affected by the winds of change, and the *kupechestvo*'s notion of bourgeois respectability was coming to include such things as good table manners, propriety of conduct in social relations, and attention to clothing and personal cleanliness. According to N. A. Naidenov, already in the first half of the century there had appeared a distinction in the *kupechestvo* between those who dressed *po-russki* (in the Russian style) and those who dressed *po-nemetski* (in the German style). While the former continued to wear long coats, boots, and beards, the "Germans" put on short coats and more fashionable footwear and shaved off their beards.[5] A few rich businessmen were building fashionable new homes, abandoning the old merchant style (or lack of it) and copying the palaces of the nobility. At the same time, merchant sons and daughters began to appear occasionally at the theater, and the Merchants' Club began to sponsor balls, masquerades, concerts, and even literary evenings to satisfy a growing desire for secular forms of entertainment. As early as 1814, the Merchants' Club was already holding balls every Sunday during the winter season. The club's regulations specified that gentlemen who wished to dance had to wear gloves and appropriate footwear and that each member was entitled to bring three women to a ball, but they had to be women "of good name."[6]

No doubt in the early years of the century many merchants and their wives and daughters still had only the vaguest notions about how they ought to conduct themselves at a ball. One outsider who attended the Merchants' Club's social functions left the following unflattering description of the ladies of the *kupechestvo*:

> The merchant daughters, at a ball or a masquerade, are usually very silent; the married women are almost inaccessible to conversation, though permitting themselves to be invited to move in silence to the music. Here you see opulent rows, but everything reflects their lack of taste. Often the heads of merchant daughters shimmer with diamonds and attract the fond glances of eligible bachelors from the military and civil service—who often purposely visit the Merchants' Club in order to look for brides for themselves.[7]

But in spite of the crudities that remained, the merchant world was beginning to feel the effects of the process of Westernization that Peter the Great had set underway in the eighteenth century. If that far-reaching process of cultural change in the past century had affected chiefly the nobility, in the nineteenth century it would transform the urban business community. Certainly many of the old types, with their long beards, coarse habits, and general ignorance, remained at the end of the century; but they were a dying breed, and Zamoskvoreche no longer belonged to them.[8]

Thus, the founding fathers brought their families into a milieu that was gradually undergoing a process of cultural evolution in the direction of increasing adaptation to the Russian version of Western culture. But if the youth who would make up the older generation of the 1890s could simply absorb from the atmosphere around them the rules of proper dress and behavior, it was still extremely difficult for them to break out of the stultifying and narrow intellectual and cultural horizons typical of the early nineteenth-century merchant milieu. The process of Westernization within the *kupechestvo* made itself felt first in regard to externals, as had also been the case with the nobility in an earlier period. Changes in beliefs, values, in the whole world view of the *kupechestvo*, came more slowly than changes in external appearance and behavior.

One of the major obstacles standing in the way of cultural and intellectual change within the *kupechestvo* was the traditional merchant antipathy toward education, an old and deeply rooted attitude that was only gradually overcome. If many *kuptsy* in the early years of the nineteenth century were prepared to admit that a knowledge of reading, writing, and arithmetic was necessary for the conduct of business, they were nonetheless profoundly convinced that education beyond that point was both useless and dangerous. M. Ia. Riabushinskii, who "did not attribute special importance to the book learning of his children," told his sons that life itself would be their best teacher—an attitude widely shared by businessmen in the earlier part of the century. As a result of their father's attitude, the Riabushinskii heirs learned only to read and write, and at that point their formal education came to an end.[9]

But if book learning was considered useful for business, it was also seen as highly dangerous. Many merchant fathers feared above all that education of their sons would prevent them from becoming good businessmen, capable of taking over the family firm. One representative of the older generation of the 1890s, N. P. Vishniakov, described the attitudes of the Zamoskvoreche of his childhood as follows:

The *kupechestvo* then did not trust enlightenment and did not recognize it as necessary. Until the mid-1850s there was not one person with a university education among our numerous family and acquaintances. The old people believed that learning only distracted from business, and from their point of view they were unconditionally right. The conditions in which the *kupechestvo* lived were so primitive that a man who received any education was bound to show a desire to leave this milieu. There were, of course, many examples of this. The old generation recalled them and became incensed, not being able to evaluate the reason for this alienation.[10]

Education, it seemed, posed the threat of opening new horizons, creating visions of a better way of life, and seducing merchant sons from their predestined role.

P. M. Vishniakov, the founder of the Vishniakov dynasty, shared the typical views of the time and gave his sons a very meager education. As his son Nikolai Petrovich later wrote:

Really, from the point of view of my father, what was necessary for his sons? Only that they should become good *kuptsy*, support him in his old age and continue his business, which fed the family and gave a good profit. And for that what was necessary? It was necessary to be able to write in Russian not so much correctly as beautifully, in office style, and to be able to count, i.e., to know the four arithmetical rules . . . it was also useful to know a little German. . . . If sons were educated further, it would only make them "scholars" who would scorn their father's business, and so sooner or later it would perish . . . the point was not scholarship but good morals, piety, following the will of the older people. Such was the catechism of success.[11]

Besides a fear that education would distract from business, the *kupechestvo* in the early nineteenth century also tended to see book learning as subversive of the established order. In discussing the circumstances that shaped his father's attitude toward books, N. P. Vishniakov wrote that numerous individuals among the *kupechestvo*

> believed that there was poison and infection in books; they called educated people Voltaireans, atheists, masons . . . and said that such people, because they were harmful, must be removed from society, persecuted in all sorts of ways, put in prison, even sent to hard labor. All this was necessary so that these dangerous people should not read books and should not communicate their contents to others. So said the local policeman and the priest . . . all the petty "intelligentsia."[12]

In such an atmosphere, Vishniakov's father soon came to feel that perhaps it would be best to stay as far away as possible from books. Thus, the strong current of obscurantism of the early nineteenth century had its effect on the politically uninformed and instinctively conservative *kuptsy*, finding its way to them through the local representatives of authority.

One other factor that affected merchant attitudes toward education was the strong attachment to religion typical of the Moscow *kupechestvo* in the early 1800s. If books were somehow subversive of the political order, many felt that they also posed a threat to orthodox religious belief. And the religious objections to education were undoubtedly even more serious than the political objections. The merchant milieu was very far removed from the world of politics and government and gave scant attention to it, but religion was another matter. Religion was something very close to them, an important element of their daily lives, and any threat to the foundations of religious belief was bound to be viewed with a good deal of alarm.

But, paradoxically, religion in some cases served as a stimulus to education as well as a deterrent. Vishniakov remarked that frequently the individuals most hostile toward education were those who identified religiosity with *tserkovnost*—regular attendance at church and public displays of piety.[13] On the other hand, those who sought content as well as external form in their practice of religion were sometimes stimulated to seek deeper religious understanding through reading and conversation. Religion provided for some individuals not only spiritual but intellectual experiences. For men and women with an inquiring turn of mind, living in a milieu which looked upon secular learning with grave suspicion, the reading of religious books and discussion of religious problems was their only legitimate intellectual outlet, and many took advantage of it.

In the history of the Moscow dynasties, it is not unusual to find even founding fathers who displayed not only devotion to religion but an intellectual interest in it. For example, the founder of the Prokhorov family, according to his son's biographer, had a reputation as a great reader of books of "spiritual and moral content" and often gathered friends at his home to read to them or to discuss the books he had read. His wife, equally pious, also occupied herself by reading psalms and lives of saints and other religious material. Both Prokhorovs were firm believers in the education of their children on a religious basis, but they saw no need for extensive secular education.[14] They are an excellent example of a recurrent situation in which religiosity provided a stimulus for enlightenment, but enlightenment within a very restricted sphere.

In spite of business, political, and religious reasons for mistrusting education, merchant fathers, as noted above, frequently realized that a modicum of secular education was good for business. In fact, as the decades passed, the notion of how much education a businessman needed gradually expanded. In the memoirs and family histories of the Moscow dynasties, there emerges a definite pattern regarding educational opportunities given to sons (and frequently to daughters as well). In the first decades of the nineteenth century, educational arrangements were meager, and most often merchant sons were sent for a few years to a parish school or given lessons at home by a priest or perhaps by one of their father's clerks. But as the decades passed, it became increasingly frequent for substantial merchant families to employ the services of tutors and governesses, either Russians or, very often, members of Moscow's German colony.[15] Finally, in about the 1840s, in addition to being tutored at home in their younger years, more and more merchant children began to attend secondary schools, either private or public gymnasia, or, frequently, the Lutheran school in Moscow, which had an excellent reputation. In all but a very few exceptional cases, the university was still out of the question. It was traditional to give sons responsible positions in the family business by at least the age of fifteen or sixteen, and before the 1860s and 1870s the education of merchant sons was brought to an abrupt halt when they reached this traditional age of business maturity.

Another significant innovation in the education of merchant sons was the gradually spreading practice among well-off families of sending them abroad, to Western Europe, so that they could acquaint themselves with European business methods and European technology. In fact, not only did they send their sons abroad, but increasing numbers of already established merchants and industrialists began to make European pilgrimages, chiefly for business reasons, in the 1840s and 1850s. E. F. Guchkov, for instance, went abroad for the first time in 1842,"with a scientific goal." He visited industrial and commercial centers in Germany, France, and England, and returned home with dyers recruited from Alsace and Holland, as well as with new ideas which were soon adopted at the Guchkov factory. Guchkov returned to Western Europe for the World's Fair in London in 1851 and made his third trip in 1857, this time taking the waters at Wiesbaden on the advice of his doctor.[16] Similarly, K. V. Prokhorov went abroad in 1851 for the London fair and returned to Russia via France, Switzerland, and Germany, where he visited factories. Prokhorov took with him his two sons, two future members of the older generation of the 1890s, both of whom he left off in Mulhouse to learn Alsatian methods of cotton printing and machine building.[17]

Another family which early sent its sons abroad for practical education was the Krestovnikovs. When their father died, the Krestovnikov boys were removed from the gymnasium they had been attending by their mother, who was anxious to put them to work in the family business.[18] But their uncle, G. A. Moskvin, proved more farsighted and in 1845 sent Valentin Konstantinovich to England, where he worked in various offices in Manchester, Liverpool, and London. Valentin spent a total of four years in England, and soon after his return to Moscow in 1848, his younger brother Nikolai Konstantinovich departed for the British Isles. The Krestovnikov family was not a little concerned about the effects such a sojourn abroad might have on its sons and heirs. As Nikolai later wrote, "how all the relatives worried about brother Valentin, about his morals, as if he might be corrupted in foreign parts! In letters to him they mentioned their concern that he should not forget to go to church and should not drink port wine and so on."[19] When Nikolai himself left for England, his godfather sent him off with the warning: "Learn everything English, but remain Russian!"[20]

The fears of the Krestovnikovs that some foreign ways might rub off on the family heirs during their sojourn abroad were not groundless. In spite of the fact that merchant sons were sent abroad chiefly for the purpose of becoming better businessmen, they could hardly avoid being affected by the culture of the host countries. Nikolai Krestovnikov told of meeting two newly arrived Russian friends in London, both dressed in dreadful Russian costumes and knowing only one English phrase: "I say!" He and other Russian youths who had already been to some extent anglicized immediately took them round to the tailors and haberdashers and fitted them out in English style, right down to and including gloves.[21] Their linguistic deficiencies were also no doubt soon remedied. Krestovnikov himself, though he was able to remain in England only a short time because of the sudden death of the head of the family, managed not only to study English but to visit Parliament, attend the opera at Covent Garden, and indulge in other English entertainments. He wrote to his uncle in 1850: "At times I am overcome with a feeling of delight that I walk on the soil of such an ancient, such a cultured country! The more I become acquainted with it, the more it conquers my sympathy!"[22] One of the Moscow friends whom Krestovnikov met in London, V. I. Iakunchikov, had become a complete anglophile and remained one all his life.[23] Krestovnikov himself, while perhaps basically "remaining Russian," nonetheless developed a taste for European travel. During his lifetime he made eight separate trips abroad, visiting numerous European countries, chiefly for purposes of pleasure and health rather than business.[24]

Even in families who were slow to adopt the practice of sending sons abroad to study European business methods, the sons sometimes took the initiative themselves, and their interest in foreign travel was not always dictated by the needs of business. Perhaps the first to travel abroad on his own initiative with ambitious educational purposes was T. V. Prokhorov (1797–1854), one of the most remarkable figures of the early nineteenth-century Moscow *kupechestvo* and in many respects an interesting precursor of the older generation of the 1890s. Interested in both education and prison reform, Prokhorov sought to supplement his own meager education first by studying with various teachers in Moscow and then, in 1832, by traveling in Germany and France. There he visited not only factories but schools and prisons, and he returned home with renewed faith in the value of education, both for factory workers and for merchants and industrialists themselves.[25] In 1846 he made a second trip abroad, visiting factories, schools, prisons, and hospitals, as well as various other public and private institutions, and "seeking out people from whom he could learn something useful." Prokhorov carefully noted both the virtues and the vices of the Germans, but he returned home with the conviction that the secret of the Germans' many admirable virtues lay in their superior education and that Russia must follow Germany in this respect.[26]

Others followed in Prokhorov's footsteps, traveling to Europe in search of knowledge and, increasingly, pleasure, and these European trips played an important part in the continuing self-education of the older generation of the 1890s. No doubt in most cases it had been their fathers' idea that once their secondary education and perhaps a brief stay abroad had been completed, they should dedicate themselves entirely to business. In fact, things did not usually work out that way. In most cases, the sketchy education this generation had received from tutors and in secondary schools, supplemented by trips abroad, simply whetted their appetite for further enlightenment. Perhaps very much to the point is Vishniakov's observation that conditions of life in the merchant milieu were "so primitive" that anyone exposed to any education at all immediately desired to find a way out of that milieu. Education opened broad new horizons, gave a glimpse into a world of learning, of art and literature, of history and languages—in a word, a world of culture—whose existence had previously gone largely unnoticed in the *kupechestvo*. And those affected by this broadening of horizons did indeed manifest a desire to leave Zamoskvoreche or the Old Believer communities behind them forever, both in a physical sense (most members of this older generation moved out of the old merchant quarters into new homes on fashionable streets) and, more importantly, in an intellectual sense.

In many cases, the manifestation of a desire for further education by merchant sons and daughters led to family conflict. When M. Ia. Riabushinskii discovered that his son was secretly learning to play the violin, he smashed the instrument and put an end to the clandestine lessons, though without in any way inhibiting his son's developing love of music.[27] Much more serious was the tension among the Vishniakovs resulting from the different cultural levels attained by different generations of the family. N. P. Vishniakov's memoirs reveal the development of a huge cultural gap between the children of P. M. Vishniakov's two wives, who were separated in age by several decades. Of the two eldest sons, though they assimilated the external manifestations of "culture," one was distinguished primarily for his ugly displays of temper and his unspeakably crude practical jokes, while the other was given to wine, women, and heavy-handed displays of his authority as head of the family after his father's death. Their younger stepbrothers, subject to the fortunate influence of their younger mother, from their earliest years imbibed her love for music and her respect for both learning and humane and decent behavior. The eldest of her sons cut his intellectual eyeteeth on Voltaire, whose writings had a considerable influence in shaping his views, and, repelled by the domestic atmosphere created by his stepbrothers, he first rebelled against their authority and finally left the family and the business for a job in a St. Petersburg government office. In 1853, an irrevocable split occurred, and the two families of the late P. M. Vishniakov went their separate ways, no doubt with a sense of relief all around.[28] Such intrafamily tensions developed in other merchant families, though certainly not in all. The recollections of N. A. Naidenov and of N. K. Krestovnikov give no indication of major family conflict, and in both these cases the older generation seem to have offered no resistance to the cultural aspirations of their children. Everything seemed to depend on the willingness of the older generation to accept change and to recognize the right of their juniors to a way of life somewhat different from their own.

In a few cases, the elders' worst fears were fulfilled, and some educated sons simply lost any desire to remain businessmen and gave up active participation in the family firm as soon as possible. N. S. Abrikosov, for instance, developed a great passion for chemistry; as soon as his father died, he left business and went to Paris to attend lectures at the Sorbonne.[29] Generally speaking, however, such instances were rare enough in the older generation of the 1890s. In the majority of cases educated merchant sons obediently followed in their fathers' footsteps, entered their family firms, and usually became excellent businessmen. Unlike their fathers, however, they were not content to dedicate their whole lives to business and sought as best they could to fill the gaps in their early education and so enter the world beyond Zamoskvoreche, the world of educated people.

Many members of this generation suffered from serious gaps in their education to the very end of their lives, however impressive their achievements in self-education. Among others, P. M. Tretiakov, the famous collector of Russian art, was largely self-educated. Although he received a domestic education of sorts in his youth, his artistic taste and his considerable knowledge of art were entirely the result of self-training. Tretiakov, however, recognized the limitations of his knowledge. When he first became interested in art, he purchased several paintings reputed to be the work of old European masters. He soon realized that it would be difficult for him to determine the genuineness of European works of art and foreswore any further attempts to buy European paintings, since his lack of artistic knowledge made him easy prey for swindlers. He restricted himself chiefly to the purchase of contemporary Russian works, whose authenticity was more easily ascertained.[30] Similarly K. T. Soldatenkov, who in his youth had no formal education whatsoever, recognized the deficiencies in his knowledge and attempted to remedy them in a variery of ways.[31] At one time he attended a private series of lectures given for him by the well-known Westerner and professor, T. N. Granovskii.[32] In later years, he sought out other members of the intelligentsia to assist him in his publishing and collecting activities. The artist A. A. Ivanov served as his advisor in the purchase of paintings for his extensive collection, and M. P. Shchepkin edited the series of important but financially unprofitable scholarly works which Soldatenkov published.[33] Neither Soldatenkov nor Tretiakov ever mastered any foreign languages, in spite of numerous sojourns abroad. Soldatenkov was forced to travel with an interpreter; Tretiakov, on his visits to European art galleries, was accompanied by his wife, who was from the extraordinarily well-educated Mamontov family and who had an excellent command of both French and German.[34] But whatever the remaining deficiencies in their education, both Tretiakov and Soldatenkov won recognition as men of culture, became friends with numerous artists and writers, and were able to hold their own in conversation with the likes of I. E. Repin and V. D. Polenov, Ivan Turgenev and Count Leo Tolstoi.

Fairly typical of this generation were two memoirists, Petr Ivanovich Shchukin and Anna Ivanovna Volkova. P. I. Shchukin, born in 1853, received his early education at home, from German governesses, and then for a brief time attended a Moscow private school run by a Frenchman. At the age of ten he was sent to a boarding school in Vyborg, operated by

Germans, and in 1867 was transferred to the Girst boarding school in St. Petersburg. In 1872 his father took him to Berlin, where he went to work in the office of a German firm. After two years in Germany, Shchukin moved on to Lyons, where he worked for a French textile firm and then in 1875 took a position in the office of the P. D. Warburg company. Shchukin finally returned to Moscow in 1878.[35]

Shchukin's life abroad was rather drab, and the people with whom he associated were mostly clerks and accountants, persons occupying the same low status as he in the business world. Nonetheless, he sought in various ways to supplement his education outside the office. He traveled extensively, attended lectures and concerts, took private lessons in French, and studied the manufacture of silk with a former French silk manufacturer. It was also in France that he first acquired an interest in collecting.[36] Beginning with the collection of French books, Shchukin soon laid the foundations for one of the most extensive and impressive collections in Moscow, consisting chiefly of books, manuscripts, and documents, but including a wide variety of other objects as well (mostly objects representing the applied art of Russia and the Near and Far East). When he began collecting, Shchukin embarked on a program of reading and study that would eventually make him one of the most knowledgeable collectors in Moscow. A fellow collector, A. P. Bakhrushin, praised Shchukin as "the most serious collector of all known to me, because he does not collect anything without first gathering a whole bibliography about this object and studying it in books." Bakhrushin observed that Shchukin was capable of giving "a whole lecture on the spot" about any of the items in his collection.[37]

If Shchukin, through self-education, made himself into an extremely knowledgeable collector, his memoirs nonetheless show that the author was a man of spotty education, unaccustomed to abstract thought of any sort, and totally lacking in analytical abilities. His lack of formal training was also apparent in his historical publications: his published volumes of documents from his collection,[38] which contain few attempts at analysis or synthesis or even at providing historical background, and the brief notices he occasionally published in *Russkii arkhiv*, simply announcing the existence of certain documents in his collection but making no attempt to assess their historical significance. Shchukin undoubtedly performed a valuable service simply by gathering and preserving his collection and by his multivolume publications of documents, as well as by the freedom he allowed scholars in making use of his collection. Nonetheless, he did not have the education or training to go beyond mere collecting, even if he had so desired.

Shchukin at one point in his life had wanted to enter the university, but a professor whom he consulted had told him that his previous education was insufficient and that he would require considerable tutoring in order to be able to pass the entrance examinations. Shchukin studied with tutors for a brief time but then, for some reason, dropped the whole project,[39] and many of the gaps which the professor had spotted in his education remained with him until the end of his life. These did not, however, prevent him from performing considerable services for the world of scholarship or from playing a certain role in educated society. Especially after he donated his collection to the Historical Museum in 1902, Shchukin played an important role in the affairs of the museum and often served as its representative on official occasions.[40] Entirely taken up with his collecting and his involvement with the Historical Museum, Shchukin gave less and less attention to the family business, which remained chiefly in the capable hands of his brother S. I. Shchukin, one of the most dynamic businessmen of his generation as well as a collector of French impressionist paintings and financial angel of the Psychological Institute of Moscow University.[41]

Anna Ivanovna Volkova is an even more interesting example of the educational trials and tribulations, as well as the cultural achievements, of the older generation—and evidence of the fact that the process of cultural change at work within the *kupechestvo* affected women as well as men. Born in 1847, Volkova received her earliest education from her mother, a woman of some education and culture, who played the piano, read Voltaire, and suffered bitterly from the boorishness of her husband.[42] When her mother became fatally ill with cancer, Volkova was put into the hands of German and Russian governesses and later attended several private schools in Moscow. She was enthralled by the new world her lessons and books opened to her and became a passionate reader, finding escape in books from her oppressive home life.[43] Married at the age of sixteen to a banker who neither shared nor encouraged her newly developing intellectual interests, a man who went so far as to refuse her money for books, she continued to seek solace in reading and soon also began to write.[44] She became intensely interested in the subject of the education and upbringing of children and an advocate of the emancipation of women, these interests no doubt reflecting her own disappointments in life—her extremely unhappy childhood and her miserable marriage. In 1883 and 1884 she edited a journal devoted to the "woman question." After the journal closed down, because of financial difficulties, she continued to write voluminously, chiefly articles bringing to the attention of Russian readers the latest theory and practice of European education. She contributed a total of 486 articles to various journals during her lifetime, but, as in Shchukin's case, her intellectual limitations were apparent simply from the type of articles she produced, mostly translations and summaries of various European works on education.[45]

In spite of her intellectual and literary achievements, Volkova never overcame a feeling of inferiority before truly educated people. She recognized the deficiencies of self-education and regretted all her life that being a *kupchikha* had imposed serious limitations on her own intellectual development. In 1887, reacting to a recommendation of conversation as an excellent means of self-education, Volkova wrote in her diary:

> My family situation and the very conditions of merchant life do not permit me to make use of this means of self-education. The people with whom I might talk do not visit [us], being squeezed out [by those who] do not at all desire "to make minds spin, to sharpen understanding, to enlighten feelings, to awaken and nourish thought"; with these others there is nothing to talk about. . . . And so it goes from day to day, but I am dying to share my thoughts, to talk. Yes, we make acquaintances outside the home, but it seems to me that they look down upon me. Of course, this is perhaps my imagination! Sometimes I do not feel this heaviness with these people, but at times it is so difficult for me, so bitter, that my lips tremble and I begin to feel confused. All this is bad, foul! Oh, my *soslovie*, my *kupecheskoe soslovie*!

Later she added to this entry: "What a stupid remark! It is stupid, very stupid, but the weight of my *soslovie* lies on me like a heavy burden, and I feel it precisely as such. With an educated husband, my position would not be so utterly isolated."[46]

Generally speaking, her diary, parts of which were published after her death, is a touching document, attesting to the tremendous mental and emotional strain involved in trying to raise herself above the milieu into which she was born, a feat which was perhaps doubly difficult for a woman, especially for one who received no encouragement either from her father or, later, from her husband.[47] In spite of the miseries she suffered from her unhappy marriage, Volkova not only stayed with this husband with whom she had nothing in common, but after he suffered a paralytic stroke, she both cared for him and took over the management of his banking business.[48] She thus combined intellectual strivings with a talent for business, a combination not rare in her generation, among either men or women.

If Volkova and Shchukin are fairly typical of their generation, some attention should be given to the extremes at either end of the educational and cultural scale. Even within the best of families, this older generation of the 1890s contained some rather crude types. Thus, M. F. Morozova, who inherited from her husband a controlling interest in the huge Nikolskaia factory, was once described by her son Savva in most uncomplimentary terms. According to Savva, she dressed and acted like a gentlewoman, loved to read novels, was acquainted with many Slavophiles, and yet would not permit electricity in her home because she considered it a supernatural force. She busied herself with philanthropy and yet, according to her son, loved no one, could not even find a tear to shed at the death of her husband, and ruled over her sons with an iron fist. She lived in a large new home, in neo-Russian style, all alone in her twenty rooms, receiving no one except priests from Rogozhskoe cemetery and, on major holidays, a few relatives. Her son insisted that she never bathed for fear of colds but simply drenched herself in cologne.[49] Although there was no love lost between Savva Morozov and his mother, there seems little reason to doubt that such types as M. F. Morozova, combining the externals of culture with inner coarseness, continued to exist in the older generation.

At the other extreme, one finds a few families far in advance of the other business dynasties in regard to education and culture. Most notable in this respect were the Botkins, whose rapid educational and cultural advancement stemmed largely from the efforts and enlightened attitude of one member of the family, V. P. Botkin. Born in 1810, son of the founder of the Botkin tea firm, Vasilii Petrovich was profoundly affected by the Moscow intellectual climate of the 1830s. He strove through a process of self-improvement to remedy the gaps in his own meager education and fought a hard battle with his father to ensure formal education, up to and including the university, for his younger stepbrothers, who were born in the 1830s. The results of his efforts were brilliant. In the 1830s and 1840s, Vasilii Petrovich himself was a leading member of the select group of Moscow Westerners that included V. G. Belinskii, A. I. Herzen, and T. N. Granovskii, and made a reputation for himself as an interpreter of Hegel, an art critic and historian, and the author of a series of travel letters. One of his stepbrothers, Sergei Petrovich, became a doctor and medical researcher and was in his time perhaps Russia's foremost medical man. Another stepbrother, Mikhail Petrovich, became a well-known painter and member of the Academy of Art. A fourth member of the family, Dmitrii Petrovich, ran the family business and collected European paintings. In later generations, the Botkins continued to produce individuals who made notable careers in various fields outside business: several diplomats and military men, another painter, a singer, and the like. One of the sons of Sergei Petrovich followed in his father's footsteps and became a doctor. He was appointed personal physician to the Imperial family and perished with them at Ekaterinburg in 1918.[50]

The rapidity of the Botkins' cultural and educational advancement was exceptional. Most notably, their early pursuit of higher education, display of independent talent, and development of careers outside the field of business would be more typical of the younger generation of the 1890s than of the older generation who were the contemporaries of these brilliant Botkins. The men and women of the older generation, who, as we have seen, rarely had the opportunity for higher education or systematic training outside the field of business, but who nonetheless desired to expand their horizons beyond the business world, for the most part turned to activities more suitable to wealthy dilettantes—philanthropy, patronage, and collecting—though many also dedicated considerable time and effort to public affairs.

OF these various activities, all extremely popular and highly respected in Moscow, philanthropy in particular occupied a very special place in the life of the city and in the view the upper layers of Moscow society had of themselves and their city. Indeed, the number of philanthropical societies and charitable institutions in Moscow was somewhat startling. In 1889 there were 495 public and private charitable institutions in the city, extending help to a total of 430,466 people. In that year these institutions spent a total of 5,325,457 rubles, a large part of this money coming from interest on the 24,961,925 rubles in capital which they controlled. The largest number of institutions (142) were associated with the Orthodox church, but the 130 institutions maintained by the city gave help to the largest number of persons (178,331). Only 40 institutions were supported by private charitable societies, and 20 by private individuals, the remainder being controlled either by various *soslovie* organizations or governmental departments.[51] But whether the institutions were public or private, a large amount of their funds came from individual contributions. Given the existence of this extensive philanthropical apparatus, it is not surprising to learn that in 1900 Moscow was spending more per capita on charity than Paris, Berlin, or Vienna.[52] The magnitude of Moscow's charitable efforts was a testimony both to the generosity of Muscovites and to the extreme poverty of the lower strata of the city population.

Many Muscovites regarded the inhabitants of their city as being particularly sensitive to the needs of the poor and the suffering and had long prided themselves on their generosity. Charitable impulses were hardly restricted to any particular *soslovie* but affected all groups of the population. The Moscow press almost daily published reports of charitable contributions from representatives of all social groups, and in addition the newspapers itemized particularly needy individual cases toward which philanthropists were urged to direct their attention. The city government in the 1890s put considerable effort into the creation of a municipal welfare system that depended on contributions of both time and money from the more fortunate members of all *sosloviia*. Leading philanthropists became well-known public figures, and at least one of them, A. N. Strekalova, achieved a position of great respect in Moscow society entirely on the basis of her innumerable charitable activities. After Grand Duke Sergei became Moscow's governor-general, his wife, the Grand Duchess Elisaveta, dedicated a considerable amount of her time and attention to

philanthropy and headed a number of the city's more important philanthropical societies. Both she and her husband put their considerable prestige behind the cause of philanthropy in Moscow and could be counted
on to grace with their presence the opening of any major new charitable
institution. If by the end of the century some intellectuals were beginning
to question the wisdom of allowing private philanthropists, rather than
public agencies, to make crucial decisions regarding disposition of the
money they allotted for the public welfare, most Muscovites still looked
with admiration upon philanthropists and regarded private philanthropy
as a legitimate means of attempting to alleviate the poverty and suffering
of the lower classes.[53]

Of almost equal importance in Moscow's public life were patronage and
collecting. When the industrialist Baron Alexander Stieglitz donated a
million rubles for the creation of a technical drawing school in St. Petersburg, residents of the capital were profuse in expressions of admiration
for his gift and "crowed about it for almost half a year." Muscovites were
puzzled by all the excitement, since in Moscow, as N. O. Rakshanin
commented, "gifts of millions astonish no one."[54] Indeed, Moscow art,
science, and education were the beneficiaries of so many huge gifts that·
Muscovites could afford to be somewhat blasé about them. And although
by the end of the century most of the millions for patronage and for the
creation of collections were coming from the business elite, businessmen
entering this field were only taking over a tradition of generosity already
established by the Moscow nobility.[55] One of Moscow's first private art
museums had been the Golitsyn Museum, established in 1865 but closed
in 1887, when most of the Golitsyns' collection was sold to the Hermitage
Museum in St. Petersburg.[56] Like the Golitsyns, other noble families,
because of their reduced circumstances, were perhaps finding it increasingly difficult to continue patronage and collecting on a broad scale,
though they continued active participation in Moscow's dozens of private
societies formed for the encouragement of the arts and sciences. But more
and more they began to be joined in these groups by businessmen who,
in becoming active benefactors of art and science, inherited much of the
respect Moscow had earlier accorded to patrons and collectors from the
nobility.

Although patronage and collecting were of relatively recent origin in
Russia, philanthropy had a long history, reaching back to the time of the
introduction of Christianity into Russia. The Orthodox church had from
the beginning lauded the virtues of giving alms to the poor, not so much
for the material benefit of the recipient as for the spiritual benefit of the
donor. The historian V. O. Kliuchevskii, in a public lecture on the origins
of Russian philanthropy, described its religious foundations in pre-Petrine
Russia as follows:

> Philanthropy . . . was more necessary to the benefactor of the poor
> than to the beggar. . . . The ancient Russian philanthropist, a "lover
> of Christ," thought less about his good deed raising the level of social
> well-being than about raising the level of his own spiritual perfec-
> tion. . . . "To paradise one will go with holy alms," they said in the
> old days: "the beggar is fed by the rich, and they are saved by the
> prayers of the beggar."[57]

Besides giving alms to the poor, the Orthodox believer concerned about
the fate of his soul also frequently gave large bequests to churches and
monasteries. Such grants were again intended largely for the benefit of
the donor and were accompanied by requests for eternal prayers for his
salvation.

These religious forms of philanthropy were very old, but in the early
nineteenth century they were still the predominant forms of philanthropy
among the merchant community. Alms were freely distributed to the
poor, usually on special occasions such as the major church holidays or a
death in the family. When a rich merchant died, the news quickly spread
among Moscow's poor, and a huge crowd of beggars soon gathered in the
courtyard, awaiting their due (usually a small handout of a ruble or so).[58]
One favorite form of charity was grants of dowries to poor brides, frequently accompanied by the request that the recipients pray for the soul
of their benefactor. Besides distribution of alms, the money of Moscow
kuptsy decorated numerous churches in munificent style and went to the
support of various monasteries.

Such types of philanthropy were still much alive in some sections of
the *kupechestvo* even at the end of the nineteenth century. All Moscow
talked for weeks about the will of A. K. Medvednikova, widow of a rich
Siberian gold mine owner, who died on her estate near Moscow in 1899.
She left her entire fortune, more than 5 million rubles, to charities, both
secular and religious. Typical of the old forms of philanthropy was a
bequest of 100,000 rubles to the Christian poor of Moscow, the interest
on this capital to be distributed three times a year to the designated
recipients. But the most astonishing part of Medvednikova's will was her
grant of 100 rubles to every church in both Moscow and her native town
of Irkutsk, as well as grants of 10,000 rubles apiece to sixteen monasteries.
All these bequests to religious institutions were accompanied by a request
for the remembrance of the soul of the benefactress.[59]

Thus, the concern for personal salvation long remained a motive behind
the philanthropy of the *kupechestvo*. Throughout the nineteenth and early
twentieth centuries, many contemporaries continued to stress this motive
as the primary one behind the charitable activities of the business community, and some later writers have upheld this view. Buryshkin told of
an incident which occurred when his father was making plans to build a

hospital for the benefit of a village near his estate: having received a request from the elder Buryshkin to donate land for the hospital, the local peasants replied that since Buryshkin was only interested in saving his own soul, he could provide the land himself.[60] One Soviet writer on Moscow life, himself a scion of the lower strata of the population of pre-revolutionary Moscow, reiterated this common belief that desire for personal salvation was the chief motive behind merchant philanthropy as well as the widespread conviction that the large proportions assumed by merchants' charitable contributions were simply a sign that the merchants had much to repent of. He recalled that

> the *kuptsy* loved to go on sprees—to visit the gypsies, to eat well, to drink, while sternly observing Lent, and at the same time—to cheat, to deceive, to drive someone, as they said, "to the wall," not to pay their debts.
> And although the *kuptsy*, from a religious point of view, considered all this a sin, and accumulated many such sins, nevertheless they had many ways of redeeming themselves before God for these sins: they knew how to observe fasts, and to pray, and their capital permitted them to do good deeds—here is the origin of broad merchant philanthropy.[61]

The Soviet historian P. A. Liashchenko likewise attributed the extensive philanthropical activities of Moscow businessmen chiefly to concern for their souls.[62]

Such explanations of the extensive philanthropy of Moscow's businessmen fail, however, to take into consideration certain definite changes that occurred during the nineteenth century both in the motives behind the charitable activities of the *kupechestvo* and in the forms their philanthropy assumed. Even in the first half of the century, some notable changes were apparent. Besides religion, patriotism became another spur to large contributions. The merchant community responded to the Napoleonic invasion and the destruction of Moscow with donations totalling 1,718,764 rubles.[63] These contributions established a tradition of patriotic readiness to respond to any national crisis, and the Moscow *kupechestvo* thereafter distinguished itself repeatedly by large donations, both from individuals and from the *soslovie* as a whole, not only for war relief work but for famine relief, assistance to victims of epidemics, and the like. In January 1904, for instance, the Exchange Society and the Merchants' Society jointly pledged 1 million rubles from the Moscow *kupechestvo* to aid casualties of the Russo-Japanese War and their families.[64]

The government encouraged contributions to worthy causes by members of the *kupechestvo* in a variety of ways. In some cases, state officials exerted very direct and rather crude forms of pressure in order to part the merchants from their money. Thus, at the time of the Crimean War,

Moscow's despotic governor-general, Count A. A. Zakrevskii, simply summoned to his office representatives of all the well-to-do business families and announced to them the sums they were expected to contribute.[65] But in addition to these cruder forms of encouragement, the government also appealed to the merchants with all sorts of medals, orders, ranks, and titles as rewards for large donations to either religious or secular institutions and causes, and there were many *kuptsy* who could not resist this bait.

In such a way, motives other than religion had come into play in the early part of the century. And at the same time, even if religious motives long remained dominant in merchant philanthropy, there was in process a subtle change of emphasis in the religious rationalizations of philanthropy. If previously the soul of the donor had been regarded as the primary beneficiary of giving alms to the poor, some philanthropists were now beginning to stress the benefit to the poor themselves. The religious injunction to care for one's neighbor gradually came to be at least as important to some philanthropists as concern for their own salvation.

An early example of this changing emphasis can be found in the activities and theories of T. V. Prokhorov, already mentioned as one of the most remarkable products of the Moscow *kupechestvo* in the early nineteenth century. Prokhorov was probably the first industrialist in all of Russia to establish a technical school at his factory. His pupils came chiefly from among the sons of poor *kuptsy* and *meshchane*. At the school Prokhorov subjected them to a benevolent paternalistic regime, giving attention not only to their technical training but to their moral and spiritual training as well. He devoted to the school considerable personal attention and energy and sincerely believed that he was fulfilling the religious injunction to care for one's fellow man.[66] No doubt Prokhorov himself benefited very directly from the school, through the acquisition of well-trained workers, but, in fact, he became so deeply involved with his pupils that he neglected his business, which suffered accordingly. One of his brothers, after repeatedly bailing him out of financial difficulties, finally wrote him in despair that the only thing left for him to do was to enter a monastery—he was simply too idealistic to survive in the real world of business.[67]

Prokhorov gave an ideological foundation to his philanthropy in a pamphlet he wrote and published, entitled *O bogatenii*. In it, he set forth the idea that men of wealth have a moral responsibility to use that wealth for the benefit of those less fortunate than themselves. Prokhorov believed that all wealth accumulated by an individual beyond that necessary for the satisfaction of basic needs ought to be used to help his fellow man.[68] He wrote that "it is permissible to possess wealth only if it is used to help the needy or assist in some way or another in the spiritual and moral improvement of mankind."[69] Certainly, he argued, the industrialist had an obligaton to use a certain part of his profits for the improvement of his business, which would contribute to the public welfare. But like all wealthy individuals, he also had an obligation to direct part of his money toward philanthropical purposes. Not only would he thus help his fellow man, but the philanthroper would be rewarded by the moral satisfaction of knowing that "he lives 'in God.' "[70]

Prokhorov further discussed the forms philanthropy should take and here also parted company with traditional notions. He advocated going beyond the mere donation of money—which was generally as far as merchant philanthropy went in his day—and believed that the philanthropist should give earnest consideration to the choice of both the recipients and the forms of charity. Instead of simply placing alms in the hands of any beggars who came along, the philanthropist should visit the dwellings of the poor, become acquainted with their needs, help those who most needed help, and give them aid not only in the form of money but through personal attention and advice.[71]

Prokhorov was an interesting precursor of the businessmen-philanthropists of the later part of the nineteenth century in a number of respects. For one thing, he gave not only money but time, energy, and the benefit of his own creative imagination to his charitable enterprises. Such a practice was extremely unusual in the first half of the century, though it would become typical later on. The most respected philanthropists of the older generation of the 1890s were almost without exception distinguished by some degree of personal involvement in their charitable undertakings. One of the best examples of this was the Rukavishnikovs and their correctional home for juvenile delinquents. N. V. Rukavishnikov personally took over the management of a small home for wayward children in 1870 and during the few remaining years of his life dedicated almost all his time and energy to making the home into a model institution.[72] As a result of his work with the home, Rukavishnikov achieved not only a national but an international reputation in this field, and the Dean of Westminster Abbey once commented, after meeting Rukavishnikov: "I can die happy since I have succeeded in seeing a saint."[73] When N. V. Rukavishnikov died in 1875 at the age of thirty, his brother K. V. Rukavishnikov took upon himself the continuation of his work and with the help of one Dr. Fiedler succeeded in maintaining the home as a model of its kind.[74] K. V. Rukavishnikov also played an instrumental role in the creation of a national organization for those involved in correctional work with children and was for many years president of this body.[75] Like many of the creations of Moscow philanthropists, the Rukavishnikov home was eventually turned over to the city of Moscow, but K. V. Rukavishnikov still continued to take a direct and personal interest in its fate and to contribute generously to the financial support of the home.[76] Such a high degree of personal involvement in a philanthropical undertaking was as usual for the Rukavishnikov brothers' generation as it had been rare in Prokhorov's time.

Prokhorov also foreshadowed the philanthropy of the later generation in the form he gave to his good works. By creating a school for the children of the poor and attempting to give them an education that would prepare them to make a decent living, he undoubtedly made a greater contribution to the betterment of social welfare in Russia than the mere distribution of alms could ever accomplish. The next generation followed in his footsteps and sought to alleviate poverty and suffering through the creation of institutions to care for and educate the poor, the sick, the old, the unfortunate. Thus, the institutions created by merchants and indus-trialists of the older generation of the elite and managed by the city included not only the Rukavishnikov home but the following institutions as well: the Mazurin orphanage, the Arnold-Tretiakov school for deaf-mute children, the V. E. Morozov children's hospital, the Soldatenkov hospital, a public reading room and a trade school created by V. A. Morozova, the Varvara Lepeshkina teachers' training school, a trade school and an eye clinic financed by V. A. Alekseeva, the Bakhrushin hospital for the chronically ill, the Bakhrushin orphanage, the Bakhrushin complex of free apartments for poor widows and female students, and, finally, a psychiatric hospital named after former mayor N. A. Alekseev, who both contributed generously to it and collected the rest of the funds needed chiefly from other wealthy businessmen.[77] This list of municipal institutions hardly begins to exhaust the full complement of philanthrop-ical establishments created by the older generation. It gives only some idea of the type of charitable activity in which they engaged.

This change in the forms of philanthropy practiced by the *kupechestvo* was in part a reaction to the running critique of Moscow philanthropy kept up by writers interested in the question. Ridiculing such primitive types of charity as giving dowries to poor brides (which, according to one writer, had the chief effect of bringing about numerous marriages that would otherwise not have occurred),[78] the critics of Moscow philanthrop-ists urged them to undertake types of philanthropy that would have more lasting and beneficial effects both for the individual recipients of charity and for society as a whole. Some critics, particularly those who repre-sented the liberal intelligentsia, stressed secular considerations in urging the creation of useful institutions upon the wealthy and emphasized the need to promote general social betterment.[79] On the other hand, conserv-ative writers dealing with questions of philanthropy still frequently con-tinued to emphasize religious considerations, though they increasingly stressed the Christian obligation to help one's fellow man rather than saving one's own soul through good works.[80] But whether they sought to rationalize philanthropy on the basis of religious or secular considerations, almost all writers concerned with problems of philanthropy in the later nineteenth century put the emphasis on creating useful institutions rather than on distributing alms or decorating churches.

In many cases it would be difficult to say whether secular or religious considerations were paramount in the mind of any individual businessman-philanthropist in the later decades of the century. Religion still played an important role in the lives of most members of the business elite's older generation, although it was not so all-encompassing as it had been for their fathers and grandfathers, and for some philanthropists religious considerations were still important. But there seems little doubt that secular motives and secular rationalizations of philanthropy came increasingly to dominate the thinking of many philanthropically inclined merchants and industrialists. One indication of this secularization of philanthropy in the business elite was simply the fact that donations to churches and monasteries were rare, though not entirely unheard of, in the older generation of the 1890s. P. M. Tretiakov's will left a considerable sum to secular charities and institutions, but nothing for religious institutions. K. T. Soldatenkov willed large sums to various charities, only two of which had any religious connections. Soldatenkov did maintain the old traditions to the extent of leaving a small sum to be distributed to brides and an additional 100,000 rubles to be distributed as alms to the poor. Otherwise, the vast majority of the several million rubles disposed of by his will went to various secular charitable and educational institutions and organizations.[81]

Many of the nonreligious factors that seem to have come increasingly to motivate the philanthropy of the elite were also significant in motivating the patronage of art and science and the collecting so widely practiced by the older generation, as well as their participation in public affairs, and can best be examined by considering all these fields of activity together. Certainly one factor that came to account for the activity of members of the elite in these various fields was a theory of the responsibility of wealth. Here again, T. V. Prokhorov was ahead of his time. He was the first Russian businessman-philanthropist to formulate the idea that all individuals have an obligation to employ wealth beyond a certain level for the benefit of their fellow men. In fact, Prokhorov's pamphlet was a rare statement of this belief—most Moscow philanthropists unfortunately did not discuss their motives in public. Nonetheless, there were numerous indications that many members of the older generation of the 1890s shared Prokhorov's views. For instance, the Riabushinskii family history noted the "philanthropical obligations accompanying created wealth."[82] Rakshanin once described as typical a philanthropist of his acquaintance, a woman from a business family, noting that she accepted the view that "millions have their obligations," obligations that she fulfilled willingly and "with Christian love."[83] Also, when Professor I. I. Ianzhul delivered a public lecture on Andrew Carnegie's theories regarding the responsibility of wealth, leading philanthropists and patrons from Moscow's business community were present and gave the lecture a warm reception. K. T. Soldatenkov was so enthusiastic that he later came to see Ianzhul and asked him for permission to publish the lecture.[84]

One great philanthropist, patron, and collector from the older generation clearly formulated a view of the social obligations of wealth in a letter to one of his daughters. This was P. M. Tretiakov, who wrote:

> My idea from my very youngest years was to make money in order that what is accumulated from society would be returned to society (to the people) in some sort of beneficial institutions; this thought has never deserted me during my whole life.

Tretiakov went on to explain that both he and his wife had received around 100,000 rubles each from their respective parents, and he felt obliged to leave the same amount to each of his children. But having fulfilled that obligation to his offspring, Tretiakov believed that the remainder of his wealth should be employed for socially beneficial purposes, for philanthropy and the creation of his art gallery, which from the very beginning he planned to give as a gift to his native town.[85]

Tretiakov's letter is noteworthy, first of all, in that he seems to indicate that his sole motive in making money was a desire to benefit society, an idea that even goes beyond the notion that wealth, however and for whatever purpose it was accumulated, ought then to be used in part for socially beneficial purposes. Also, Tretiakov's letter made no connection between the uses of wealth and religious teachings. Tretiakov, although he was a religious man, seemed to think more in terms of the social obligations of wealth than in terms of religious and moral obligations. Thus, if the concept of the responsibility of wealth originated partly in the Christian emphasis on love for one's fellow man, as was true in Prokhorov's case, by the later nineteenth century the concept seems to have been largely secularized.

Closely allied with the idea of responsibility of wealth as a motive for the good works of Moscow businessmen was the concept of "public service," a notion undoubtedly secular in origin. Although the desire to serve was repeatedly attributed to philanthropists, patrons, collectors, and public figures from the business elite, the term "public service" never received precise formulation, and, indeed, exact definition was hardly required. The term was common coin in the language spoken by educated Russians and reflected the dedication to the ideal of service long professed by both the nobility and the intelligentsia. The whole concept of public service was an integral part of the world view of the upper levels of Russian society. The idea that the purpose of their existence was to serve had been inculcated in Russian noblemen since the time of Peter the Great. If they did not always live up to the ideal, nonetheless in the later nineteenth century spokesmen for the nobility sought to justify their special position and privileges almost entirely on the grounds that the *dvorianstvo* fulfilled the special responsibility of serving the public good. Likewise, the Russian intelligentsia was imbued with the idea of service, though where the nobility tended to think chiefly in terms of service to the state, the intelligentsia thought in terms of service to their country, or service to the *narod*.

Given the great emphasis placed on the concept of service by the two socially and intellectually dominant groups in Russia, it would perhaps have been odd if the *kuptsy* had not been increasingly affected by this ideal, especially as they more and more began to rub elbows with representatives of both groups and, breaking away from the isolated world of Zamoskvoreche, became more and more open to the ideas and values of these other social groups. Of particular importance is the fact that the older generation of the 1890s came to maturity during the years of the Crimean War and the Great Reforms. Many members of what was then the younger generation of the *kupechestvo* were deeply affected by the idealism and intellectual excitement of the late 1850s and 1860s, and the acceptance of the ideal of service by leading representatives of the business community would seem to date chiefly from these decades. A case in point is N. A. Naidenov, about whom V. P. Riabushinskii once wrote that "his chief occupation was public service."[86] Naidenov's memoirs are a testimony to the importance that the concept of public service came to have for many members of the older generation of the 1890s and to the effect the atmosphere of the 1850s and 1860s had in bringing about acceptance of this idea. His reminiscences concentrated almost entirely on what he referred to as his "public service," only very rarely mentioning his business activity. In the conclusion of his memoirs, Naidenov noted that he had covered the first fifteen years of his "public service" (primarily in the municipal duma and certain business organizations), without even noting the fact that these were also the first years of his business activity.[87] Though others might question whether Naidenov was really interested in service to the public, as opposed to service to his own *soslovie*, he himself was convinced that all his activities, particularly in the city duma and in the Exchange Committee, were motivated by a desire to serve the public good. It is also clear that the period of the late 1850s and early 1860s was crucial in the development of Naidenov's dedication to public service and that the enthusiasm of the Moscow nobility and intelligentsia for service to their native town through the newly created municipal organs of self-government was a particularly strong influence on him.[88]

Another interesting example of acceptance of the service ideal is Savva Ivanovich Mamontov, the dilettante and great patron of the arts, the center of the so-called Abramtsevo circle, which included many noted

Russian artists. Coming to intellectual maturity in the 1860s and 1870s, Mamontov was affected by the intelligentsia's enthusiasm for helping the masses, as were many of the artists with whom he associated and who believed that art should be for the masses, that it should assist in their education and general betterment.[89] The notion of somehow helping the people through art remained with Mamontov all his life. Thus, he decorated his company's rail terminal in Moscow with Korovin's murals of the Far North, maintaining that "the eye of the people must be trained to see beauty everywhere—in streets and railroad stations."[90] By creating his private opera he hoped both "to raise the level of culture in Moscow and to introduce young people to opera."[91] The latter aim he fulfilled partly by distributing free tickets to students.[92]

Mamontov's wife, the former Elizaveta Sapozhnikova, was in some respects affected by the general diffusion of populist ideas in the 1860s and 1870s even more deeply than her husband. After the Mamontovs purchased the estate of Abramtsevo in 1870, they established there a hospital and school for the benefit of neighboring peasants.[93] Some years later they created a workshop on their estate which had the dual purpose of reviving the old *kustar* handicrafts and providing peasants with both education in a craft and employment. The workshop existed for several decades and, chiefly through the efforts of Elizaveta Mamontova and the artist E. D. Polenova, became well known for its products, which were sold in a shop in Moscow. To Mamontova, the workshop's avowed aim of helping the local peasantry was just as important as its artistic purposes.[94] Mamontova took a great interest in the local peasants, frequently visited the villages, and distributed help and advice.[95] Through the workshop she hoped especially to provide employment that would allow peasant youths to remain in the village rather than being forced to seek work in the city, with its corrupting influences.[96] If this seems a strange view for someone born and raised in the city, it is an indication of the depth of the influence current populist thought had on Elizaveta Mamontova.

Undoubtedly Mamontova was much more strongly influenced by the views of the intelligentsia than were most of her contemporaries within the business elite, but nonetheless many of the older generation emerged from the 1860s and 1870s with at least a vague ideal of service to guide them in their activities. Not only the philanthropists, patrons, and public figures but even the collectors from the elite tended to view their activities as a form of service to the public. The collector A. P. Bakhrushin, in a small book he wrote describing Moscow's major collections, strongly emphasized the idea that collecting was not merely a personal pleasure but constituted a service to Russia and to Russian science and learning.[97] P. I. Shchukin took a similar view, and one of his associates at the Historical Museum wrote of Shchukin that his collecting activity "soon stopped being an object only of personal pleasure and was infused with the idea of public service, with the conscious goal of creating within the limits of his personal taste a collection for science and for his native town."[98] Similarly, S. I. Shchukin, the collector of French impressionist paintings, explained to Buryshkin at some time during the 1920s: "I collected not only and not so much for myself, but for my country and my people. Whatever happens in our land, my collection must remain there." As a result, Shchukin, then living in exile in Western Europe, refused to follow the example of certain other Russian collectors and did not try to get his paintings out of the Soviet Union.[99]

While there seems little doubt that a service ideal motivated many members of the older generation, some commentators on the good works of the Moscow business elite, searching for their motives, went beyond the concepts of responsibility of wealth and public service and introduced the idea of repentance, though of a secular rather than a religious form. Sergei Sharapov, a well-known publicist around the turn of the century, wrote that the businessman's philanthropy was essentially a way to restore to the people what the businessman had earlier taken from them and that it stemmed from consciousness on the part of the businessman-philanthropist that he had lived a predatory and senseless life.[100] Also, one of the best, and least-known, novels about the life of the Moscow business elite, Mark Basanin's *Torgovyi dom Bakhvalova synov'ia*, stressed repentance as the motive behind the good deeds of the fictional Bakhvalov family, one of whose members even went so far as to argue that the family's money did not belong to it but was money stolen from the people.[101] Further, a Soviet author has claimed that P. M. Tretiakov once confessed to torment about his position as an industrialist and an unwilling exploiter of his workers; he is said to have admitted that the money he had made belonged not to him but to the workers.[102] This claim is somewhat credible in regard to Tretiakov, who was one of the most idealistic philanthropists and patrons in his generation. But if other members of the business elite suffered from feelings of repentence for exploiting the people and desired to make restitution, they did not confess to such perturbation in public.

Actually, one cannot entirely rule out the possibility that some of the older generation were affected by such feelings. Given the general hostility of Russian society toward businessmen and the constant accusations of exploitation and predatory activity that resounded in the press, it may well have been difficult for some more sensitive souls to come to terms with their conscience, and they might have been led to seek some form of restitution. However, it seems likely that such tender consciences were the exception rather than the rule. If many representatives of the Moscow dynasties came to feel that they had a responsibility to serve and to use their wealth for the social good, that is still a far cry from saying that they regretted the means they had used to make their money in the first place.

In fact, most industrialists tended to view themselves as the benefactors of their workers, rather than as their exploiters,[103] and there is certainly no evidence that any of them suffered any qualms of conscience for exploiting the Russian consumer.

Perhaps fairly typical of their attitude is a story that N. P. Vishniakov told about himself. Vishniakov recalled that as a child, he could not comprehend why some people should be rich and others poor. The religious explanations given by his nurse did not satisfy him, and he long worried about this question. But, he later wrote, "of course, at that time I could not understand the significance of the productive forces of trade and industry and their necessary result—the accumulation of capital."[104] No doubt for most businessmen the need for economic development and capital accumulation justified a good deal. There seems no reason to question the sincerity of their frequent assertions that businessmen were only doing their patriotic duty and contributing to the general welfare by developing trade and industry in Russia. Even Prokhorov, the precursor of this older generation in so many respects, included the development of industry along with philanthropy as a socially beneficial use of wealth, and most businessmen of the older generation appear to have felt a quiet pride in their business accomplishments, even if the general social hostility toward business did not allow them to crow about their achievements.

If feelings of repentance were rare, the older generation's belief in the responsibility of wealth and in the ideal of service was very real and was, in fact, one of the most sympathetic characteristics of this generation. But it would, of course, be an oversimplification to imagine that all their philanthropy, their patronage, their collecting, their participation in public affairs were motivated solely by altruism. Whatever their views in regard to the responsibility of wealth and public service, the good deeds of many members of the business elite's older generation could also be attributed to a desire for fame and immortality and for greater social acceptance. If there were some true idealists among the older generation, like Tretiakov and Mamontova, one could find at the other end of the spectrum individuals whose primary goal was to make a name for themselves, to rise on the social ladder, through the practice of philanthropy or patronage or other forms of "service." In many cases, ideals and ulterior motives were inextricably mixed, and it would be most frequently impossible to untangle them and to determine which were the more important to any given individual.

Savva Mamontov was again an excellent example of this mixture of motives. In addition to wanting to serve the people, Mamontov also hoped to make a reputation for himself, to be "known and respected by more people than if he were nothing more than a tycoon," and to win immortality of a temporal sort. In view of the low esteem in which businessmen were held, Mamontov was aware that even the most successful of them would never achieve real fame and would be soon forgotten after they died. Although he did hope to be remembered as the man who opened up the Russian North through his railroad building, Mamontov decided that his chances for fame and immortality were better if he patterned himself after the Medici and became a patron of the arts. He also hoped to make a name for himself as the author of plays and opera libretti, as a sculptor and a ceramicist,[105] but in the end, Mamontov achieved lasting fame not as a writer or artist but as a patron, as the center of the Abramtsevo circle, and as the creator of a private opera which provided a stage for the new works of Russian composers and for the first time gave Fedor Chaliapin an opportunity to exhibit his magnificent talents.

Mamontov's great concern for the immortality of his name is clear from the preface to a brief autobiography he composed in the 1860s, chiefly for the benefit of his own descendants. Lamenting the brief memory of mankind, he wrote:

> You live, you work, you overwork, and one fine morning they cart you off and put you outside the city limits. In a month, or maybe in a year if someone needed you, you are forgotten. Your name becomes an empty sound and no one feels anything toward you. Once in a while the grave keeper bothers your bones with a coarse jest when some well-meaning relative of yours asks him to tidy up your grave.

Mamontov then went on to explain his reason for writing his autobiography:

> I take up this task for my own self-assurance, and I have a definite reason for it. I am not a literary figure, not a great societal figure; nothing would remain after me to positively show how or for what purpose Savva Mamontov lived, and this wounds my pride. I will die, and my grandchildren will know only my name. The small facts of my life (and it consists only of such small facts) will be lost to them. . . . This is a pity. Take up this little book in a free minute and find out about me.[106]

Of course, Mamontov in later years created much more solid foundations for his remembrance by his children and grandchildren than this small autobiography, but the desire expressed here for eternal remembrance never deserted him.

Another seeker of immortality through service was N. A. Alekseev, mayor of Moscow from 1885 to 1893. Practically from birth, Alekseev was groomed by his family to carve out a secure place for the Alekseev name in Russian history. All Moscow heard about this up-and-coming "genius" of the Alekseev family from his earliest years and followed his career closely.[107] Alekseev chose municipal government as the arena in which he would immortalize the family name, and indeed he showed enough ability and political talent to be elected mayor at the young age of thirty-seven. Once in the mayoral office, Alekseev initiated one of the most active and colorful periods in the history of Moscow municipal government, and hopes soon arose that he would be the first statesman of national stature to emerge from the Moscow *kupechestvo*.[108] All the hopeful plans of his family and friends were laid to rest by the madman's bullet that killed Alekseev in 1893, though by this time his activities as mayor had assured the Alekseev name at least a small niche in Russian history.[109]

The cases of both Mamontov and Alekseev would seem to demonstrate that, if once *kuptsy* had sought through their good deeds eternal remembrance of their souls, many now hoped to attain a temporal immortality that would ensure the survival of their memories in later generations. This strong desire for immortality can be seen also in the insistence by almost all members of the older generation that the institutions they created bear their names. Soldatenkov, for instance, specified in his will that all his books and pictures, which he left to the Rumiantsev Museum, were to be put in a special hall named after him. He further gave over a million rubles to the Merchants' Society for the establishment of a trade school to bear his name and an even larger sum to the city for the Soldatenkov hospital.[110] In some cases, philanthropists went to great lengths to ensure remembrance not only of themselves but of various members of their families. One could find in Moscow such institutions as a home bearing the names of six members of the Mazurin family (*Dom prizreniia imeni Alekseia Vasilevicha i Anny Alekseevy Mazurinykh i synovei ikh Nikolaia, Pavla, Alekseeia i Konstantina*).[111]

The desire to be remembered by posterity is a common human motive, but the intensity of this desire seems uncommonly strong in many of the Moscow dynasties. One is tempted to suggest that the strength of their yearnings for immortality may have resulted partly from certain feelings of injustice: these families had, after all, achieved a great deal in the field of trade and industry and yet were perfectly aware that such accomplishments went for the most part unappreciated by their contemporaries and, barring a major change in Russian attitudes toward business and businessmen, seemed unlikely to be remembered by future generations. It must have seemed unfair; and so the deserved immortality that eluded them in one field, they sought doubly hard to achieve in others. In the end, of course, it was all in vain. While many of their creations still exist in Moscow, few now bear the names of their creators.

Closely related to the desire for fame and immortality was the hope of winning a certain social position and respect from one's contemporaries. Again, neither wealth nor successful business activity alone could bring the esteem and social recognition that many of these families must have felt they deserved, and so they were forced to conquer it in other ways. Philanthropy, patronage, collecting, participation in public affairs all provided to members of the older generation an entrée into society, created opportunities for them to hobnob with nobles and intellectuals, and brought them undoubted social esteem. Philanthropists were drawn into charitable societies, where they sat side by side with representatives of the nobility and intelligentsia. K. V. Rukavishnikov, for example, was a leading figure in the prestigious committee formed in 1898 to coordinate all philanthropical activities in Moscow. Chairman of the group was the Grand Duchess Elisaveta, and among its other members were various nobles, bishops, professors, and the like.[112] Patrons and collectors joined various artistic and scientific societies, where they mingled with both artists and scholars, as well as with other patrons and collectors from the nobility. Prominent *kuptsy* could be found as members and officers of the Society of the Lovers of Art, the Architectural Society, the Archaeological Society, the Bibliographical Society, the Musical Society, the Philharmonic Society, the Polytechnical Society, the Imperial Technical Society, and practically any other similar group in Moscow. Members of business families interested in public affairs sat in the municipal duma alongside representatives of the nobility and the intelligentsia, worked with them in various municipal committees and organizations, and served with them as trustees of numerous public and private institutions.

The contacts established with nobles and intellectuals through such activities frequently ripened into social relationships, and sometimes into close friendships. Savva and Elizaveta Mamontov had warm personal relations with all the artists included in the Abramtsevo circle and with their families.[113] P. M. Tretiakov and K. T. Soldatenkov received innumerable artists and writers in their homes and became close friends with some of them.[114] S. M. Tretiakov and N. A. Alekseev, both active in the Musical Society, frequently entertained leading figures of the musical world, and Tretiakov maintained a particularly close friendship, dating from childhood, with Nikolai Rubinstein, founder and director of the Moscow Conservatory.[115] Several of the Mamontovs also were deeply involved in the musical world of Moscow and enjoyed close friendships with both Rubinstein and the composer P. I. Tchaikovsky.[116] Varvara Morozova, patroness and philanthropist, became the "unofficial wife" of one of the editors of *Russkie vedomosti*, V. M. Sobolevskii, and received in her home many outstanding literary figures and members of the liberal intelligentsia.[117] The Perlov brothers, as a result of their philanthropical and agricultural activities, had a wide acquaintance in philanthropical and agricultural circles and were undoubtedly highly gratified when A. N. Strekalova, a noblewoman and the grande dame of Moscow philanthropy, appeared to deliver the major address at the jubilee of their trade firm in 1887.[118] (The fact that a notable philanthropist should be the major speaker at a business jubilee is in itself, of course, an interesting indication of the great value Moscow businessmen placed on their philanthropy.)

However warm the relationships that developed between members of the business elite, on the one hand, and nobles and intellectuals, on the other, representatives of the elite's older generation respected the barriers still separating them from the nobility and, unlike some of their offspring, never sought to be recognized as *intelligenty*. In relations with the intelligentsia, most were satisfied with the position of businessmen-patrons who counted many intellectuals among their friends. Indeed, many members of this generation were acutely aware of the barriers still separating them from *intelligenty*—barriers resulting partly from their own deficient educations. Perhaps fairly typical in this respect was P. G. Shelaputin, who emerged in the 1890s as one of Moscow's most prominent philanthropists and patrons. As the founder of a gynecological institute, several schools, and a pedagogical institute, Shelaputin came into contact with many members of the medical and teaching professions and became a particularly close friend of Dr. V. F. Snegirev, professor of gynecology at Moscow University. Another friend, Prince B. A. Shchetinin, recalled that Shelaputin "was attracted to science, to enlightenment, treated with respect all educated people and loved to mingle with circles of professors." Nonetheless, according to Shchetinin, Shelaputin's professorial acquaintances "could not, however much they wished it, become 'true' friends with him, in view of his 'domestic education.' " Using a phrase not infrequently employed to describe many members of the older generation, Shchetinin wrote that Shelaputin "had left one shore and not quite reached the other"—in other words, while having raised himself above the generally low cultural level typical of the old *kupechestvo*, Shelaputin had still not succeeded, because of his deficient education, in reaching the intellectual and cultural level typical of representatives of the intelligentsia.[119]

In any case, a not unwelcome side effect of the philanthropy, patronage, collecting, and participation in public affairs of the business elite was the opening of many doors which heretofore had been tightly closed to *kuptsy* and a greater degree of social acceptance than was possible for mere businessmen. If some individuals cared little for the social prestige that resulted from their activities, others were conscious social climbers. For example, all who knew him agreed that P. M. Tretiakov was an extremely retiring, even unsociable, individual, who cared little for the fame and prestige that came to him through his gallery. It was typical of him that after announcing he was making a gift of his gallery to the city, he immediately departed for Western Europe in order to avoid the ensuing publicity.[120] By contrast, his brother, S. M. Tretiakov, was something of a social butterfly, and his brother's second wife a social climber. Though the two brothers remained on good terms, the snobbery and social pretensions of Sergei Mikhailovich's wife created tension within the family.[121]

Some of the intellectuals who benefited from the good deeds of patrons from the business elite took a very ironic view of the social climbing of their benefactors. Nemirovich-Danchenko was not particularly kind to his patrons from the business elite's older generation when he came to write his memoirs. For instance, he told of soliciting funds for the Art Theater from one of the Ushkovs, who agreed to contribute only on the condition that Nemirovich reported his contribution directly to the Grand Duchess Elisaveta. Ushkov was a director of the Philharmonic Society, and Nemirovich wrote of him and his fellow directors that they valued the society only for its concerts, "at which they occupied seats in the front rows and could flaunt before all Moscow their patronage."[122] Another critic of Moscow patrons from the business elite's older generation was S. P. Melgunov, a journalist and writer, who directed his barbs chiefly at Varvara Morozova. Melgunov wrote that Morozova patronized only big names, who could bring her immediate prestige. She gave money to the populist Nikolai Mikhailovskii for his journal *Russkoe bogatstvo*, conducted a salon attended by "decadents" such as Andrei Belyi and Valerii Briusov, but was unwilling to back "unknowns" such as Melgunov, whose request for financial backing for a small journal she had turned down—or, it might be added, such as Nemirovich and Stanislavsky, whose request for funds for the Art Theater she had also refused. Melgunov insisted that all she really cared about was her social standing and that her patronage was entirely directed by the thought of achieving greater social prestige in the right circles.[123]

In spite of the fact that some individuals took a very jaundiced view of the motives of patrons and philanthropists from the business elite, their good deeds also provoked admiration in many quarters and resulted in increased social respect and prestige. For every negative evaluation of the patrons of the older generation one can find a matching positive evaluation. For instance, Melgunov's comments on Varvara Morozova must be balanced by those of the historian and liberal politician P. N. Miliukov, who wrote of her as follows:

In the "Portuguese" castle reigned Varvara Alexeevna Morozova, a lady well-known to the Moscow intelligentsia. She was a person of amazing energy and readiness to serve the social cause in the spirit of the 1870's. Everything about her, from her modest appearance and unassuming dress to her personal entourage, created amidst surrounding splendor, attested to her profound faith in the immutable ideal of social progress and in the necessity of sowing the seeds of "everlasting reason and goodness." . . . People of our type, already old-fashioned, felt at home here. All sorts of "liberal" organizations held their meetings and found true asylum at V. A. Morozova's.[124]

Similarly positive appreciations of other patrons from the elite's older generation could be cited—though it seems unquestionable that Savva Mamontov was the recipient of by far the greatest amount of praise from intellectuals who benefited from his patronage, many of whom were, of course, his close personal friends.[125] While Mamontov was in prison awaiting trial on charges arising from the financial collapse of his railroad company, his artist-friends stood staunchly by him and were profuse in their expressions of support.[126]

Moreover, Mamontov's subsequent acquittal in court can probably be attributed at least in part to his fame as a patron of the arts.[127] Certainly, public opinion was with him throughout the trial, and it is difficult to avoid the conclusion that such public sympathy as was extended to him resulted entirely from admiration for his activities as a patron rather than admiration for his business achievements. His case vividly illustrated the fact that businessmen who were denied respect as businessmen could indeed achieve social respect and prestige through patronage and similar activities.

In this regard, Rakshanin's attitudes were perhaps fairly typical of the attitudes of many contemporaries toward Moscow's business elite. While in general he did not think highly of the Moscow *kupechestvo* or its elite, Rakshanin nonetheless frequently commented on the good they had accomplished through their patronage and philanthropy. After the death of P. M. Tretiakov, who was without question the most widely respected of Moscow's patrons and philanthropists, Rakshanin wrote that "we have lost the most glorious of our citizens: Pavel Mikhailovich Tretiakov has died." He went on to say that "Moscow has a right to be proud of the patrons of the contemporary *kupechestvo*" and commented that Tretiakov, Soldatenkov, Mamontov, and P. I. Shchukin were probably the greatest of them all. Their greatness, he believed, was "the result of many years of glorious work, work done quietly, without the least desire to push themselves forward, work burning with true love for the affair, with modesty and purity, with the most genuine sincerity."[128] High words of praise, indeed, from a man who rarely found a kind word to say about the Moscow *kupechestvo*.

Such social admiration was probably more important to the Moscow business elite than visible marks of distinction meted out by the government in the form of orders, medals, ranks, titles, and the like. If these had been important to the *kuptsy* of an even earlier generation, by the end of the nineteenth century they were in somewhat bad odor, at least in the upper ranks of the *kupechestvo*.[129] Too many jokes had been made about

merchants who would sell their own mothers for the sake of a medal—
and the government in previous decades had dispensed such signs of
distinction with too free a hand—for them to remain worthy of general
respect. Donald Mackenzie Wallace noted as early as the 1870s that the
"traffic in decorations has had its natural result. Like paper money issued
in too large quantities, the decorations have fallen in value. The gold
medals which were formerly much coveted and worn with pride by the
rich merchants—suspended by a ribbon round the neck—are now little
sought after."[130] In their memoirs, scions of the Moscow dynasties frequently noted that they, or their fathers, if they had earned medals, would
never have dreamed of wearing them.[131] How much secret pride was
hidden behind their external insouciance in regard to medals, orders, and
titles is hard to say, but it seems entirely probable that to most businessmen the respect of educated society was much more important than any
medal.

One other factor which deserves mention as a motive of the philanthropists, patrons, collectors, and public figures from the older generation
of the business elite is simply that many of them loved what they were
doing and in some cases found it more satisfying than their business
activities. Whatever his other motives, there is no question that Savva
Mamontov loved art, as did P. M. Tretiakov.[132] The degree to which
many of the collectors became totally wrapped up in their collections can
perhaps be understood only by other collectors. A. P. Bakhrushin told of
a Moscow collector whose house caught fire. When the collector discovered the fire and found that the room containing his collection had already
burned, he refused to leave the burning house, preferring to perish along
with his beloved collection. Bakhrushin, a collector himself, found this
attitude entirely sympathetic and understandable and wrote that "once a
man collects something, he puts his soul into his collection, and God
preserve us should all this perish from fire—no money received from
insurance could fill the emptiness in a man's heart, could fill his orphaned
soul, could replace the collection!"[133]

In any case, the motives behind the good works of the older generation
of the business elite were a complex mixture of personal enjoyment, altruism, and social ambition. However great the latter in some individuals,
the altruism of many of the philanthropists in particular should not be
underestimated. It might be noted that the social doctrines based on the
theories of Thomas Malthus and Charles Darwin that accompanied the
earlier stages of industrialization in the West were never accepted in Russia, not even by its "middle class." Perhaps the poverty in Russia was too
great, and its causes too obvious, to make possible the acceptance of any
theory which advocated leaving the poor to their fate on the grounds that
they somehow deserved their poverty. Perhaps the long tradition of philanthropy and the feeling of responsibility for the *narod* shared by nobility

and intelligentsia alike were too strong to permit the development or acceptance of a cold-blooded Malthusianism or Social Darwinism. Whatever the case, there is a notable contrast between the nineteenth-century Western businessmen and their spokesmen who saw poverty as a manifestation of natural laws and denied in advance the efficacy of any measures intended to relieve it and, on the other hand, the Moscow business elite who accepted (however well or badly they may have fulfilled) a responsibility for the alleviation of poverty and suffering and ignorance. Whether they took up this responsibility chiefly because to do so was what educated society expected of them—and might, therefore, be a means of achieving acceptance in that society—or whether they believed in their hearts that it was a mission laid upon them by Providence, the results were the same: a multitude of institutions—for the care of the poor, the sick, the old, for the promotion of the arts and sciences, for the spread of education—which were only the most visible signs of the extensive good works of the Moscow business elite.

C H A P T E R 4

THE OLDER GENERATION OF THE 1890s: PARTICIPATION IN PUBLIC AFFAIRS

IN addition to their broad involvement in philanthropy, patronage, and collecting, the business elite's older generation was also active in public affairs, on both a local and a national scale. Although their participation on the local level took many forms, including, for instance, service as trustees or members of the boards of various societies and institutions, the most visible form of their public activity occurred within the organs of Moscow's municipal self-government. Many of them served in the city duma and in various municipal bodies ranging from the draft board to the sanitary inspectorate. Some served as mayors; some were justices of the peace; many were trustees of town schools, hospitals, and various other worthy institutions. A few also served as representatives of the Moscow duma in the district and provincial zemstvos.

In addition to service in municipal institutions, the older generation was active in various organizations whose chief function was to promote and defend the interests of industry and trade. Those who served as members of the Exchange Committee shared with the Moscow Merchants' Society the responsibility for defending the interests of the business community on a local level and at the same time acted as the chief spokesmen of Moscow business before the central government. Some big businessmen also belonged to the local section of the Russian Industrial Society and to the Moscow Council of Trade and Manufacturing, both of which bodies, though not nearly so active as the Exchange Committee, also on occasion voiced the opinions of Moscow businessmen to the government chancelleries in St. Petersburg. Finally, many members of the business elite participated in government conferences or served on committees established in St. Petersburg to deal with the problems of trade and industry and belonged to official boards handling matters affecting business, such as the assessment of taxes on industry or the conduct of the factory inspectorate.

Though there was a profound difference between participation in the activities of the Exchange Committee, essentially a *soslovie* institution seeking to promote and defend the interests of businessmen, and participation in the city duma, an "all-*sosloviia* institution" working for the general good of Moscow inhabitants, the curious fact is that members of the Moscow elite persisted in regarding both these forms of participation in public affairs as constituting public service. We are faced here with two different conceptions of public service—one old, one new. Within the terms set down by the *soslovie* system, representation of the interests of local trade and industry did indeed constitute public service—the only kind of meaningful public service with which the *kupechestvo* had any experience, since it was the only kind that had been expected in the past. The type of public service expected from them in the reformed duma represented an altogether new experience for them and placed upon them expectations that they did not immediately comprehend. The fact that the older generation of the 1890s was never quite able to make the distinction between duma service to the community as a whole and *soslovie* service demonstrated the continuing hold of the *soslovie* mentality; it also accounted in part for their different degrees of effectiveness in the two arenas. In regard to the representation of their own interests before the government, the businessmen of the older generation made their voices heard and their influence felt and were able to exert some effect on state policies relating to trade and industry. On the other hand, the older generation made few notable contributions to the conduct of Moscow's municipal affairs and tended to be, with a few exceptions, extremely passive and lethargic in regard to fulfillment of the civic responsibilities accompanying the municipal offices they held.

A further contrast can be drawn between their achievements as philanthropists, collectors, and patrons and their failure to contribute effectively to municipal self-government. In the former areas, the older generation accommodated a striking degree of change, as compared with earlier generations of the Moscow *kupechestvo*. Not only did they increasingly remove themselves from the influences of the old merchant culture and begin to absorb the Europeanized, "higher" culture heretofore restricted to the nobility and the intelligentsia, but they also gave evidence of having acquired an understanding of and concern for the public good. Whatever their other motives, all the philanthropists, collectors, and patrons were actuated by a desire to use their wealth in ways that would benefit Russian society. But as participants in municipal affairs the older generation proved much less capable of thinking in terms of public benefit and of devising ways to promote the public good.

In other words, as private individuals functioning in areas where state involvement was minimal, they seemed to have no difficulty assimilating and fulfilling a desire to promote the general welfare. In the area of public affairs, where they still continued to function as a group and where they found themselves dealing with the state, they were very slow to throw off *soslovie* habits and to assimilate a new conception of their public role. Indeed, the state made this difficult by placing different expectations upon them when they functioned in different capacities. The terms of their relations with the central government underwent no essential change in the last half of the nineteenth century (the only real change was simply that the government was far more concerned about industrial and commercial development than ever before, and therefore businessmen were given far more opportunities to present their views in a more vigorous manner). Their relations with the central government were still cast in the old *soslovie* mold—the government desiring their advice and opinions only on matters directly related to trade and industry but still adamant that they were not to concern themselves with any issues transcending their immediate *soslovie* interests. At the same time, in the municipal arena, the *kuptsy* were expected to ignore their *soslovie* identity and to act on matters affecting a variety of local concerns in such a way as to promote the welfare of all Moscow inhabitants. It was far easier to continue to function in old, familiar ways than to make the transition to the new ways of thinking and behaving implied in the creation of all-*sosloviia* institutions such as the duma. And lack of change on the one level served to impede change on the other, so that only very gradually did the Moscow business elite achieve a new understanding of its role in public affairs, either on the national or on the local level. In fact, this new understanding would come to full fruition only with the younger generation of the 1890s and only after 1905.

HOWEVER ineffective the older generation of the elite may have been in municipal affairs, the mere fact that they should have sought to participate at all in the institutions of municipal government denoted a major change in the psychology of the *kupechestvo* after 1861. Before the reform of Moscow's municipal self-government in 1862, the Moscow merchants were notorious for using all means, fair or foul, to avoid the responsibility of holding public offices of any kind. This extreme repulsion toward assuming public duties stemmed in large part from the structure and conduct of the pre-reform municipal institutions. Before 1862, all power and authority in the city administration rested with local members of the bureaucracy representing the central government in St. Petersburg. But the law nonetheless imposed municipal tasks on the Moscow *kupechestvo* as part of their *soslovie* obligations. It required the election of a mayor and of duma members, who were to be chosen from among the more substantial *kuptsy*. Merchants were also required to serve in the Orphans' Court and other less important institutions and in a large assembly whose 120 members, exclusively from the *kupechestvo*, transacted both town and *soslovie* business (and without always drawing a firm line between the two).[1]

The holding of these various offices brought a certain amount of honor within the *kupechestvo*, but the incumbents had no real power and were in effect simply the executors of the decisions of the bureaucracy. Moreover, such positions often proved onerous in terms of the demands they made on the time and the money of their occupants—much of the money being paid out in the form of bribes, without which little could be accomplished in the pre-reform administration. Elected officials were also faced with the prospect of being taken to court after their term of service was completed if the bureaucrats to whom they were responsible found their performance in any way unsatisfactory. Under such conditions, it is not surprising that most *kuptsy* considered it a great misfortune if they were unable to argue or buy their way out of election to public office.[2]

Recalling the circumstances in which municipal service had to take place before 1862, N. P. Vishniakov wrote that such service was simply a "trap" for the *kupets*, threatening him with "extortion, humiliation and the danger of ending up in court."[3] Vishniakov described the merchant attitudes typical of the 1850s as follows:

> The word "bribe" I became acquainted with very early. It was necessary to pay up *in order not to be elected to any sort of duties* to which one somehow might be elected; it was said that these duties were extremely unpleasant and dangerous, that they did not have the least relevance to our immediate needs, and that they had been thrust upon us from without, by reason of some sort of laws and regulations thought up by the nobles and officials with the particular goal . . . of doing us a bad turn, destroying us, ruining us utterly. It was dangerous to serve, because the officials demanded bribes, and if you did not pay them, then they could destroy you; if you paid, then they would suck at you like leeches, extracting money, and also would ruin you. Not to serve was best; this was difficult, but not impossible. It was necessary only to see someone on the quiet, to invite someone, to cajole, to entertain, to "slip it" to someone, and then a person with power could bypass all laws and regulations so that you would not be disturbed and would not be called to service.

As an additional reason for avoiding municipal service Vishniakov mentioned the fact that "they could take anyone to court, whenever they pleased, if you did not get along with them." "They," of course, referred to the officials, the feared *chinovniki*, who in this period held the *kuptsy* at their mercy and were seen by them as "something evil and hostile to us, but also strong and merciless."[4]

It would be difficult to deny that the very structure and method of conduct of pre-reform municipal government gave the *kuptsy* convincing reasons for seeking to avoid public office, but other factors were involved as well. The extreme aversion of the *kuptsy* to any form of participation in municipal affairs was frequently taken as a sign of their lack of public-spiritedness and of their egotistical absorption in their own affairs. Although these opinions were hotly disputed both by Vishniakov and by N. A. Naidenov in their memoirs, there was a certain amount of truth in them. The desire to dedicate all one's time and efforts to the development of the family business was undoubtedly an important reason for avoiding involvement in public affairs in the minds of early representatives of the Moscow dynasties, many of whose businesses in this period were not yet solidly established and therefore required a good deal of attention. One of the Konovalov family histories admitted as much. When P. K. Konovalov, we are told, was threatened with election as mayor of his native town of Kineshma, he joined with another local factory owner in contributing 6,000 rubles to the town, on the condition that neither they nor their sons could be elected to public office for a specified number of years. The family history explained frankly that "the complexity of the business he had created demanded of Petr Kuzmich constant attention and did not permit him to give any part of his time, experience, and influence to public service." But it went on to add that "after the enterprise was consolidated, his son and heir Aleksandr Petrovich worked much and with great success for the benefit of society."[5]

For the Moscow dynasties, this reason for objecting to public service was largely removed as the decades passed and as their businesses were established on sound foundations, thus allowing them more time to devote to other activities. But the chief obstacle to their participation in civic affairs was still the dangers it involved. This obstacle was removed only by the Moscow municipal reform of 1862, which gave the organs of municipal self-government greater independence from bureaucratic supervision and at the same time eliminated the most onerous facets of municipal service.[6]

In addition, the reform broadened the social base of the Moscow city government to include representatives of all town *sosloviia* and at least temporarily undermined the former dominance of the *kupechestvo*. The reformed municipal institutions attracted the participation of many of Moscow's leading citizens, and in the 1860s and early 1870s, the duma, a large body of 175 members, was dominated by representatives of the nobility and the intelligentsia—men such as Prince A. A. Shcherbatov and Prince V. A. Cherkasskii, both of whom served as mayor, the Slavophiles A. I. Koshelev and Iu. F. Samarin, and the historian M. P. Pogodin. These men were much respected in Moscow, and their leadership of the municipal self-government gave it a glamour and prestige that it did not possess when it was made up entirely of *kuptsy*. Moreover, nobles and intellectuals brought to the city duma the same sort of public-spiritedness and enthusiasm for self-government that they brought to the new zemstvo institutions, and this public-spiritedness and enthusiasm without doubt rubbed off on many members of the *kupechestvo*. For at least the younger *kuptsy*, membership in the duma now became something to be sought rather than avoided, though the older men frequently remained dubious.[7]

Even if many *kuptsy* now sought membership in the new duma and in other municipal bodies under its control, they tended for many years to defer to the leadership of the nobility and the intelligentsia, who were more experienced in public affairs, more accustomed to public speaking, and generally better prepared to take the initiative in the duma. These groups dominated municipal affairs in the 1860s, with little challenge from the representatives of other *sosloviia*,[8] but the picture began to change in the 1870s, as the *kuptsy* came to manifest a growing desire to achieve preponderance in municipal institutions. In 1871 the *kupets* I. A. Liamin made a successful bid for the post of mayor. He was the first businessman to be elected to that position by the duma since the municipal reform had gone into effect. Liamin, however, won the mayoral post only by culti-vating the support of the nobility and, once in office, had to rely on the Slavophile I. S. Aksakov to write his speeches. Moreover, he was forced to resign in 1873 under conditions which many considered proof of the inability of the *kuptsy* to act effectively in town affairs. Summoned to appear before the provincial governor, Liamin showed up in a frock coat rather than in his uniform. The governor lost his temper and subjected Liamin to a severe dressing down, whereupon Liamin resigned in great embarrassment.[9] Probably the only things that the incident actually proved were the unfamiliarity of the *kupechestvo* with bureaucratic protocol and the governor's general hostility toward municipal self-government, but it was nonetheless an unpropitious beginning for the *kupechestvo*'s attempt to play a major role in municipal affairs.

Liamin's successor as mayor, D. D. Schumacher, did little to improve the image of the *kuptsy* as public activists. Schumacher was a banker and railroad magnate whose reputation was irretrievably tarnished by the col-lapse of the Commercial Loan Bank, with which he was closely associated. The collapse occurred while Schumacher was serving as mayor, and he was taken to court, along with other outstanding representatives of the Moscow *kupechestvo* who were involved in the affairs of the bank. All were eventually acquitted,[10] but the unfortunate conjunction of Schumacher's service as mayor and the collapse of his bank only confirmed the opinion of many Muscovites that *kuptsy* were unsuitable for high office.

In spite of these sorry beginnings, the *kuptsy*, greatly assisted by a new municipal statute issued in 1870, continued their drive for hegemony in the duma. This second reform of the Moscow municipal self-government changed the method of electing members of the duma. Whereas the old law had given a specific number of seats to each of the five town *sosloviia*, the new statute set up three electoral curia, whose membership was determined on the basis of property qualifications. The law of 1870 had the effect of bringing relatively more representatives of wealth into the duma, and this trend was even further advanced by a third reform of municipal self-government in 1892. The statute of 1892 did away with the former curia and gave the right to vote to all individuals meeting certain property qualifications and also to all members of the first guild of the *kupechestvo*. The number of voters, never large, was further reduced so that under the 1892 statute not even 1 percent of the population of Moscow was permitted to vote. The effect of the new statute was to ensure the more substantial *kuptsy* an easy numerical predominance in the duma, a predominance which they had already achieved under the law of 1870.[11]

The *kuptsy* had attained their majority in the duma for the first time in the elections of 1876, and thereafter were able to control the mayoral elections.[12] S. M. Tretiakov, occupying the mayor's post from 1876 to 1882, was the first civic leader of any significance from the *kupechestvo*. He came to office with broad plans for the development of the city, but realization of his plans was difficult, partly because of constant obstructionism from the representatives of the *meshchane* and artisans. Tretiakov, unable to work effectively with this unruly duma, resigned in disgust in 1882.[13] His immediate successor, Professor B. N. Chicherin, was elected with the support of the *kuptsy* in the duma, who acknowledged the lack of any suitable mayoral candidates from the business community. Chicherin was forced to resign soon after his election and, with no acceptable candidates yet in sight from among the *kuptsy*, was succeeded by a colorless official, S. A. Tarasov.[14] Not until the advent of N. A. Alekseev as mayor in 1885 did the *kupechestvo* finally produce a truly capable and dynamic municipal leader.

If before 1885 the *kuptsy* in the duma had difficulty finding real civic leaders within their midst, they also exhibited a certain lack of imagination in regard to the uses of the power they had achieved in city government. The record of the duma in the 1870s and early 1880s was something less than impressive,[15] and it is difficult to avoid the conclusion that the *kuptsy*, in struggling to achieve numerical predominance in the duma, had no particular goals in mind beyond pure and simple control of the duma. In a retrospective view of the struggle between *kuptsy* and *meshchane* in the duma of the 1870s, one journalist summed up the apparent lack of purpose of both groupings, writing that both one and the other party, in essence, had little concern for the public "benefits and needs"; they were both chiefly occupied with settling personal accounts, with a struggle for predominant influence, and neither of them gave themselves an exact, definite accounting of why, really, they needed this influence and how they would use it. Whole sessions of the duma passed in reproaches between the councillors of the two parties, in mutual attacks on one another, in the settling of personal accounts, in examination of statements and "special opinions" having the character of slander. . .they pushed one another to the wall not for the sake of any definite, thoughtfully established tasks, but for the sake of the very process of mindless struggle.[16]

In any case, the failure of Tretiakov to achieve many of his plans for the development of Moscow can only partly be blamed on the obstructionist tactics of representatives of the *meshchanstvo*. A good deal of the blame must rest on the shoulders of the *kuptsy* in the duma. In spite of their demonstrated desire to win seats and achieve control of the city council, the inescapable impression is that having acquired much of the responsibility for the conduct of municipal affairs, the *kuptsy* in the duma had no idea how to proceed. While not all the bureaucratic tutelage of the past had been removed, considerable freedom had been given to the city council. Such relative freedom in determining municipal projects was a new experience for the *kuptsy*, and without guidance from above, they seemed to flounder about, not at all sure in which directions they ought to be moving or exactly what their responsibilities were. Being asked to concern themselves with the general welfare was indeed a new and unprecedented commission from the government, and that the *kuptsy* were slow in perceiving how they ought to go about it is understandable.

Tretiakov was unable to overcome the immobility of the duma majority, but the experience of his successor seemed to show that if they were incapable of taking the initiative in duma affairs, the *kuptsy* were at least willing to be led. N. A. Alekseev was a different breed of mayor altogether from any that Moscow had yet seen, and he quickly galvanized the lethargic duma into action. His election initiated one of the stormiest and most creative periods in the history of Moscow self-government. An ambitious man, Alekseev had long ago determined that he would make a name for himself and for his family through participation in municipal affairs. He thus became a unique exception, the only member of his generation of the elite to throw himself wholeheartedly into municipal concerns. Having been a member of the duma for several years before his election as mayor, Alekseev came into office with a program of municipal improvements that he was determined to put into effect. An extremely energetic and competent individual, Alekseev was also something of a despot and would brook no opposition to his plans. He kept all power and initiative entirely in his own hands and seemed to regard the duma as merely a bothersome rubber stamp. His methods gave rise to considerable criticism and controversy. One journalist complained that Alekseev well might have said, in the manner of Louis XIV, "I am Moscow."[17] Cries of *samodurstvo* (petty tyranny in the fashion of Kit Kitych) resounded in the halls of the duma and in the press, some members of the duma refused to attend duma meetings or even threatened to resign their seats by way of protest, and all Moscow divided into pro- and anti-Alekseev camps.[18]

However just the criticism of his methods, Alekseev got things done. Under his administration many new beginnings were made in various fields of municipal life. Moscow acquired a new city hall, designed according to Alekseev's wishes (it is the present Lenin Museum, a lamentable monument to Alekseev's architectural tastes). More important, the duma finally took important steps toward the badly needed extension of the water supply system and the creation of a sewerage system, effected improvements in the organization of the city hospitals, and expanded the municipal school system. One of his successors as mayor, Prince V. M. Golitsyn, gave Alekseev considerable credit both for his total dedication to municipal affairs and for getting the town administration moving.[19] Many of his defenders, besides emphasizing his real achievements, also insisted that his energetic despotism was the only method by which the lethargic duma could be budged at all.[20]

Alekseev's career was brought to an untimely end when he was assassinated in 1893, but the work he had begun was continued and expanded by his successors. K. V. Rukavishnikov, elected mayor in 1894, was careful not to repeat the sins of his predecessor and, as a result, came in for criticism not on the grounds that he was a despot but on the grounds that he was too concerned with maintaining correct relations with the duma and therefore moved too slowly and lost the dynamism the duma had experienced under Alekseev.[21] Nonetheless, he continued what Alekseev had begun in many fields, and the achievements of the city self-government during his term were especially impressive in education and welfare.[22]

When Rukavishnikov's term expired, he refused to run again, and the *kupechestvo* found itself in the familiar situation of not being able to come up with a *kupets* both willing and suitable to occupy the mayoral office. They therefore helped to elect Prince V. M. Golitsyn, highly popular among all levels of the Moscow populace, especially for his refusal to kowtow to St. Petersburg, an attitude that had earlier led to his resignation from the state service. Golitsyn was an easygoing and affable man. He got along well with almost everyone, and the *kupechestvo* in general liked him and referred to him as "our prince." He did not, however, take much initiative in town affairs but left it to the various factions of the duma to determine policy.[23]

With both Rukavishnikov and Golitsyn leaving a considerable amount of initiative to the duma, the *kupechestvo*, with its majority, was in the 1890s in a position where they could easily have dominated duma politics. But, in fact, if Alekseev had managed to move the inert majority, he did not entirely overcome its inertia. It is obvious from reading press accounts and minutes of duma meetings during the 1890s that the *kuptsy* of the older generation were still extremely lethargic and unimaginative in regard to their civic responsibilities. (The representatives of the younger generation, until the end of the decade, were still too few in number and too inexperienced to make much of an impact in the duma.) Most duma members from the older generation of the *kupechestvo*, including those from families of the business elite, primarily distinguished themselves either by persistent absence from duma meetings or, if they were physically present in the duma hall, by total silence. The few members of the older generation who occasionally spoke out usually did so only when some pet project or cause was under consideration. N. A. Naidenov took the floor whenever some matter affecting local trade and industry was being discussed, and V. A. Bakhrushin overcame his normal state of silence when discussion revolved around any of the charitable institutions donated to the city by the Bakhrushin family.[24]

In the absence of leadership from representatives of the majority, the duma meetings during the 1890s were completely dominated by the few members from the intelligentsia, men such as Professors V. I. Gere and M. V. Dukhovskoi, the lawyers V. M. Przhevalskii, F. F. Voskresenskii, A. I. Hennert, and S. A. Muromtsev (a future president of the State Duma), and especially the energetic N. N. Shchepkin, for many years an activist in municipal affairs, vice-mayor under Rukavishnikov, and later a leading Kadet (i.e., a member of the liberal Constitutional Democratic party, founded in 1905) and member of the State Duma. The important duma committees, where most of the real work of the duma was accomplished, were also usually led by members from the intelligentsia.[25] Similarly, the city board (*uprava*), which was the executive organ of the duma, was strongly influenced by its employees from the intelligentsia—engineers, architects, pedagogues, doctors, and other professional and technical people.[26] Under Rukavishnikov, N. N. Shchepkin, as vice-mayor, played a leading role in the *uprava*, while under Golitsyn leadership was provided by N. A. Astrov, town secretary from 1897 until 1905, a liberal and later a leading Moscow Kadet. Thus, the situation in the Moscow city self-government in some ways resembled the situation in the zemstvos, where the "third element" from the intelligentsia played such a large role.

If the intelligentsia deservedly received much of the credit for the accomplishments of the duma, the *kuptsy* of the majority received a large share of the blame in the press and in public opinion for the defects of the

Moscow municipal administration. The Moscow duma, like the Moscow *kupechestvo*, had many critics and few defenders. While the local press occasionally praised the organs of municipal self-government for specific accomplishments, its overall attitude toward their performance was a negative one. In the absence of any definitive study of the functioning of the Moscow city government in this period, it is impossible to determine the validity of either the charges made against the duma and its majority by contemporaries and by later critics or of the laurels awarded them by the duma's few defenders.

For example, the duma's critics repeatedly charged that the duma majority was primarily concerned with defending the interests of the large property owners, from whom both voters and duma members were chiefly drawn, and of neglecting the interests of other groups of the population, particularly the poor.[27] Rakshanin wrote that "the preponderant majority of duma members are moneybags, whom you may suspect of whatever you like except superfluous anticipation of the needs of the poor."[28] One Soviet critic of the Moscow duma, N. Karzhanskii, put the case even more forcefully when he wrote that

the history of the Moscow city duma is a story about how the upper bourgeoisie of Moscow, using the laws of the tsarist government, took into their own hands all the communal economy of the city, how they ruined and robbed Moscow, transferred the tax burden from the big industrialists and property owners to the shoulders of the working people.

Karzhanskii's chief complaint against the duma was that it failed to tax large property owners to the limits made possible by the municipal statute but instead charged high prices for municipal services, thus shifting the largest part of the financial burden of municipal government onto the poorer classes of the population.[29] Similar charges, emphasizing the property owners' extreme restraint in imposing taxes on themselves, had occasionally been made by contemporaries.

By contrast, N. A. Astrov, who in his memoirs strongly defended the Moscow duma, insisted that the duma stood above classes, that it was concerned with the welfare of all Moscow citizens, and that its work "acquired a more and more democratic character."[30] In support of his opinion, one could point to the increasing number of municipal undertakings, such as free medical care, free primary education, evening and Sunday classes for workers, a municipal pawnshop, a municipal system for the distribution of financial aid to the poor, and a *Narodnyi dom* ("House of the People"), all designed to benefit primarily the poorer groups of the population. Concerning the duma's perpetual financial difficulties, Astrov argued that the major problem of city finances was limitations placed on the city's revenue-collecting powers by the municipal statute and by the authorities. In general, Astrov tended to blame most of the defects in the town administration on the restrictions implicit in the law regulating its activities and, in particular, on constant interference by the bureaucracy, which thwarted many of the duma's best efforts.[31]

In spite of his generally favorable evaluation of the duma and its work, Astrov admitted that the municipal administration was at times forced to come to terms with the interests of the property owners who controlled the duma. He did not, however, consider this a serious problem or a major obstacle to the "above-class" work of the duma. Astrov's belief that the need to cater to the self-interest of property owners was more a petty annoyance than a major problem was well illustrated by an example he gave of the property owners in the duma coming to the defense of their own interests. On one occasion, S. A. Muromtsev presented a report on the status of cattle sheds in Moscow and requested that the duma act to require of their owners measures to ensure elementary cleanliness. This proposal caused an immediate outcry from Naidenov and others, who protested that, in Astrov's words, Muromtsev's project was "a violation of the sacred right of property, socialistic, and unacceptable to the Moscow duma." It was accordingly voted down.[32]

Others took a more serious view of this sort of obstructionism in the name of the "sacred right of property." Rakshanin was a constant critic of the self-serving duma majority and regarded their pursuit of their own self-interest as a serious obstacle to civic improvement in Moscow. He wrote, for example, of the deplorable conditions existing in many Moscow apartment buildings and excoriated the duma for its failure to act in this matter, a failure he blamed on the fact that the duma members were property owners themselves and therefore more sympathetic to landlords than to tenants.[33] He also expressed repeated criticism of duma members from the *kupechestvo* for putting the interests of local trade and industry above those of the city as a whole. If Rakshanin's accusations were justified, it may well be that the chief contribution of the duma's *kuptsy* majority was to block measures that would have promoted the public welfare at the expense of imposing restrictions on business, but at the same time one must keep in mind the numerous institutions the duma did create for the public good and financed largely through taxes on business.

Perhaps even more common than accusations of acting out of self-interest leveled against the duma majority were press complaints about the extreme slowness of action of the duma in regard to provision of the basic municipal services. (Some of these complaints were undoubtedly justified: it took twenty-four years of discussion in the duma before the first steps were made toward creation of the city sewerage system.)[34] Reading the Moscow press in the 1890s and early 1900s, one comes away with the impression that in regard to the creation and management of such basic services as water, sewerage, transportation, and the like, the city administration was hopelessly incompetent and that the population suffered grave wrongs at its hands. By contrast, P. V. Sytin, a later investigator of the work of the Moscow duma in these fields, gave the performance of the Moscow city administration a high rating. He wrote that the work of the duma and the *uprava* until the early 1890s could be characterized as "unplanned, without any looking to the future," and entirely designed to meet immediate needs. However, he concluded that from the early 1890s on, the activities of the organs of municipal self-government could be described as "work planned on a large scale for the radical improvement of the town and for giving it a European appearance." He especially praised the city administration in this later period for carefully following innovations introduced in European cities and quickly introducing them in Moscow.[35]

In contrast to the disagreement on these points, there was one fact of municipal life on which all commentators were agreed—the extreme apathy and indifference not only of most members of the duma but of the vast majority of the electorate. Accusations of apathy on the part of duma members were easily proved simply by citing attendance records or referring to the silence of the majority of duma members. The apathy of the electorate could be statistically demonstrated with figures on the number who actually participated in elections. As *Russkie vedomosti* reported in 1904, approximately 25 percent of the eligible voters had taken part in each of the past three elections.[36]

This apathy was hardly restricted to voters from the *kupechestvo* but applied to electors from all social groups, though no doubt each had somewhat different reasons for not appearing to vote. But voters from all groups were put off by the method of elections, which could not have been better designed to discourage voter participation. In the 1890s, voters had to elect 160 duma members and 20 candidate-members. At first the seats were distributed among three electoral districts, each of which thus had to elect 60 members and candidate-members. Later on, six electoral districts were created, each to elect 30 members and candidate-members. The number of candidates in each district, even after the creation of six districts, was sometimes more than 100, and each voter had to vote either for or against each candidate. Given such a situation, the individual elector was in most cases unacquainted with the majority of the candidates on whom he was expected to cast his ballot. His task was made even more difficult by the fact that no real campaigning preceded the elections. Until the elections of 1904, issues were never discussed by the candidates, and so the elections were reduced largely to a matter of personalities. Some duma factions drew up lists of candidates whom they supported and circulated these lists among electors, who frequently followed them for lack of any better guide to their voting. Electors from the *kupechestvo* tended to cast their ballots on the basis of the social status of the candidates and so voted for eminent *kuptsy*, known to all the business community, and for possessors of titles such as commercial or manufacturing councillor or honored citizen. Thus, election to the duma frequently had more to do with social position than with the personal merits of the successful candidates.[37]

Among the *kupechestvo* in particular, election to the duma was considered a mark of honor, and very often electors from the business community decided on their candidates chiefly on the basis of who they felt were deserving of this honor.[38] One *Russkie vedomosti* columnist gave the following sarcastic description of an electoral meeting; it is probably not too wide of the mark:

> "I ask that so-and-so be inscribed as a candidate!" proposes one of the electors, and the answer to him is: "But for more than a year he has suffered from paralysis and cannot get out of bed."
> "It doesn't matter!" objects the first. "It is necessary to honor him with this election: he fully deserves it."
> "And I propose as a candidate so-and-so!" comes another voice.
> "What sort of candidate is he!" it is remarked. "He is almost one hundred years old and not capable of any work."
> "This is no problem," remarks the proposer. "Because he is a very good man, it is necessary to honor him."

The result of such electoral procedures, as the columnist went on to comment, was that "in the composition of our duma the huge percentage of members consist of very honorable people, respected by all, imbued, perhaps, with very fine intentions, but only, regretfully, taking little or no active part in the complicated organization of the town economy."[39]

On the pages of *Russkie vedomosti*, representatives of the liberal intelligentsia constantly agitated for a change in the municipal electoral laws that would bring more "educated people" into city government and thereby, it was hoped, remedy all the deficiencies of Moscow's municipal self-government.[40] But the duma refused even to recommend to the central authorities a reform not only advocated by *Russkie vedomosti* but endorsed by one of the duma's own committees, namely, an expansion of the municipal franchise to include persons who rented homes or apartments.[41] Such a reform would have brought more representatives of the intelligentsia into the duma, most likely with beneficial results. But the duma majority seemed satisfied with the existing electoral laws and practices, which ensured the presence of many members of the very flower of the business community in the duma. Any representative of the social elite of the *kupechestvo* who stood as a candidate for the duma was almost assured of election, because of the peculiar voting habits of the *kuptsy*, and almost all of Moscow's leading business dynasties at one time or another had representatives in the city government. Not infrequently, two or more members of the same family served in the duma at the same time. For example, in the duma sitting from 1897 to 1900 were five Bakhrushins and five Guchkovs, three Vishniakovs and three Morozovs, two representatives apiece from the Botkin, Lepeshkin, Liamin, Mamontov, and Naidenov families, and one representative each from the Abrikosov, Karzinkin, Rukavishnikov, and Shchukin families.[42]

Thus, the duma had among its members the finest representatives of Moscow's business elite, many of whom played important roles and performed notable services in other fields such as philanthropy and patronage. Moreover, because of the general respect these people enjoyed among the *kupechestvo*, they were in a position where they could easily have exercised leadership in the duma. Yet, as far as the older generation of the business elite is concerned, these men failed to leave much of a mark on municipal government. With the exception of Alekseev, the older generation produced no outstanding civic leaders, certainly none whose services in this field could be compared with the activities of the older generation in philanthropy, patronage, and collecting. As Alekseev demonstrated, the opportunity was there, but, in fact, they failed to take advantage of it, remaining content to leave initiative in the hands of the intelligentsia of the duma and *uprava*. One is forced to wonder why they did not devote some of the tremendous energy and time that they gave to the creation of private art galleries and hospitals to the betterment of the city through active leadership in municipal government. And why did they not, like Alekseev, seek fame and immortality as civic reformers rather than as patrons and philanthropists?

There are undoubtedly a number of answers to these questions, one of which might be that the chances of achieving immortal fame through participation in civic affairs were extremely slim. If a mayor like Alekseev might have a hospital named after him, this was a rarity, and, in any case, not everyone could be mayor. And even Alekseev is mostly forgotten today, but who does not know of P. M. Tretiakov and his art gallery? Membership in the duma carried with it a certain amount of honor and prestige, and duma activists achieved a certain respect in Moscow society. But somehow a vigorous fight for the expansion of the city schools did not bring the same degree of fame and respect—to say nothing of immortality—as the creation of an art gallery on one's own private means. Part of the problem was, of course, that the achievements of the duma were in a sense collective achievements. While a few individuals might be singled out and given credit for specific accomplishments of the city administration, the successes of the municipal self-government were credited to the duma and the *uprava* as a whole rather than to individuals. Anyone seeking individual fame would have been hard put to achieve it through municipal work.

But there were other, more basic reasons for the inertia of the older generation in civic affairs, and one of the most important was undoubtedly the narrow political and social horizons typical of the *kupechestvo* before 1861 and never much expanded by the generation born between 1830 and 1860. Astrov noted that the political physiognomy of the duma in the early 1890s was totally indecipherable. The majority of duma members, he wrote, "went about their daily affairs and were little interested in politics." In particular, he found that the *kuptsy* in the duma showed no interest in broad political problems.[43] His observations tend to support the generally held view of contemporaries that the *kupechestvo* as a whole was almost totally indifferent to political and social problems—a view which has also been repeatedly reaffirmed by Soviet historians. Certainly few members of the Moscow *kupechestvo* before 1905 gave any indication that they harbored firm political and social ideals and principles or that they held strong views on the major problems agitating much of educated Russian society in the last decades of the nineteenth century. Beyond a vague feeling that the development of trade and industry was good for the country, the mind of the Moscow *kupechestvo*, including its elite, appears to have been essentially a political blank.

V. Ia. Laverychev, the noted Soviet student of the upper ranks of the *kupechestvo*, has written that the predominant mood among them in the later nineteenth century was conservative, and the evidence would perhaps seem to support his conclusion.[44] But in many cases what appears to have been conservatism might better be regarded as indifference, a refusal to confront and to take stands on the issues of the day. If the implications of such indifferentism were conservative in nature, amounting to acceptance of the existing political and social structure, a considerable distinction must nonetheless be made between conscious conservatism, a conscious dedication to the preservation of things as they are, and unthinking indifference, which by its refusal to face political and social questions assists in the preservation of the established order. Buryshkin singled out passive acceptance of the status quo, an unconscious "reconciliation with the conditions of contemporary life," as characteristic of the Moscow business community before 1905,[45] and his characterization is probably more accurately descriptive of reality than Laverychev's label of conservatism.

Certainly, any student of the older generation of the Moscow business elite cannot help but be struck by the almost total absence of expressions of opinion on political and social matters by representatives of this group. P. I. Shchukin performed the remarkable feat of composing four volumes of memoirs without so much as hinting, either directly or indirectly, at any political or social opinions he might have held. Anyone reading his memoirs is almost forced to conclude that he was as close to being as completely apolitical as any human being can get. Similarly, two volumes of the collected correspondence of the Krestovnikov family contain exactly three letters which refer, more or less in passing, to political and social problems. The numerous students of Savva Mamontov and his circle have been unable to discover any firmly held political or social convictions on Mamontov's part—beyond his belief that art should somehow serve the people. One is forced to the conclusion that the older generation of Moscow's business elite did not hold any strong political and social views—or, if they did, those views appear to be well and truly lost to posterity.

In searching for some coherent political viewpoints among the Moscow business elite, one inevitably stumbles upon the mild flirtation between some members of the elite and a group of Moscow Slavophiles in the later 1850s and 1860s—a rare case of collaboration between businessmen and intellectuals.[46] It was the Moscow Slavophiles, led by F. V. Chizhov, who sought out the businessmen. Impelled by their intense Russian nationalism, the Chizhov group, which included I. S. Aksakov, I. K. Babst, and A. P. and D. P. Shipov, strongly advocated economic autarchy for Russia and sought allies in the business world who might help to realize their dream of Russian economic independence. These Slavophiles themselves, though all were from the nobility, had taken up business activity, partly with the goal of moving Russia closer to autarchy. They also turned to journalism to try to promote their views and secured the support of a number of Moscow businessmen—including T. S. Morozov, the Tretiakov brothers, I. A. Liamin, K. T. Soldatenkov, V. A. Kokorev, the Mamontovs, and the Khludovs—for two short-lived journals, *Vestnik promyshlennosti* (1858–1861) and *Aktsioner* (1858–1865), both edited by Chizhov.

This association might lead one to believe that the Moscow elite had been converted to some form of Slavophilism, but such an assumption simply cannot be sustained. The alliance was always an uneasy one. The Slavophile intellectuals propounded grandiose schemes for national economic development and also advocated reforms in areas outside the economic sphere, such as the abolition of serfdom and the institution of freedom of expression, which they saw as necessary for both economic development and national greatness. But they could not overcome the determinedly narrow viewpoint of their associates from the *kupechestvo*, who never shifted their focus away from measures necessary to promote the well-being of Moscow trade and industry. Moscow *kuptsy* were not to be easily dislodged from their *soslovie* viewpoint. However irritating this was to their Slavophile associates, at the same time, ironically, the continuing *soslovie* orientation of the businessmen from the elite was both a major point of contact between them and the Slavophiles and the factor chiefly responsible for the one lasting achievement of this strange alliance.

Admittedly, the common views of the two groups regarding tariffs—that they had to be kept high to protect Russia's nascent industries—was the chief cement holding them together; indeed, Moscow businessmen might very well have offered financial support to any group or journal advocating a high protective tariff, so important was it to them. But in addition, there was a certain compatibility between the by-now almost instinctive and habitual *soslovie* viewpoint of Moscow businessmen and the political views of the Slavophiles. Stressing Russia's uniqueness and the differences between Russian tradition and the practices of Western European countries, Slavophiles propounded a highly idealized interpretation of the seventeenth-century Russian political system as a guide to future political reform. They accepted the idea of an all-powerful tsar, who sustained an almost mystical communion with his people and who governed in accord with both the desires and the best interests of all his subjects. Such a relationship between tsar and people, they argued, had prevented class conflict in the past and could do so again in the future if the relationship were restored in its pure form. Unfortunately, from their point of view, the growth of bureaucracy had served to interject an unnecessary intermediary between the tsar and his people and had destroyed the communion of earlier centuries. Though idealized, the Slavophiles' political theories rested on an acceptance of the basic principles of the *soslovie* system and served as a point of intellectual contact between them and Moscow *kuptsy*.

The most successful venture undertaken by this alliance of Slavophiles and *kuptsy* was the development of a more effective and vigorous method of urging businessmen's points of view upon the government. It was this group that was largely responsible for the eventual revision of the charter of the Moscow Exchange that permitted the creation of an Exchange Society with the rights to petition the government and to send representatives to participate in government deliberations on economic policy. In future years the Moscow business elite would make good use of the Exchange Society in their attempts to influence state policies, and much of the credit for their effectiveness in the use of this organization should probably go to their Slavophile allies, who, as noblemen, understood far better than did the *kupechestvo* how to exert influence in the councils of state. But it was much easier for Moscow businessmen to accept this new institution which continued to function along old lines—the *soslovie* petitioning the government to give consideration to its views in setting policies involving business interests—than it was for them to imbibe the entire Slavophile philosophy, which would have led them outside their narrow *soslovie* sphere onto the dangerous ground of politics.

The nationalism of the Slavophiles may have left a faint mark on the consciousness of Moscow businessmen of the older generation: at least they easily fell into the habit of arguing that higher tariffs, or easier credit, or whatever at the moment appeared to be in the best interests of Moscow business was in the best interests of the nation (though they never made any very serious efforts to demonstrate why this was so). But for the most part, the nationalism of the Moscow elite's older generation had little in common with the intense, highly intellectualized nationalism of the Slavophiles. An emotional sort of attachment to "Mother Russia" surely existed among them, a patriotism of a very rudimentary kind. One recalls S. I. Shchukin's insistence that his art collection must remain in Russia, even after the Bolsheviks had taken over and he had fled the country: Russia was still Mother Russia, no matter who might be in charge of its political fortunes at any particular moment. But this vague, emotional sort of nationalism coexisted with an admiration for Western culture, and the two combined to produce a surprising degree of cosmopolitanism even in this older generation—a cosmopolitanism that would be much accentuated in the younger generation and that would greatly ease the exile of many members of both generations to Western Europe after the revolution of 1917.

The absence of a principled nationalism as an important ideological influence on the business elite is exemplified by the collectors among the older generation. For every collector of Russian art, such as P. M. Tretiakov, there was another who concentrated on Western European paintings, such as S. I. Shchukin, who almost single-handedly introduced the Russian art world to French impressionism.[47] (It should also be recalled that Tretiakov's first purchases were Western European paintings, which he thereafter avoided only because of his inability to determine their authenticity; he continued his frequent pilgrimages to the art museums of Europe.) P. I. Shchukin collected objects intended to illuminate everyday life in the Russian past, but at the same time he collected similar objects from Western Europe with the intention of demonstrating European influence on Russian culture.[48] The architecture of the older generation's homes was similarly eclectic, some building in the neo-Russian style popular in the later nineteenth century, others inhabiting neo-classical mansions that once belonged to the nobility or building in styles currently popular in Western Europe.[49]

The older generation actually encompassed a broad range of types, strung out along a scale ranging from "true Russian" to "true cosmopolitan," with the largest number bunched at the middle of the scale. There were some individuals at either extreme. I. I. Shchukin moved so far in the direction of cosmopolitanism that he came to find life in Moscow unbearably provincial and in the 1890s moved his residence permanently to Paris, where he collected Spanish paintings.[50] At the other end of the scale, N. A. Naidenov was one member of the elite who had a profound sense of Russian tradition, and of the traditions of the Moscow *kupechestvo* in particular, as indicated by his publication of historical records from the archives of the Moscow Merchants' Society.[51] But Naidenov also noted with pride in his memoirs that his family was among the first to abandon traditional Russian dress and to take up the new "German" styles when it became fashionable to do so among Moscow *kuptsy*.[52] Shchukin's attitude of scorn toward his native land was unusual. Naidenov was more typical in his ability to achieve a comfortable synthesis of Russian and Western European culture. Most members of the older generation valued both Russian and European culture in some degree, without being noticeably principled or fanatical in the defense of either. If some patrons and collectors sought particularly to support Russian art, they did so at least as much because it was good art, and more readily accessible, as because it was Russian.

The combination of patriotism and cosmopolitanism exhibited by the older generation of the elite is in no way remarkable when one considers that many of these sons of "true Russian *kuptsy*" had received a part of their education in Western Europe and that most of them made frequent European tours. Moreover, Western Europe was the source of technological progress. To keep up with technical developments in their field, businessmen had to keep a constant eye on Western European industry. Not only did most of their machinery come from Europe, but so did many of their employees as well. The Moscow elite continued for many decades to hire technical experts from Western European countries and were extremely hesitant to hire Russian engineers and technicians who had received their training in Russia. At one of the meetings accompanying the Industrial Exhibition at Nizhnii Novgorod in 1896, discussion was devoted to the question of hiring Russians in Russian industry. The session was led by N. N. Alianchikov, one of the top technical-managerial employees at the Morozovs' Nikolskaia factory. Alianchikov cited T. S. Morozov's reputation as an "anglophile" as far as his hiring practices were concerned and noted that only late in his life and reluctantly had Morozov been persuaded to hire Russians such as himself. He went on to try to convince other, still obviously reluctant, employers that the necessity for hiring foreigners no longer existed.[53] Another incident demonstrating the business elite's admiration for Western technical expertise occurred when the Moscow duma was beginning to plan the expansion of the city water supply system. The mayor, N. A. Alekseev, stubbornly insisted on consulting foreign experts—much to the displeasure of many duma members, in particular the representatives of the *meshchanstvo*, who did not share Alekseev's conviction that Western engineers were superior to those of Russia. Alekseev, as usual, had his way and requested that plans be submitted first by an English engineer and then by a Belgian expert. In the end, however, even Alekseev was forced to admit that the most practicable proposal, which was eventually adopted, was submitted by two Russians.[54] The episode indicated the increasing competence of Russian technicians, but certainly for many decades Moscow industrialists had had little choice but to look westward, and it would have been difficult for these industrialists not to conceive at least a begrudging admiration of European methods and progress.

If an intense and intellectual nationalism can fairly easily be ruled out as a factor influencing the outlook and behavior of the Moscow elite, it is much more difficult to determine their attitude regarding one other linch-pin of the Slavophiles' theories—namely, the tsar. It might seem logical to assume that, in light of their continuing acceptance of the *soslovie* system, veneration of the tsar then followed naturally. But there is practically no evidence of any sort to verify such an assumption. Perfunctory messages of congratulation to the tsar from the duma or the Exchange Society on the birth of an heir or other notable happenings within the Imperial family constituted practically the only mention of the tsar in these businessmen's public discourse. Such messages, of course, showed only that the elite did what was expected of them on such occasions. Similarly, the fact that a number of Moscow's business elite became members of the so-called Holy Host (*Sviashchennaia druzhina*) cannot be taken as a reliable indication of their political sentiments. Founded by St. Petersburg noblemen and bureaucrats after the assassination of Alexander II in 1881, the Holy Host was a sort of counter-revolutionary secret society that attempted to buttress the autocracy and to combat the growth of the revolutionary movement. It is rather startling to find Moscow *kuptsy* in the company of such exalted names and titles as those on the membership list of the Holy Host; one imagines that if asked to join such eminent company, they could hardly have refused. In any case, if membership was open to businessmen, why did not more of them join? Out of 23 Moscow *kuptsy* who belonged to the Holy Host—its membership totalled 709— only 9 came from elite families. Of these, only S. M. Tretiakov occupied a position of leadership within the business community.[55] The membership of these few individuals from the Moscow elite in the Holy Host seems to say as little about the political convictions of the elite as does the fact that another representative of this generation, S. V. Lepeshkin, contributed to the support of several revolutionary groups.[56]

In his memoirs, D. I. Abrikosov noted the strong monarchical and religious convictions of his grandfather, founder of the Abrikosov dynasty and a representative of the generation preceding the older generation of the 1890s. He went on to remark that

> my grandfather could serve as an example of the support which the throne and the Orthodox Church could have found among the merchants, but . . . the evolution of all classes of society progressed so quickly that the second generation was already indifferent to the old traditions.[57]

Other evidence seems to support his view that the Moscow elite was increasingly indifferent toward the throne. N. P. Vishniakov indicated that in the 1820s and 1830s his parents' attitude toward the tsar and the Imperial family was one of great respect and interest and that his mother in particular rejoiced at any opportunity to see in person the tsar or members of his family. In 1826 she went to great trouble to see the arrival of Nicholas I in Moscow before his coronation, and in 1837 she was thrilled by the chance to lay eyes on the heir to the throne when he was visiting Moscow. These were two of the great events of her life, duly recorded by her son, who, however, appeared to regard his mother's fascination with the Imperial family with an affectionate indulgence.[58] Half a century later, by the time of Alexander III's coronation in 1882, this sort of respectful attitude toward the throne seems at least to have considerably diminished, as indicated by a story concerning K. T. Soldatenkov and I. V. Shchukin that circulated in Moscow at the time. Soldatenkov and Shchukin had for years regularly attended events at the Bolshoi Theater, always sitting in the same seats. Invited to be present at a ceremony at the theater that was a part of the coronation festivities, they arrived to find their customary seats occupied by two generals. When they protested, they were told that under no condition could those seats be made available to them, whereupon they left the theater and absented themselves from the ceremony.[59]

There is a striking contrast between Vishniakova's elation at the mere sight of the tsar and Soldatenkov's and Shchukin's refusal to take a back seat even to high officials in order to be present at a solemn ceremony honoring the tsar at the price of an affront to their own dignity. Even more striking is the fact that I. V. Shchukin was the *father* of the Shchukins included in the older generation of the 1890s, a member of the same preceding generation as Vishniakov's mother. Something appears to have happened in the decades between the 1830s and the 1880s to lessen the Moscow business elite's admiration for the Russian ruler. One can only surmise that Moscow businessmen were influenced by a decreasing respect for the tsar among educated society in general. In addition, having risen to a position considerably nearer the apex of the social pyramid, the members of the business elite perhaps no longer saw the tsar as the same distant, awe-inspiring figure that he appeared to be from further down the social scale.

In any case, Moscow *kuptsy* very rarely had any direct dealings with the tsar himself, whereas they were in constant contact with his representatives, members of various levels of the state bureaucracy. And here it seems safe to say that dislike of bureaucrats was a basic emotion shared by the entire business community. In his memoirs N. P. Vishniakov stressed the uncomfortable relationship existing between *kuptsy* and *chinovniki* in the Moscow of the 1840s and 1850s, describing the officials as

something "evil and hostile to us." He told of a *kupets* who, having undertaken a state contract, failed to pay the necessary bribes and as a result
was utterly ruined; his dying words to his son were "Never have any
business with the state!" Vishniakov dwelt particularly on the disregard
for either law or justice and the haughty arbitrariness of Moscow Governor-General Zakrevskii, relating the story of another *kupets* who, summoned to report to Zakrevskii regarding some minor matter, "was so
frightened that on arriving at the governor-general's house, he died of an
apoplectic stroke in his carriage." Vishniakov noted that after taking over
as governor-general, Zakrevskii "established a very definite relationship
with the *kupechestvo*" by informing the duma that the Merchants' Society
must assume responsibility for feeding and for supplying horses to twelve
regiments about to pass through Moscow. The imposition was greatly
resented, though it was not the first time such requests had been made of
the Moscow *kupechestvo*. And after 1862 the responsibility for billeting
troops in Moscow was laid squarely upon the shoulders of the Moscow
municipal self-government—perhaps the most resented, most onerous obligation imposed on the city duma by St. Petersburg and the one that gave
rise to the most persistent clashes between the duma and the central
government.[60]

Dislike and resentment of bureaucrats, of their arbitrariness and their
incessant impositions, was a definite part of the mentality of the Moscow
business community throughout the nineteenth century. In spite of their
efforts to cultivate good relationships with important officials after 1870,
the complaints that representatives of the elite voiced about government
policies not infrequently focused on deficiencies of the *chinovniki*. This
theme was a very persistent one and a major factor in the politicizing of
the Moscow elite in 1905 (see chap. 6). Though they never gave any hint
of this in their public statements, some businessmen may have realized
that the tsar was, after all, the "head bureaucrat" in the Russian government, and their irritation with the actions of lesser officials and with their
very manner of dealing with *kuptsy* may finally have been considered a
reflection on the tsar himself.

Once one rules out a principled nationalism or any strong feelings of
loyalty to the tsar and accepts the elite's passive accommodation to the
continuation of the *soslovie* system, accompanied by a strong dislike of the
very officials who were charged with making that system work, it is
difficult to find any further evidence regarding their political beliefs. Some
of their contemporaries singled out certain members of the older generation as "conservatives" or "liberals," but such labels do not seem particularly appropriate. N. A. Naidenov, for example, was regarded as a
conservative, with some justification, although his so-called conservatism
was more a mood than a well thought-out political ideology. Generally
resistant to changes of any sort unless they would specifically benefit trade

and industry, Naidenov despised "reformers" of the type of Mayor Alekseev. In a letter to K. P. Pobedonostsev, the conservative grey eminence of the reigns of both Alexander III and Nicholas II with whom Naidenov was on good terms, he expressed his hatred for Alekseev and his conviction that such people, who denigrate the old ways and want to rebuild everything anew, only cause great grief.[61] Alekseev, on the other hand, was sometimes spoken of as a liberal, but again his liberalism constituted more a mood than an ideology, consisting chiefly of a certain readiness to accept change, though change of a very moderate sort. It is difficult to envision Alekseev as a liberal just because he was ready to accept such improvements in the municipal economy as the development of sewers and expansion of the school system or even because he was prepared to support certain measures of factory reform.[62] And there is no indication that his "liberalism" ever went any further. Emperor Alexander III once reportedly praised Alekseev precisely because as mayor he avoided all "politics" and stuck to his sewers, and Rukavishnikov complimented his predecessor on the same grounds, noting the difference in this respect between Alekseev and the duma intelligentsia.[63] Certainly, the liberal intellectuals in the duma, many of whom were alienated by Alekseev's despotic methods to the point of threatening to resign their municipal offices, would have had difficulty in seeing Alekseev as a liberal in any sense of the word.

No doubt the atmosphere of the times contributed something to the refusal of Alekseev and others to confront difficult political and social questions. The late 1880s and early 1890s were not a time for political heroism in Russian society, and even the more progressive zemstvo people largely restricted themselves to "small deeds." Perhaps in another time Alekseev might have developed into a liberal worthy of the name. But the fact remains that he, like other members of his generation of the business elite, was a political babe in the woods, with no political ideology, few firm political or social convictions of any sort, and a preference for avoiding even mildly controversial questions. And it was precisely this sort of political obtuseness that made most members of the older generation unable to contribute very constructively to municipal work. Alekseev was something of an exception, but in fact he differed from his contemporaries within the elite only in his ambition, his dedication, and his determination to lead within the municipal arena. There was little originality in any of his ideas for municipal improvement, most of which had been talked about for years. Further, his proposals for the city consisted largely of a number of ad hoc measures, unrelated by any general plan for the city's development—the eventual emergence of such a plan must be credited chiefly to the intelligentsia in the duma and particularly in the *uprava*. Alekseev could lead. That ability was his great contribution to municipal affairs.

In contrast to the *kuptsy*, members of the Moscow intelligentsia entered the duma already equipped with a fairly definite ideology, with political and social goals, with a general idea of the sort of society they wanted to help create. Many of them saw municipal self-government as a forerunner of a national constitutional structure and regarded work in the duma both as preparation for engagement in national politics and as an immediate opportunity to put some of their ideas into practice. Moscow *kuptsy* brought with them into the duma few ideas on the subject of political and social improvements. As a result, if they were willing to go along with many of the suggestions emanating from the intelligentsia, they were not in a position to take the initiative in planning municipal reform. Without any coherent set of ideals or any firm vision of what the Russian future ought to hold, they could only follow others who had such ideals and vision.

T HE political indifference of the Moscow business elite's older generation was a legitimate inheritance from the past, rooted firmly in the *soslovie* system which had prevented the *kupechestvo* from broadening its horizons to include questions beyond the immediate concerns of trade and industry. The world of the *kupechestvo* in which the older generation grew to maturity had long been isolated from political and social concerns, and at no time in the nineteenth century did the government give *kuptsy* any encouragement to break out of this isolation. Quite the contrary. Every sign that some members of the business community might be developing political interests brought swift retribution from the government.

N. P. Vishniakov's memoirs deal at length with the absence of political concern within the *kupechestvo* during the years of his youth, coinciding with the reign of Nicholas I, and bring into stark relief both the *kupechestvo*'s political indifference and the reasons for it. To begin with, he noted that

in our milieu public interests were weakly developed, and political interests did not exist at all. The Crimean War thundered menacingly, but this thunder we little understood; emancipation of the serfs was being prepared and greatly agitating only noble circles; there was talk about juries; somewhere far away the remarkable unification of Italy was being completed with the help of French bayonets. . . . All this touched us very little. . . . Any sort of political rumors and news had for the inhabitants of Bolshaia Iakimanka much less significance than the death of some notable parishioner, the wedding of a local girl with a good dowry or the birth of an heir in a related family. Interests did not go further than the local circle of relatives and friends, touching only in rare cases the town.[64]

His own family was typical of the merchant milieu of the period, and Vishniakov described them as follows:

Among us no one was interested in politics. At the very most one of my older brothers might say at dinner: "In *Moskovskie vedomosti* they write that the French (or the Germans) are revolting, and they are having great disorders."
And that was all. Of course, this could not pass unnoticed. But for the inhabitants of Bolshaia Iakimanka, as it was then, such news had less interest than, for example, the recent death of Andrei Petrovich Shestov, formerly a popular mayor, and of his relative Petr Mikhailovich Vishniakov. They knew these people well, talked about them much. So what if some French or Germans are revolting! A fat lot that means to us!
Of course, we were not the exception in this, and our world view was shared by the large part of the Moscow *kupechestvo*.[65]

Vishniakov and other memoirists of the period sometimes noted that a few rare individuals of their acquaintance were interested in "politics." But in such cases politics almost always turned out to mean foreign affairs. Vishniakov singled out his brother-in-law as unique, because he read newspapers and "much loved to expand on views about politics with company." But it is clear that his political views went no further than foreign affairs. Vishniakov wrote that "from him for the first time I heard the words: diplomacy, note, congress, neutrality, European balance of power and so on." But while his brother-in-law loved to discourse on the Crimean War and other matters of foreign policy, neither he nor any other member of the family ever introduced his young relative to the vocabulary of internal politics.[66]

Seeking the sources of the *kupechestvo*'s narrow interests and avoidance of internal political questions, Vishniakov found them in the oppressive atmosphere of the reign of Nicholas I and in the very structure of the Russian state and society. His comments on this period from the *kupechestvo*'s point of view are illuminating:

The end of the forties and beginning of the fifties, the years of my childhood, were one of the most unpleasant and difficult epochs of Russian history. Never yet, it seems, had administrative-police oppression attained such limits, never was the servility of the huge majority of the Russian people so profound. The laws existed only on paper. All knew that their application depended exclusively on one's social position. The concept of rights, as such, remained only in books and among circles of idealistic characters, and in life reigned the rule: "don't fight the strong and don't mess with the rich!" The huge majority lived only for their material interests, without any sort of public or political ideals. Grief to him who tried to raise himself to the idea of fatherland and state, seeing in their present structure not only the good sides but also the defects! However well-intended his aims, he became suspect already by the very fact that he dared to enter into consideration of the foundations without a direct commission from the authorities. The least incautious step—and such a bold man could be subjected to all sorts of administrative punishments which were applied completely arbitrarily without the least fear of public opinion or the press. It was naiveté, malicious irony or pure deceit to speak of any public or national goals and tasks, about sympathies and antipathies. There existed only the goals and sympathies of the government, i.e., of a tight circle of all-powerful people in Petersburg, who were accustomed in everything to be led by their personal tastes and considerations.[67]

Thus, in Vishniakov's view of the period, involvement in political questions could be dangerous and was undoubtedly futile, in view of the fact that the government, controlled by nobles, was not open to suggestions from other *sosloviia*.

Some critics of the *kupechestvo* would have argued that narrow absorption in business and making money were the major reasons for their lack of interest in political questions. While there was some truth in this accusation, there is no question that the government did everything in its power to discourage the awakening of political and social interests among the *kuptsy* and to prevent their involvement in political questions. Before 1861, the *kupechestvo*, as Vishniakov pointed out, was made to understand that politics were none of its affair and that any meddling in political matters could have dangerous repercussions. Even in the field of municipal government where, before 1861, no great questions of politics were involved, the *kuptsy* were allowed no initiative, were subject to the tutelage of the bureaucracy, and were made to feel that they must defer to the bureaucrats or else invite immediate reprisal. Totally at the mercy of state officials, unprotected either by their social status or by any connections in higher circles, the *kuptsy* developed a habit of refusing to think for themselves and deferring to the representatives of the state power in all things—a habit which died very hard.

On the few occasions when members of the *kupechestvo* summoned up their civic courage and gave voice to political opinions, the government was quick to indicate its displeasure. One example of this, long remembered in Moscow, was the case of V. A. Kokorev and his political banquet of 1857. Kokorev, at that time still just a rich tax farmer, began to show an interest in political questions in the 1850s and became friendly with many of Moscow's Slavophiles. Soon after it became apparent that Alexander II's government seriously intended to free the serfs, Kokorev organized a huge banquet at the Merchant's Club as a demonstration of sympathy with the idea of emancipation. Present were numerous representatives of both the local intelligentsia and the upper ranks of the *kupechestvo*. This unique banquet was perhaps a first, unsure step by the *kupechestvo* in the direction of involvement with major questions of the day, but it brought an immediate rebuff. Convinced that the emancipation was no concern of the merchants, Governor-General Zakrevskii called Kokorev to his office, gave him a severe reprimand, and broke off their hitherto close and friendly relations. Kokorev was set down as a dangerous radical, subjected to police surveillance for several months, and threatened with other dire punishments. A second banquet, which he had planned to hold in February 1858, was forbidden, and his attempt to publish a speech he had written for the banquet was frustrated by Zakrevskii. Other merchants involved in the episode were visited by the police or summoned to Zakrevskii's office and various threats were made, all of which no doubt severely dampened the *kupechestvo*'s enthusiasm for futher ventures into the sphere of higher politics.[68]

If the Kokorev banquet testified to a certain awakening of political interest among businessmen during the period of the Great Reforms, this awakening did not survive the period of reaction that followed. Like the reign of Nicholas I, the reign of Alexander III was not conducive to the political enlightenment of the business community. B. N. Chicherin, well acquainted with the leading strata of the *kupechestvo* through his brief service as mayor, reflected on their position during this period in a manner that recalled Vishniakov's description of the situation of the *kuptsy* during the reign of Nicholas I. With a far more charitable attitude toward the *kupechestvo* than was typical of most liberal intellectuals, Chicherin wrote:

> Seeing how the noble Russian *dvorianstvo* conducts itself in regard to the authorities, I cannot judge too harshly the *kupechestvo*, which for centuries was trained to servile obedience, and all of whose vital interests depend on the arbitrary will of the authorities. "If we should think about creating opposition, they would make us knuckle under," one Osipov told me, in justification of their conduct.

Further, Chicherin noted that

> this dark mass could still be elevated to a completely different height if it were not constantly and unyieldingly oppressed from above by the corrupting action of the authorities. The public can be educated in noble aims by those who stand at its head. It is necessary to indicate to it the highest goals and to support in it independence of feeling; then it will be enlivened, bright and bold. But when from above everything is directed toward suppressing in society all independence and toward developing servile obedience, when independent thought is persecuted as rebellion, and at the top one sees

nothing but hypocrisy, arbitrariness and lies, then what can be demanded from the subjects[?][69]

Holding a low opinion of the political consciousness of the *kuptsy* in the duma, Chicherin, somewhat to his surprise, was nonetheless the beneficiary of one of their rare acts of political courage. When Chicherin made a speech containing some vague liberal sentiments, the government forced him to resign his position as mayor. The duma, always sensitive to unwanted interference from Petersburg, expressed its support for Chicherin in a resolution that brought immediate censure from provincial officials. Two *kuptsy*, V. D. Aksenov and S. V. Lepeshkin, made speeches in the duma expressing their sympathy for Chicherin. As a result of these bold acts, both Aksenov and Lepeshkin, along with S. A. Muromtsev, the author of the resolution, were called on the carpet by Governor-General V. A. Dolgorukov, who threatened Aksenov with exile and read him a communication from the Minister of the Interior himself, warning Aksenov to be more cautious in the future.[70]

The government's negative attitude toward the *kupechestvo*'s meddling in any political matters, exhibited in both the Kokorev and the Chicherin cases, remained unchanged right down to 1905. In that year, high state officials on at least two occasions reaffirmed the government's long-standing view on this subject. On one occasion, the Moscow governor-general commented to the *starshina* of the Merchants' Society on the deplorable recent political activity of many *kuptsy*, noting that such involvement in politics "would have bad results for trade" and adding that, in any case, "the *kuptsy* make bad politicians."[71] At the same time, when Savva Morozov, one of the politically active members of the younger generation of the business elite, called on S. Iu. Witte to try to influence him in favor of reforms, Witte told Morozov that if he truly cared about the welfare of his country, he would confine his activities to the field of industry and not play at revolution.[72] Witte made it clear that he felt industrialists had no business interfering in political matters, and his statement to Morozov neatly summed up the attitude of the government during the whole period before 1905.

THE older generation of the business elite was extremely aware of and sensitive to the government's view, and the whole force of tradition combined with the government's attitude to keep the members of this generation clear of political involvements. Undoubtedly, they frightened easily. If the intelligentsia was made for defiance and acts of political heroism, the *kupechestvo* definitely was not. Members of the older generation of the elite were sensitive to even the gentlest hints that the government did not favor their taking an interest in political matters. And not only the lack of any tradition of concern for political and social questions but also, no doubt, a continuing fear of arbitrary measures of retribution on the part of state officials and the feeling that, as Chicherin put it, "all of [their] vital interests" were dependent on "the arbitrary will of the authorities" kept them politically apathetic.

In an earlier day, *kuptsy* who offended representatives of the state power feared personal ruin at the hands of vengeful bureaucrats. By the end of the century, although such a possibility could not be entirely ruled out, it was not very likely to occur, at least in regard to members of the business elite. Their businesses were too large, too well established, too vital to the national economy for the government to seek their ruin. If state officials occasionally threatened obstreperous businessmen with exile, they never fulfilled those threats. Savva Morozov, in a deliberate act of defiance, once drove down a main street of Moscow beside a well-known Bolshevik who was wanted by the police; the authorities took no action, either against Morozov or against the Bolshevik he had taken under his protection.[73] Such a defiant act would never have occurred to any members of the older generation, still much less confident of their position vis-à-vis the authorities than the younger generation of the business elite would be. The incident nonetheless demonstrated that successful businessmen had achieved a certain degree of personal immunity not available to the average citizen. It also showed how far the upper ranks of the business community had come since the reign of Nicholas I, when K. V. Prokhorov was actually subjected to the indignity of a brief term in prison for having attempted to bribe the president of the Tariff Commission.[74]

If the possibility of personal ruin at the hands of bureaucrats had been largely removed, big businessmen had other reasons now to fear incurring the wrath of the government. By the last decades of the century, big business had achieved a highly favored position in the state. As the central government over the decades had become increasingly interested in the rapid development of the national economy, it had given more and more attention to the needs and desires of the leading representatives of the business community and had bestowed upon them many privileges and favors. As a group, big businessmen now had much to lose should the state find cause to temper its benign attitude toward them and to withdraw favors previously granted. What the state gave, it could also take away, and there is little doubt that the whole attitude of the older generation of the business elite toward political involvement was influenced by this ever-present possibility.

Probably the most valuable gift Moscow's business elite received from the government after 1861 came in the form of a special relationship between the government and the upper stratum of the *kupechestvo*, particularly the industrialists. In the 1860s, the government had initiated the practice of consulting with leading figures in trade and industry on important questions of state economic policy. First employed during review of the tariff in the 1860s, formal government consultation with important businessmen soon developed into an established practice.[75] The chief representative of the government in these consultations was the Ministry of Finance, while the spokesmen for the business world came chiefly from the local exchanges and, more rarely, the Councils of Trade and Manufacturing. The ministry, usually through the Department of Trade and Manufacturing, developed the habit of requesting opinions from these institutions on questions of economic policy currently under consideration within the bureaucracy. On increasingly frequent occasions, representatives of the business world were invited to St. Petersburg for conferences on specific problems and were sometimes requested to formulate their own proposals for legislative enactments. Further, the Exchange Societies had the right to send petitions to the minister of finance, bringing to his attention problems of trade and industry requiring government consideration. Finally, on a local or provincial level, many businessmen served on permanent boards and committees that dealt with various matters of interest to the business community, such as the assessment of taxes on industry and trade, the supervision of the factory inspectorate, the discounting policies of the State Bank, and so on.

Moscow business leaders played a large role in this interaction between business and government. Representatives of the Moscow business elite were always included in conferences touching on general problems of trade and industry and on particular problems affecting the textile industry. They frequently served as spokesmen to the government representing not only Moscow business but the merchants and industrialists of the entire Central Industrial Region. Fulfillment of this role gave them no real power but did give them a considerable amount of influence.[76] In all questions, the power of initiative and of final decision remained with the bureaucracy, which might give more or less serious consideration to the opinions of businessmen but which would reach its decisions on the basis of a variety of considerations, of which the views of the business community were only one. But if the business community was in most cases powerless to block the enactment of measures distasteful to them, it was able in certain cases, because of its special relationship with the Ministry of Finance, to mitigate the effects of these measures and occasionally to bring about certain important revisions of basic policy. For example, a substantial change in the orientation of the factory inspectorate was effected while I. A. Vyshnegradskii was minister of finance, partly because of the agitation of Moscow industrialists.[77] In a later period, the curbing of the Zubatov experiment in "police socialism" also resulted in part from the strong objections of Moscow factory owners.[78] Moreover, the mere fact that the upper ranks of the *kupechestvo* had any voice at all, any influence at all in the central government was highly unusual, given the existing relationship between state and society in tsarist Russia. As the historian P. A. Berlin has pointed out, the businessmen were practically the only group in the country who were encouraged to organize, encouraged to express their opinions, by the tsarist government.[79] It was a signal honor, a rare opportunity to have some influence on the workings of an autocratic government, and in the nineteenth century Moscow's business leaders were not about to take any actions that might jeopardize their favored position.

This special relationship seems to have been more highly valued than any specific economic benefit that Moscow businessmen received from the state. Soviet historians have tended to emphasize direct aid to business in the form of subsidies and the like as the important factor in explaining the general political submissiveness of big businessmen,[80] but this factor was much less important to Moscow's leading businessmen than it was to merchants and especially industrialists in other geographical areas and in other fields of trade and industry. The textile industrialists who played the preponderant role in the Moscow business community needed little direct aid from the state, nor did they get much. Almost all of them sold their goods on the mass market, rather than relying on state contracts. They received no assistance in the form of direct subsidies, since they were able to finance their business operations out of their own profits, supplemented by credit from the Moscow banks they controlled. The leading Moscow industrialists did not even make use of what financial assistance was offered them by the state. Though the Moscow section of the State Bank was ordered to make available large lines of credit to Moscow's big textile industrialists, they used this credit only on the rarest occasions.[81]

The one very direct benefit Moscow industrialists received from the state was the protective tariff. The textile industry benefited greatly from high tariffs which kept out foreign competition, and the same is true of other fields of industry in which Moscow businessmen were engaged, such as chemicals. Moscow's business elite highly valued the protective tariff and considered it, in fact, the single most important feature of the government's economic policy. They prepared for battle at the least hint that the tariff might be lowered and kept up continuing pressure on the government to maintain existing duties, or to change them in a direction favorable to native industry.

While Moscow's big businessmen benefited from the tariff, and from other general state measures such as the encouragement of railroad development, not a few government policies went against what these same businessmen regarded as their own best interests. If, as Soviet historians emphasize, industrialists appreciated the employment of the repressive apparatus of the state to deal with labor troubles,[82] the method of state interference in strikes and demonstrations at factories was at the same time resented by many industrialists, since the officials tended to take complete control of the situation, leaving the industrialist no freedom of action whatsoever.[83] Moreover, if the government sent Cossacks to the factories, it also sent factory inspectors, whose appearance as the enforcers of the new factory laws was roundly denounced by the majority of Moscow industrialists as sharpening relations between workers and employers and creating disorders in the factories.[84] Representatives of the Moscow business community also expressed strong disagreement with other state policies, such as the encouragement of a newly developing textile industry in Russian Poland and the strong infusion of foreign capital into the Russian economy.[85]

Thus, it would be difficult to argue that the specific economic benefits Moscow businessmen received from the state kept them politically quiescent, since these benefits were counterbalanced by state policies which had a negative effect on what the Moscow business elite considered its own best interests. What the business elite seem to have valued even more highly than any specific state policies was the special relationship between themselves and the Ministry of Finance, which gave them the rare opportunity to exert influence on the process of government legislation. The men of the older generation had been instrumental in the creation of this relationship in the first instance, through their petitions, their visits to St. Petersburg, their cultivation of good relations with important officials, their organization of the Exchange Committee as a representative group. They were aware of how far the big business community had come since the days of their youth, when the government enacted measures affecting the livelihood of businessmen with a supreme disregard for the opinions and experience of the business community. And this relationship that they had helped to create made it possible for them not to control economic policy, but to have some influence on it. The members of this generation dared not ask for more. They appreciated the favored position in which the government had placed them and were determined to preserve it.

The great value that many members of the older generation placed on this special relationship with the government, and the lengths to which they were prepared to go in order to maintain it, are obvious from the memoirs of N. A. Naidenov and from his activities as president of the Moscow Exchange Committee. In his latter capacity, Naidenov made certain that neither the committee nor the Exchange Society as a whole should go beyond consideration of economic problems. Dedicated to the preservation of the special privileges of the committee, Naidenov was convinced that the chief threat to these privileges was deviation from strictly economic concerns into the field of politics. The committee was indeed prohibited by its charter from discussing political matters, but as Buryshkin has pointed out, there was no official supervision of the committee, and no state officials were present at its meetings, so that political discussions would have been possible had it not been for the determination of Naidenov to avoid any and all subjects that he considered even vaguely political. Under his leadership, the Exchange Committee stuck strictly to specific questions of economic policy, such as the tariff, industrial taxation, and factory laws. It did not even take under consideration the basic question of which general state policies might best promote the development of the national economy. In attempting to answer such an essential question, the committee would have been forced to consider various factors outside the field of economics, such as the lack of educational opportunities and the defects of the political structure—matters which Naidenov was determined to avoid at all costs.[86]

In his memoirs, Naidenov's opinions on how the Exchange Committee ought to conduct itself are reflected in his comments on the fate of various institutions created by the Great Reforms. While he believed that the government's efforts at reform in the 1860s and 1870s constituted one of the great chapters of Russian history, Naidenov nonetheless felt that the reforms had not turned out as well as they might have, because society consistently abused the rights and privileges granted to it by the government. In regard to the newly created juries, he wrote:

> The jury courts little by little began to stray from their given path; they began to show *liberalnost* which brought with it decrease in the rights belonging to these courts and their reduction to their present position. And there the cause was immoderation in the use of rights given to them.[87]

This was evidently the chief lesson that Naidenov learned from the reforms and their aftermath, although in a sense it was a very old lesson, reflecting once again the *soslovie* mentality: the government grants rights, and it is the business of subjects to perform their duties within the sphere defined and circumscribed by those rights. He applied this lesson consistently in his management of the Exchange Committee, above all by steering the committee completely clear of all political and social questions, the discussion of which would have raised the possibility of restriction of the independence and privileges of the committee.

If the older generation refused to give attention to political questions, they did, of course, consider and discuss economic questions, on which the government both permitted and expected them to comment. Attempting to discuss economic problems without venturing into the field of politics was obviously a tricky proposition, since the line between economics and politics is often a hazy one. But ignoring as best they could the facts that most economic decisions have political and social repercussions and that most political and social policies have economic effects, the businessmen of the older generation struggled manfully to keep the two separate. If they were at all aware that the economic policies they advocated or opposed might have important political and social effects, few hints of this awareness crept into their public statements.

Moreover, if Moscow businessmen of the older generation refused in their comments on economic questions to consider political and social repercussions, they also failed to take into consideration the interests of other sectors of the economy beyond those in which they were personally involved. Their job, as they saw it, was to defend the interests of Moscow trade and industry, which in fact meant chiefly the interests of the textile industry of the Central Region. They ignored agriculture altogether, and the needs of other fields of trade and industry besides those represented in the Moscow business elite evoked little interest in them. They rarely thought in terms of the economy as a whole and tended to consider all questions from the point of view of their own needs at the moment, giving little attention to whether a particular policy, though beneficial in the short run, might have undesirable effects in the future. *Novosti*'s Rakshanin, with considerable justification, labeled the approach of Moscow's business community to all political, social, and economic events and problems "calico politics," arguing that the reactions of Moscow businessmen to current events and issues were always based solely on their evaluation of the possible effects on the price of calico.[88] And, indeed, their vision was not much broader in scope than Rakshanin made it out to be.

The older generation of the elite demonstrated its extremely narrow scope of vision again and again, in its many petitions, reports, and public statements. For instance, to choose one example in which both economic policy and foreign policy were involved, the spokesmen for Moscow's business elite in 1893 were vociferous in their support of the brief tariff war between Russia and Germany. As was obvious from their resolutions and public statements, their sole concern in the affair was that the Russian government should not give in to German demands for lower tariffs on industrial goods, even though the *quid pro quo* might be a lowering of German duties on Russian agricultural products. They talked bravely of a permanent, or at least a very protracted, severance of commercial relations with Germany, insisting that Russia could get along very well without German trade.[89] They gave no thought to the effect of the tariff war on Russian relations with Germany or other states. That Russia's hardpressed agriculturalists might benefit considerably from a lowering of tariffs did not concern them. The difficulties a long tariff war might cause for other areas of the economy besides the textile industry and the problems it would create for the government's overall program of rapid industrial development were also given no consideration. In effect, they were saying that the Moscow textile industry could get along for an indefinite period without further imports of German machinery and that the economy would therefore suffer no harm from breaking commercial relations with Germany.

Other examples of their extremely narrow field of vision are not difficult to find. When a textile industry began to develop in Russian Poland, Moscow textile industrialists, always sensitive to any threat of competition, mounted a major petition campaign against the textile manufacturers of Lodz, arguing that the government was granting unfair privileges to these potential competitors of Moscow industry and also stressing the fact that many Lodz businessmen were, after all, foreigners and Jews.[90] The fact that the development of the Lodz textile industry would be of great value to the Russian economy in general was quite overlooked. Similarly, the Exchange Committee's petition protesting against the large infusion of foreign capital into the Russian economy was based on a very narrow point of view. Although it reflected a deep-seated dislike of foreigners who evaded tariff duties by establishing their businesses in the very heart of Russia and thereby created competition for Russian businessmen, the immediate provocation for this petition was a period of rising oil prices. The rather curious reasoning of the Exchange Committee led them to the conclusions that because of foreign involvement in the Russian oil industry, Moscow industrialists were having to pay higher prices for fuel and that this situation was injurious to the Russian economy as a whole.[91] That foreign investment in the oil industry and in other parts of the economy might indeed be of great benefit to the overall economic development of Russia was ignored in their anxiety over rising fuel costs and their deeper fear of foreign competition within the boundaries of the Empire.

Another curious instance of what P. A. Berlin called the "petition politics" of the Russian bourgeoisie occurred on the occasion of the expulsion of a large part of the Jewish community from Moscow in 1882 and well illustrated the difficulty of separating economics from politics. A petition signed by representatives of many leading Moscow firms protested the government's decision to restrict Jewish rights of settlement in Moscow on the grounds that it was bad for business. The government's decision, of course, was not based on economic considerations but purely on the anti-Semitic sentiments of leading figures in the government, including the Emperor himself. But the petition of the Moscow businessmen did not even mention anti-Semitism, said nothing of the humanitarian considerations involved, nothing about religious toleration. It simply noted that Moscow's Jewish traders acted as middlemen between Moscow and the western and southern regions of the Empire and that their banishment would generally disrupt trade.[92] For the businessmen to have commented on the anti-Semitism motivating the banishment or to have expressed opinions regarding religious toleration would, of course, have been considered most improper by the government. But the resulting petition, which leaves an impression of total political and moral obtuseness, was nonetheless in part a political statement and demonstrated the difficulty of keeping politics and economics in separate spheres.

That at least some businessmen were aware of the political questions involved in many economic issues was well demonstrated by an interview with S. I. Shchukin conducted by N. O. Rakshanin for *Novosti* in 1894. In this interview, one of the extremely few ever given to the press by a member of the older generation, Shchukin struggled to keep his comments on a strictly economic plane but was nonetheless forced to admit, under the interviewer's prodding, that the economic issues he was discussing also had political and social implications. When Shchukin commented on the increasing use of factory-made textiles by the peasants and noted that they were beginning to demand better grades of cloth, Rakshanin inquired whether Shchukin thought that the manufacturers, by stimulating peasant demand for increasingly better-quality goods, were performing any sort of service for the villages. Shchukin's answer was highly revealing of the mode of thought of Moscow businessmen and deserves to be quoted at length. He commented that

if you speak from the moral point of view, then this is a vice which calico introduces into the village, spreading its use and little caring about the means of satisfying this demand. It is not possible to hide this fact from one's eyes, and I do not wish to do so. I wish to explain to you the position as it is. It is undoubted that in this respect the cloth manufacturers have a bad influence on the village. But what is to be done? This is the natural course of things. I am talking with you about the state of calico production in Russia and I cannot touch on other sides of this question. Production, developing so quickly, naturally must seek markets for sale and cannot ask questions standing outside the commercial viewpoint of business.

Further on in the interview, Shchukin returned to this subject once again and stated that

the expansion of personal demands is the natural result of any progress. Industry and trade always and everywhere have introduced and will introduce this vice. This is the natural course of things and to demand from industrialists and from merchants that they should deliberately give up regions of their sale with the goal of not accustoming the village to luxury would be, you must agree, very naive.[93]

Thus, Shchukin in effect agreed with the interviewer's implication that the demand for better and better factory-made textiles in the villages was developing faster than the peasants could acquire adequate means for

146 · THE MOSCOW BUSINESS ELITE

satisfying this demand and that, as a result, certain dislocations were introduced into village life by the development of the manufacturing industry. But if he recognized that industrial development caused dislocations in the villages, Shchukin was in effect gainsaying any responsibility on the part of industrialists to deal with these dislocations or even to consider them.

Besides the development of peasant demand, Shchukin also briefly discussed efforts to expand the export of Russian textile goods. In the past, the government had tried to encourage Moscow manufacturers to develop export markets in Persia, in the Far East, and in the Balkans. Though a few firms were involved in the export trade, Moscow textile industrialists, generally speaking, gave something less than an enthusiastic response to the urgings of the government.[94] The government's goals in this matter were, of course, chiefly political, while Moscow businessmen looked on the question from an economic point of view. In commenting on this issue, Shchukin showed himself not unaware of the political implications involved but still insisted on approaching the question primarily from the economic viewpoint. He noted that Russian textile manufacturers still had to conquer many internal markets which as yet had not been opened to their goods. This being the case, he saw little need to try to develop export ties with foreign countries. He commented that

> I speak from the commercial point of view and do not desire to inject politics into this matter. If we begin to bring patriotism into this affair, then, of course, the conversation changes completely. For the sake of patriotism the Moscow *kupechestvo* has thrown away huge sums and made huge sacrifices. But in such a case it is necessary to call these things by name. And I am talking with you about commerce and there is no need for us to bring in politics and patriotism.[95]

Government officials interested in the expansion of Russian influence in Persia and the Balkans might well have been annoyed with Shchukin's refusal to consider politics and patriotism in his analysis of foreign markets and might well have insisted that it was indeed the patriotic duty of Moscow manufacturers to undertake the conquest of these markets. But having helped to accustom Moscow businessmen to think only of economic factors and to ignore politics in all matters they were forced to consider, state officials could hardly expect them now to overcome their deliberate political blindness and to place politics above economics in this particular case.

Even if some members of the older generation, like Shchukin, were aware of the political implications of economic issues, in practice, as the

Shchukin interview demonstrates, they insisted on reaching decisions on economic questions entirely on the basis of economic factors, ignoring all political and social factors. They also ignored the fact that in taking stands on what were basically economic questions for them, they were also often taking political positions. Berlin has commented on the inability of Russian businessmen even after 1905 to realize that many times when they thought they were speaking only the language of economics, they were in fact speaking the language of politics as well.[96] This same generalization is entirely applicable to the older generation of the Moscow business elite before 1905. When Shchukin and other Moscow businessmen failed to show any interest in the expansion of exports into Eastern and Balkan markets, they were in effect taking a political position of refusal to support the government's efforts to create spheres of influence. When businessmen signed the petition protesting the expulsion of Moscow Jews, they appeared to be taking a stand in the political controversy regarding government persecution of Russia's Jewish population. Similarly, when businessmen fought the introduction of factory legislation, they were involving themselves in what was, to the government, primarily a political and social question and only secondarily an economic one.

But even if businessmen were unwillingly forced into taking positions on what were essentially political and social questions, it would be absurd to try to deduce their political views from the positions reflected in their petitions and public statements. While most Moscow businessmen, as businessmen, had a negative attitude toward expansion of exports to Persia and the Balkans, it may well be that as private citizens they favored or, more likely, were indifferent to the government's imperialistic policies, as long as those policies did not involve any exertions or sacrifices from the textile industry. Similarly, it would be incorrect to see their petition protesting the banishment of the Jews as a reflection of opposition toward anti-Semitism in the Moscow business community. There was indeed a good deal of anti-Semitism among Moscow businessmen, though anti-Semitism of a mild sort; the petitions resulting from their campaign against the Lodz textile industry, stressing as they did the Jewishness of many businessmen in Russian Poland, indicated that they were more than ready to make use of anti-Semitism when it served their own purposes.[97]

Finally, to try to deduce any sort of political views at all from Moscow businessmen's stand on factory legislation would be quite impossible. In effect, they might be interpreted as arguing in favor of continued oppression of the lower strata of the population and as saying that a policy of repression was better calculated to assure their quiescence than an attempt to satisfy some of their grievances and to improve their working and living conditions. But one must contrast the industrialists' opposition to factory legislation with the very real efforts that many of them made individually to improve conditions at their factories and also with the desire to help the less fortunate and improve conditions for the poorer classes that was demonstrated by their private philanthropy. One is thus left with a paradox, and the only way to resolve it is to acknowledge that Moscow industrialists simply did not recognize the issue of factory legislation as a political and social question but saw it only as a question of "their dominant control over the workers, which had proved so profitable in the past."[98] What was at issue was not politics, but profits.

The fact is that while Moscow businessmen of the older generation, in the course of their attempts to elucidate their views on economic questions, were often forced in an oblique manner to throw their weight on one side or another of a political or social question, they did so without devoting any conscious thought to the political or social issue involved or to the resultant political position in which they were placing themselves. Their politics were in effect a sort of "politics by default," arrived at not by conscious deliberation of political issues but appearing as an unconscious by-product of their economically motivated reactions to current questions. Whether the matter at hand was basically a political or social question or an economic one, or all of these combined, they saw all issues which they deliberated as economic issues and reached their conclusions on the basis of economic factors. Their public postures reflected their conviction that, as Shchukin put it, businessmen "cannot ask questions standing outside the commercial viewpoint of business."

Even if the refusal of Moscow businessmen to confront the political and social implications of their views on economic matters and their habit of judging all issues from a narrow economic point of view was partly a consequence of government pressure on them to steer clear of all non-economic considerations (and partly, of course, the natural tendency of many businessmen at all times and in all places to put immediate economic considerations above all others), their approach was so narrow as occasionally to irritate even officials in the Ministry of Finance. Witte reacted very sharply to the Moscow Exchange Committee's resolution protesting against the large amounts of foreign capital invested in the Russian economy and accused Moscow businessmen of being unable to see further than their own profits.[99] But such outbursts from government officials were rare, and usually even the most trivial and inane requests and opinions of Moscow's business leaders were received with courtesy and consideration. Much more frequent were negative reactions to the petitions and statements of Moscow businessmen from the press, whose comments invariably dwelt on the extremely narrow viewpoint of Moscow businessmen and on their apparent attitude that, for all they cared, "the world may perish so long as the cotton textile industry flourishes."[100]

THE narrowness and egotism of Moscow businessmen was in large part responsible for the general hostility toward them as a group found among the educated Russian public and reflected in journals and newspapers of all political leanings. In a country where the press was largely controlled by, and public opinion largely determined by, intellectuals who consistently thought in the broadest terms of the welfare of the Russian people as a whole and noblemen who were dedicated to service of the state and its higher interests, the contempt evoked by the extremely narrow approach of Moscow businessmen is no cause for surprise. The hostility was both wide and deep, but whatever its extent and depth, it had seemingly little effect on Moscow businessmen and certainly did not cause them to moderate their views. The government was also apparently unconcerned about the general dislike of the *soslovie* responsible for the development of national trade and industry. Not until 1903, on the occasion of his retirement from his ministerial post, did Witte sound a note of alarm regarding public hostility toward the "commercial and industrial *soslovie*." Perhaps somewhat sobered by the strength of the opposition to his plans for industrial development which he had faced and which had finally led to his forced resignation, Witte commented to a group of businessmen that they were not well liked by their fellow citizens and that they ought to make some effort to overcome the widespread hostility directed toward them and their views. Among other things, he suggested that they should make use of organs of the press to argue their views before the public and to influence public opinion in their favor.[101]

The suggestion was not a new one. During the Nizhnii Novgorod fair of 1895, a Vichuga textile industrialist by the name of A. F. Morokin, who was himself a frequent contributor of articles on economic questions to various journals and newspapers, publicly called upon the *kupechestvo* to make a concerted effort to put its views across in the press. Morokin noted that

in recent years we have remained without an organ which would be a worthy representative and strong defender of national industry and trade, in all its totality, and which would oppose the detraction and abuse that are showered upon us by our open and hidden enemies and especially by the periodical press, with very rare exceptions, and that are showered upon us almost without answer, since there is no one anywhere to say a word in defense of the industrialist.[102]

But Morokin's plea for a defense of businessmen and their views in the press remained without result, as did Witte's later suggestion.

Actually, in earlier years Moscow industrialists had subsidized a number of journals and newspapers designed to promote their point of view on certain subjects. After both *Vestnik promyshlennosti* and *Aktsioner* had ceased publication, a group of Moscow capitalists, including T. S. Morozov, I. A. Liamin, P. Maliutin, and K. T. Soldatenkov, undertook in 1866 to finance the newspaper *Moskva*, whose editor was I. S. Aksakov. Aksakov, however, soon got into trouble with the authorities, and the paper was very short-lived. Almost twenty years later, in 1884, T. S. Morozov took the initiative in founding another newspaper, *Golos Moskvy*, to express the views of Moscow businessmen, but the paper was not a success and soon passed into other hands. In 1887, D. I. Morozov, N. P. Konshin, and A. F. Morokin began to publish a paper called *Russkoe delo*, edited by the publicist S. I. Sharapov. Morozov tried to retain control over the content and management of the paper, but persistent clashes with Sharapov over financial matters caused him to withdraw his support in 1889.[103] Morozov and his brother Arsenii Ivanovich also financed the journal *Russkoe obozrenie*, published in the late 1880s and 1890s.[104]

The fact that some of Moscow's leading businessmen had on several occasions taken the initiative in creating journals and newspapers to promote their own views would perhaps indicate that the Moscow business elite was not entirely indifferent to the uses of the periodical press. However, the interesting fact that emerges from their few forays into the field of publishing is that each one of these various organs was created as a response to a momentary "crisis" of some sort. As soon as the crisis had passed—or at least somewhat lessened—the interest of Moscow businessmen in publishing ceased. Further, these various crises all had to do with some action of the government that was seen as threatening the self-interest of Moscow trade and industry.

For example, the financing of Aksakov's *Moskva* was undertaken at a time when the tariff was under review and when Moscow businessmen rightly feared that government opinion had turned in favor of lowering tariff duties. The businessmen supported Aksakov's paper because he argued for a high protective tariff. When a new and lower tariff was confirmed, and there seemed little likelihood of effecting higher tariffs in the immediate future, Moscow businessmen lost all interest in financing any further publications.[105] Similarly, the various publications financed by Moscow businessmen in the 1880s and early 1890s appeared soon after the first factory legislation was put into effect and at a time when Moscow businessmen were beginning their campaign against the textile industry of Lodz. Sharapov was hired to wage war on both these fronts, against the factory inspectors and against the Lodz manufacturers, while the economic section of *Russkoe obozrenie* concentrated chiefly on factory legislation. (One of its most imaginative articles was an attempt to prove, entirely on the basis of biblical quotations, that a government proposal for the insurance of factory workers was contrary to Christian teachings.)[106]

Russkoe obozrenie, the only one of these publications to survive until the end of the 1890s, began losing interest in problems of factory legislation after 1893, at a time when Moscow industrialists had begun to reconcile themselves to the presence of inspectors in their factories and when there was no further legislation under serious consideration by the government. The economic section of the journal began to concentrate on other topics, including a great many pertaining to agriculture, and Moscow business-men once again found themselves without any organ of the press to argue their views.

Thus, in spite of the fact that leading Moscow businessmen of the older generation at various times financed organs of the press to purvey their point of view on economic questions, they never undertook any continu-ous public relations effort to influence educated opinion. In fact, they do not appear to have been interested in influencing public opinion at all but rather seem to have aimed their propaganda efforts chiefly at government circles. The fact that their major undertakings in the field of publishing appeared at times when the government was considering various measures directly affecting Moscow trade and industry would seem to indicate that their main interest was to influence the bureaucrats in the Ministry of Finance rather than the public at large. Naidenov stated directly that it was fear of the spread of "free trade" ideas in high government circles that led to the support of Aksakov's *Moskva* by Moscow businessmen,[107] and it seems likely that their later subsidization of other newspapers and journals was also undertaken primarily with the idea of influencing bureaucratic opinion. Their experiments in the use of the press, sporadic as they were, should probably be seen as an extension of the petition politics growing out of the *soslovie* system rather than as an attempt to influence public opinion.[108]

If Morokin, in his statement at the Nizhnii Novgorod fair and in his own writing and publishing activities, showed himself aware of the need for a press organ that would consistently express the views of businessmen and attempt to defend them against persistent attacks in other journals, he was seemingly exceptional in his recognition of the need for a contin-uous public relations effort. Anxious as they were to influence govern-mental opinion, Moscow's business elite of the older generation showed no interest in influencing the opinion of the public at large even on eco-nomic questions, nor did they seriously try to change the extremely neg-ative image of themselves held by educated society. In fact, not only did they refrain from an out-and-out public relations campaign, but they generally followed a policy of secrecy in regard to their activities and opinions. This policy, of course, made it difficult even for those few journalists who were interested in what was happening in business circles to get any good copy.

This policy of secrecy, which was pursued in regard to both their business activities and the activities of various organizations of business-men, stemmed partly from the habits of the past. The Russian businessmen had traditionally been as close-mouthed as possible regarding their busi-nesses, partly out of fear of competitors, partly out of fear that any infor-mation that they divulged would lead to new or higher taxes.[109] The innate secrecy of Russian businessmen made it extremely difficult to get any accurate information about their business dealings, and the compilation of trustworthy statistics on trade and industry was almost impossible.[110] When in the 1890s an attempt (one of many) was made to gather detailed statistics about business transacted at the Nizhnii Novgorod fair, the statisticians hired to complete the task immediately ran up against the clandestine tendencies of the Russian *kupets* and soon found that their efforts produced more frustration than information.[111]

This traditional secrecy also manifested itself in the conduct of the Merchants' Society, the *soslovie* organization of Moscow *kuptsy*, as well as in the conduct of the Exchange Committee. The Merchants' Society was the only *soslovie* organization in Moscow that did not admit representatives of the press to its meetings and wanted no publicity for its activities.[112] The Exchange Committee under Naidenov pursued a similar policy. Nai-denov, who in his memoirs specifically approved of secrecy as a general principle in the conduct of affairs, avoided any publicity concerning the committee's activities and, like many other businessmen of his generation, persistently refused even to give interviews to interested journalists.[113] When K. V. Rukavishnikov became mayor, he introduced the same prin-ciple of secrecy into the Moscow municipal *uprava*, admonishing city employees as follows:

> Above all, I ask you most earnestly not to hobnob with journalists and not to let them in on your plans or the details of the activity of the institutions under your supervision. Let them write whatever comes into their heads—you should not pay the least attention to this. Also do not pay any attention to what people will say about you. In this respect, follow my example. Believe me, so-called pub-lic opinion is simply nonsense and we haven't the least need to heed it. We must follow our own path.[114]

Such secrecy outraged both citizens who believed that their city govern-ment ought to be responsive to public opinion and journalists who were accustomed to much greater openness during Alekseev's administration. Rukavishnikov's attitude was rooted in his commercial background, but it also reflected the influence of the example set by the central government, known for its extremes of official secrecy and disregard for public opinion, as well as the lingering grip of the *soslovie* system, in which the opinion of other social groups was never a factor that needed to be considered.

In view of the generally narrow approach of Moscow's leading businessmen of the older generation to the problems of the day, it seems probable that neither greater openness with representatives of the press nor publication of their own journals and newspapers would have done much to change public opinion toward them. However that may be, there can be no doubt whatsoever of their supreme disregard for the public's reaction to their views and for the public's opinion of businessmen as a group—even though, as was stressed in the preceding chapter, many of them were indeed sensitive to what the public thought of them as individuals. In general, the businessmen of the older generation believed that only bureaucrats were worth influencing and that what the educated public thought of business and businessmen mattered little, as long as they enjoyed the good will of the minister of finance. In the short run, they were undoubtedly right. Before 1905, the Russian public had little opportunity to exert influence on decisions regarding matters of interest to Moscow businessmen. But in the long run, their scorn of public opinion had disastrous consequences.

Perhaps the businessmen of the older generation should not be blamed for failing to foresee a revolution and a major change in the political and social structure of the Russian state. In any case, before 1905, they essentially accepted the autocracy on its own terms and sought to deal with it within the limitations set down by the government itself. In their willingness to work with the autocracy and to accept its terms, the older generation was again in effect making a political judgment for economic reasons. However dissatisfied they may have been with certain aspects of governmental economic policy—the only field of state policy with which they concerned themselves—still, it was the only government they had, and cooperation seemed to them the policy best calculated to preserve and promote their own economic interests.

Whether in accepting the tsarist government and all it stood for they were truly acting in their own best economic interests is of course a debatable question. Lenin before 1917 and Soviet historians after 1917 have repeatedly pointed out that the autocracy, though it followed a general policy of promoting industrial development in the later nineteenth and early twentieth centuries, did not pursue a consistently "bourgeois" line. If it directly encouraged industrialization, the government also followed a policy of support for the nobility, which involved the retention or creation of numerous obstacles to capitalistic development, and failed to create the bourgeois infrastructure that would have insured rapid capitalistic development. And, their argument goes, by failing to provide a "bourgeois democratic" political structure, general educational opportunities, freedom of movement, and the like, the government held back the development of industrial capitalism with one hand while promoting it with the other.[115]

There would seem to be a good deal of truth in this Marxist view, particularly as it related to the years preceding 1905 and to the older generation of the Moscow business elite. But whether they would indeed have been better off in the long run had they engaged in political opposition to the autocracy is one of history's unanswerable questions. As it happened, they accepted the government's prohibition of their engaging in political activity and would never have dreamed of creating political opposition lest it jeopardize their privileged relationship with the government and thereby do harm to what they perceived as their own best economic interests. Certainly, they were in a far better position than the preceding generations of businessmen, in that they had gained some influence in governmental circles. Dedicated to preserving what had been gained, they entertained no thought of further changes in the system. Whether in the municipal or the national arena, they held themselves aloof from political and social questions and through their indifference became a passive pillar of support for the autocracy. The awakening of political interests and political opposition among the Moscow business elite had to await the emergence of a younger and more daring generation.

CHAPTER 5

THE YOUNGER GENERATION OF THE 1890s

BY the early 1890s, observers of the Moscow scene had already begun to discern the emergence within Moscow's business elite of a younger generation, sometimes called simply the *molodoe kupechestvo*. While feuilletonists might debate whether the new generation was better or worse than its elders, its members were recognized as being unquestionably different, and their points of dissimilarity with the older generation became increasingly obvious as the years passed. Where the older generation had produced dedicated philanthropists, this new generation was, if not indifferent, at least much more casual in its approach to charitable activities. Although continuing to bring forth notable patrons and collectors, the new generation also gave birth to innumerable painters, sculptors, actors, directors, and writers, as well as politicians and members of the liberal professions. The *molodoe kupechestvo* was rich in men and women of independent talent who were more concerned with making personal contributions to art, science, or politics than with supporting the talents of others. Where the older generation had tended to think in terms of duty, responsibility, and service to society, this younger generation was much more individualistic, more dedicated to the pursuit of individual interests and the development of individual talents than to furtherance of the public good.

In addition, the younger generation also continued to produce dynamic industrialists and merchants, who were in some respects far more conscious of themselves as businessmen than their fathers had been and more aware of the importance of the business community in the Russian state and Russian society. Overcoming the traditional political indifference of the *kupechestvo*, they actively sought political influence and political power for their *soslovie*. If their approach to political and social questions remained somewhat narrow, based above all on economic considerations, they were nonetheless drawn into the political drama of 1905 and thereafter remained prominent figures on the Russian political stage.

Perhaps the most remarkable family of the Moscow business elite in this generation was the Riabushinskiis, whose achievements well illustrate the broad range of activity of their generation. The Riabushinskii brothers were among the most imaginative and innovative businessmen in Moscow in the early twentieth century, but they excelled in many other fields as well.[1] Pavel Pavlovich, the eldest brother and recognized leader of the family's business and political activities, emerged as one of the most outstanding political figures of the Moscow business community after 1905 and was a member of the State Council, an important figure in the creation of the Progressive party in 1911, and spokesman for the left-leaning liberals among Moscow businessmen. In addition to his political activities, P. P. Riabushinskii played an influential role in both old and new organizations of businessmen. He became a member of the Moscow Exchange Committee in 1905 and was its president from 1915 until its demise after the October revolution, while at the same time serving as president of a new organization of cotton textile manufacturers of the Moscow region. In 1917 he was a founder of the new All-Russian Union of Industry and Trade. Finally, Riabushinskii also published the newspaper *Utro Rossii*, which preached the legitimate right of the *kupechestvo* to a major role—if not *the* major role—in national affairs.[2]

Among Pavel Pavlovich's brothers, the most renowned was Dmitrii Pavlovich Riabushinskii, who took little part in the family business but who established the first aerodynamics laboratory in Russia and achieved a solid reputation as a scientist and scholar both in Russia and, after 1917, in France.[3] Another brother, Fedor Pavlovich, became fascinated with Siberia early in his life, built up a large library on the region, and sponsored an important scientific expedition to Kamchatka.[4] Nikolai Pavlovich was an amateur painter and aesthete, the publisher of *Zolotoe runo*, a magazine dedicated to new movements in the arts.[5] Mikhail was a collector of paintings, while Stepan assembled a magnificent collection of icons.[6] Vladimir Pavlovich, like his eldest brother, was very active in politics; he also shared Stepan's interest in icons and after 1917 created in France a society to promote the appreciation of Russian icons in Western Europe.[7] As a whole, the Riabushinskiis were also noteworthy for their patronage of Moscow's most innovative architects. Their new residences and office buildings were outstanding examples of contemporary styles of architecture and interior decoration. Most notable, and most controversial, was Nikolai Pavlovich's fanciful dacha, known as the Black Swan, in Petrovskii Park. It represented an extreme variation of the so-called modern or decadent style associated with the Art Nouveau period.[8]

The vocations and avocations of the Riabushinskii brothers and other

members of their generation represented in most cases a natural development stemming from the surroundings in which they grew to maturity
and the type of upbringing they had received from their parents. For the
most part, they passed the years of their childhood and adolescence not
in the Zamoskvoreche or Rogozhskoe cemetery districts but in fashionable
sections of town where wealthy and respected businessmen now lived side
by side with nobles and members of the intelligentsia. As patrons and
collectors, philanthropists and public figures, many of their parents had
achieved a wide acquaintance in all sectors of educated society, and to
their homes came notable personages in the cultural and social life of
Moscow. Their parents were, in the words of one member of the younger
generation, "people who had already crossed the threshold of culture, and
who although they did not receive the benefits of higher education . . .
still made much of culture their own."[9] The children of these parents
grew up in homes in which art and music, philanthropy and public affairs
frequently received more attention than business.

Vera Pavlovna Ziloti, the daughter of P. M. Tretiakov, has described
in her memoirs the cultivated atmosphere which surrounded her and
many members of her generation during their formative years. The circle
in which the Tretiakov family moved included not only other wealthy
and cultured families of the business elite but, above all, innumerable
artists, who were drawn to Tretiakov not simply by his patronage but by
his deep love for Russian art. Such luminaries of Russian painting as I. E.
Repin, V. D. Polenov, V. M. Vasnetsov, V. V. Vereshchagin, V. G.
Serov, and V. I. Surikov were constantly in the Tretiakov home, and
many of them became close friends of the family. The ties binding the
Tretiakovs to the world of art were further strengthened when Vera's
aunt married the architect A. S. Kaminskii, builder of the Tretiakov
gallery, and her younger sister Liubov married a painter, N. N. Grit-
senko. In addition to her associations with numerous artists, Vera met the
leading figures of Moscow's musical world—and eventually married one
of them—through regular attendance at concerts and other musical events
and through her uncle Sergei, a leading musical patron. The Tretiakovs
became particularly good friends with the composer P. I. Tchaikovsky as
a result of his brother's marriage to Vera's cousin.

Vera's father was also well acquainted with many Moscow intellectuals
and writers, some of whom occasionally visited the Tretiakov home. Like
many businessmen of his generation, P. M. Tretiakov was on good terms
with Moscow's leading Slavophiles, who often came to visit with their
families. An especially frequent visitor was the Slavophile Iu. F. Samarin,
whose sister lived across the street from the Tretiakovs. I. S. Turgenev
came occasionally, and Tretiakov and his wife so admired this writer that
they made a special trip to see him in Paris shortly before his death.

Tretiakov often called on L. N. Tolstoi when he was in Moscow, and the two men argued over their different philosophies of life. On a number of occasions Tolstoi and his daughter had tea with the Tretiakov family.

Business intruded very little into the world of Vera Tretiakova's childhood. Conversations at the family dinner table, where guests were usually present, revolved chiefly around art, music, and literature, while business was rarely mentioned. P. M. Tretiakov continued the old practice of maintaining an office in his home, where he and several employees worked long hours. But his daughters had little idea what went on behind the closed doors of the office and showed little interest in it. Vera visited the Tretiakov factory in Kostroma province only once in her life, found it a strange and terrible place, and evidently gave no more thought to the source of the family income. Perhaps if she had been a son rather than a daughter, the business world might have played a larger role in her upbringing. But even Nikolai Sergeevich Tretiakov, the sole male heir to the Tretiakov business in this generation, was evidently more influenced by the atmosphere of art and culture typical of Tretiakov home life than by the professional concerns of his father and uncle. The younger Tretiakov became an indifferent businessman but a passionate painter, a student of the Moscow School of Painting, Drawing and Architecture.[10]

Although the Tretiakovs' contacts among artists and intellectuals were perhaps broader than those of most families of the elite, the cultured atmosphere of the Tretiakov home was hardly unique. The son of parents who led a somewhat secluded life, Konstantin Sergeevich Alekseev nonetheless was exposed to similar influences from his youngest years—he appeared in his first amateur theatrical at the age of two or three and began regular attendance at the Italian opera when he was only six years old.[11] Alekseev has given a rather humorous description of his family life, writing that

in order to keep us children near to the home hearth, our parents listened willingly to all our demands. Thanks to this, our house often changed its physiognomy in accordance with what was going on there at any given time. For instance, my father, who was well known as a philanthropist, founded a dispensary for the peasants. My oldest sister fell in love with one of the doctors in the dispensary and the entire house began to manifest an extraordinary interest in medicine. Sick people came from all the corners of the earth and all the comrades of my brother-in-law would gather for interminable consultations.

Soon my second sister fell in love with a neighbor, a young German merchant. Everybody in the house began speaking German and the house itself became filled with foreigners. We youngsters tried to dress in European fashion, and all who were able grew wide beards and changed the manner of combing their hair.

But then my oldest brother fell in love with the daughter of a simple Russian merchant who wore long Russian boots, and the entire house became a model of simplicity. The samovar never left the table; all of us drank too much tea; we forced ourselves to go regularly to church; we arranged solemn services, invited the best church choirs and sang early mass in chorus ourselves. Then my third sister fell in love with an expert bicyclist, and all of us donned woolen stockings, short trousers, bought bicycles and learned to ride.

At last my fourth sister fell in love with an opera singer, and the entire house began to sing. Many of the famous singers of that time were guests in our house and especially on our estate.[12]

Raised in such a receptive atmosphere, the Alekseev sons and daughters could not help but grow up with a broader spectrum of possible careers and avocations before their eyes than had been the case with their parents, who had grown to maturity within the still largely closed merchant culture. But whatever the current enthusiasm of the moment in the Alekseev household, the life of the family always revolved around their amateur theatricals, performed in a theater specially built on their estate.[13] In the end, the theater exercised a greater fascination over the young Alekseevs than medicine or opera or bicycling. The stage of the Alekseev family theater eventually gave to the world the author of the above lines, the famed director and actor better known under his stage name of Stanislavsky, as well as a number of other capable actors and actresses, and a producer and a director, all from among Alekseev-Stanislavsky's nine brothers and sisters.[14]

If the cultured and receptive atmosphere existing within the family circle helped to shape the men and women who made up this generation, their education also suggested new interests, while at the same time providing them with the knowledge and skills requisite for the pursuit of these interests. In spite of their own limited formal education, the parents of this generation displayed a profound belief in the value of education for their children and tried to give them every educational opportunity.[15] As a result, the male members of the younger generation attended private or public gymnasia, and many of them continued their studies at both Russian and foreign universities or in specialized types of higher educational institutions. The old practice of educating wealthy merchant sons at home almost entirely disappeared in this generation, partly because the regulations governing the new universal military conscription permitted shorter terms of service to graduates of formal educational institutions.[16]

Of the sons who received higher education, some chose to study in fields related to their business activities. A. I. Konovalov, for instance, received a higher technical education in Mulhouse, in the heart of the Alsatian textile industry.[17] Savva Morozov studied chemistry both in Russia and Western Europe.[18] Many others studied in the law faculty of Moscow University, which was a suitable preparation for both business and non-business careers. N. S. Tretiakov earned a law degree before going on to study painting, and N. N. Abrikosov, later a director of the Abrikosov firm, also graduated in law.[19] However, not a few law graduates pursued careers or interests outside the field of business. B. I. Abrikosov became a lawyer, while his brother D. I. Abrikosov pursued a career in the diplomatic service.[20] N. I. Guchkov, another law graduate, became a professional public servant and politician, serving as mayor of Moscow from 1905 to 1912 and taking an active part in the affairs of the Octobrist party.[21] Sergei Morozov, Savva's brother, had a degree in law but after leaving the university became an amateur painter, a patron of the arts, and a dedicated advocate of the preservation of *kustar* industries.[22]

Some members of the younger generation decided against a business career before embarking on their higher education and concentrated their studies in fields with no conceivable relation to business. A. I. Abrikosov studied medicine at Moscow University and made a brilliant career as a physician and scientist under both the Imperial and Soviet regimes.[23] A. M. Remizov, whose mother was a Naidenov, studied natural sciences at Moscow University, although he later turned into a prolific writer whose works were well known in Russia before 1917 and in the Russian emigration after 1917.[24] Two students at the School of Painting, Drawing and Architecture were M. A. Mamontov, who became an artist, and A. S. Mamontov, whose planned career as an architect was cut short by his death at an early age.[25] F. I. Guchkov was a graduate of Moscow's Aleksandrovskoe Military School and pursued a career as a professional army officer.[26] His brother A. I. Guchkov, later a founder of the Octobrist party and minister of defense for a brief period in the Provisional Government, studied history at Moscow University, where he participated in P. G. Vinogradov's history seminars along with P. N. Miliukov, one of his future political opponents. Guchkov also studied at several German universities and returned to Moscow with something of a reputation both as a scholar and as a duelist.[27]

While the men of this generation generally passed through formal educational institutions, the women were more likely to be educated at home by private governesses and tutors. A. I. Abrikosova, later a convert to Roman Catholicism and martyr to her religion under the Soviet regime, graduated from a Moscow gymnasium and continued her studies at Cambridge University, but she appears to have been exceptional in the extent of her formal education.[28] Probably more typical was Vera Tretiakova, who was given an excellent private education. Among her teachers were some outstanding pedagogues, such as A. N. Ostrovskaia, sister of the dramatist. Professors from various Moscow institutions gave Tretiakova periodic examinations before her teachers and parents, and in later years, when she had outgrown her tutors, a number of Moscow professors gave her private lessons.[29] Likewise, N. K. Ushkova, who became the wife of the famous orchestral conductor S. A. Koussevitsky, received a private education. She first studied with tutors who taught her history, literature, three foreign languages, mathematics, music, and religion. Later she was put into the hands of E. F. Kreiman, daughter of the director of one of Moscow's most renowned private gymnasia. Together they traveled extensively abroad and lived for several months in Paris, where Ushkova attended the lectures of M. M. Kovalevskii and other notable Russian scholars living in the French capital.[30]

Other daughters of this generation who showed special talents or interests were given the appropriate special education. M. K. Morozova (born Mamontova) was a talented amateur pianist who took lessons from a number of Moscow's outstanding musicians, including the composer A. N. Scriabin.[31] E. A. Karzinkina studied with the painter V. D. Polenov at the School of Painting, Drawing and Architecture and later continued her artistic education in Paris.[32] M. V. Iakunchikova, who early revealed great artistic talent, was tutored by several notable painters and later studied at the School of Painting. She became in her time a very well known artist, though her career was cut tragically short by her death from tuberculosis at the age of thirty-two.[33]

As a result of their education and upbringing, this younger generation of the business elite displayed a tremendous variety of amateur and professional talent in the arts and sciences, in politics and the professions. Much less impressive, however, was their record as patrons and philanthropists, and their apparent failure to live up to the standards set by their parents' generation in this respect occasionally called forth hostile comment. For example, one journalist who was a keen observer of the Moscow scene wrote early in the 1890s that this *molodoe kupechestvo* compared poorly with the older generation, especially in regard to patronage of the arts and sciences. After praising the efforts of the older generation to promote the development of Russian culture, he noted that "the young generation of the *kupechestvo*, which is acquiring civilization and beginning to live in the 'English' manner, looks on patronage as something almost shameful, something even almost sinful for themselves, the young merchant millionaires." According to him, the younger generation was wont to say that "they have already swindled our fathers enough."[34]

Perhaps this journalist might have somewhat softened his opinion in later years, as members of the younger generation gradually became more active as patrons. It would certainly be erroneous to leave the impression that the *molodoe kupechestvo* produced no patrons whatsoever. Savva Morozov was the mainstay of Stanislavsky's Art Theater,[35] and his brother Sergei extended his personal patronage to the artist I. I. Levitan, while at the same time spending a considerable amount of money for the encouragement of *kustar* industries and the establishment of the Kustar Museum in Moscow.[36] The patronage of several of the Riabushinskiis has already been mentioned. And like the Riabushinskii brothers, many members of this generation were enthusiastic clients of Moscow's architects. Some also assembled small collections of paintings, one side effect of which was to support Russian artists.[37] Thus, the younger generation was not entirely without its patrons, but it is indisputable that it contained no patrons or collectors of the stature of P. M. Tretiakov, K. T. Soldatenkov, Savva Mamontov, and P. I. Shchukin, for whom patronage and collecting had become, in effect, a way of life. Instead of making careers out of patronage, the younger generation more typically sought to become artists themselves.

Moreover, like Savva Mamontov before them, the patrons of the younger generation were rarely content to restrict themselves to mere financial support of certain artists or projects but sought a deeper involvement. Sergei Morozov subsidized Russian painting but at the same time became an amateur painter himself. Savva Morozov did not simply hand money over to Stanislavsky but became intimately involved in the operation of the Art Theater. As Stanislavsky recalled:

> On coming to know better all the good qualities of Morozov, we brought him nearer to the purely artistic side of the Theatre. And this was done not because he controlled the financial nerves of the Theatre, but because he evinced much taste and understanding in the fields of literature and artistic creativeness. Problems of the repertoire, of the distribution of roles, of the examination of the faults of the performance and their production were solved with the aid of Morozov, who proved himself a useful worker in this field also.[38]

In addition, Morozov took charge of certain technical facets of the theater. Again, as Stanislavsky remembered,

> he undertook the supervision of the electrical lighting of the stage and the auditorium. . . . As soon as his family would leave for the country, he changed the parlor of his home into a laboratory for his scenic experiments and the trials of various systems and methods of electrical light were made there prefatory to their introduction into the Theatre. The great bathroom of the mansion was turned into a chemical laboratory in which were prepared lacquers of various tones and colors for the painting of electric bulbs and glass, so that more artistic tones of stage lighting could be achieved. Trials of all sorts of electric effects which demanded a space were made in the large garden that surrounded the house. Morozov was not afraid of hard work, and dressed in working apparel, labored side by side with the electricians and smiths, astounding specialists with his

knowledge of electricity. With the beginning of the season Morozov would enter on his duties as the supervisor of the lighting in the Theatre, and he placed his department on a very high footing.[39]

Stanislavsky attributed Morozov's active participation in the Art Theater to the fact that he was a "born artist," but it seems clear that Morozov's education had prepared him to play a role in the theater which most of the businessmen-patrons of the preceding generation could not have sustained, for lack of knowledge and skills.

In regard to philanthropy, there is little evidence concerning the charitable contributions of the younger generation, and this very lack of evidence would incline one to believe that they were nowhere nearly so active as philanthropists as their elders had been. Certainly, almost all the major charitable institutions in Moscow bearing the names of Moscow business dynasties were the creations of the older generation. It seems likely, from what slender evidence is available in published sources, that the new generation contributed to the support of various charities and causes, but on a smaller scale than the older generation. And with very few exceptions, they showed little interest in the organization of major new charitable institutions such as were frequently the personal creations of members of the older generation.

It might be added, however, that the industrialists of this younger generation in many cases accomplished a great deal more than their fathers in the creation of "philanthropical" institutions for the benefit of their own employees. Perhaps in part reacting to occasional criticism of industrialists who gave millions to hospitals and art galleries but neglected the most pressing needs of their own workers, many members of this generation evidently decided that charity should begin at one's own factory. As a result, in many industrial establishments owned by Moscow dynasties, the major development of schools, hospitals, and various amenities for factory workers occurred after the transition of management from the older to the younger generation. The most impressive record compiled by any member of the Moscow elite in the field of factory philanthropy belonged to a member of the younger generation, A. I. Konovalov. The Konovalov family had been considered the most enlightened of employers for many decades, but Aleksandr Ivanovich far outdid his predecessors in bettering the position of his workers.[40] He assumed leadership of the family industrial enterprises in 1897 and thereafter introduced improvement upon improvement. In 1900 he instituted a nine-hour day, in addition to opening a library and reading room. In later years Konovalov enlarged and reorganized the factory school, built a new and elegant hospital with 100 beds, and created a nursery school and a home for chronically ill and aged workers. He also superintended the building of 120 small, individual dwellings and made them available for purchase by workers, thus removing at least some of them from the factory barracks. In addition, he sponsored the organization of a consumers' cooperative for workers and other factory employees and created a scholarship fund for children of office personnel.[41]

Such improvements benefiting the factory workers and other employees were not, of course, undertaken entirely for altruistic reasons but also helped to attract workers to the factory and to maintain discipline and peace among the factory population. Some who criticized members of this generation for their absorption in their individual concerns and failure to serve the public good might well have noted that it was typical of them to undertake their major "philanthropical" effort in the area that would bring them the greatest personal benefits. In any case, except for these semi-philanthropical activities at their factories, members of the younger generation showed little desire to be known as great philanthropists. They preferred to rest their reputations on other activities; and considering their numerous other accomplishments, their philanthropical undertakings, however large or small, indeed read as merely incidental footnotes to their biographies. The fact that Savva Morozov founded a maternity home in Moscow is almost inconsequential in comparison with his innumerable other achievements, whereas for many members of the older generation, such an undertaking might well have been one of the major accomplishments of their lives.

In addition to their relatively poor showing as patrons and philanthropists, the *molodoe kupechestvo* were occasionally criticized before 1905 for their failure to live up to the record of the older generation in terms of public service through participation in Moscow's public affairs. One *Novoe vremia* feuilletonist, in a bitter diatribe against Moscow's younger businessmen, argued that they showed "scornful indifference" toward everything except their business and financial interests and had lost the desire to serve society that had typified the older generation. He commented that

> the generation of the Moscow *kupechestvo* which grew to adulthood in the sixties and seventies stood in this respect much higher. The people who belonged to it, whether well or badly, all the same served their town and their *soslovie* both in the city duma and in *soslovie* institutions. It is impossible to say that this service was especially productive and successful, but all the same it is better than complete indifference to public affairs.[42]

Again, it would be wrong to give the impression that no members of the younger generation served in the duma or occupied other positions of trust in either municipal or private institutions. But as Stanislavsky has testified, this younger generation was as a whole undoubtedly much less interested than the preceding one in occupying positions of public responsibility. Recalling his own experiences at the time that he reached young adulthood, Stanislavsky wrote:

"In order to create a position for oneself," my uncle and cousin told me, "it is necessary for you to occupy yourself with some sort of social work. You must become the honorary president of some school or of a poorhouse, or a member of the Duma." And from that time on my sufferings began.

I went to some sort of meetings and tried to look imposing and important. I feigned interest in the question of what kind of waists or bonnets were made for the old women in the poorhouse and in the progress made by my school. . . . It seems that I played the part very well[,] for every charitable institution in the city began to ask for my services. I never had time to attend to everything, I became tired, and my soul was filled with coldness and sourness and a feeling that I was engaged in evil work. I was not doing my own work, and I could find no satisfaction in what I was doing. I was making a career of which I stood in no need whatsoever.

Stanislavsky's dilemma was finally resolved when he was made a director of the Musical Society and of the conservatory and was able to resign his other public positions on the plea of lack of time. He was satisfied with this solution and thought it "better to occupy myself with a strange affair in artistic circles among interesting people than in poorhouses and schools which were not only alien to me, but unbearable."[43]

Stanislavsky's attitudes toward public work were probably fairly typical of the attitudes of his generation. As his statement makes clear, members of this generation felt little pressure to make "careers" for themselves in public service positions which held for them little intrinsic interest. Nonetheless, a feeling of responsibility to serve the public interest was not entirely absent, as shown by the fact that Stanislavsky believed he was obliged to hold some public position, whatever it might be. Moreover, Stanislavsky would later prove that he was not entirely lacking in the desire to contribute toward social betterment when he became one of the leaders of a group dedicated to the creation of theaters for the *narod*.[44] But for him, as for so many members of his generation, participation in Moscow public affairs and the desire to serve society was hardly the major concern that it had been for many of the older generation. Like their patronage and their philanthropy, the contributions of the younger generation to public affairs in most cases were a minor part of their lives.

Novoe vremia's feuilletonist attributed the lessening of the desire to serve their fellow citizens among the younger generation of the Moscow business community partly to the nature of the times. While the older generation, he noted, was much influenced by the enthusiasm for social betterment that had accompanied the era of the Great Reforms, the younger generation had come to maturity in a relatively quiet period of public life, when repression and reaction from above helped to produce apathy and resignation below. "The present position of public activity in the Moscow *kupechestvo*," he wrote, "is only one of many signs of the period of social stagnation that we are living through."[45]

Undoubtedly there was considerable truth in this generalization. Certainly few members of the younger generation exhibited any of the vague populist sympathies typical of many of their elders. Indeed, it is difficult to avoid the impression that the older generation had, generally speaking, a more intimate understanding of the poverty and misery that afflicted the Russian masses and a more genuine sympathy with their plight than did their sons and daughters. In part, their greater sympathy may have stemmed from the intellectual influences of the 1860s and 1870s, but it may also be that greater proximity to their own families' humble origins influenced them in this direction. Many of the members of the older generation were themselves the sons and daughters of former peasants. In most cases they had been raised in more modest circumstances than their own offspring and had been exposed more directly to poverty and suffering.

In any case, the younger generation exhibited a certain snobbishness and a degree of alienation from the life of the popular masses which was not so noticeable in their parents. It is almost inconceivable that any member of the older generation would have found (or at least admitted to finding) poorhouses and schools "unbearable," as did Stanislavsky. Moreover, D. I. Abrikosov's memoirs serve as a testament to the isolation of the younger generation of the business elite from the life of the Russian masses. Abrikosov, for instance, recalled walking home from school along "dark, crooked streets, the sight of which made me miserable." In particular, he "hated one corner, where a cheap eating place for droshky drivers was situated. When we passed it, the door would usually open to admit some new arrival and the smoke of cheap tobacco and the smell of cabbage soup would fill the whole street. It was the real Russia"—a Russia with which Abrikosov had little contact.[46] On another occasion, he traveled with his aunt and uncle to Perm, whence his ancestors had come a century ago. Abrikosov found the scenes of provincial life to which he was for the first time exposed quite revolting. "With what pleasure I returned to The Oaks [the family estate]," he remembered. There "everything was so clean and cultured."[47]

Growing up in the lap of luxury, isolated in their palatial mansions from the masses of the population, separated from the popular culture by their own cultural and educational achievements, the younger generation appears to have lost contact to a large degree with the simple realities of everyday life for the vast majority of the Russian people. And this separation from the life of average Russians may in part help to explain the attenuated enthusiasm for public service of any sort observable in the younger generation. In their parents, it would seem that perhaps a more intimate knowledge of popular life combined with the idea of service to the people so prevalent in the 1860s and 1870s to help produce their dedication to the idea of public service, which in turn caused them to endow so many schools, hospitals, almshouses, and other charitable institutions of the type so unbearable to Stanislavsky and to take an active interest in the work of Moscow's municipal government. Whatever the causes, it is clear that the younger generation found much less inspiration in the ideal of service than did their parents. This ideal, which figured prominently in the memoirs of the older generation, was notably absent in those of the younger generation. And insofar as they engaged in philanthropy or public service work, the *molodoe kupechestvo* gave the impression that they did so chiefly because it was expected of them, or out of a sense of *richesse oblige*.

Only in regard to patronage of the arts and sciences does one find some of the same enthusiasm and dedication in certain members of the younger generation such as was typical of many of their elders in their attitudes not only toward patronage but toward philanthropy and public service as well. Undoubtedly, it was a field much more suited to the new generation, with its aesthetic tastes and artistic and intellectual interests. Through patronage they could indulge these interests and pursue their own individual bents. And much the same might be said of the few representatives of the younger generation who participated in municipal government before 1905. The Guchkov brothers, very active members of the city duma, obviously found participation in Moscow public affairs attractive not as a fulfillment of any desire to serve but rather as a means of furthering their own political ambitions.

An additional factor that may help to explain this generation's decreased interest in philanthropy, public service, and, to a lesser degree, patronage, was perhaps the fact that, unlike their parents, they had almost from birth possessed a sense of social security and did not feel the pressure that many of their elders had felt to win respect and acceptance in Moscow society. The move from Zamoskvoreche to Tverskaia had already been made, and in spite of continuing prejudices against merchants and industrialists as a group, the cultured families of the business elite, thanks to the efforts of the older generation, had gained recognition as a legitimate part of Moscow educated society. The younger generation, attending the same schools as representatives of the nobility and intelligentsia and finding friends among members of these groups, still, to be sure, faced certain social barriers, but none to compare with those confronting members of the *kupechestvo* several decades earlier. With their cultured upbringing and superior education, the younger generation easily moved into and improved upon the social positions already achieved by their parents. Undoubtedly many of them felt as Stanislavsky did when he wrote:

> The majority of our generation of rich people received a good education and were acquainted with world literature. We were taught many languages, we traveled very extensively, and in a word we were plunged into the very heart of the maelstrom of culture. Having become equal in education to the nobles and aristocrats, class distinctions disappeared as if of themselves. Common political and social work brought together all cultured people and made of them the Russian "intelligentsia."[48]

Stanislavsky's sense of being an integral part of the intelligentsia appears to have been shared by many of his contemporaries among the families of the business elite. Certainly, those men and women who took up careers in the arts and sciences or in the professions had a right to consider themselves members of the Russian intelligentsia, but even many of those who remained primarily businessmen tended to regard themselves as being, in some sense, *intelligenty*. For instance, Buryshkin wrote of himself and an associate, also a businessman, that "properly speaking, we both were more *intelligenty* than representatives of the class of 'exploiters.' "[49] Although he did not elaborate, Buryshkin seems to have based his claim to recognition as an *intelligent* chiefly on his educational and cultural achievements and on his liberal politics. In any case, the younger generation showed every evidence of feeling quite at home in the world of cultured people and mixed easily with representatives of the Moscow intelligentsia.

Close friendships and marriages between intellectuals and members of elite business families were indeed common in this generation, but it is nonetheless apparent that certain barriers still remained between the two groups and that members of the intelligentsia were wary of accepting representatives of the business world as full-fledged *intelligenty*. Interesting in this respect are the comments of Vladimir Nemirovich-Danchenko concerning the representatives of the younger generation of businessmen with whom he was acquainted, chiefly through the Art Theater. While he had few kind words to say for the patrons of the older generation of the business elite, generally regarding them as seeking only fame and uncomprehending of true art, Nemirovich was usually much more generous in his evaluation of his acquaintances among the younger generation. He did not fault them for cultural or intellectual reasons but repeatedly expressed admiration for their "good taste." He was particularly fond of the young Tarasov, an aesthete and devotee of the Art Theater, of whom Nemirovich recalled: "He was quite himself: simple, candid, tender—yes, even tender—but bold; he approached everything with taste, giving the impression that there was nothing he feared so much as vulgarity."[50] Good taste was also a characteristic that drew Nemirovich to the Alekseev family and to Savva Morozov, whom Nemirovich complimented on knowing "the good taste and value of that simplicity which is more costly than luxury."[51]

Nonetheless, Nemirovich noted certain qualities in his acquaintances among the "*kupecheskaia* intelligentsia" which continued to set them apart from the true Russian *intelligent*. Although he became quite friendly with Savva Morozov and admired him for his intelligence and his broad knowledge of literature, Nemirovich also noted in Morozov certain offensive "mercantile" traits. "His mind," Nemirovich wrote, "was always preoccupied with some sort of mathematical and psychological calculation. The expression 'a merchant's shrewdness' fitted him admirably." In addition, Nemirovich reacted negatively to the sense of power Morozov radiated. His eyes, Nemirovich claimed, "gleamed with ruthlessness, with the consciousness of capitalistic might." And Morozov, he believed, "by no means exaggerated when he said of himself: 'If anyone should stand in my way, I would ride right over him without blinking.' "[52] Needless to say, ruthlessness and calculation were not among the qualities most admired by Russian intellectuals. And while Nemirovich's perception of Morozov was perhaps somewhat distorted by his admitted general dislike of capitalists, his attribution of these qualities to Morozov stood, nonetheless, as a barrier to acceptance of him as a fellow and an equal.

While impressing Nemirovich with certain repugnant qualities, Savva Morozov at the same time, through his relationship with the writer Maxim Gorky, participated in what was perhaps the closest of all friendships established between any member of the business elite's younger generation and a representative of the intelligentsia. Recalling Morozov many years later, Gorky wrote of him simply: "He was a good friend, a man close to my heart, I loved him very much."[53] While greatly admiring Morozov for his broad education and knowledge, Gorky was undoubtedly drawn to him chiefly by a deep intellectual and emotional sympathy. Baring his soul to Gorky, as he had not to Nemirovich, Morozov shared with the writer his own growing revulsion against the existing social and economic system and his increasing attraction to Marxism in general and Bolshevism in particular. As is clear from his recollections of their friendship, Gorky immediately understood the paradoxical and difficult nature of Morozov's position as, on the one hand, a leading representative of Russian capitalism—a position he could never bring himself to renounce—and, on the other hand, as a secret "traitor to his class," a man increasingly troubled by the social and economic consequences of his actions as a capitalist. Fascinated by this complex personality, sympathetic to the inner conflicts of this troubled soul (conflicts which were chiefly responsible for Morozov's suicide in 1905), Gorky established with this "class enemy" a friendship of rare warmth and mutual understanding.

The extremely close relationship between these two men was perhaps the only friendship in which a perfect understanding was achieved between a businessman and an *intelligent*, and in conjunction with Nemirovich's comments, it helps to throw light upon what was probably the major factor in maintaining a certain seemingly unbridgeable distance between businessmen and intellectuals. If many of their parents had been kept apart from the intelligentsia by reason of their deficient educations, members of the younger generation did not usually suffer from the same deficiency and, as is clear from the comments of both Nemirovich and Gorky, could even evoke a certain admiration from intellectuals for their educational and cultural attainments. What kept the younger generation still at a distance from the intelligentsia was not cultural deficiencies but certain basic differences in experiences and attitudes.

Most Russian intellectuals certainly brought to their relationships with businessmen a deep-seated prejudice against capitalists, a prejudice bound to color their relations with representatives of Russian capitalism, no matter how much they may have liked certain individual businessmen. But such prejudices may well have been reinforced by certain attitudes exhibited by their businessmen-friends on subjects close to the heart of every Russian *intelligent*. Nemirovich's comments about Stanislavsky are particularly revealing in this respect. He wrote of his friend and colleague that Stanislavsky

> had always lived in Moscow. As a Moscow manufacturer, he possessed an immense fund of impressions of the life of the mercantile class. Later he began to associate with the artistic world, again that of Moscow. . . . Of the immense mass, however, of the Russian provincial intelligentsia and semi-intelligentsia, of all that many-millioned stratum of Russian life which served as material for Chekhov's productions, he knew nothing. Equally alien to him were their perturbations, their tears, envies, grudges, quarrels, all that which makes up life in the provinces. And of the meaning of need, of earning one's livelihood, he was also ignorant.[54]

As a result of his limited experiences and his limited understanding of the existence of ordinary Russians, Stanislavsky, according to Nemirovich, found it difficult to appreciate the "workaday realities" of Chekhov's plays, realities which were familiar to and engaged the immediate sympathy of the "true" *intelligent*, responsive to the *narod*, to its needs and sufferings. In Stanislavsky, as in other members of the elite's younger generation, it would appear that separation from and, frequently, indifference toward the masses of the Russian people were qualities antipathetical to the intelligentsia and stood as continuing barriers between businessmen and *intelligenty*. Only in rare cases, such as the friendship between Morozov and Gorky, could this basic difference in mentality be completely overcome.

But whatever the barriers still standing between businessmen and intellectuals, or businessmen and nobles, most members of the younger generation certainly shared Stanislavsky's sense of social acceptance and moved with ease in all but the most exalted circle of Moscow society. Thus, insofar as the desire for social respect and prestige was a factor in motivating the philanthropy, patronage, and public service of the older generation, this motive was at least greatly weakened in the younger generation, which perhaps helps to explain their more casual attitude toward all forms of public service. As Stanislavsky commented, a "career" in public service positions was a "career" for which they had no need.

Finally, an additional reason for the younger generation's lesser enthusiasm for good works may simply have been that they had more confidence and pride in themselves as businessmen than did the older generation. If the older generation had more or less accepted society's scorn for them as businessmen and had sought respect chiefly as philanthropists and patrons raher than as businessmen, the younger generation expected to be appreciated for its business achievements. This change of attitude called forth hostile comments in the press, with one feuilletonist noting of the older generation: "No one knew very much about the affairs and enterprises of these people, their dividends or losses. They knew and spoke about what pictures P. M. [Tretiakov] bought, and what Alekseev said and did in the duma, but where their factories were, what was made at their factories, very few knew and no one was interested." Now, he went on to complain, instead of being known for their good works as philanthropists and patrons, the younger generation, for whom the ruble constituted "the whole content and·meaning of their life," made sure that "all Moscow" knew what sort of enterprises they operated, the size of their dividends, how much they were worth.[55] Thus, it may be that at least some members of the younger generation, while continuing to engage in philanthropy and patronage simply because it was expected of them, felt no need to establish reputations as great philanthropists, patrons, or collectors simply because they expected to be accorded social respect on the basis of their position in the business world.

One of the most interesting figures of this generation, who well illustrates some of the major differences between the "fathers" and the "sons" (or, in this case, between "mothers" and "sons") was Mikhail Abramovich Morozov, son of the redoubtable Varvara Morozova. Morozov first achieved fame (actually, notoriety) as the model for the leading character in A. I. Sumbatov's play *Dzhentlmen*. In the play, the "gentleman" in question was a millionaire who sought to win public recognition through literature but who, for the most part, succeeded only in making a fool of himself. Like the character in Sumbatov's drama, Morozov tried his hand at literature, producing several historical works,[56] a series of travel letters, and articles on various subjects which he published in journals and newspapers under the pen name of Mikhail Iurev. Whether Morozov's literary output was motivated by a desire for fame, as Sumbatov saw it, or whether he was simply possessed by an overwhelming desire to express himself is difficult to determine, but it seems likely that Sumbatov's interpretation had some merit. Certainly, Morozov's travel letters and essays reveal only mediocre literary talent, while his historical works read like seminar papers left over from his student days at Moscow University and undoubtedly would never have been published if their author had not been a millionaire.

But whether Morozov's motive was a desire for fame or an inner urge or, to give him the benefit of the doubt, a combination of both these factors, it is striking that he should have sought fame and self-fulfillment through literary creation. The resulting contrast between Mikhail Abramovich and his mother sums up a major difference between the two generations they represented. Whereas Varvara Morozova, in addition to running the family business, practically made a career out of doing good works—through her innumerable contributions to educational, artistic, and literary undertakings and her support of all sorts of liberal causes— her son and heir devoted himself to literary composition.

This is not to say that Morozov was entirely lacking in the impulse toward philanthropy, patronage, and public service. On the contrary, he compiled one of the most creditable records of any member of his generation in this area and, in fact, was himself very critical of his own generation for its self-absorption and its comparative indifference toward serving the public good.[57] Inspired by the belief that it was his duty to serve, Morozov was a treasurer of the Musical Society, a generous benefactor of the conservatory, a member of the board of the Alexander III Hospital, founder of a home for 100 unfortunates, and a contributor to Moscow University's cancer clinic, which was the collective creation of the Morozov clan. Also, as a *starosta* (elder) of Uspenskii Cathedral, he contributed a considerable amount to its renovation and collected materials for a history of this monument of Russian architecture.[58]

It was an impressive record for a man who died at the age of twenty-six, and in an earlier day, he might well have rested on his laurels as a philanthropist, patron, and public servant. But times had changed, and this new generation of which Morozov was a part seemingly contained within itself an almost irresistible urge toward individual creativity, toward the display of individual talent—an urge to which even its relatively untalented members, like Morozov, could not remain immune. However much truth or fantasy was contained in Sumbatov's caricature of Morozov, the dramatist seems to have grasped an essential feature of the *molodoe kupechestvo*—their desire to develop their unique individual talents and to excel as individuals of talent rather than as contributors to the public good. D. I. Abrikosov expressed this desire very clearly when, recalling his difficulties in deciding what to do with his life, he wrote that "I could always participate in the different industrial and commercial enterprises in which my family was engaged, but I was ambitious and wanted to build my own career rather than follow in a path well trodden by others." Like Morozov a man of no particular talents, Abrikosov fell more or less by chance into a diplomatic career.[59]

Abrikosov was one of the fairly large number of individuals in this generation who entirely gave up personal involvement in the family business. The pursuit of a career in another field, or the pursuit of outside interests, did not necessarily entail retirement from business activity. Stanislavsky, for instance, continued to serve as a director of one of his family's companies and went to his office every day, even after the opening of his Art Theater.[60] Nonetheless, not a few individuals in this generation ended all direct involvement with family business concerns, though they usually continued to receive income from the family enterprises.

Actually, the surprising thing is not that so many members of this generation left the business world altogether but, on the contrary, that so many of them continued active participation in the family business. In some of the Moscow dynasties, this younger generation of the 1890s represented the fourth or fifth generation of the family, and it seems remarkable, especially given the rather high mortality rate of Russian business enterprises, that these families in their third or fourth or fifth generation still continued to carry on their business activity and to produce capable, and sometimes outstanding, businessmen. The only two families who, as noted earlier, completely liquidated their family concerns in this generation were the Guchkovs and the Iakunchikovs, but representatives of both families still remained active in other non-family enterprises. The enterprises headed by most of the other Moscow dynasties continued to flourish, in spite of the fact that their young directors now frequently combined business activity with professional or amateur participation in other fields.

D. I. Abrikosov, apparently judging largely by the experience of his own family, regarded a three-generational cycle as typical of Moscow business dynasties. He wrote that the third generation of a business dynasty was given to "starting independent careers unconnected with commerce or leading a life of leisure, but generally supporting the most extreme movements in art or politics and usually squandering the inheritance received from its hard-working grandfathers and parents." He further noted that "our family passed through this same evolution"[61] and indeed it is true that the third generation of Abrikosovs, most of whom became involved in other fields, allowed the family business to decline and no doubt reduced the size of the family fortune. However, what was true of the Abrikosovs was not necessarily true of other business families. One could point to the Prokhorovs, for instance, a family in which control of the business rested in the hands of the fourth and fifth generations by the turn of the century.[62] The Alekseevs were likewise into their fifth generation by the early twentieth century. Although one branch of the family had long ago been ruined and passed into oblivion, other Alekseevs were carrying on in good order.[63] Not a few families were well into their fourth generation, and of those who had passed through only three generations, one might point to the Riabushinskiis as a refutation of Abrikosov's argument. If two of the Riabushinskii brothers (Dmitrii and Fedor) had no interest in the business, others (particularly Pavel, Vladimir, and Mikhail) were excellent businessmen who, far from squandering their inheritance, increased it many times over. In some of the older families it is true that the third generation was a relatively weak generation in regard to its business talents. But in those cases, interestingly enough, the fourth generation once again produced capable businessmen who repaired the damage done by the incompetence or indifference of their fathers. This pattern held true in the Prokhorov, Tretiakov, and Konovalov families, among others.[64]

Whether any of these dynasties might eventually have matched the Du Ponts' record of twelve generations of businessmen, had it not been for the revolution, is of course impossible to say. But there is no doubt that Moscow's business dynasties were, with very few exceptions, still thriving in the early years of the twentieth century and still capable of producing excellent businessmen. The fact that the younger generation participated, and often excelled, in so many fields of activity outside the business world should not lead to the conclusions that the Moscow dynasties were on the decline and that all of their talent was being drained into fields other than business. The younger generation of the Moscow business elite showed itself capable of contributing to the arts and politics, among other fields, while at the same time carrying on the family business traditions.

CHAPTER 6

THE YOUNGER GENERATION OF THE 1890s: POLITICS AND THE LABOR QUESTION

IF the cultural achievements of the younger generation were strikingly different from those of their predecessors, the differences between the younger and the older generations of the Moscow business elite in their approach to politics were equally notable. The *molodoe kupechestvo*, in contrast to their elders, became deeply involved in the political life of the nation and from 1904 until the Bolshevik revolution were active participants in Russian politics. Prior to 1904, however, the younger generation gave little indication of any greater degree of political activism than was exhibited by their elders. They appeared to be the willing heirs of the relationship created between the older generation of the elite and the tsarist government, one of the conditions of which was that businessmen refrain from political activity. And while discontent with many features of that relationship was maturing in the years before 1905, it seems unlikely that the younger generation would have sought to change the terms of the relationship through open political activity had it not been for the development of a revolutionary movement, in whose initiation they took little part. Much less would they have sought to change the very nature of the government with which they were dealing, had it not been for the appearance of this revolutionary movement that drew them along in its wake.

Undoubtedly, the members of the younger generation were much more amenable to being incorporated into the political opposition than their elders, since a major difference between the two generations was a difference in their basic political mood. If the basic mood of the older generation was conservative, that of the younger generation was liberal. As a whole, this generation contained probably an even broader spectrum of political tendencies than the preceding generation, ranging all the way from reactionary to radical. The center of gravity, however, was a liberalism which during the period from 1904 to 1917 would veer from left to right and again back to the left, in reaction to the unfolding of political and economic events on the national scene. But if the basic mood was different from that of the older generation, this new generation, like its predecessor, contained few true political ideologues. It would be an exaggeration to identify members of the younger generation as true Russian liberals, dedicated to the principles of constitutional government and individual freedom. Moscow businessmen prided themselves on being pragmatists, and their approach to politics, like their approach to business, was indeed a pragmatic one. When in 1904 the elite's younger generation espoused liberal programs, they did so because these seemed the best means to the ends they sought—because, most basically, this generation believed that the adoption of liberal programs would have beneficial results for business. In this respect, they much resembled their elders, who also accepted a certain political system because it seemed to offer the best means for achieving their own economic and professional ends. But the two generations had somewhat differing conceptions of both the ends they sought and the means to be used to achieve them.

A combination of factors contributed to the politicization of the younger generation in 1904, but among these various factors, the labor question played a predominant role. Faced with a nationwide strike movement of mammoth proportions and with renewed government efforts to enact factory legislation, the young Moscow industrialists in 1905 concentrated considerable attention on problems of labor relations, and any discussion of their activities during that year must necessarily reflect the primacy of the labor question, a question of fatal significance for the future of Russian capitalism and Russian capitalists.

IN discussing the political activities and attitudes of the younger generation, one must make a distinction between those members of the generation who remained active businessmen and those who devoted themselves primarily to other interests or other careers. The most politically active members of this generation were the businessmen among them, while those whose primary interests lay in other fields tended to be more politically apathetic (with the obvious exception of the two Guchkov brothers who became professional politicians).[1] In particular, those individuals who were involved in the arts, either as professionals or as dilettantes, showed little interest in political life, perhaps partly because contemporary currents in the artistic world were antipathetical toward political involvement. Stanislavsky was an excellent illustration of this trend. He stayed away from politics and firmly held to the belief that art and politics should not mix. In his memoirs he wrote that "many attempts were made to drag our Theatre into politics, but we, who knew the true nature of the Theatre, understood that the boards of our stage could never become a platform for the spread of propaganda, for the simple reason that the very least utilitarian purpose or tendency, brought into the realm of pure art, kills art instantly."[2] Stanislavsky's determination to keep his theater free of politics even included a ban on any sort of political meetings on the premises.[3]

Probably typical of the aesthetically inclined members of this generation was Margarita Kirillovna Morozova, the widow of Mikhail Abramovich Morozov, who was a member of the philosophical circle of Vladimir Solovev and one of the creators of the Literary Circle, where the poet Valerii Briusov and other decadents reigned. For a brief period in 1905 Morozova showed some interest in politics and courted the liberal politician P. N. Miliukov. Miliukov was invited to address a gathering in her home and soon thereafter received a contribution of several thousand rubles from Morozova toward the creation of a political party. Morozova attended a number of political meetings at which Miliukov was also present and finally invited him to her palatial home for private conversations. If Miliukov had expected to discuss politics with his new-found admirer, their talks in fact took an entirely different direction. Somewhat to his surprise, Miliukov found himself "met face to face by the new trends in literature and art among the Moscow merchant Maecenas." He and Morozova discussed the philosophy of Solovev, the literary works of Andrei Belyi, the latest trends in music, but, Miliukov related,

> there was one subject which we did not touch upon at all. This was politics, a subject which the new trends regarded either neutrally or negatively. I had absolutely no reason to consider myself her mentor. I was an examinee, and one who failed the exam at that. Marguerite Kirillovna's interest in our conversations weakened, as the antithetical nature of our ideological positions became apparent. As a result, the absorbing tête-à-têtes in the Egyptian room of the palace ceased as abruptly as they had begun.[4]

If politics in 1905 became momentarily fashionable, Morozova, like many members of her generation who had only very slight connections with the business world, apparently could not evoke any truly deep interest in the subject.

Such individuals who were no longer deeply involved in business became, in effect, simply rich people living off their dividends, little concerned with the political situation as long as the money kept coming in. They were not directly affected by the problems active businessmen faced every day while attempting to do business within a framework created by the combination of Russian economic backwardness and political autocracy. As a result, they had little reason to give much thought to economic conditions or to pay much attention to political questions. Such *rentiers* simply were not subject to the same influences that moved the business-men of the younger generation to throw in their lot with the political opposition to the autocracy.

One of the politically apathetic representatives of the younger genera-tion, the diplomat D. I. Abrikosov, feeling out of step with his own age group within the business elite, wrote of them that they "with few excep-tions, joined the ranks of the intelligentsia, whose opposition to any sort of conservative authority and abnormal craving for change contributed to the destruction of Old Russia."[5] In fact, if members of the younger gen-eration did indeed from late 1904 onward show themselves favorable to basic changes in Russian life, their participation in the revolutionary movement beginning at that time would have been difficult to predict on the basis of their behavior during the preceding decade. To all appear-ances, the *molodoe kupechestvo* was as politically listless as its elders during this period. Almost the only visible exceptions were N. I. Guchkov, who became a member of the Union of Liberation, formed in 1902 by left-wing liberals, and Savva Morozov, who was involved with various liberal and radical groups.[6] But the participation of these two individuals in various oppositional groupings was hardly sufficient to indicate any broad political awakening or widespread thirst for change among the younger generation of the elite as a whole. As late as November 1904 the journal *Promyshlennyi mir* remarked on the continuing prevalence of political apa-thy in the Russian business community and singled out for special criti-cism the well-educated "sons of Moscow *kuptsy*." "Why," the journal asked, "do these *intelligenty* among the *kupechestvo* remain silent and why do they not awaken the 'all-Russian *kupechestvo*' from its peculiar somno-lence?"[7] Yet even as *Promyshlennyi mir's* editor penned these lines, the "sons of Moscow *kuptsy*" were preparing to make their debut in the open political arena.

The appearance of representatives of the Moscow business elite's younger generation as active participants in the political struggle between the autocracy and its opponents was conditioned by numerous factors, some of which had been at work within the Moscow elite for several decades. Among the most important of these factors that propelled Mos-cow's young businessmen into the political struggle was a growing self-confidence and a new feeling of their own importance which they had begun to exhibit in the 1890s. During that decade, encouraged by the increasing concern for industrial development shown in official circles and among the educated public and by the increasing weight of trade and industry in the Russian economy, Moscow businessmen began to display a new and firmer realization of the tremendous importance of business and businessmen to the future of Russian society as a whole and a growing confidence in themselves and their own future. In particular, the younger generation of the Moscow business elite evinced a new sense of pride in themselves and in their accomplishments in the field of trade and industry and, for the first time, began to demand recognition of the importance and value of their profession from other sectors of Russian society.

The changing attitude of Moscow's young businessmen did not go unnoticed. Beginning in the 1890s, the press occasionally carried articles expressing the conviction that *kuptsy* were now seeking greater political and social influence and debating whether history would elevate businessmen to a predominant position in the Russian state and Russian society. The new aggressiveness of certain businessmen was also reflected in Gorky's novel *Foma Gordeev*, in the character of the merchant Maiakin, who expressed his views as follows:

> "Who is it that contributes most of all for the benefit of the poor, to all these houses, asylums, philanthropic institutions? The rich people, the merchants, our trading class. Very good, sir! But who commands and arranges their life? The nobles, the officials, and all other sorts of people, only not our people. The laws and the newspapers and the sciences come from them—everything is from them. In former days they were landed proprietors, now the land has been jerked out from beneath them—they have entered government service. All right! But who are the most powerful people now-a-days? The merchant is the greatest power in the Empire, because the millions are his!"

Still reflecting on the plight of the masses at the hands of nobles and officials, Maiakin continued:

> "Their life has not been arranged by us merchants, and down to the present day, we have no voice in its organization, we can't lay a hand on it. Others have arranged that life, and they have bred in it all sorts of shabbiness, in the life of these sluggards, unfortunates, paupers—and if they have bred it, they have defiled it, and they— judging as God would judge—should purify it. But it is we who purify it—we contribute to the wants of the needy, we take care of them. Judge for yourself, pray; why should we sew patches on the rags of another man, if we have not torn them? . . . Wouldn't it be more sensible if we were to step aside, and stand there and watch for a while, how every sort of rottenness multiplies, and strangles the man who is a stranger to us! He can't manage it—he has no means. So he turns to us, and says: 'Pray help, gentlemen!' And we reply to him: 'Please give us room to work in! Include us among the organizers of that life!' And as soon as he does include us, then, with one sweep we must purify life from every uncleanness and divers excesses. Then our Sovereign the Emperor will perceive clearly with his bright eyes who are his faithful servants, and how much sense they have acquired while their hands were idle."[8]

Maiakin met with a mixed reception among businessmen. N. A. Bugrov, an old and very wealthy Nizhnii Novgorod merchant who could have come straight from the pages of Ostrovskii, objected to Gorky that he had never in his life met a man like Maiakin. But Savva Morozov agreed with Gorky that such businessmen were beginning to appear, though he was not very optimistic about their future.[9]

The new sense of pride that was beginning to permeate not only the Moscow elite's younger generation but certain other sectors of the Russian business community was very much in evidence at the government-sponsored Industrial Exhibition which took place in Nizhnii Novgorod in 1896. The Exhibition, an official celebration of the achievements of Russian industry, provided businessmen with an opportunity for self-glorification and for putting forth their demands for recognition. Their growing self-esteem was expressed most concisely by *Volgar*, a newspaper closely connected with the Nizhnii Novgorod Fair Committee, headed at that time by Savva Morozov. To greet the opening of the Exhibition, *Volgar* published an article praising the Russian *kupechestvo* to the skies and arguing, in effect, that it was high time they replaced the nobility as Russia's leading *soslovie*. The *Volgar* article stressed the fact that the *kupechestvo* now contained many people with "European educations" and that many of its members were capable of serving, and did serve, in high positions in both the state administration and the armed forces. The article went on to argue that the *kupechestvo*

> is also uniquely strong in our time in its wealth. It is capable of anything. . . . At a time when many *sosloviia*, because of the changing social conditions of life, cannot now, as in the blessed past, exert their strength and position for the development of popular productivity, the *kupechestvo* . . . emerges as that support on which the government may justifiably rely.[10]

This paean to the *kupechestvo* accurately reflected the increasing self-confidence of at least some sections of the Russian business community and their conviction that businessmen were entitled to a larger role in public life. Behind this new self-confidence was a growing belief on the part of many businessmen that in industrial development lay the only guarantee of a happy and prosperous future for Russia and that the business community therefore held the key to Russia's future in its hands. This belief was first announced to the public at large in a speech delivered by Savva Morozov in 1893 in his capacity as president of the Nizhnii Novgorod Fair Committee. In his speech, Morozov in effect offered industrialization as a panacea which would cure numerous of the ills affecting the country. Directing attention to the recent famine which had afflicted large sections of the Russian Empire, Morozov boasted that in spite of the drop in peasant purchasing power occasioned by crop failures, the textile industry had survived the crisis in good order. No textile firms had been forced into bankruptcy, and, Morozov insisted, workers employed in textile factories had suffered no hardships during the famine years. Wages had remained steady, and food had been made available to the factory population at low prices. The lesson to be drawn from this experience, according to Morozov, was that broad industrial development could prevent any future repetition of the catastrophe of 1891 and 1892. Arguing that Russia could easily become "one of the foremost industrial countries of Europe," he concluded that a "strong, well-developed, stable industry would serve as a powerful regulator of popular well-being."[11]

There were indications that Morozov's strong belief in the benefits to be derived from industrial development was increasingly shared by other members of the Moscow business elite. Most interesting was a letter written in 1898 by I. K. Krestovnikov to one of his brothers, in which he attempted to articulate a vision of industry as the major force for progress in Russia. Krestovnikov wrote:

It is impossible to introduce book culture and stop at that. Language and literacy undoubtedly play a big role—this is one of the most powerful cultural weapons! It is necessary, however, that literacy should find application in life, that life should demand from the literate uninterrupted reading, in a word, the development of knowledge by means of books. Simple literacy is not necessary and there is no doubt that it is soon forgotten after learning. Culture must be implanted in a country through many channels: through improvement of means of communication, through telegraphs, telephones, through factories, plants, handicrafts and so on. All this destroys both physical and intellectual stagnation! In a word, if we will ourselves do everything that our level of culture demands, then the very culture of the people will begin noticeably to increase even without the help of foreigners, and will call forth new demands. The development of demands brings with it an upsurge of culture, etc.; and here we already are in a circle of eternal progress, like a squirrel on a wheel, which is seen in the very life of the people.[12]

If he expressed himself somewhat awkwardly, Krestovnikov's main thought was clear enough: that the development of industry and communications was the chief means for raising the general level of popular culture in Russia.[13]

The vision of progress contained in Morozov's speech and Krestovnikov's letter is interesting not only as an indication of Moscow businessmen's growing sense of their own importance but as a demonstration of a considerable broadening of the viewpoint of Moscow industrialists. In earlier years they had, in effect, advocated the development of industry more or less for its own sake. Though they had frequently asserted that industrial development was a good thing for the country as a whole, they never seemed able to explain exactly why this was so. Now they began consciously to develop an ideology of progress which made the development of industry appear as the key to the future improvement of Russian life. And if, on the one hand, this belief in progress through industrial development only seemed to increase their egocentricity and make more urgent their incessant demands for benefits and privileges to industry and industrialists, on the other hand, this same belief in progress also implied a recognition of the need for change, the need for basic improvements in Russian life.

Although it is perhaps somewhat risky to generalize on the basis of the very few pronouncements, public or private, that Moscow businessmen offered regarding the state of the nation, nonetheless, all the indications are that dissatisfaction with the status quo was spreading among them in the later 1890s and the early twentieth century—and not among the younger generation alone. Even the older generation of the elite was not immune to this mood of growing discontent with the general state of things in Russia. I. K. Krestovnikov, whose vision of "eternal progress" was cited above, belonged to the older generation. And a very clear statement of distress over Russia's general situation, plus a recognition of its bad effects on business, came from the pen of his brother K. K. Krestovnikov. In a letter from Kazan in 1899, Krestovnikov informed another brother in Moscow that

> all the grain intended for those suffering from famine lies on the banks of the Volga; there is no transport. . . . Perhaps it will lie there until spring, in which case the fields will remain unplanted. Here for a whole month the inhabitants have been without sugar and without fish. . . . Businessmen are depressed. . . . Cattle and fowl in the villages are dying! In general it is something unpleasant! Agriculture is so exhausted that philanthropy alone will not correct the matter![14]

In another letter written later in the same year, Krestovnikov continued his complaints:

> I feel that here, in Russia, something is not right; there is neither money nor grain nor firm guiding principles—there is only cultural empty-light, which tries to pass for culture. I think that now industrial people are convinced that it is impossible to spend a greater part of their basic capital on factory property.[15]

These expressions of discontent found in the Krestovnikovs' letters from the last three years of the 1890s are all the more striking in that they are the only letters in the family's collected correspondence, covering the better part of the nineteenth century, which express any views on the general situation of the country at all, much less feelings of discontent. Thus, while Naidenov, still firmly ensconced at the Exchange Committe, continued to hew to a strong conservative line, even among his supporters of the older generation discontent with the status quo was developing.

It need hardly be mentioned that this discontent with the general state of things in Russia was, as K. K. Krestovnikov's letters clearly implied, closely connected with a concern over future economic development. The fact remains, however, that the Moscow elite in the later 1890s was developing a considerably broader view of the conditions necessary for successful development of the economy. It occurred to at least some of their representatives that high tariffs and state loans were not enough to ensure a favorable climate for industrial and commercial activity. Certainly in their resolutions of 1905 the younger generation of the elite would show clear awareness of, as they expressed it, "the direct dependence of the fate of industry on the cultural and political conditions of popular life."[16] And it appears, particularly on the basis of K. K. Krestovnikov's letters, that in the years before 1905 many members of the Moscow elite gradually were coming to realize that conditions the intelligentsia constantly complained about—mass poverty and illiteracy, the depressed state of agriculture, the lack of basic freedoms among the masses of the population—were holding back industrial development. Krestovnikov's conviction that "something" was "not right" in Russia indicates that some members of the elite were coming to share the intelligentsia's sense of malaise over the general condition of the country, though, again, this sense of malaise overcame them only as they gradually began to realize that Russian political and cultural backwardness retarded economic development.

Such general dissatisfaction was reinforced by the recession of the early twentieth century, which put an abrupt end to the steady forward movement of the economy in the 1890s. Although the textile industry was not hit so hard as some other areas of the economy, the profits of many textile enterprises suffered, and Moscow manufacturers held concerned meetings to discuss how to deal with this sudden setback.[17] In the press, the recession provoked articles attributing the crisis to exhaustion of peasant purchasing power and containing gloomy predictions about the future of Russian industry, in view of the increasing impoverishment of its chief mass of consumers. That the backwardness of Russian agriculture and the poverty of the peasantry, the major market for Moscow textiles, could well prove a major obstacle to further development of the industry was recognized by at least one "well-known manufacturer" of cotton textiles who communicated his fears anonymously to *Promyshlennyi mir* in 1900. Expounding an extremely pessimistic view of the market situation for textile goods, this industrialist commented that the numerous burdens on the Russian masses had "drained" them "to such an extent that one is forced to recall the fable about the goose which laid the golden eggs." In his extreme agitation over the poverty of the mass of the population and its limiting effects on the market for textiles, he was even brought to question the sacred cow of high tariffs, which had contributed their share to impoverishment of the masses through raising the prices of goods they purchased.[18] His letter is only one further indication of growing concern over the conditions of Russian life on the part of businessmen and their dawning realization that general Russian backwardness stood as an obstacle to industrial development.

WHILE Moscow businessmen's increased sense of their own importance and their growing discontent over general conditions in the country help to explain the participation of the younger generation of the elite in the oppositional movement of 1905, there were still other more important factors drawing these young businessmen into opposition to the tsarist government. At the most basic level, discontent among the Moscow business elite, in the years before 1905, stemmed to a very large extent from defects in their relationship with the government and from unhappiness over certain government policies toward industry, especially in the field of labor relations. If they were increasingly recognizing that Russia's general cultural backwardness was an obstacle to industrial development, nonetheless, Moscow businessmen were still much more sensitive to the problems they faced every day on a very personal basis in their relationship with the government and in their own factories. As their behavior in 1905 made evident, it was these immediate problems that were foremost in their minds when they began putting their signatures to revolutionary manifestoes.

Of the grievances that led the younger generation of Moscow businessmen into revolt, two can easily be singled out as by far the most important. Neither of these grievances was exactly new, though as the years passed and events developed, they came to be felt more and more keenly. The first of these basic grievances was a long-established dislike of bureaucracy and of the red tape with which it sometimes seemed to be trying to bind and gag Russian industry and commerce. One of the first and strongest statements of businessmen's antipathy toward bureaucrats came from the pen of V. A. Kokorev as early as the 1880s. Kokorev, who will be remembered as the organizer of the banquet to support a proposed emancipation of the serfs in 1857, published a long article in *Russkii arkhiv* in 1887. In it he outlined fifteen "economic failures" attributable to the misguided policies of the bureaucracy. Kokorev referred to the bureaucrats as "the firm of 'they' " and castigated them for lack of knowledge of Russian conditions and indiscriminate adoption of Western liberal thought and Western models. Typical of the opinions he expressed on the working of government chancelleries was the following:

> The compilers of statistical and industrial surveys, on which the "financiers" base their projects, without doubt would be horrified by those misfortunes which they have caused in recent times if they would look into the life of the *narod*. It is time to stop compiling surveys of Russian economic life based on official reports which do not at all reflect reality, and, after sincere repentance, it is time to establish the rule of studying above all Russian life in the villages, in order to make one's views coincide with popular needs, without which bitter results will occur, even with the very best intentions.[19]

Kokorev insisted too that if the bureaucrats themselves were unacquainted with the conditions of life in Russia, they also refused to take advice from "people of experience."[20] The result was, in his view, fifteen major failures of economic policy, ranging from the evil effects produced by the monetary reform of 1837 to the bad results obtained by the mistaken policy of granting nobility to successful businessmen.

In the conclusion of his article, Kokorev drew a contrast between the sad state of the Russian economy, whose future he regarded very pessimistically, and Russian successes in other fields, such as art, medicine, and engineering. Failure in the one area and success in the others, he argued, occurred because the economy was managed by heavy-handed bureaucrats, while art, medicine, and engineering were free of bureaucratic dictation and had close ties with the *narod*. These areas had progressed because "they are not oppressed by the weight of chancellery formalism," while in the economic field the bureaucrats persistently stifled all inspiration and initiative.[21]

Kokorev's complaints against the bureaucracy reflected a very real source of dissatisfaction among the Moscow business elite. In the early 1890s, the Morozov-financed *Russkoe obozrenie* took up the cudgels against the bureaucrats, repeating and expanding upon complaints first voiced by Kokorev. Like Kokorev, *Russkoe obozrenie* writers condemned officials in charge of industry for lack of knowledge of the field and argued that officials responsible for preparing legislation concerning trade and industry had no practical preparation for this task but were simply "impractical theoreticians," far too inclined to follow Western examples without reference to peculiar Russian conditions.[22] In addition, the journal complained about the government's frequent failure to consult businessmen in regard to important decisions affecting business. According to *Russkoe obozrenie*, the tariff negotiations with Germany in 1893 caused particular distress within the business community, because they were conducted in complete secrecy, the government failing either to keep businessmen informed or to ask their advice.[23] Thus, like Kokorev, the journal in effect argued that "people of practical experience" should be given greater influence over the decision-making process insofar as it affected business.

Russkoe obozrenie also concentrated on other sore points in the relationship between the government and the Moscow business community. It complained of the innumerable officials who were given some share of authority over the factories. "The factory," said the journal, "is subject at the same time not only to the authority of the governor, the *gradonachalnik* or chief of police, the district police officer, the town duma, the zemstvo board, but to numerous committees, commissions, inspectors, doctors, and sanitarians. Many of these authorities issue regulations on various subjects which are binding on the factories but which contradict one another and are completely unrealizable."[24] The interference of so many different officials in the running of factories held back the development of industry, the journal claimed, as did archaic industrial legislation. *Russkoe obozrenie* insisted that it had long been time to reform the whole body of law relating to industry, parts of which dated back to the eighteenth century and were totally inapplicable in contemporary conditions.[25] Finally, *Russkoe obozrenie* also considered the responsibility of the industrialists for so many "philanthropical" undertakings for the benefit of their workers to be a brake on industrial development. In England, it was pointed out, factory owners were not saddled with the responsibility for providing schools and hospitals; it was instead assumed by governmental bodies.[26] Thus, the journal implied that bureaucrats, with all their rules and regulations, should stop making a nuisance of themselves in the factories and should instead devote themselves to various undertakings that would facilitate industrial development, such as legal reform and the creation of schools.

If *Russkoe obozrenie* complained endlessly about the incompetence of government as it attempted to "manage" industry, it did not go so far as to suggest that the government ought simply to leave industrialists to their own devices and entirely abandon industrial regulation. But it seems undoubtable that, if they were not advocates of total laissez-faire in regard to the economy, Moscow businessmen wanted a greater degree of freedom from governmental control at the most basic level of management of their own factories and in the conduct of their own businesses. One of the few persistent voices in Russia calling for greater freedom for business enterprise was *Promyshlennyi mir*, the Petersburg journal which began publication in 1899. That the journal's views had awakened some sympathy in business circles was indicated by the letter it received in 1900 from the unidentified textile manufacturer whose opinions on the condition of the textile market were previously cited. In addition to the fears he expressed over the state of consumer demand, this same manufacturer showed considerable sympathy with the journal's crusade to free business from bureaucratic red tape. Among other things, he complained that the officials who attempted to "manage" industry with all their papers, memoranda, and circulars were not in touch with the realities of the business world, and so textile manufacturers often found themselves in a position where "life demands from them one thing, and the papers something else." He clearly implied that government interference in trade and industry was frequently in itself an obstacle to economic growth.[27]

Later in the same year *Promyshlennyi mir* published another letter whose author, identifying himself only as a "Moscow *kupets*" and a member of the Moscow provincial zemstvo, voiced a different type of complaint about the relationship between the bureaucracy and industry. He condemned the current method of conducting relations between the government and businessmen, in which representatives of business all too often had to try to make their influence felt "from the back porch." Instead of the existing relationship, in which businessmen either had to await a summons from the government in order to voice their opinions or attempt to make themselves heard through sporadic petitions and the exploitation of personal connections with government officials, this *kupets* proposed as a substitute the development of permanent organizations of businessmen which would attempt to exert continuing influence on state policy in a more open and regular manner.[28]

Thus, on the eve of 1905, some members of the Moscow business community were entertaining new doubts about the effectiveness of existing methods of influencing government policy, in addition to nursing long-standing grievances over bureaucratic interference with industry and trade. But if Moscow businessmen had long resented bureaucratic interference in general, the most heinous form of this interference, in their view, came in regard to labor relations in the factory. For decades this had been a problem fraught with possibilities for major conflict between industrialists and the state, since their apparent interests in the matter were diametrically opposed—the industrialists wanting to maintain their own autocratic powers in the factories, which, they insisted, were necessary to ensure industrial progress, while the state insisted on its right to interfere in relations between employers and workers in order to secure some improvement in the position of the factory population. The industrialists saw state attempts to regulate labor relations as a threat to their own power and profits, while government officials saw such regulation as essential in order to alleviate working-class discontent which might otherwise become disruptive of political and social stability. In the early 1900s the tensions between government and industrialists over this issue would finally become uncontainable and would play a major role in driving Moscow's young businessmen into the arms of the opposition.

As noted earlier, Moscow industrialists had reacted to the first serious attempts to regulate factory labor in the 1880s with dismay, almost with disbelief that the government could be so brazen as to interfere in relations between employers and their workers. I. I. Ianzhul, the Moscow region's first factory inspector, related that many industrialists thought bribery of factory inspectors was all that was required of them. Others refused to believe that the government seriously intended to carry through with its regulatory attempts and were convinced that it would all blow over in a short time.[29] But when the seriousness of the government's intentions finally became apparent to them, Moscow factory owners started a petition and newspaper campaign against factory legislation in which they stressed, above all, the "patriarchal" relationships existing in Russian factories as their first line of defense against outside interference.[30] They further insisted that there was no basic conflict of interests between capital and labor and that factory laws and factory inspectors only destroyed the natural harmony of interests between these two productive forces. *Russkoe obozrenie*, repeating the arguments made by Moscow industrialists in an 1887 petition to Minister of Finance Vyshnegradskii, summarized their position as follows:

> The workers represent material labor and the factory owners, intellectual labor and capital. The former cannot get along without the latter and vice versa. . . . The joining of these two types of labor can occur only on the basis of a *similarity* of interests. . . . If the owner receives a significant share of the benefit from the enterprise, this is because without his intellectual labor and capital the physical labor of the workers would be futile, and because he bears the risk of the business, while the workers and employees, as hired people, do not share in this risk. . . . It is impossible therefore to construct a doctrine around the opposition of interests of workers and factory owners only because the owner receives a significant part of the income of the enterprise in good years. It is also impossible to base such a doctrine on the belief that the lower the salaries and wages that the factory owner pays his employees and workers, the greater his income from the enterprise. This contradicts the most basic principle of political economy. Low salaries and wages naturally result in a decline in the quality of work, and the income of the enterprise depends on this quality of work. It would be mistaken to think that the income of an enterprise depends on cutting salaries or wages. . . . In practice competition among factory owners removes any possibility of arbitrariness on the part of the employer in the determination of wages.

In sum, the Moscow industrialists "[saw] in the cooperation of employers and workers at the factory a union based on *similarity* of interests and *differences* in capabilities, which are complementary to one another." Such a union, they believed, would be destroyed by the new factory laws, which assumed not harmony but opposition of interests between labor and capital.[31]

Notwithstanding the anguish it produced among industrialists, the factory legislation promulgated by the tsarist government before 1905 was extremely modest in its dimensions.[32] Two laws, one enacted in 1882 and the other in 1885, attempted to regulate the labor of women and children and created the factory inspectorate to enforce their provisions. A law of 1886 regulated labor contracts between the employer and the individual worker, while an 1897 enactment established a maximum working day of eleven and a half hours and put some limitations on overtime work. The government then completed its pre-1905 legislation with two laws promulgated in 1903, one requiring employers to provide compensation in cases of industrial accidents which resulted in the disability or death of a worker and the other providing for the election of "factory elders" (*starosty*), who would represent the workers before their employers. One stimulus to the passage of these laws, it should be noted, was strikes that occurred at factories owned by Moscow businessmen, in particular a violent outburst by workers at the Khludovs' Iartsevskaia factory in 1880 and another, even more serious disturbance at the Morozovs' Nikolskaia plant in 1885, both ignited by lowering of the workers' wages.

These laws were only loosely enforced, in part simply because the factory inspectors were so overburdened in terms of the territory they had to cover and the number of factories they were required to inspect that it was impossible for them to catch all violations. Furthermore, many of these factory laws came to be so hedged round with exceptions and qualifications that, in practice, they had little impact. The restriction on overtime work contained in the law of 1897, for instance, was so qualified by subsequent amendments that it had no practical effect. Finally, in addition to lax enforcement and significant numbers of exceptions, the penalties provided for employers who violated factory laws were merely nominal. Violations of the provisions of the law of 1897, for example, brought only fines of no more than fifty rubles.

Both the limited scope of the factory laws and the leniency with which they were enforced helped to mitigate the initial shock and horror with which Moscow industrialists reacted to factory regulation. While they continued to resent any sort of state interference in their factories, the industrialists nonetheless learned that they could live with factory legislation. By the early 1890s a more or less satisfactory working relationship had been achieved between factory owners and factory inspectors in the Moscow region, as a result of compromises on both sides.[33] In contrast to their anguished opposition to the first factory laws, Moscow industrialists offered no determined opposition to the 1897 law regulating working time, although Witte was forced to raise the maximum legally permissible working day from the eleven hours that he had originally proposed to eleven and a half hours, partly to satisfy the objections of industrialists.[34]

This relatively stable situation in regard to government regulation of factory labor was rudely shattered in the early 1900s with the advent of the *zubatovshchina* in Moscow. The brainchild of S. V. Zubatov, an official of the Okhrana, or security police, this experiment in "police socialism" was intended to combat political sedition among the workers and turn them into loyal supporters of the tsarist regime. In Moscow, the Zubatov experiment took two forms: a series of lectures and discussions held for the benefit of local factory workers and the creation of several workers' organizations, led by police agents. Whatever the original intention had been, these new labor organizations ended up leading several strikes at Moscow factories, and it was this activity of Zubatov and his agents which called forth the wrath of Moscow industrialists. They were particularly outraged by the Zubatov-inspired strike at the silk textile factory owned by Jules Goujon and other notable Moscow Frenchmen, during which Goujon was threatened with exile by the authorities if he did not give in to the demands of his workers.[35]

That the government itself should be stirring up agitation and strikes among factory workers and bullying employers into granting strikers' demands was simply more than could be borne by Moscow industrialists. They reacted to the *zubatovshchina* with a long and bitter note directed to the Ministry of Finance, in which many of their long pent-up resentments against the government's labor policies came to the surface and in which they roundly condemned the experiment in police socialism as illegal and dangerous adventurism. It was, they insisted, extremely perilous to try to deflect the working class from participation in political activity directed against the government by involving it instead in "anti-capitalist" activity. The note made it clear that Moscow industrialists believed the government was trying to save itself at their expense; and they, of course, deeply resented being used in such a manner.[36]

This note provoked by the *zubatovshchina* was an extremely interesting indication of the basic views of Moscow industrialists on the labor question as of 1902 and outlined their principal grievances in this field. Among other things, the industrialists insisted that trouble at the factories was most frequently caused not by permanently employed workers but by various "vagabonds" and "hooligans" who hung around the factory settlement, doing occasional odd jobs at the factory and generally bent on causing trouble. Another dangerous element at the factory, they claimed, was former workers who had lost their jobs because of participation in disorders. Like the vagabond element, they had nothing to lose, and, partly motivated by a desire for revenge, they were at all times ready to participate in any sort of disturbances. The employers were aware that

these former workers were not basically dangerous people and were frequently willing to renew their employment, but they were prevented
from doing so by the police. All in all, the factory owners were convinced
of the basic peaceableness and docility of the core of factory workers and
were inclined to blame troubles at the factories entirely on outside agitators, unemployed elements, and meddling by the police.

Indeed, the industrialists believed that their workers had little cause for
complaint and stoutly denied Zubatov's accusation that they exploited
their workers. Their note argued that Russian workers had little to complain of as regarded working time, since the observance of numerous
religious holidays by Russian industry meant that Russian workers spent
10 percent less time on the job than did their counterparts in Western
Europe. As for material circumstances, the industrialists insisted that
factory workers were incomparably better off in relation to other workers
such as coachmen and waiters, particularly as they received all sorts of
fringe benefits, such as free education and medical care, in addition to
their wages.

The industrialists included in their note a mild protest against the factory inspectorate, arguing that the inspectors all too often tried to instill
in the workers the idea that they were being exploited by their employers,
and then went on to condemn, in much stronger terms, Zubatov's idea
that workers should be organized into unions. Unions might work well
enough in America or Australia, but, the note claimed, they were obviously unsuitable in Russian conditions. Unions would simply provide
an opportunity for ill-intentioned agitators to gain influence over the semi-
literate mass of workers and to stir up trouble in the factories while
pursuing their own political ends. To grant the workers freedom to strike
as well as to organize would be even worse, since again the right to strike
would only facilitate the machinations of agitators who would cause completely unnecessary ruptures of factory peace.

Adding a few gratuitous comments on the difficulties of running a
factory when factory managers were constantly besieged by a huge army
of officials and subjected to their endless demands, the industrialists' note
in conclusion repeated a complaint frequently made by *Russkoe obozrenie*,[37]
to the effect that factory workers, who represented less than 1 percent of
the population of the Empire, were being singled out for special treatment
as compared with the other 99 percent of the populace. They were being
unreasonably pampered by the authorities and were being turned into
"spoiled children." And, the note added with dismay, not only were
government authorities pampering workers, but even the religious authorities acted in the same spirit, "forgetting that before the church there are
neither workers nor factory owners but only Orthodox people."

This note on the labor question better than any other document
summed up the state of mind of Moscow businessmen on the eve of 1905

and testified to their profound discontent with government handling of industry and especially of the labor question. But if such documents made their feelings of discontent explicit, before 1905 Moscow industrialists proposed no clear solutions to the problems which they recognized. As far as one can determine from the nature of their complaints, their program, had they drawn one up, probably would have included the following points: an immediate end not only to "police socialism" but to all police meddling in the factories, except when directly requested by the factory owners; disbandment of the army of officials who interfered in all aspects of factory work (in which demand they might have included the factory inspectors); greater influence for "men of practical experience" in the decision-making process where trade and industry were concerned, as well as an end to government secrecy in all matters affecting business; and action by the government to facilitate the development of the economy in ways deemed necessary by businessmen themselves, including legal reform and assumption by the government of responsibility for providing schools, hospitals, and other facilities for the factory population. Some might also have included a demand that businessmen be allowed to create more effective organizations in order to exert constant, continuing pressure on government, or even called for a major effort to overcome general Russian backwardness, which acted as a brake on industrial development. As for the labor question, while Moscow industrialists did not regard highly the efforts of the government to deal with this problem, it is difficult to deduce any proposed solutions from their statements on the subject. Specifically rejecting police socialism, unions, and strikes, and not holding a high opinion of the factory inspectors or the regulations they tried to enforce, Moscow industrialists to a very large extent appear to have been trying to convince themselves that no *rabochii vopros* (labor question) existed in Russia, even as late as the early twentieth century. The message that seemed to be coming through from their various statements on the labor question was that the factory workers were basically peaceable and benefited from the paternal care of their employers in the form of comparatively good living and working conditions. Therefore, all would be well if only the inspectors, the police, and outside agitators would leave the factories alone.

If they could not offer convincing solutions to all the problems they faced, it is nonetheless a striking fact that Moscow's business elite came increasingly to recognize and to face up to problems in the relationship between business and the state. In the note provoked by Zubatov's activities, Moscow businessmen spoke out with considerable vehemence against various government policies and practices. It would seem that at least a significant group of Moscow industrialists had finally been provoked beyond endurance. If in earlier years a rather delicate balance had been maintained in their relationship with the government, with the favorable (from the point of view of the businessmen) aspects of this relationship outweighing the unfavorable, now it seemed that the balance was being tipped in the opposite direction and that, more than any other single factor, it was the *zubatovshchina* that made the difference.

T HE increasing dissatisfaction of Moscow businessmen with the government's handling of industry coincided with a rising level of discontent in other sectors of the community, and the growing mood of opposition demonstrated particularly by the intelligentsia most probably rubbed off on businessmen to some extent and encouraged them to express their own displeasure with the government in the years before 1905. Certainly the discontent of the business community, like that of other sectors of educated society, intensified with the outbreak of the Russo-Japanese War in 1904. While participating in the general patriotic enthusiasm that greeted the beginning of the war and promising large sums for war relief work, Moscow's merchants and industrialists soon began to experience the adverse effects of war on their own businesses, and, as a result, their patriotism was sorely tried. The Zündel factory reported that February 1904 was "the worst February for commerce within living memory." At the Nizhnii Novgorod fair, in August and September, business was extremely slow.[38] The press unanimously blamed the bad state of commerce on two factors: lack of transport, which had largely been commandeered for military purposes, and lack of credit, resulting from the vast sums sopped up from the capital market by big state loans to finance the war.[39] One foreign visitor to Russia in 1904 and 1905, who studied the effects of the war on Russian society, found that businessmen in general, and those of Moscow in particular,

> always regarded the war as an unmitigated curse, and the policy which led up to it as criminal folly, for it has proved disastrous to trade and manufactures, and undermined the whole credit system on which Russian national economy is based. They denounced the action of the Government in no measured terms, they laughed at the Russian generals, they delighted in anecdotes illustrating official corruption or military inefficiency, and never believed in the future of Manchuria.[40]

Thus, the war, bringing with it both business and military disasters, served as a catalyst in the business community, as in other sectors of Russian society, and turned discontent into sheer outrage at the incompetence of the government.

The first indications that businessmen would support an oppositional movement came in November 1904, when a number of leading Moscow businessmen of the younger generation (including most prominently

Savva Morozov and V. P. Riabushinskii) participated in the zemstvo congress held in Moscow and supported its resolutions.[41] At the end of the month, businessmen in the city duma voted for a resolution which in effect repeated the demands of the zemstvo congress, though in somewhat more moderate form. This duma resolution called for the inviolability of the individual; freedom of speech, press, assembly, and religion; and expansion of the responsibilities of the zemstvos and city dumas. On the question of political structure, the resolution was closer to the position of the minority at the zemstvo congress and merely stated the need to assure permanent participation of elected representatives of the people in the legislative process.[42] The historian V. Ia. Laverychev, regarding this duma resolution as a landmark in the political development of the Russian bourgeoisie, called it "the first organized political act of a significant group of industrialists of Central Russia."[43] And although the duma intelligentsia played a large role in the drafting and adoption of the resolution, it was, nonetheless, as Laverychev has indicated, the first significant step of the Moscow business elite into the open political arena.

In spite of business support for the zemstvo and duma resolutions, there was hardly a consensus within the business elite on political questions. Two definite groupings soon emerged. One was headed by Naidenov and by the man who would soon succeed him as president of the Exchange Committee, the somewhat more progressive G. A. Krestovnikov. The spokesman for the other faction, until his suicide in May, was Savva Morozov, ably seconded by P. P. Riabushinskii. The division between these two groupings represented a division between Right and Left, conservative and liberal, and also a division between generations. In spite of a few mavericks, such as S. I. Chetverikov, who generally supported the younger generation rather than his own age group, the two factions developed largely along generational lines—a fact recognized by contemporaries when they christened the Morozov-Riabushinskii group the *molodye* (the young ones). Both groups shared many of the same grievances, but the Naidenov faction for the most part rejected the solutions proposed by their younger colleagues, particularly concerning political questions, and refused to go along with them in supporting a political *fronde*. Indeed, it should be emphasized that the most basic point of disagreement between the "old" and the "young" in 1905 concerned the methods to be used in seeking redress for grievances often shared by both generations. The older generation preferred to cling to the tested method of exerting influence through channels of communication long established between the government and the business community, while the younger generation joined the opposition to the autocracy and regarded this avenue as the more promising path toward achievement of their goals.

This split, insofar as it concerned political questions, was first demonstrated by the reactions of the Moscow elite to the events of January 1905. While Naidenov appealed for preservation of the autocracy, members of the younger generation, headed by Morozov, drew up statements demanding the creation of a national assembly of elected representatives of the people.[44] The split again surfaced at a June meeting of the permanent assembly of 100 representatives of the Exchange Society (*vybornye*), which convened to discuss the political issues brought to the fore by recent events. By this time, the Naidenov faction had managed to adapt itself to the idea of an advisory state duma, which had already received official sanction from the government. Still firmly in control of a majority of the *vybornye*, Naidenov was able to put through a resolution endorsing the creation of a purely advisory body. But the minority, led by P. P. Riabushinskii, N. D. Morozov, and Vl. S. Bakhrushin, all representatives of the younger generation, came out strongly in favor of a duma with independent legislative powers. At the end of July, this minority publicly disassociated itself from the resolution passed by the *vybornye* and declared its support for a truly legislative, rather than a merely advisory, national assembly.[45]

If they disagreed on political questions, another source of disagreement between the two generations was the question of creating a national organization of businessmen. In spite of repeated requests from businessmen of other towns that the Moscow Exchange Society should take the lead in forming such a national organization, Naidenov persistently refused to act.[46] But the idea had considerable support outside Moscow, particularly in St. Petersburg, and even Naidenov could not keep the question off the agenda of a July congress of Russian industrialists meeting in Moscow. This congress did not live out its full term: when it appeared likely that the "radicals" at the meeting would seek to gain its endorsement of a legislative assembly, Naidenov denounced the assemblage to the governor-general for having strayed from its officially approved agenda, and the congress was accordingly disbanded by the authorities. But the "radicals," in defiance of the government ban on their meeting, continued as a rump congress in the home of P. P. Riabushinskii, where, besides endorsing a legislative assembly and universal suffrage, they also established a bureau of twenty-two members (including, from Moscow, Riabushinskii, A. I. Konovalov, A. S. Vishniakov, S. I. Chetverikov, and Jules Goujon). This bureau was to be based in St. Petersburg, and its purpose was to prepare for an all-Russian congress of trade and industry, which in turn would organize a permanent association of Russian businessmen. However, the efforts of the bureau were not crowned with success, again partly because of the interference of Naidenov. The president of Moscow's Exchange Committee continued his attempts to sabotage the creation of a national organization and turned once again to the Moscow governor-general with denunciations of the whole project. Partly as a result of his opposition, the authorities refused permission for the planned congress to take place.[47]

In such a way, Naidenov and the government combined to delay the formation of a national union of businessmen until 1906. And because of Naidenov's refusal to involve the Moscow Exchange Committee in such an undertaking, it was, in the end, St. Petersburg businessmen who were chiefly responsible for the creation of the new Association of Industry and Trade. In this undertaking they had the support of the Moscow *molodye*, but an interesting split developed between St. Petersburg business leaders and the young Muscovites, chiefly over the question of what form the new organization was to take. Moscow's young businessmen wanted an association which would take as its proper sphere of action not only economic but also political questions. P. P. Riabushinskii was particularly insistent that the new organization should represent the views of the business community on political issues and should be geared to exert political pressure. His position was reflected in a resolution adopted by the bureau created at the Moscow congress in July which stated that

> the existing industrial organizations are concerned exclusively with economic questions. But recent events show that the solution of economic questions without discussion of political questions is impossible. Therefore it is necessary that industrialists and merchants join and act in common for achievement of exactly defined goals.[48]

But Riabushinskii's approach was decisively rejected by the other founders of the new association, who insisted that its sole function should be to study and illuminate economic problems and to try to win acceptance of its views in circles of power only on questions involving industry and trade.[49] Riabushinskii's unsuccessful effort to politicize the business community's new national organization was both an indication of the higher level of political consciousness existing among the younger generation of the Moscow elite, as compared with their colleagues elsewhere, and a warning of future conflicts between Moscow and St. Petersburg businessmen.[50]

The basic position of Moscow's younger generation on the questions confronting the country in 1905 was clearly stated in two notes which they drew up early in the year. The notes appeared in January and February and were very similar in their phrasing and almost identical in their content. The January note purported to represent the views of Moscow industrialists, while the February note emanated from representatives of the trade and industry of the entire Central Industrial Region. The guiding hands behind the drafting of these resolutions belonged to Savva Morozov, P. P. Riabushinskii, and S. I. Chetverikov.[51] The February note bore the signatures of representatives of almost fifty commercial and industrial enterprises in the Central Region. Among the signers were leading figures of Moscow's younger generation: besides Morozov and Riabushinskii, they included A. I. Konovalov, I. A. and N. D. Morozov, V. P. Riabushinskii, M. N. Bardygin, and I. S. and S. S. Prokhorov.[52]

These two notes represent both the first occasion on which members of the Moscow business elite offered definite solutions for the problems of concern to Moscow businessmen and the first occasion on which the younger generation of the elite ventured to act as spokesmen for Moscow industry and trade. The solutions recommended in the notes were in many respects quite different from the solutions implied in earlier statements of the views of the Moscow business elite. On some issues, these notes indeed appeared to make a complete about-face, turning away from positions taken earlier by spokesmen for the Moscow business community. But if there were striking differences between these notes and earlier statements emanating from the Moscow business elite—differences reflecting disagreements between the two generations of the elite—there were equally notable similarities, indicating a sharing of views on some subjects between the two generations.

The authors of these notes, the vast majority of whom were industrialists, made it clear that their statements were provoked by the numerous strikes which had occurred in January and that they were speaking as "one of the most interested parties" in those strikes. Seeking the causes of the factory disorders, they argued that "purely economic factors could not have played an essential role in the recent strikes." The workers had indeed put forth economic demands, but the majority of these demands "were so immoderate, so clearly unrealizable, that the workers themselves did not attribute any serious significance to them." Moreover, the industrialists, praising themselves for making a determined effort not to curtail production or to lower wages in spite of the long economic crisis of recent years, argued that the workers had no cause to complain of any recent worsening in their material position. The industrialists admitted that "it is impossible to deny the fact that the living conditions of our factory worker demand improvements," though they added that "his economic position is higher than the position of the agricultural hired worker and the majority of the peasant population." And whatever the condition of the factory worker, "the industrialist cannot change this situation with good intentions, since living conditions are a result of the development of the whole national economy."

Having dismissed the economic demands of the workers as not worthy of serious consideration, the industrialists insisted that the real causes of the strikes were not to be found in the realm of economics but in the realm of politics. Here they adumbrated a position to which they would adhere throughout 1905—that the major reasons for discontent among the factory workers were political rather than economic and that pacification of the workers could be achieved only through political reform. (Needless to say, this position found little favor with government officials, who were equally insistent that the reasons for working-class discontent were to be found in the factories.) The January note also added that it would be a profound error to attribute factory disturbances to the influence of agitators rather than to political grievances deeply felt by the workers themselves.

In their notes, Moscow's young businessmen, striking out on what was clearly a new path for the Moscow business elite, outlined what they considered to be the basic causes of political discontent, not only among factory workers but in Russian society as a whole. According to their February note,

> the absence of a firm law in the country, the guardianship of the bureaucracy, which extends into all fields of Russian life, the preparation of laws in moribund chancelleries, far from everything that is happening in real life, the fetters placed on the free voice of the country, which is deprived of the opportunity to speak to the Supreme Bearer of power about its needs, the ignorance of the people, which is deliberately preserved by those obstacles in the way of opening schools, libraries, reading rooms, in a word, of everything that could increase the cultural development of the people, the worse position in which the *narod* finds itself before the courts and the authorities, in comparison with others—all this holds back the development of the economic life of the country and gives rise in the *narod* to smoldering protest against that which oppresses and suffocates it.

Whether or not the factors here isolated by the industrialists were indeed those primarily responsible for profound popular discontent may be open to question, but what is most interesting about their statement is their clear recognition that these various manifestations of Russian backwardness were obstacles to economic development. The January note made this point even more strongly, stating that

> it is undoubted that industry is closely tied with stable legal organization of a country, with the guarantee of freedom to science and scientific truth, with the enlightenment of the people from which it recruits its working hands, which are less productive, the more ignorant they are.

The industrialists in their two notes then moved on to the labor question, which was, indeed, the major subject of these statements. Renewing their attacks on government attempts to "manage" the labor question in general and on the experiment in police socialism in particular, they attributed to the *zubatovshchina*—that "most illegal and abnormal movement"—a large share of responsibility for provoking the current factory disorders. The Zubatov experiment, they argued, had only succeeded in demonstrating to the workers that the present government had no real intention of improving the workers' position and, further, in convincing the workers that "they could achieve fulfillment of their desires only when they had acquired political power." Since the government's attempt to manipulate labor relations had backfired and had achieved results diametrically opposed to those which it had sought, the argument continued, the government, having amply demonstrated its incompetence in this matter, should withdraw from the field and permit the workers themselves to seek resolution of their own problems.

Here the young industrialists went on to make startling new demands in regard to the labor question—they asked that the workers should be given freedom to organize unions, as well as the right to strike, in order to defend their own interests. This demand, of course, represented a striking change from the note of a few years back, when Moscow industrialists had specifically condemned the "importation" of unions and recourse to strikes. Now the industrialists were offering legalization of labor organization and the strike as the best solution to the whole labor question, as well as one of the best means for achieving rapid pacification of the agitated masses. Even more remarkable was the fact that Moscow's young industrialists in their 1905 notes definitively renounced the earlier insistence on harmony of interests between workers and employers and instead spoke of the necessity for allowing "a free struggle of interests" between labor and capital.

But strikes and unions alone were not enough. The industrialists commented that "only under different conditions of state life, with guarantees for the individual, with respect of the authorities for the law, with freedom for unions of various groups of the population joined by common interests, can the legal desire of the workers to improve their position assume a peaceful, legal form of struggle, which could only assist in the flourishing of industry, as is seen in Western Europe and America." They then stated their demands for political reform, which, they believed, would not only help to normalize relations between workers and employers but would promote "the success of industry itself in Russia, its victory on the world market." Specifically, they called for the equality of all citizens before a firm and stable law; inviolability of person and dwelling; freedom of speech and press; the introduction of universal compulsory education; and the participation of representatives of all classes in the legislative process.

In stating these demands, the authors of the notes particularly emphasized the benefits such reforms would bring to industry. They noted, for instance, that freedom of speech and press was necessary in order to facilitate "clarification of the workers' needs, improvement of their existence and the correct, successful growth of industry and popular well-being." Similarly, compulsory schooling was necessary since "in the enlightenment of the people lies the strength and power of the state and of its industry." Thus, if their political demands were similar to those of the liberal movement in general, the industrialists were moved to support such demands primarily because they believed that reforms of this nature would benefit industry. The pragmatism of the authors of these notes is apparent throughout—these were not ideologues but practical men of business who were uninterested in theories of representative government but who believed only that the creation of a popular assembly would be of benefit to themselves and to Russian industry.

One of the most interesting features of these resolutions was the considerable stress placed on "legality" as a basic principle to be introduced into Russian life. In earlier decades, Moscow industrialists had shown no great regard for the law. Vishniakov noted that in the 1850s the merchant attitude was that "the law . . . existed only to be evaded," and I. I. Ianzhul, the first factory inspector of the Moscow district, discovered the same attitude among industrialists in the 1880s. The majority of factory owners, he reported, "were accustomed to regard any talk about the law as just so much hot air and not worthy of their attention."[53] In view of their somewhat cavalier attitude toward the law in the past (an attitude partly bred by the bureaucracy's own frequently demonstrated disregard for the laws of the land), the sudden conversion of Moscow industrialists to the principle of legality was remarkable. And though they drew no direct connection here, it seems likely that the *zubatovshchina* was to a large degree responsible for this conversion. In both their 1902 note and their 1905 resolutions, Moscow businessmen put considerable stress on the illegality of the Zubatov movement, emphasizing the point that government agents were themselves violating the laws of the land by promoting strikes and other worker activities. The Zubatov incident seems to have been largely responsible for a dawning realization, at least among the younger members of Moscow's business elite, that the law could be a powerful protection against arbitrary acts by the government, not only in regard to its "management" of the labor question but in all its relations with industry. In other words, the adherence of Moscow businessmen to the principle of legality, espoused by the entire liberal movement, was probably again in large part based on practical experience: had the government itself obeyed the law, Zubatov's agents would have been prevented from stirring up trouble at Moscow factories.

If the January and February notes of the younger industrialists were notable for their political demands, their greatest interest nonetheless lies in their proposed solution to the labor question. Their demand for legalization of unions and strikes sounded very radical indeed, compared with past attitudes of Moscow industrialists toward labor relations. But this demand must be considered within the context of other statements on the *rabochii vopros* emanating from representatives of Moscow industry during 1905 and of the actions they took in regard to their own workers. And in that context, the notes of January and February lose much of their radicalism.

Early in 1905, the Exchange Committee established a special commission to consider labor problems. S. I. Chetverikov headed the commission, and representatives of the *molodye*, in particular Savva Morozov and P. P. Riabushinskii, took a leading role in its deliberations.[54] The commission's report, which appeared in April, demonstrated that the basic position of Moscow industrialists on the labor problem had changed little in substance and that they were still extremely reluctant to effect many of the changes in the factory order considered desirable by either the government or the workers. On the question of the length of the working day, the commission concluded that it should be lowered only to eleven hours, thus making it clear that Moscow industrialists were not inclined to give any serious consideration to the current demand of the workers for an eight-hour day. On the subject of wages, the commission insisted that for a variety of reasons it was impossible to establish a minimum wage or any sort of guaranteed wage. The commission likewise rejected other current demands of working-class spokesmen, finding it impossible to abolish the fines levied on workers for bad work or violation of factory regulations, or to allow workers to participate in the determination of wages, in decisions regarding the hiring or firing of personnel, or in the resolution of other questions involving the internal order of the factory. Many other problems which had been raised by working-class spokesmen were simply ignored in the report, including the question of insurance for workers and the need to regulate overtime work.

The commission's report did take up the question of strikes in some detail. It favored changing existing legislation in order to remove strikes from the sphere of criminal law: a strike should be regarded as a civil wrong, a simple violation of contract, rather than as a criminal act. At the moment of a strike, the workers would be considered to have violated the terms of their individual labor contracts with their employer. All such contracts would immediately become null and void, and the employer would therefore not be required to pay workers during a strike. But if unauthorized work stoppages were to be relegated to the field of civil law, and if the only penalty to be visited upon peaceful strikers was loss of pay, the use of violence during the course of a strike, the commission argued, should be subject to the severest penalties as a criminal act. The commission's definition of violence was broad. It encompassed the destruction of factory property, including "any unavoidable damage of property resulting from the suddenness of the work stoppage," and also the use of either force or threats against members of the factory management. In addition, the presentation of workers' demands during the time of a strike by a large crowd of people was to be included within the definition of "violence."[55]

While the report dealt with the question of strikes in some detail, it had little to say on the subject of unions, beyond giving them its stamp of approval. And, indeed, assuming that this report was fairly representative of the views of the Moscow elite on labor problems, one is left wondering where the unions proposed by the *molodye* would find a place for themselves in the scheme of things envisaged by Moscow factory owners. The report specifically rejected workers' requests to participate in decisions on wages and personnel and denied the possibility of establishing any sort of guaranteed wage for factory employees. It envisaged the continuation of the system whereby the workers as individuals, rather than in a group, entered into labor contracts with their employers. What, then, were the new unions supposed to do? The question is difficult to answer, since at no time did any representative of the Moscow business elite ever define precisely the functions which unions might assume in Russian industry. It appears, however, that Moscow businessmen saw unions chiefly as a means to allow workers to discuss and clarify their own needs, which would then be reported to the factory administration. There is no indication that any Moscow industrialist of whatever generation looked forward to the participation of workers' representatives in the making of essential decisions regarding the workers' living and working conditions. Such decisions, it seems, were to be left entirely to the discretion of management. Moscow employers also gave no indication of proposing national as opposed to purely local or company unions, whose effectiveness in the conduct of strikes would be open to question.[56]

For all their readiness to approve the legalization of strikes, Moscow industrialists at the same time sought to assure the creation of a situation in which such strikes would be totally ineffective. From the time of the January strikes in 1905, they began to show a new determination to create a united front against their workers. A January meeting of Moscow industrialists took a united stand against the strikers, pledging themselves to solidarity in refusing all of the workers' demands.[57] In their January and February notes, the industrialists commented that if workers were granted the right to organize unions, the same right must also be made available to their employers.[58] In May, *Promyshlennyi mir* reported that efforts were already being made in Moscow to create an all-Russian union of employers to conduct the struggle with workers' unions. The journal noted that in Moscow business circles it was hoped that such a union would protect employers from unreasonable demands made by the projected workers' unions, the fulfillment of which could have "harmful effects" on the industrial development of the country.[59] In fact, such a union did not appear until 1906, when industrialists of the Central Region came together for the purpose of struggle against their workers. This new organization of employers then proceeded to use such familiar methods as lockouts and black lists against troublesome factory workers.[60] Thus, it would be difficult not to agree with *Russkie vedomosti*'s pronouncement that the Moscow industrialists, in advocating a free struggle of interests, "forget only that the chances in this struggle are not equal"[61] (though to say that they "forgot" is certainly giving them the benefit of the doubt).

In the same issue, *Russkie vedomosti* also noted that the attitude of Moscow industrialists toward the labor question, as it emerged in 1905, was a vestige of the "old liberalism" that favored laissez-faire, and there was a good deal of truth in this observation. It seems entirely probable that the chief motive behind Moscow industrialists' demands for the creation of workers' and employers' unions and for the legalization of strikes was a hope of getting the government almost entirely out of the field of labor relations. The industrialists' January and February notes were most insistent on the point that the government's attempt to "manage" the labor question had only led to disaster and that government management should now give way to a "free struggle of interests." Their opposition to further government regulation of factory conditions was also manifested in May 1905, when industrialists from all over Russia, led by Moscow's G. A. Krestovnikov, walked out of the so-called Kokovtsov commission, established by the government to consider further factory regulation measures.

As an excuse for their sudden departure from the commission, Krestovnikov offered the destruction of the Russian fleet at Tsushima Straits, news of which arrived in St. Petersburg soon after the commission convened. Referring to this "terrible injury" that Russia had suffered, Krestovnikov maintained that the commission had no right to continue "to occupy itself with peaceful discussion of questions of our everyday, petty life."[62] But it is difficult to believe that the industrialists left the commission entirely because of the Tsushima disaster. Two days previously, before news of the naval defeat had been made known, Krestovnikov had already made a speech strongly objecting to the consideration of new factory laws. In his speech, Krestovnikov urged upon Minister of Finance V. N. Kokovtsov the view that what was needed in the field of labor relations was not further government regulation of factory life but the creation of conditions which would permit "freedom of economic struggle for the interested parties."[63] Thus, from the beginning the industrialists had attempted to obstruct the work of the commission. This fact, combined with their continuing emphasis on the necessity of creating a "free struggle of interests," clearly indicated that the industrialists were determined to do everything in their power to prevent further interference by the tsarist government in the labor question.

204 · THE MOSCOW BUSINESS ELITE

One particularly striking fact to emerge from the proceedings of the Kokovtsov commission was that it was Krestovnikov, a representative of Moscow's older generation, who was chosen to lecture the Minister of Finance on the necessity of creating a "free struggle of interests" between capital and labor. Krestovnikov's advocacy of this concept indicates a basic agreement between both generations of the Moscow business elite on the labor question. Indeed, it appears that dislike of government "management" of the labor question was the one issue on which there was the greatest unanimity within the Moscow elite and that many members of the older generation were prepared to accept the new solutions to the labor question proposed by their juniors. There were still some holdouts—Naidenov evidently never accepted the idea of unions and strikes and a "free struggle of interests," and no doubt others of his generation found such proposals too radical.[64] But Krestovnikov's endorsement of unions and "economic struggle" at the Kokovtsov commission on behalf of all the industrialists present is a good indication that these ideas, first expressed in the resolutions of Moscow's young industrialists, had won the sympathy of a large section of the Russian business elite, irrespective of age or geographical location.[65]

Thus, in spite of their numerous differences and disagreements, the two generations of the Moscow business elite gave evidence of considerable similarity in their approach to the labor question. Both were united in their dislike of government regulation of labor relations and in their determination to rid themselves of this regulation insofar as possible. Both were equally determined to hold the line against workers' demands and to maintain their autocratic control of their own factories. The area of labor relations was, in fact, the only one in which the similarities between the two generations were more striking than their differences in 1905.

THE position taken by Moscow industrialists on the labor question in 1905, though it was self-seeking, was perhaps neither so hypocritical nor so totally divorced from reality as it might appear at first glance. They did undoubtedly believe in the basic peaceableness of their workers and were convinced that troubles at the factories were more often than not the result of political or other factors over which the industrialists had no control. While there was some wishful thinking involved in their interpretation, no one could deny that political factors played a major role in the massive outbreak of strikes in 1905. Moreover, the industrialists' insistence that many of the workers' demands were so extreme that the workers themselves did not take them seriously should not be dismissed entirely out of hand. Certainly by the end of 1905 many liberal organs of the press, in normal times sympathetic with the workers and hostile toward employers, had come to find it difficult to put much credence in the demands presented by the factory workers and were beginning to agree with the industrialists both that the demands of the workers were completely unrealistic and that their realization would lead to the collapse of Russian industry.[66] And in later years, certain Mensheviks involved in the labor movement reached approximately the same conclusion as had the industrialists in 1905. Some Mensheviks believed that "strikes ostensibly economic in character often demonstrated by the unrealistic character of their objectives and the impatience and violence of the tactics with which they were conducted that they merely provided an excuse for the expression of political unrest."[67] Thus, not only the industrialists but many intellectuals who were close to the Russian labor movement viewed with some skepticism the seriousness of many of the workers' economic demands.

One also cannot peremptorily dismiss the industrialists' contention that the factory population was basically peaceable and docile. If the history of Russian industry was punctuated with innumerable examples of *buntarstvo*, which eventually gave way to an organized labor movement, nonetheless, in the nineteenth century many Russian workers, as some labor agitators discovered, were resigned to unquestioning acceptance of their fate and accepted the paternalistic premises on which the factory regime was based. The workers' acceptance of their role in a paternalistic system was clearly illustrated in Rakshanin's description of his visit to the Morozovs' Nikolskaia factory. When Rakshanin accompanied Savva Morozov into the courtyard of the factory, he discovered that it was filled with people, workers and others, who had requests to make of Morozov. As Morozov approached the crowd, one man went down on his knees in the snow before the great industrialist and began bowing low to the ground. Somewhat embarrassed by it all, Morozov dealt with their requests hurriedly and sent them to the factory office, promising he would give the necessary orders—a job for one, a grant of money for another. One tearful and persistent old woman followed Morozov as he moved away, pleading for a job and calling her potential benefactor *batiushka* (little father).[68] Other visitors to the Nikolskaia factory reported similar experiences. One, for example, told of an old woman who came to Morozov with her family problems, complaining about the behavior of her drunken son-in-law, a clerk in the factory office. Morozov promised to deal with the situation without delay.[69] Thus, to a certain extent a father-to-children relationship did exist between employers and their workers, similar to the relationship existing earlier between lords and serfs, and it seems likely that many industrialists counted on this relationship to keep their workers loyal and docile. Though this type of relationship was becoming increasingly precarious as the workers gained in education and in general awareness of the world around them, it had not entirely perished by 1905. It was still very much in evidence in the strike at the Nikolskaia factory in that year, when the workers' first request was to speak with Savva Timofeevich, who, they were sure, would listen sympathetically to their complaints and try to meet their demands.[70]

One should keep in mind, in considering the position of Moscow industrialists on the labor question, that conditions in many of the factories which they owned were far better than conditions in the average Russian factory. Chetverikov, one of Moscow's more progressive employers, related with pride that there was no strike at his factory in 1905 until December, when the workers struck not because of economic grievances but only to demonstrate their sympathy with the political goals of the Moscow uprising.[71] Other relatively enlightened Moscow employers had similar experiences in 1905.[72] Certainly, for an industrialist who dedicated himself, willingly or unwillingly, to the creation of schools, libraries, hospitals, tearooms, consumers' cooperatives, insurance funds, and so on, all for the benefit of his employees, and in addition perhaps voluntarily lowered working hours and raised wages beyond the norms common in Russian factories, it must have been difficult to understand why his workers should be dissatisfied with their working and living conditions.

Moreover, there was no doubt a good deal of truth in the contention of the industrialists that the material conditions of their workers were in most respects superior to those of the inhabitants of the Russian villages from which the workers came. The historian T. H. Von Laue has commented that the factories compared very favorably with the villages, since they offered a steady wage, provided medical care, and stimulated literacy and a broadening of cultural horizons. The comparatively good conditions existing at the factories led Von Laue to explain working-class discontent chiefly on the basis of a sense of alienation which the workers experienced when economic circumstances forced them to leave their villages to seek work in the factories. Never reconciled to this exile from the village, they experienced deepening discontent, which gradually assumed explosive proportions.[73]

Von Laue may well be right in indicating that some of the major factors at the base of working-class discontent should be sought outside the realm of purely political and economic factors. Anyone acquainted with conditions in Moscow factories cannot fail to be impressed with the incredibly unequal distribution of power within the factory order and with the fact that the workers were rendered almost totally unable to control their own lives. The exercise of autocratic powers by the factory administration, not only over the working life of the factory employees but over their nonworking time as well, creates, in anyone on the outside looking in, a sense of total oppression, quite irrespective of any economic exploitation. With the most minute details of the workers' lives being regulated by the factory managers, it is not difficult to understand the resigned complaint of a Morozov worker who explained simply, "we are all serfs of the Morozovs."[74] If for many years a sense of oppression was mitigated by the paternalistic relationship between employers and workers, with greater education and broader horizons many workers would have come to feel the weight of management's power more acutely and would have sought to regain control over their own lives.

In any case, the working-class discontent which eventually contributed so substantially to the destruction of Russian capitalism and the personal ruin of Moscow's business elite can only be attributed to a wide variety of factors, some of which were totally outside the ability of industrialists to control. There was little they could do to remedy the political discontents of their workers or to deal with the alienation of peasant-workers. All the same, it is impossible to avoid the conclusion that Moscow's industrialists more or less deliberately blinded themselves to very real economic dissatisfactions of their workers, as well as to other dissatisfactions arising out of the factory order—sources of discontent over which they did have some control. Blaming troubles at the factories on "hooligans," outside agitators, factory inspectors, the police, Zubatov agents, the workers' lack of political rights, they persistently chose to ignore very real problems within the factory order itself. Their attitude was not one which made a peaceful resolution of such problems likely. Their constant talk of "struggle" in 1905 and the measures they took to organize themselves for struggle with their workers made it clear that they would fight the demands of the workers every inch of the way. *Russkie vedomosti* undoubtedly was too kind when it wrote that the employers *"forget* only that the chances in this struggle are not equal." It seems unlikely that they "forgot" the inequality of the struggle which they proposed: it is more likely that they were perfectly aware of this inequality and were relying on it as a safeguard against any changes in the factory order which would reduce either their power or their profits. With government regulation of labor relations greatly reduced, if not eliminated entirely, and with the workers left to rely only upon their own unaided efforts, the industrialists no doubt believed that they would soon emerge as complete masters of their own factory domains.

If the Moscow business elite was somewhat obtuse in its approach to the *rabochii vopros*, they also miscalculated in drawing up their political plans in 1905. The Moscow industrialists who supported the constitutional movement, and particularly the group of *molodye* around P. P. Riabushinskii, believed that under a representative system of government industrialists would have greater power and find greater favor with other holders of power than under the autocratic regime. At the end of 1905 members of the Moscow business elite optimistically formed their own political parties and went forth into the electoral battle with high hopes. But their hopes were soon confounded as they met with decisive rejection at the hands of the voters. It is, in truth, difficult to imagine any reason why they should have expected electoral victories, given the small size of the "middle class" in Russia and the lack of any other substantial sector of society which would cast its votes for parties representing big business. The widespread hostility toward business and businessmen, the depth and enduring quality of which Moscow businessmen (particularly those of the younger generation) perhaps never fully grasped, virtually assured in advance that the permanent conquest of substantial political power by the business community would be, at the very best, a long and uphill struggle. And if hatred of the *kuptsy* came to haunt their political ventures, so too did the *kupechestvo's* own age-old reluctance to get involved in politics. Riabushinskii's hope for the creation of a national organization of businessmen which would act as a major political force was wrecked by the unwillingness of many businessmen to engage in direct political activity. If Riabushinskii and others of the *molodye* expected that political power would by historical right fall to them as representatives of Russia's bourgeoisie, if they believed that the forces of history were on their side, then history soon proved them sorely mistaken.

FROM the point of view of social development, Russia's businessmen had made great strides during 1905 and the years preceding. To argue, as Soviet historians have done, that they emerged as a "class" in 1905 seems, however, to be a bit premature. At best, their behavior indicated that they had progressed to a stage intermediary between *soslovie* and class, between *kupechestvo* and bourgeoisie, exhibiting a fascinating mixture of old and new.

New was the creation of a national organization of businessmen—an especially important step, as some form of national organization is generally considered a necessary attribute of the modern social class. New also was the relative unanimity of opinion that emerged in the resolutions and petitions of businessmen from all over the Empire in 1905, a sign of an emergent "class consciousness" transcending the concentration on purely local concerns inherent in the *soslovie* system. The businessmen who participated in the Kokovtsov commission in particular provided an impressive example of unanimity in both beliefs and actions. They seemed ready to accept a modern conception of the relationship between labor and management, eschewing the old paternalism and notions of the natural harmony of interests between the two groups in favor of engaging in "class struggle." Further, seen against the background of the *soslovie* mentality, the businessmen's actions during the sessions of the Kokotsov commission constituted what was, for the *kupechestvo*, almost unprecedented behavior. In effect, representatives of the *kuptsy* refused to accept the judgments of a representative of the tsar. Rather than do so, they broke up the meeting, determined to have their way and to find new means of forcing the tsar's government to turn their opinions into state policy. Such defiance did not even arise as a possibility within the confines of the *soslovie* system. Questioning the judgment of the tsar's officials was tantamount to questioning the accepted understanding that only the tsar could determine what was best for the nation.

Indeed, the statements emanating from Russian businessmen, and especially from the Moscow *molodye*, during 1905 implied that the *kuptsy* had their own ideas as to appropriate government policies touching on broad areas of Russian life and that their ideas did not necessarily concur with those of the tsar and his representatives. While these statements still approached political questions somewhat gingerly, they all the same reflected what Savva Morozov's speeches in the 1890s stated more clearly: the beginnings of the elaboration by businessmen of a view of progress that made industrial development the key to Russia's future, not simply the particular function of their own *soslovie*. This claim constituted another significant step in their social development. Certainly a central feature of the bourgeoisie's drive for hegemony in Western societies was advancement of its claim that only the acceptance of its value system—with an emphasis on sustained economic development prime among those values—could assure the future prosperity and happiness of the nation. Acceptance of this bourgeois scale of values, in one degree or another, by other social groups eventually signified the bourgeoisie's achievement of social and political dominance. Russian society was assuredly a long way from experiencing "bourgeois hegemony," in view of the continuing resistance or indifference to all-out capitalistic development in important sectors of the populace. But the basic question still remains: are we yet dealing here with a true bourgeoisie?

Impressive as these new ways of thinking and acting were, there was much in the behavior of Russian businessmen to indicate that they had not entirely broken out of the confines of the *soslovie* system to emerge, reborn, as a modern bourgeoisie. The reluctance of many of the founding members of the new national Association of Trade and Industry to involve the group in politics was essentially a reluctance to move beyond the rules of the *soslovie* system that limited *kuptsy* to an expression of opinion on narrowly defined economic questions. The language of many statements by businessmen in 1905—for instance, the January and February resolutions of Moscow industrialists—have a hauntingly old-fashioned ring. Such modern, bourgeois notions as civil liberties and representative government were urged not in the "interests of humanity"—as was common with the bourgeois liberals of Western Europe—but only in the best interests of trade and industry. Clearly, the spokesmen for Moscow business were still in a state of some confusion as to whether they were speaking out in the interests of "mankind" or even "the nation" or only in the interests of Russian business. There was still much of the *soslovie* mentality in these statements, a hesitancy to claim that they could speak for the nation rather than only for the *kupechestvo*.

The most convincing demonstration of the hold that the *soslovie* mentality still exercised on the minds of Russian businessmen came late in 1905, when they attempted to form political parties in preparation for election of members of the new State Duma. Not only in Moscow, but in St. Petersburg and elsewhere, members of the business elite created strictly local political groups, which appealed only to businessmen. It was almost as though they were trying to re-create local corporate *soslovie* organizations to choose delegates to a new zemskii sobor. Faced with an electorate composed not of *kuptsy* but of representatives of all social groups, such parties met with a speedy demise. In any case, they had nothing in common with modern bourgeois political parties which, even though they may represent narrow class interests, still try to present themselves as the best alternative for all the people, the true representatives of the best interests of all mankind.

Moscow's business elite, and, indeed, the entire Russian *kupechestvo*, had undergone an impressive period of development in the decades before 1905, moving them further and further away from the old-fashioned Russian *kupets* and transforming them at a relatively rapid pace into modern businessmen. There is no denying their progress in education, in cultural development, and in their understanding of their role in an emergent capitalistic society. Nonetheless, in 1905 their rebirth as a part of a modern bourgeoisie was still hampered by the lessons learned under the tutelage of the *soslovie* system, lessons that could be unlearned only gradually, or, as it turned out, annihilated by a total social cataclysm that would ruthlessly erase the last vestiges of the curious system that had served as the organizing principle of Russian society for so long.

APPENDIX

THE following abbreviated genealogical charts for four families are fairly representative of genealogies of the Moscow business elite as a whole. They are perhaps especially interesting as an indication of the extent of intermarriage among elite families. In fact, most of the marriage partners of elite families, particularly in earlier generations, came from among the *kupechestvo*. Spouses who are known to have come from other *sosloviia* or who had other occupations are so identified, but in some cases their origins are unknown.

Other genealogies may be found in A. S. Beliajeff's dissertation, "The Rise of the Old Orthodox Merchants of Moscow," and in Thomas C. Owen's *Capitalism and Politics in Russia*. Beliajeff gives detailed charts for the Riabushinskiis, the Guchkovs, and the Morozovs, while Owen's condensed genealogies for numerous families are intended chiefly to indicate links created by intermarriage.

PROKHOROV

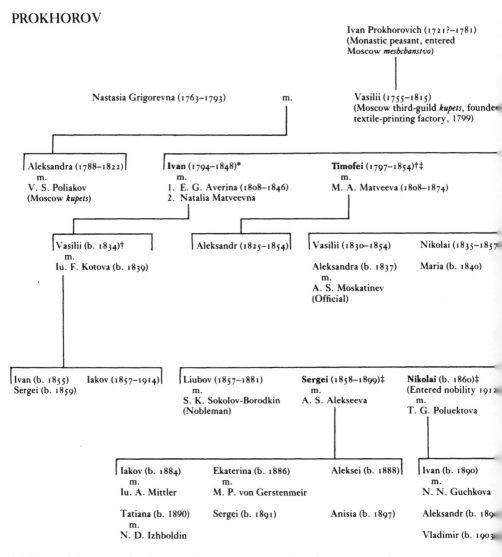

Ivan Prokhorovich (1721?–1781)
(Monastic peasant, entered
Moscow *meshchanstvo*)

Nastasia Grigorevna (1763–1793)   m.   Vasilii (1755–1815)
(Moscow third-guild *kupets*, founded
textile-printing factory, 1799)

Aleksandra (1788–1822)
m.
V. S. Poliakov
(Moscow *kupets*)

Ivan (1794–1848)*
m.
1. E. G. Averina (1808–1846)
2. Natalia Matveevna

Timofei (1797–1854)†‡
m.
M. A. Matveeva (1808–1874)

Vasilii (b. 1834)†
m.
Iu. F. Kotova (b. 1839)

Aleksandr (1825–1854)

Vasilii (1830–1854)

Aleksandra (b. 1837)
m.
A. S. Moskatinev
(Official)

Nikolai (1835–1857)

Maria (b. 1840)

Ivan (b. 1855)   Iakov (1857–1914)
Sergei (b. 1859)

Liubov (1857–1881)
m.
S. K. Sokolov-Borodkin
(Nobleman)

Sergei (1858–1899)‡
m.
A. S. Alekseeva

Nikolai (b. 1860)‡
(Entered nobility 1912)
m.
T. G. Poluektova

Iakov (b. 1884)
m.
Iu. A. Mittler

Ekaterina (b. 1886)
m.
M. P. von Gerstenmeir

Aleksei (b. 1888)

Ivan (b. 1890)
m.
N. N. Guchkova

Tatiana (b. 1890)
m.
N. D. Izhboldin

Sergei (b. 1891)

Anisia (b. 1897)

Aleksandr (b. 189)

Vladimir (b. 1903)

Boldface type indicates those individuals who bore primary responsibility in later generations for the family's business affairs.

*Honored citizen.
†Hereditary honored citizen.
‡Manufacturing councillor.
Sources: *Materialy k istorii prokhorovskoi manufaktury* and Buryshkin.

m.   Ekaterina Nikiforovna Mokeeva (1778–1851)
(Moscow second-guild *kupchikha*)

Konstantin (1798–1885)†‡
m.
1. E. A. Shelaputina (1809–1838)
2. P. N. Troilina (1818–1872)

Iakov (1804–1858)†
m.
1. V. V. Shaposhnikova (1811–1838)
2. L. I. Gubkina (1817–1888)

Anna (b. 1806)
m.
P. N. Pribylov

Sergei (b. 1834)

Konstantin (1842–1888)
m.
P. G. Khludova

Ekaterina (1828–1850)
m.
I. A. Bykovskii
(Kazan and later
Moscow *kupets*)

Ivan (1836–1881)
m.
A. A. Alekseeva
(1840–1909)

Varvara (1831–1901)
m.
V. S. Lepeshkin
(Moscow first-guild
kupets)

Anna (b. 1834)
m.
S. V. Perlov

Elizaveta (1832–1905)
m.
N. E. Ivanov
(Manager of Chetverikov factory)

Sofia (b. 1833)
m.
I. I. Burkhart

Aleksei (1847–1888)
m.
V. S. Mazurina

Anisia (b. 1861)
m.
A. I. Alekhin
(Nobleman)

Varvara (b. 1864)
m.
S. K. Sokolov-Borodkin
(Nobleman, widower of
her sister Liubov)

Ekaterina (b. 1866)
m.
1. V. Ia. Gvozdanovich
2. V. A. Beklemishev
(Sculptor)

Tamara (b. 1892)
m.
N. V. Lezhnev

Grigorii (b. 1892)

Liudmila (b. 1898)

Timofei (b. 1902)

Tatiana (b. 1905)

KRESTOVNIKOV

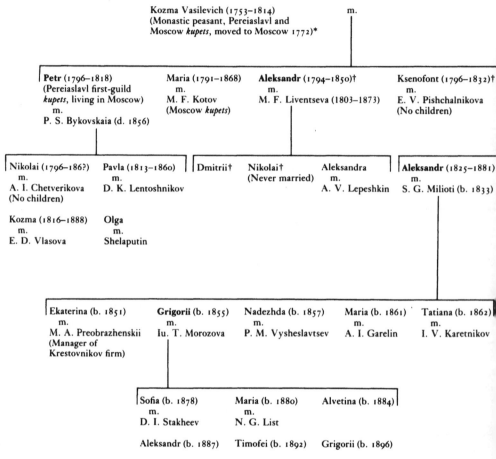

Kozma Vasilevich (1753–1814)   m.
(Monastic peasant, Pereiaslavl and
Moscow *kupets*, moved to Moscow 1772)*

Petr (1796–1818)   Maria (1791–1868)   **Aleksandr** (1794–1850)†   Ksenofont (1796–1832)†
(Pereiaslavl first-guild   m.   m.   m.
kupets, living in Moscow)   M. F. Kotov   M. F. Liventseva (1803–1873)   E. V. Pishchalnikova
m.   (Moscow *kupets*)   (No children)
P. S. Bykovskaia (d. 1856)

Nikolai (1796–186?)   Pavla (1813–1860)   Dmitrii†   Nikolai†   Aleksandra   **Aleksandr** (1825–1881)
m.   m.   (Never married)   m.   m.
A. I. Chetverikova   D. K. Lentoshnikov   A. V. Lepeshkin   S. G. Milioti (b. 1833)
(No children)

Kozma (1816–1888)   Olga
m.   m.
E. D. Vlasova   Shelaputin

Ekaterina (b. 1851)   **Grigorii** (b. 1855)   Nadezhda (b. 1857)   Maria (b. 1861)   Tatiana (b. 1862)
m.   m.   m.   m.   m.
M. A. Preobrazhenskii   Iu. T. Morozova   P. M. Vysheslavtsev   A. I. Garelin   I. V. Karetnikov
(Manager of
Krestovnikov firm)

Sofia (b. 1878)   Maria (b. 1880)   Alvetina (b. 1884)
m.   m.
D. I. Stakheev   N. G. List

Aleksandr (b. 1887)   Timofei (b. 1892)   Grigorii (b. 1896)

Boldface type indicates those individuals who bore primary responsibility in later generations for the family's business affairs.

*Kozma Vasilevich founded a trading firm. His sons established the Krestovnikov textile factory in 1814, and the sons of Konstantin Kozmich created the chemical plant in 1855.
†Hereditary honored citizen.
‡Manufacturing councillor
§Commercial councillor.
Source: *Semeinaia khronika Krestovnikovykh.*

Agapia Vasilevna (b. 1755)

Konstantin (1796–1841)†
m.
N. A. Moskvina (1806–1862)

Valentin (1827–1896)‡	Konstantin (1830–1899)	Nikolai (b. 1831)§	Vladimir (1830–1899)
m.	m.	m.	m.
E. I. Bona	1. Iu. I. Osipova (d. 1887)	A. S. Ermakova	M. P. Shelkovnikova (b. 1843)
(No children)	2. N. I. Sokolovskaia	(No children)	
	(No children)		

Iosif (b. 1834)†	Sergei (1837–1891)
m.	m.
A. E. Fedorova	P. M. Shibalova
(No children)	(No children)

Nadezhda (b. 1865)	Vera (b. 1868)	Ekaterina (b. 1870)	Aleksandr (b. 1873)	Sergei (b. 1874)
m.			m.	m.
A. N. Miliaev			O. I. Kutina	N. K. Polivanova

MAMONTOV

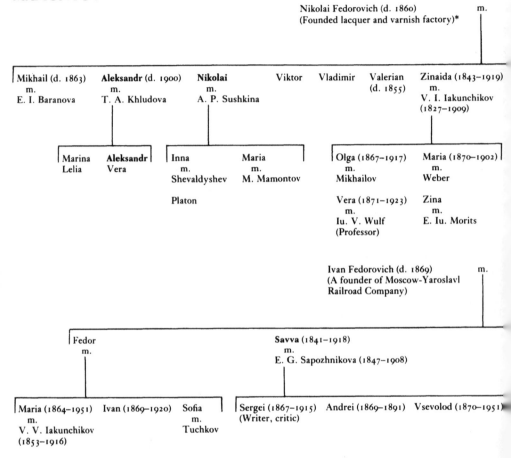

Boldface type indicates those individuals who bore primary responsibility in later generations for the family's business affairs.

*Fedor Ivanovich Mamontov, the progenitor of the Mamontov clan, was a liquor tax farmer. His two sons, Nikolai and Ivan, pursued their business careers independently. (A third son, Mikhail, left no children.)

†See Tretiakov genealogy for issue of this marriage.

Sources: *Promyshlennoe i torgovoe t-vo Mamontovykh*, Botkina, Buryshkin, Sakharova, Ziloti, Grover.

V. S. Vagina (d. 1864)

Vera (1844–1899)	Kirill	Ivan	Evdokia	Savva
m.	m.	m.	m.	m.
P. M. Tretiakov†	M. O. Levenstein	E. A. Rober	K. V. Rukavishnikov	E. F. Dmitrieva

Margarita	Sergei	Mikhail	Nikolai	Natalia
m.	m.			m.
M. A. Morozov	N. S. Sheremetevskaia			S. N. Tretiakov
	(Later Countess Brasova,			
	wife of Grand Duke			
	Mikhail Aleksandrovich)			

Maria Tikhonova

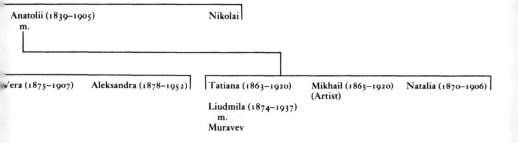

Anatolii (1839–1905)		Nikolai
m.		

Vera (1875–1907)	Aleksandra (1878–1952)	Tatiana (1863–1920)	Mikhail (1865–1920)	Natalia (1870–1906)
			(Artist)	
		Liudmila (1874–1937)		
		m.		
		Muravev		

TRETIAKOV

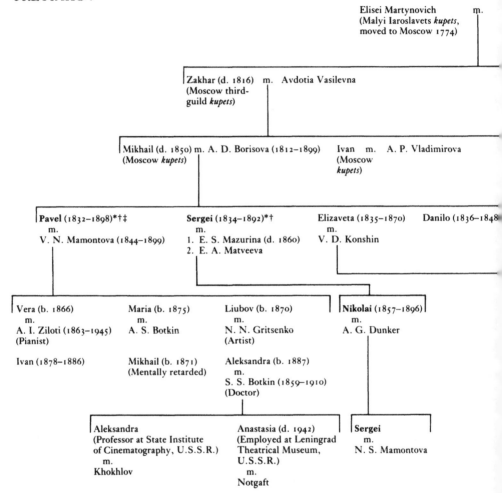

Boldface type indicates those individuals who bore primary responsibility in later generations for the family's business affairs.

*Pavel and Sergei Mikhailovich founded the Tretiakov linen-textile factory in 1866. Earlier, the Tretiakovs had engaged in trade in linen goods.
†Hereditary honored citizen.
‡Commercial councillor.
Sources: Botkina, Buryshkin, Ziloti.

Vasilisa Trifonovna

Osip

Petr

Sofia (1839–1902)	Aleksandra (1843–1848)	Nikolai (1844–1848)	Mikhail (1846–1848)	Nadezhda (1849–1939)
m.				m.
A. S. Kaminskii				Ia. F. Gartung
(1829–1897)				(Industrial chemist)
(Architect)				

Vladimir	Aleksandra (d. 1903)	Praskovia	Nikolai
m.	m.	m.	
M. N. Slatina	N. A. Alekseev (1852–1893)	A. I. Tchaikovsky	
(Noblewoman)		(Nobleman)	

NOTES

INTRODUCTION

1. Theodore H. Von Laue, *Sergei Witte and the Industrialization of Russia* (New York, 1969), pp. 269–71.

2. Ibid., p. 270.

3. Ibid., pp 268, 270.

4. G. F. Semeniuk, *Krupnaia moskovskaia tekstil'naia burzhuaziia i ekonomicheskaia politika tsarizma v kontse XIX veka* (Moscow, 1964), p. 12.

5. As late as 1913, 51.4 percent of Russia's national income came from agriculture, 28.0 percent from industry, and the remainder from trade, construction, transportation, and communications. P. I. Liashchenko, *Istoriia narodnogo khoziaistva SSSR*, vol. 2, *Kapitalizm*, 3rd ed. (Moscow, 1952), p. 697.

6. K. Kocharovskii, *Sotsial'nyi stroi Rossii* (Prague, 1926), p. 23.

7. Liashchenko, 2: 439–40. Useful summaries of Moscow's economic development in the later nineteenth and early twentieth centuries may be found in A. S. Nifontov, *Moskva vo vtoroi polovine XIX stoletiia* (Moscow, 1947); and Akademiia Nauk SSSR, Institut Istorii, *Istoriia Moskvy*, vol. 4, *Period promyshlennogo kapitalizma* (Moscow, 1954), and vol. 5, *Period imperializma i burzhazno-demokraticheskikh revoliutsii* (Moscow, 1955).

8. See Roger Portal, "Industriels moscovites: Le secteur cotonnier (1861–1914)," *Cahiers du monde russe et soviétique* 4, nos. 1–2 (1963): 11.

9. See I. F. Gindin, "Russkaia burzhuaziia v period kapitalizma, ee razvitie i osobennosti," *Istoriia SSSR*, no. 3 (May–June 1963), pp. 46–47; Ia. I. Livshin, "'Predstavitel'nye' organizatsii krupnoi burzhuazii v Rossii v kontse XIX—nachale XX vv.," ibid., no. 2 (March-April 1959), p. 101.

10. P. A. Buryshkin, *Moskva kupecheskaia* (New York, 1954), p. 112. Buryshkin was the son of a peasant who had become a wholesale trader in textile goods in Moscow and had quickly accumulated a modest fortune. Though the Buryshkin family never made it into the elite of the Moscow business world during the nineteenth century, after 1905 P. A. Buryshkin played an important role in civic affairs and in the political activities of the Moscow elite. His memoirs attempted to provide not only his personal recollections but an outline history of the leading business families of Moscow and of their professional and politi-

cal activities in the later nineteenth and early twentieth centuries. They are perhaps the single most valuable published source on the Moscow business elite in this period.

11. See I. F. Gindin, "Russkaia burzhuaziia," *Istoriia SSSR*, no. 2 (March-April 1963), p. 70; and "Sotsial'no-ekonomicheskie itogi razvitiia rossiskogo kapitalizma i predposylki revoliutsii v nashei strane," in *Sverzhenie samoderzhaviia* (Moscow, 1970), p. 58.

12. The only partial exceptions in the later nineteenth and early twentieth centuries were the journals *Russkii arkhiv* and *Promyshlennyi mir*. *Russkii arkhiv* published a small number of brief articles relating to certain outstanding Moscow businessmen of the past or containing genealogical information on Moscow business families. *Promyshlennyi mir* regularly covered current happenings in the business world, but contrary to what the title of the journal might lead one to expect, it was primarily concerned with discussion of state policies and economic problems of a general nature rather than with the activities of industrialists. In 1905 the title of the journal was changed to the more appropriate *Russkii ekonomist*. In addition, the Moscow journal *Russkoe obozrenie* gave a certain amount of space to matters of concern to Moscow businessmen, by whom it was subsidized (see chap. 4).

13. Among other things, Haxthausen noted that "if one now asks, 'To whom does that palace belong?' he gets as a reply, 'the manufacturer N, or the merchant O, etc. but formerly Prince A. or G.'" August von Haxthausen, *Studies on the Interior of Russia*, ed. S. Frederick Starr, trans. Eleanore L. M. Schmidt (Chicago, 1972), p. 25.

14. Quoted in Henry Rosovsky, "The Serf Entrepreneur in Russia," in Hugh G. J. Aitken, ed., *Explorations in Enterprise* (Cambridge, Mass., 1965), p. 343.

15. Ostrovskii depicted merchant life in a number of his earlier plays, including *Svoi liudi—sochtemsia, Prazdnichnyi son—do obeda, Svoi sobaki gryzutsia chuzhaia ne pristavai,* and *Zhenit'ba Bal'zaminova.* In some of his later works, appearing after 1860, he continued to portray the negative sides of merchant life but at the same time recognized that education and culture were beginning to penetrate the *kupechestvo,* a fact often overlooked by later writers who used Ostrovskii as their authority on the Russian business community. Such later plays included *Groza, Serdtse ne kamen', Ne vse kotu maslianitsa,* and *Pravda khorosho, a schast'e luchshe.* See Ts. P. Baltalon, "Tronulos'-li vpered temnoe tsarstvo?" *Artist,* no. 36 (April 1894), pp. 183–201.

16. *It's a Family Affair—We'll Settle It Ourselves,* in George Rapall Noyes, ed., *Plays by Alexander Ostrovsky* (New York, 1969), pp. 237–38.

17. Ibid., p. 258.

18. See P. S., "Moskva," *Novoe vremia,* 18 Sept. 1893; A. P. Lukin ["XII"], "Moskovskie pis'ma," *Novosti i birzhevye vedomosti,* 22 June 1891; A. Skabichevskii, "Konets temnogo tsarstva," ibid., 12 Nov. 1902. (*Novosti i birzhevye vedomosti* will hereafter be cited as *Novosti,* the name by which it was familiarly known to contemporaries.)

19. The use of this stereotype was so pervasive in the contemporary Russian press, both conservative and liberal, as practically to defy documentation. Perhaps the single most representative article is G. Startsev, "'Chumazye' vozgordilis'," *Novosti,* 19 July 1903. Also, in the latter months of 1893, statements by representatives of the business community regarding the current tariff war with Germany gave rise to innumerable articles in the press attacking the *kupechestvo* on every conceivable ground and making full use of this stereotype.

20. For a useful summary of the treatment of the *kupets* in Russian fiction see Eugen Häusler, *Der Kaufmann in der russischen Literatur* (Königsberg, 1935).
21. Petr Boborykin, *Kitai-gorod*, 2 vols. (St. Petersburg, 1883), 2: 266, 272.

CHAPTER I

1. Portal, "Industriels moscovites," pp. 7, 12–13.
2. Buryshkin, p. 109.
3. Ibid., pp. 110–11.
4. Ibid., p. 100.
5. Ibid.
6. Colorful descriptions of some of Moscow's more uncivilized but wealthy businessmen may be found in V. A. Giliarovskii, *Moskva i moskvichi* (Moscow, 1968), pp. 117–18, 299–302, 326–27.
7. N. O. Rakshanin [N. Rok], "Iz Moskvy," *Novosti*, 25 Nov. 1894; Ne fel'etonist, "Moskovskaia zhizn'," *Novoe vremia*, 25 March 1903.
8. Rosovsky, p. 363.
9. I have omitted from this list a number of families which Buryshkin included in his listing of the leading Moscow business dynasties. Some of the families he mentioned (Kumanins, Shelaputins, Mazurins), while very prominent in earlier decades, had by the end of the century lost much of their significance in the business elite. Some of the Kumanins and Shelaputins had been elevated into the nobility, and those who continued to maintain contact with the business world were rather unremarkable individuals (except perhaps for P. G. Shelaputin, a philanthropist of some note). The Mazurins, as Buryshkin recognized, were declining, both in regard to business and to social standing, and played little role in the social or business worlds of Moscow by the end of the century, though the Mazurin name still retained a certain glamour. Three other families whom Buryshkin included (Krasilchikovs, Shvetsovs, Tarasovs), if they were, as Buryshkin claimed, families of some importance in the business milieu, have left almost no traces of themselves in published sources; I can find nothing to indicate that they were families of the first rank. Finally, I have not included the Vtorovs chiefly because the family came to Moscow from Siberia only in 1897 and consolidated its claim to social significance only after 1905.
10. Conversely, a number of Moscow-based families of the business elite could be considered a part of the elite of other towns. For example, the Krestovnikovs, who owned a chemical plant in Kazan, played an important role in the civic and business life of that community. Several Krestovnikovs were at all times permanent residents of Kazan. *Semeinaia khronika Krestovnikovykh*, 3 vols. (Moscow, 1903–1904), 1: 98.
11. Rakshanin, "Iz Nizhniago," *Novosti*, 25 July 1898.
12. *K stoletiiu chainoi firmy "V. Perlov s synov'iami" (1787 g.–1887 g.). Istoriko-statisticheskii ocherk* (Moscow, 1897), pp. 71–74.
13. *Materialy k istorii prokhorovskoi trekhgornoi manufaktury i torgovo-promyshlennoi deiatel'nosti sem'i Prokhorovykh gody 1799–1915* (Moscow, n.d.), p. 449.
14. In fact, the only exceptions worthy of note were the Tarasovs, who were Armenian, and the Bostandzhoglos, who were of Greek nationality. But neither of these families were "foreign": both originated as members of non-Russian national minorities within the Russian Empire.
15. *Vospominaniia P. I. Shchukin [sic]*, vols. 3 and 4 (Moscow, 1912), 3: 36; P.

M. Shestakov, *Rabochie na manufakture T-va "Emil' Tsindel'"* v Moskve (Moscow, 1900), p. 1.

16. John P. McKay, *Pioneers for Profit: Foreign Entrepreneurship and Russian Industrialization, 1885–1913* (Chicago, 1970), p. 53n.

17. *Istoriia Moskvy*, 5: 36.

18. Ch. M. Ioksimovich, *Manufakturnaia promyshlennost' v proshlem i nastoiashchem* (Moscow, 1915), sec. 1, pp. 204–7; Buryshkin, pp. 61–67.

19. William L. Blackwell, *The Beginnings of Russian Industrialization, 1800–1860* (Princeton, 1968), p. 242.

20. McKay observed of the Goujons, one of Moscow's most prominent "foreign" business families, that even though they had been active in Russian industry since the 1830s, they had managed to preserve their French identity. "The family," he wrote, "reflects both the foreign origins of much of the Russian business class and the tenacious preservation of ethnic identity without assimilation" (McKay, p. 53n.). Jules Goujon, the family's leading representative at the turn of the century, was still a French citizen; on one occasion, when he irritated officials in charge of the so-called *zubatovshchina* in Moscow, he was narrowly saved from deportation by the intervention of the French ambassador. A. Morskoi, *Zubatovshchina. Stranichka iz istorii rabochego voprosa v Rossii* (Moscow, 1913), pp. 77, 91.

21. The activities of the Germans, French, and Swiss in particular were frequently mentioned in Moscow newspapers. See *Russkie vedomosti*, 10 Jan. 1893 and 16 Jan. 1897; *Moskovskie vedomosti*, 25 May 1896.

22. Vladimir Polunin, *Three Generations: Family Life in Russia, 1845–1902*, trans. A. F. Birch-Jones (London, 1957), p. 181.

23. Among the large textile factories controlled by Moscow businessmen, both the Danilovskaia and Zündel factories, as well as the Kränholm factory founded by Knoop, were owned by groups of Russian and "foreign" (mostly German) businessmen. Particularly active in this sort of joint venture on the Russian side were the Khludovs, the Shchukins, and K. T. Soldatenkov (Ioksimovich, sec. 1, pp. 61–62, 207–8, 284). At least in the case of the Shchukins and Soldatenkov, common business interests with German businessmen were accompanied by social intercourse. *Shchukinskii sbornik*, vol. 10 (Moscow, 1912), pp. 255–56; *Vospominaniia P. I. Shchukin*, 3: 23–24, 36.

24. V. P. Ziloti, *V dome Tret'iakova* (New York, 1954), p. 198.

25. Buryshkin, pp. 235, 237.

26. See L. Rabenek, "Moskva i eia 'khoziaeva' (Vremeni do pervoi mirovoi voiny 1914 g.)," *Vozrozhdenie*, no. 105 (Sept. 1960), pp. 101–4; and "Moskva vremeni do pervoi mirovoi voiny," ibid., no. 107 (Nov. 1960), pp. 101–12.

27. *Sochineniia Sergeia Sharapova*, vol. 1, *Moi dnevnik* (Moscow, 1900), sec. 1, p. 11.

28. See Blackwell, pp. 212–26; and Anton Serge Beliajeff, "The Rise of the Old Orthodox Merchants of Moscow, 1771–1894" (Ph.D. diss., Syracuse University, 1975).

29. The adherents of *edinoverie*, mostly former Old Believers, could retain the old forms of ritual in their worship while at the same time becoming communicants in the Orthodox church and accepting its authority.

30. Louis Menashe, "Alexander Guchkov and the Origins of the Octobrist Party: The Russian Bourgeoisie in Politics, 1905" (Ph.D. diss., New York University, 1966), pp. 17–20.

31. See *Torgovoe i promyshlennoe delo Riabushinskikh* (Moscow, 1913), pp. 32–33.

32. Buryshkin, pp. 118–19.

33. *Vospominaniia P. I. Shchukin*, 3: 22.

34. Regulations relating to the *sosloviia* may be found in the *Polnoe svod zakonov*, but much more readily accessible are articles under the relevant headings in the *Entsiklopedicheskii slovar'* and compilations and explications of the laws in various handbooks. Most useful has been S. A. Pros'bin, *Torgovo-promyshlennyi sbornik (Svod deistvuiushchikh uzakonenii po chasti promyshlennosti i torgovli)* (St. Petersburg, 1904). On social structure, see also V. O. Kliuchevskii, *Istoriia soslovii v Rossii* (Hattiesburg, Miss., 1969); Kocharovskii, cited above; G. B. Sliozberg, *Dorevoliutsionnyi stroi Rossii* (Paris, 1933); and Robert A. Feldmesser, "Social Classes and Political Structure," in Cyril E. Black, ed., *The Transformation of Russian Society: Aspects of Social Change since 1861* (Cambridge, Mass., 1960), pp. 338–50.

35. Quoted in Tibor Szamuely, *The Russian Tradition*, ed. Robert Conquest (New York, 1975), p. 35.

36. On the Legislative Commission, see Paul Dukes, *Catherine the Great and the Russian Nobility: A Study Based on the Materials of the Legislative Commission of 1767* (Cambridge, Eng., 1967); and Pavel N. Miliukov, "Voices of the Land and the Autocrat," in Marc Raeff, ed., *Catherine the Great: A Profile* (New York, 1972), pp. 113–55.

37. N. Vishniakov, *Svedeniia o kupcheskom rode Vishniakovykh (s 1848–1854 g.)*, 3 vols. (Moscow, 1903–1911), 3: 89.

38. *Moskovskie Kupecheskoe Sobranie. Istoricheskii ocherk* (Moscow, 1911), pp. 23–26.

39. V. Golitsyn, "Moskva v semidesiatykh godakh," *Golos minuvshego*, nos. 5–12 (May–Dec. 1919), pp. 119–20.

40. M. P. Shchepkin, *Soslovnoe khoziaistvo moskovskogo kupechestva. Istoriko-statisticheskii ocherk* (Moscow, 1872), pp. 3–49.

41. Walter S. Hanchett, "Moscow in the Late Nineteenth Century: A Study in Municipal Self-Government" (Ph.D. diss., University of Chicago, 1964), pp. 361–66, 480–87.

42. See note 34 above.

43. Buryshkin, pp. 87–88, 254–55.

44. Some businessmen held public positions under the auspices of a ministry or government department and were accordingly allotted a rank from the Table of Ranks. Buryshkin noted that "the Table of Ranks created broad opportunities for state service. Many were honorary justices of the peace—this was service under the Ministry of Justice. Trustees and creators of schools 'served' either in the Ministry of Education, or of Trade and Industry. For municipal leaders the road was opened through the Ministry of the Interior and, finally, 'philanthropists' could enter very light service in the Department of the Institutions of the Empress Maria." Buryshkin, p. 97.

45. The elite families also lost contact with relatives who had remained behind in the provinces even when these relations remained active in some field of business. See M. A. Rybnikova, *Gorbovskaia khronika po arkhivu sem'i Shchukinykh* (Moscow, 1919), p. 11. Rybnikova, born into the branch of the Shchukin family that remained behind in Borovsk, was aware of her family's relationship with the famous Moscow Shchukins, but it is clear from her memoir that no contact was maintained between the two branches of the family.

46. See Nikolai Naidenov, *Vospominaniia o vidennom, slyshannom i ispytannom*, 2 vols. (Moscow, 1903–1905), 2: 66ff.; A. S. Nevzorov, "Russkie birzhi. Otchet po komandirovke vo vnutrennie gubernii Rossii na letnie mesiatsy 1896 goda," *Uchenye zapiski Imperatorskogo Iurevskogo Universiteta*, no. 3 (1897), supp., pp. 45–48; no. 4 (1897), supp., pp. 49–69; and Livshin, 97–101.

47. Buryshkin, p. 234.
48. See S. Sef, *Burzhuaziia v 1905 godu. Po neizdannym arkhivnym materialam* (Moscow, 1926), pp. 86–100.
49. See Hanchett, pp. 47–49.
50. On the fair, see A. P. Mel'nikov, *Stoletie nizhegorodskoi iarmarki* (n.p., 1917). Equally informative are occasional pieces in the Russian press generally appearing during August, at the height of fair activity.
51. "Zapiska predstavlennaia 14 avgusta nizhegorodskim iarmarochnym kupechestvom g. ministru finansov," *Moskovskie vedomosti*, 16 Aug. 1893.
52. *Moskovskoe Kupecheskoe Sobranie*, pp. 190–97.
53. V. N. Storozhev, ed., *Istoriia Moskovskogo Kupecheskogo Obshchestva, 1863–1913* (n.p., n.d.), vol. 5, part 1, supp., pp. 65–66.
54. Hanchett presents some contradictory evidence on this point, while also placing the disputes in a framework of "class conflict." Hanchett, pp. 105–6, 186–89.
55. *Russkie vedomosti*, 14 June 1893.
56. Thomas C. Owen, *Capitalism and Politics in Russia: A Social History of the Moscow Merchants, 1855–1905* (New York, 1981), p. 101.
57. Giliarovskii, *Moskva gazetnaia*, in *Sochineniia*, 4 vols. (Moscow, 1967), 3: 84–109.
58. See Lenore O'Boyle, "The Middle Class in Western Europe, 1815–1848," *American Historical Review* 71 (April 1966): 826–45.
59. For a Russian intellectual's interpretation of bourgeois culture, see D. Protopopov, "O burzhuaznosti," *Zhizn'*, bk. 2 (Jan. 1899), pp. 17–29.
60. S. A. Shcherbatov, "Moskovskie metsenaty. Iz vospominanii," *Sovremennye zapiski* 67 (1938): 162.
61. Ibid., pp. 167–71.
62. *Vospominaniia D. Nikiforova. Moskva v tsarstvovanie Imperatora Aleksandra II* (Moscow, 1904), p. 63.
63. See A. I. Elishev, *Dvorianskoe delo. Sbornik statei* (Moscow, 1898), pp. 6–7, 10–13, 19.
64. Evgenii Trubetskoi, *Iz proshlogo* (Vienna, n.d.), pp. 19, 36; and *Vospominaniia* (Sofia, 1922), p. 6.
65. Trubetskoi, *Vospominaniia*, p. 6.
66. Buryshkin, pp. 84–86.
67. Vishniakov, 3: 92n.
68. *Vospominaniia D. Nikiforova*, p. 106.
69. Vishniakov, 3: 91–92.
70. Constantin Stanislavsky, *My Life in Art*, trans. J. J. Robbins (Boston, 1935), p. 22.
71. Ziloti, pp. 245–46, 249.
72. A. P. Botkina, *Pavel Mikhailovich Tret'iakov v zhizni i iskusstve* (Moscow, 1951), p. 236.
73. Ziloti, pp. 299–301.
74. Ibid., pp. 290, 344.
75. Ibid., pp. 162–63.
76. Vladimir Nemirovitch-Dantchenko, *My Life in the Russian Theatre*, trans. John Cournos (Boston, 1936), p. 123.
77. Ibid., pp. 130–31.
78. Quoted in Buryshkin, p. 290.
79. Ibid., pp. 190, 289–91, 322.
80. See Valentine T. Bill, *The Forgotten Class: The Russian Bourgeoisie from the Earliest Beginnings to 1900* (New York, 1959), p. 151.

81. Rakshanin, "Iz Moskvy," *Novosti*, 11 June 1894.
82. V. A. Kokorev, "Ekonomicheskie provaly po vospominaniia s 1837 goda," *Russkii arkhiv*, no. 5. (1887), bk. 2, pp. 141–44.
83. Ibid., p. 142.
84. Buryshkin, p. 128. Only A. A. Bakhrushin received a patent of nobility, when he donated his Theatrical Museum to the Academy of Science.
85. Kokorev, 142; *Semeinaia khronika Krestovnikovykh*, 1: 62.
86. Elishev, p. 201.
87. See ibid., pp. 201–4.
88. Trubetskoi, *Vospominaniia*, p. 127; A. N. Naumov, *Iz utselevshikh vospominanii 1868–1917*, 2 vols. (New York, 1954–1955), 1: 105.
89. Naumov, 1: 298.
90. See P. V. Sytin, *Iz istorii moskovskikh ulits (Ocherki)*, 2nd ed. (Moscow, 1952).
91. Giliarovskii, *Moskva i moskvichi*, pp. 150–51; *Vospominaniia D. Nikiforova*, p. 98.
92. Boborykin, 2: 238, 243.
93. Sergei Atava, "Oskudenie (Ocherki, zmetki i razmyshleniia tambovskogo pomeshchika)," *Otechestvennye zapiski* 249 (March 1880): 207–13.
94. D. Pokrovskii, "Ocherki Moskvy," *Istoricheskii vestnik* 51 (Feb. 1893): 793–94.
95. Giliarovskii, *Moskva i moskvichi*, 295–96.

CHAPTER 2

1. N. P. Chulkov, "Moskovskoe kupechestvo XVIII i XIX vekov," *Russkii arkhiv*, no. 12 (1907), p. 492.
2. Out of a group of 33 leading families, for whom fairly definite information on family origins is available, 16 came originally from the peasantry and 17 from the various urban *sosloviia*. Of the families of peasant origin, 10 were descended from serfs belonging to members of the nobility; 4 came from the monastic peasantry; and the exact origin of 2 families is unknown, though they most likely had been privately owned serfs. In the case of families belonging to the town *sosloviia*, 4 identified their ancestors as members of the seventeenth-century *posadskie liudi*, 12 as members of the *kupechestvo*, and 1 family came from the *meshchanstvo*.
   Chulkov, in the article cited in note 1 above, compiled a listing of the social status of a large group of leading Moscow business families at the time that their ancestors first registered in the Moscow *kupechestvo*. Of 74 families, 24 came to the Moscow *kupechestvo* from the peasantry, 41 from either the *posadskie liudi* or the provincial *kupechestvo*, and 9 from the *meshchanstvo*. It is impossible to tell how recently many of these families may have made the transition from the peasantry to provincial urban *sosloviia*, but the figures do seem to emphasize the importance of the provincial *kupechestvo* as a source supplying the Moscow *kupechestvo* with a large proportion of its more outstanding businessmen.
3. S. I. Chetverikov, *Istoriia vozniknoveniia i razvitiia gorodishchenskoi sukhonnoi fabriki* (Moscow, 1918), p. 3.
4. *Torgovoe i promyshlennoe delo Riabushinskikh*, pp. 7–12.
5. Bill, pp. 16–20.
6. Naidenov, 1: 6–7, 47; *Ocherk torgovoi i obshchestvennoi deiatel'nosti manufaktur sovetnika pochetnogo grazhdanina i kavalera byvshego moskovskogo gorodskogo golovy E. F. Guchkova* (Moscow, 1895), pp. 3–5.
7. *Piatidesiatiletie bumago-priadil'noi fabriki, nyne prinadlezhashchei vysochaishe*

utverzhdennomu Tovarishchestvu egor'evskoi bumago-priadil'noi fabriki brat'ev A. i G. Khludovykh (Moscow, 1895), pp. 3–9.

8. Portal, "Industriels moscovites," pp. 14–16, and "Aux origines d'une bourgeoisie industrielle en Russie," *Revue d'histoire moderne et contemporaine* 8 (1961): 56–59.

9. See Gindin, "Sotsial'no-ekonomicheskie itogi," p. 53.

10. According to government statistics published in 1900, the annual turn-over of goods handled by commercial establishments in the Moscow region was valued at 1,181,000,000 rubles, while the comparable figure for industrial en-terprises of the Moscow region was 961,000,000 rubles. In European Russia as a whole, the turnover of commercial enterprises was 64 percent higher than the turnover of industrial establishments, and in Moscow itself the corresponding figure was 168 percent. Liashchenko, 2: 439.

11. For example, the net profit of the Botkin tea firm for 1894–1895, an average year, was 229,602 rubles (*Moskovskie vedomosti*, 26 Jan. 1896). At the same time, the profits of many of the large textile factories were well over the million ruble mark.

The only truly large fortune accumulated in commerce rather than in indus-try by any business family associated with Moscow was that of the Vtorovs (whose Moscow mansion presently houses the American ambassador to the Soviet Union). In the 1860s, A. F. Vtorov, a native of Kostroma province, began wholesale trade in manufactured goods in Irkutsk. In the following dec-ades, the business expanded to include retail as well as wholesale trade and offices and stores in a number of Siberian towns. In 1900, the Vtorovs estab-lished their business as a stock company with a basic capital of 3 million rubles, a figure which was increased to 10 million by 1915. In that year the firm had a turnover of 30 million rubles. But having made their fortune originally in trade, the Vtorovs, like the Shchukins, also moved into industry. N. A. Vtorov, son of the family founder, became involved both in the textile industry and in the manufacture of munitions. Ioksimovich, pp. 3–5, 7; Liashchenko, p. 441; I. F. Gindin, "Moskovskie banki v period imperializma (1900–1917 gg.)," *Istoricheskie zapiski* 58 (1956): 58–60.

12. Ioksimovich, sec. 1, p. 207, and p. 61.

13. Ibid., sec. 1, p. 47.

14. Buryshkin, p. 147.

15. *Moskovskie vedomosti*, 27 Aug. 1904; *Promyshlennyi mir*, no. 41 (7 Oct. 1901), p. 911; no. 37 (12 Sept. 1904); p. 729.

16. Chetverikov, pp. 12–13.

17. Ibid., pp. 12–13, 17.

18. Ibid., p. 17; *Moskovskie vedomosti*, 11 April 1896.

19. *Torgovoe i promyshlennoe delo Riabushinskikh*, pp. 50–51.

20. See Buryshkin, pp. 58–59.

21. See *Istoriia Moskvy*, 4: 213.

22. *Moskovskie vedomosti*, 8 March 1904; *Piatidesiatiletie fabriki Khludovykh*, pp. 25–26.

23. Ioksimovich, sec. 1, pp. 196–98.

24. Ibid., sec. 1, pp. 61, 66.

25. Ibid., sec. 1, p. 284.

26. Ibid., sec. 1, pp. 45, 47.

27. *Semeinaia khronika Krestovnikovykh*, 1: 40.

28. S. G. Budagov and P. A. Orlov, eds., *Ukazatel' fabriki i zavodov evropei-skoi Rossii. Materialy dlia fabrichno-zavodskoi statistiki*, 3rd ed. (St. Petersburg, 1894), pp. 168, 173–74; Buryshkin, p. 129.

29. *Moskovskie vedomosti*, 10 April 1896; *Promyshlennyi mir*, no. 24 (10 June 1901), p. 574.

30. Ioksimovich, sec. 7, p. 3.

31. Stuart R. Grover, "Savva Mamontov and the Mamontov Circle, 1870–1905: Art Patronage and the Rise of Nationalism in Russian Art" (Ph.D. diss., University of Wisconsin, 1971), pp. 243–44, 343–51.

32. Liashchenko, 2: 460–61.

33. Gindin, "Moskovskie banki," p. 55.

34. *Istoriia Moskvy*, 4: 209, 214.

35. Gindin, "Moskovskie banki," p. 39.

36. Ibid., pp. 51–52; Liashchenko, 2: 456; *Istoriia Moskvy*, 4: 210, and 209.

37. Gindin, "Moskovskie banki," pp. 38–39, 43, 54, 103.

38. Buryshkin, p. 110; Vladimir Riabushinskii, "Kupechestvo moskovskoe," *Den' russkogo rebenka* 18 (April 1951): 178.

39. See "Pervyi vserossiiskii birzhevoi s"ezd," *Novoe vremia*, 25 Nov. 1903.

40. Ne fel'etonist, "Moskovskaia zhizn'," ibid., 9 Sept. 1900.

41. *Torgovoe i promyshlennoe delo Riabushinskikh*, p. 53.

42. Rakshanin, "Iz Moskvy," *Novosti*, 9 Dec. 1900; A. K. Golubev, ed., *Russkie banki. Spravochnye i statisticheskie svedeniia o vsekh deistvuiushchikh v Rossii gosudarstvennykh, chastnykh i obshchestvennykh kreditnykh uchrezhdeniiakh* (St. Petersburg, 1899), pp. 77, 208.

43. Buryshkin, pp. 205, 208; "Nekrolog. V. A. Kokorev," *Novosti*, 24 April 1889.

44. *Promyshlennyi mir*, no. 16 (15 April 1901), p. 393; *Russkie vedomosti*, 28 March 1903 and 22 March 1904.

45. *Moskovskie vedomosti*, 6 May 1905, 12 May 1905.

46. Sytin, *Iz istorii moskovskikh ulits*, p. 94; Giliarovskii, *Moskva i moskvichi*, pp. 296–97; *Moskovskie vedomosti*, 9 May 1896.

47. N. V. Polenova, *Abramtsevo. Vospominaniia* (Moscow, 1922), p. 5ff.

48. Ziloti, pp. 137–39; *Vospominaniia P. I. Shchukin*, 3: 22.

49. Ioksimovich, sec. 1, p. 37.

50. *Kratkoe opisanie bumagopriadil'noi i tkatskoi fabriki prinadlezhashchei Tovarishchestvo egor'evskoi bumagopriadil'noi fabriki brat'ev A. i G. Khludovykh* (Moscow, 1900), p. 7.

51. *Vospominaniia P. I. Shchukin*, 3: 46, 47, 49.

52. *Promyshlennyi mir*, no. 43 (10 Sept. 1900), pp. 1005–6. The same Morozov family also owned the estate of Gorki outside Moscow, where Lenin later lived and died. Shcherbatov, p. 162.

53. Ioksimovich, sec. 1, p. 149.

54. *Promyshlennyi mir*, no. 32 (25 June 1900), p. 745.

55. "Bogorodskoe imenie I. S. Perlova," *Moskovskie vedomosti*, 4 Feb. 1900.

56. The larger of the Ushkov estates consisted of 42,000 *desiatiny* of land in Simbirsk province, while their smaller estate, which had once belonged to the Trubetskoi family, included 13,500 *desiatiny*. Naumov, 1: 161–78.

57. Buryshkin, p. 60. Buryshkin pointed out that one reason for the slow and weak development of "professional organizations" (he refused to recognize them as syndicates) among textile manufacturers, especially in the field of cotton textiles, was that the Moscow Exchange Committee represented the manufacturers' interests very well and brought them together for discussion of common problems. He also insisted that even after 1905 the new Society of Cotton Textile Manufacturers of the Moscow region did not achieve the same importance as groupings in other fields such as linen or woolen textiles, again because the Exchange Committee continued to serve as an effective organ of

the cotton textile industrialists. Buryshkin, pp. 74–75, 261, 264–5. See also V. Ia. Laverychev, "Nekotorye osobennosti razvitiia monopolii v Rossii (1900–1914 gg.)," *Istoriia SSSR*, no. 3 (May–June 1969), pp. 80–85.

58. Liashchenko noted that the "development of finance-monopolistic tendencies" did not achieve the same degree of development in the textile industry of the Moscow region as it did in many fields of heavy industry. Nonetheless, he found that the "transformation of Moscow 'textile' capital into bank and finance capital and its transition from limited credit-financial operations in the textile industry onto the path of broad investment" was beginning in the early twentieth century. He singled out the activities of the Riabushinskiis and of Vtorov as manifestations of this trend. Liashchenko, 2: 453, 460.

Gindin, however, has disputed Liashchenko's conclusions and has refused to recognize the Riabushinskiis as true representatives of monopoly capitalism, partly on the grounds that their only attempts at monopolization came in the field of trade (lumber and flax) rather than in heavy industry and partly on the grounds that they simply lacked both the spirit and the technique of the true monopoly capitalists of St. Petersburg. Gindin accepted N. A. Vtorov as a "monopoly capitalist" but did not consider him typical of Moscow business. Gindin argued that the typical Moscow capitalists stood aside from the movement toward creation of monopolies and bank financing and takeover of industrial concerns and were, in fact, threatened by it rather than participating in it. Gindin, "Moskovskie banki," pp. 54–60, 103–4.

59. Portal has provided a useful summary of the development of the cotton textile industry of the Moscow region during the course of the nineteenth century in his "Industriels moscovites." See also K. A. Pazhitnov, *Ocherki istorii tekstil'noi promyshlennosti dorevolutsionnoi Rossii. Khlopchato-bumazhnaia, l'no-pen'kovaia i shelkovaia promyshlennost'* (Moscow, 1958); and Michael O. Gately, "The Development of the Russian Cotton Textile Industry in the Pre-Revolutionary Years, 1861–1913" (Ph.D. diss., University of Kansas, 1968).

60. Rosovsky, p. 360; Budagov and Orlov, pp. ix, 41, 43; Liashchenko, 2: 444.

61. Bill, for instance, subtitled his chapter on the Morozov family "The Archetype of the Russian Bourgeoisie." Bill, p. 16.

62. Budagov and Orlov, p. ix; *Materialy k istorii prokhorovskoi manufaktury*, p. 141.

63. Ioksimovich, sec. 1, pp. 18–19.

64. Ibid., sec. 1, pp. 46–47.

65. Naidenov, 1: 55.

66. Buryshkin, p. 177. After liquidation of their industrial concern, the Guchkov brothers (Nikolai, Aleksandr, and Konstantin) became, to a large extent, simply *rentiers*. In the early twentieth century, one or more of the brothers had an interest in the following enterprises: the Moscow Discount Bank, the Moscow Private Commercial Bank, the Petersburg International Bank, the Nizhegorod–Samara Land Bank, the Northern Insurance Company, the "Russia" Insurance Company, the Petersburg Discount and Loan Bank, and the Russian Steamship and Trading Company. Aleksandr also held shares in *Novoe vremia* and, after 1905, published the Octobrist paper *Golos Moskvy*. Menashe, p. 23n.

67. *Istoriia Moskvy*, 4: 94–95.

68. Naidenov, 1: 47–56.

69. Buryshkin, p. 173. In the second generation of Abrikosovs, the only son interested in the business died at an early age. The third generation produced a famous doctor, a diplomat, a Tolstoyan idealist, and several lawyers and

mathematicians, but no outstanding businessman. George Alexander Lensen, ed., *Revelations of a Russian Diplomat: The Memoirs of Dmitrii I. Abrikossow* (Seattle, 1964), pp. x–xi, 6–8.

70. Buryshkin, pp. 154–55.

71. Budagov and Orlov, pp. 41, 42–43, 80, contains the data for the Nikolskaia, the Vishniakov-Shamshin, the Khludov, and the Danilovskaia factories. *Istoriia Moskvy*, 4: 95, is the source of the Guchkov figures. Budagov and Orlov, p. 80, also provides the Sapozhnikov data.

72. Budagov and Orlov, p. 87; *Prokhorovskaia trekhgornaia manufaktura v Moskve, 1799–1899. Istoriko-statisticheskii ocherk* (Moscow, 1900), p. 45.

73. *Kratkoe opisanie fabriki Khludovykh*, p. 1.

74. Budagov and Orlov, p. 50; *Kratkii obzor uchrezhdenii kul'turno-prosvetitel'-nykh i po okhrane zdorov'ia rabochikh i sluzhashchikh pri fabrikakh Tovarishchestva manufaktur Ivana Konovalova s synom* (Moscow, 1913), p. 1.

75. Many of the factory histories and informative pamphlets published under the auspices of firms owned by the Moscow dynasties give detailed descriptions of all these institutions and activities connected with the factories, but perhaps the most detailed and informative among them are three publications of the Konovalovs: *Torgovo-promyshlennaia deiatel'nost' firmy Ivana Aleksandrovicha Konovalova, 1812–1896 g. (Istoriko-statisticheskii ocherk)* (Moscow, 1896); *Tovarishchestvo manufaktur Ivana Konovalova s synom, 1812–1912 g. Kratkii istoricheskii ocherk* (Moscow, n.d.); and the work cited in note 74 above.

76. F. Pavlov, *Za desiat' let praktiki (Otryvki vospominanii, vpechatlenii i nabludenii iz fabrichnoi zhizni)* (Moscow, 1901), p. 13.

77. Ibid., p. 14. The lengths to which factory owners and managers went in exercising control over the workers are well illustrated by this excerpt from nineteenth-century factory regulations pertaining to the behavior of workers and their families in the factory barracks: "During the working hours it is forbidden to sing or to dance. At night it is forbidden to use the samovar. The workers must always assume a humble and courteous attitude and treat the women decently without insulting them either by action or in words. After ten o'clock at night every worker must remain in his room. Except in case of necessity, he may not enter other rooms or walk around the hall." Quoted in Reinhard Bendix, *Work and Authority in Industry: Ideologies of Management in the Course of Industrialization* (New York, 1963), p. 182.

78. See "O vvedenii starost na moskovskikh fabrikakh," *Russkie vedomosti*, 9 Nov. 1903.

79. Semeniuk, pp. 16–17.

80. Figures for the profit comparisons are from *Moskovskie vedomosti*, 4 March 1896, 12 March 1904, 22 May 1896, 25 May 1904, 3 March 1896, and 8 March 1904. Soviet historians have argued that Moscow textile manufacturers tended to understate their profits. Gindin believed that because of peculiar accounting practices, the reported net profits of textile firms generally were grossly understated (Gindin, "Sotsial'no-ekonomicheskie itogi," p. 47). Semeniuk accused Moscow textile manufacturers of outright falsification in the reporting of income, in order to avoid taxation (Semeniuk, p. 16).

On the other hand, at least one contemporary student of the Moscow textile industry argued that the profit rates of textile firms were grossly exaggerated. He contended that determination of rates of profit ought to take into account the fact that textile manufacturers had reinvested a considerable amount of their past profits in their enterprises without raising their basic capital. He estimated, for instance, that by 1899 a total of 27,780,000 rubles had actually been invested in the Morozovs' Nikolskaia enterprise, most of that total, above the original 5 million rubles basic capital, having come from profits that were reinvested rather than distributed as dividends. Using that figure, he found that Nikolskaia's rate of profit in 1899 was only 12 percent, rather than 66 percent (the figure arrived at by calculating on the basis of basic capital alone). V. U., "Manufaktura nashikh glavnykh raionov," *Moskovskie vedomosti*, 1 Aug. 1900.

The only conclusion that can be drawn from these opposing arguments is that rates of profits cited for Russian concerns should be handled with some care. There may well have been "concealed profits," as Gindin and Semeniuk argue; but given the considerable amount of profits which was reinvested, without increases in basic capital, it would perhaps be more indicative of the actual profitability of Moscow firms to calculate their rate of profit on the basis of net worth rather than basic capital.

81. Buryshkin, pp. 109, 134-35.

82. Moskvich, "Kupecheskaia Moskva," *Novoe vremia*, 11 June 1903; *Birzhevye vedomosti*, 30 Dec. 1893.

83. Pokrovskii, "Ocherki Moskvy," *Istoricheskii vestnik* 52 (May 1893): 395; *Novoe vremia*, 11 June 1903.

84. *Tovarishchestvo manufaktur Ivana Konovalova*, p. 19.

85. *Materialy k istorii prokhorovskoi manufaktury*, p. 269.

86. *Semeinaia khronika Krestovnikovykh*, 1: 34.

87. Quoted in Grover, p. 18.

88. Ibid., p. 19.

89. See Naidenov, 1: 15-16; *Ocherk E. F. Guchkova*, p. 6; Buryshkin, pp. 101-2.

90. See Vishniakov, 2: 31; *Ocherk E. F. Guchkova*, p. 6; Naidenov, 1: 11.

91. Naidenov, 1: 77.

92. *Piatidesiatiletie fabriki Khludovykh*, pp. 15-16. The Khludov agreement dated from 1846. The Prokhorov brothers drew up a similar agreement in 1843, requiring that the major part of their profits were to be reinvested in the enterprise and strictly limiting the amount they could take out in salaries. *Materialy k istorii prokhorovskoi manufaktury*, p. 141.

93. Nemirovitch-Dantchenko, p. 116.

94. Maxim Gorky recalled that Morozov's personal expenditures were only around 100,000 rubles a year and that Morozov contributed about 24,000 rubles annually to the Russian Marxist newspaper *Iskra*, plus unspecified amounts to the "Political Red Cross" and other left-wing causes. M. Gor'kii, *Literaturnye portrety* (Moscow, 1959), p. 305. Accounts for 1901 show that the personal and household expenses of M. A. and M. K. Morozov for that year amounted to 196,675 rubles. N. Zhuravlev, "Na rospisi lichnykh raskhodov fabrikanta M. A. Morozova," *Krasnyi arkhiv* 83 (1937): 227.

95. Alexander Gerschenkron, *Economic Backwardness in Historical Perspective* (New York, 1962), pp. 9-47; Beliajeff, pp. 236-39.

96. *Promyshlennoe i torgovoe tovarishchestvo br. A. i N. Mamontovykh v Moskve 1854-1909* (Moscow, n.d.), p. 3.

97. *Tovarishchestvo manufaktur Ivana Konovalova*, pp. 28-29; *Torgovo-promyshlennaia deiatel'nost' Konovalova*, p. 7.

98. *Materialy k istorii prokhorovskoi manufaktury*, p. 249.

99. *Prokhorovskaia trekhgornaia manufaktura*, p. 24.

100. Ibid., p. 25; *Materialy k istorii prokhorovskoi manufaktury*, pp. 451, 455.

101. Mikhail I. Tugan-Baranovsky, *The Russian Factory in the 19th Century*, trans. Arthur Levin and Claora S. Levin (Homewood, Ill., 1970), p. 322; see

also V. P. Litvinov-Falinskii, *Fabrichnoe zakonodatel'stvo i fabrichnaia inspektsiia v Rossii*, 2nd ed. (St. Petersburg, 1904), pp. 106–7; S. A. Fedotov, "Obshchii obzor khlopchatobumazhnoi promyshlennosti," *Novoe vremia*, 14 Aug. 1896, and 15 Aug. 1896; Gindin, "Sotsial'no-ekonomicheskie itogi," pp. 45–46; Portal, "Industriels moscovites," pp. 14, 16–17. Von Laue noted considerable modernization of equipment in the textile industry in the 1890s and pointed out that much of this new machinery remained in operation for decades after the revolution of 1917. For example, at the Trekhgornaia factory, once the property of the Prokhorovs, "the average age of mechanical looms in 1955 was sixty years, of the cloth-printing machines sixty-one years." Von Laue, *Sergei Witte and the Industrialization of Russia*, pp. 268–69.

102. See Alain Besançon, "La Russie et 'l'Esprit du capitalisme,'" *Cahiers du monde russe et soviétique* 8, no. 4 (Oct.–Dec. 1967): 509–27.

103. I. I. Ianzhul, *Mezhdu delom. Ocherki po voprosam narodnogo obrazovaniia, eknomicheskoi politiki i obshchestvennoi zhizni* (St. Petersburg, 1904), pp. 449–53.

CHAPTER 3

1. N. A. Kablukov quoted in Anna Ivanovna Volkova, *Vospominaniia, dnevnik i stati* (Nizhnii Novgorod, 1913), pp. xxiii–xxiv.

2. In the majority of cases, the older generation of the 1890s represented the second generation of Moscow's business dynasties. However, in some families these men and women constituted the third, or even fourth, generation of a dynasty.

3. *Torgovoe i promyshlennoe delo Riabushinskikh*, p. 30.

4. Menashe, p. 20.

5. Naidenov, 2: 11–12.

6. *Moskovskoe Kupecheskoe Sobranie*, p. 67.

7. Quoted in ibid., p. 69.

8. A good description of social and cultural change in the lower strata of the Moscow *kupechestvo* can be found in Valerii Briusov, *Iz moei zhizni. Moia iunost'. Pamiati* (Moscow, 1927). Briusov, the famous "decadent" poet, was the grandson of a peasant who had enriched himself through trade in cork and the son of a merchant whose preoccupation with education and culture contributed to his eventual financial ruin. Of equal, if not greater, interest are the memoirs of Vladimir Polunin, cited previously, and those of I. A. Slonov, *Iz zhizni torgovoi Moskvy (Polveka nazad)* (Moscow, 1914). Slonov, son of a Kolomna gardener, made a modest fortune in trade and became a European traveler, but he never quite approved of the numerous changes occurring during his lifetime in the business milieu.

9. *Torgovoe i promyshlennoe delo Riabushinskikh*, p. 13.

10. Vishniakov, 2: 92.

11. Ibid.

12. Ibid., 2: 32.

13. Ibid., 3: 19.

14. *Manufaktur-sovetnik, moskovskii kupets Timofei Vasil'evich Prokhorov* (n.p., n.d.), pp. 3–5.

15. The prevalence of Germans among the tutors and governesses employed by Moscow merchant families is quite striking. If the nobility of the past had sought out Frenchmen, Moscow merchants seemed to prefer Germans as teachers for their sons and daughters. The prevalence of German tutors was perhaps based partly on sheer availability, Germans being the largest group of Western Europeans in Moscow's foreign colony. But Vishniakov suspected that his

father may have preferred a German tutor because he was impressed with the German families in Moscow—especially with their love of order, a passion which Vishniakov's father shared (Vishniakov, 2: 95). Some special qualities of Moscow's German businessmen may have recommended them to Russian merchants, though their preference for German tutors probably stemmed in part from the fact that a knowledge of German was becoming increasingly useful for Moscow *kuptsy*.

What effects this German influence in the education of the children of Moscow's substantial businessmen may have had is difficult to discern. In later life, few, if any, of the older generation of the 1890s showed any great admiration for German culture, and their foreign visits took them to France, Italy, and England at least as frequently as to Germany. Whether German tutors and governesses may have played some role in helping to inculcate or to reinforce the "bourgeois values" of Moscow businessmen is impossible to determine, but in some cases this may well have occurred. Certainly not, however, in the case of the Vishniakovs—their German tutor, who came to be greatly loved by the whole Vishniakov family, was an absent-minded intellectual, who showed no Germanic passion for order, discipline, or hard work.

16. *Ocherk E. F. Guchkova*, pp. 8–10, 14.

17. *Materialy k istorii prokhorovskoi manufaktury*, pp. 126–27, 190.

18. *Semeinaia khronika Krestovnikovykh*, 1: 63.

19. Ibid., 1: 76–79; see also *Materialy k istorii prokhorovskoi manufaktury*, p. 191.

20. *Semeinaia khronika Krestovnikovykh*, 2: 12.

21. Ibid., 2: 54–55.

22. Ibid., 2: 21.

23. Ziloti, p. 74.

24. *Semeinaia khronika Krestovnikovykh*. Krestovnikov's travel record pales in comparison with those of other individuals of the older generation such as P. M. Tretiakov, who for many years made biennial trips to Italy, later extending his itinerary to include other Western European countries. Ziloti, pp. 145, 270, 306–7.

25. *Manufaktur-sovetnik Prokhorov*, p. 21.

26. Ibid., pp. 45–48.

27. *Torgovoe i promyshlennoe delo Riabushinskikh*, p. 13.

28. Vishniakov, 3: passim.

29. Lensen, pp. 6–7.

30. Botkina, pp. 16, 36.

31. "Nekrologi. Soldatenkov, K. T.," *Istoricheskii vestnik* 85 (July 1901): 378. Properly speaking, Soldatenkov was not, in terms of age, a member of the older generation of the 1890s but belonged to an even earlier generation. In fact, Soldatenkov was practically a whole dynasty in himself, as his life spanned nearly a century (1818–1901), and both his predecessors and successors were unremarkable. But Soldatenkov was a man determined to keep up with the times, and he transcended the educational and cultural limitations which most of his own generation, measured in terms of age, never overcame and made himself an integral part of a younger generation in terms of his education, his interests, his cultural activities. In the 1890s, when he was almost the only surviving member of his age-group among the elite, he was so much a part of the activities of the business elite that I have taken some liberty with his birth date and feel justified, on the grounds of education and culture, in including him as an honorary member of the older generation of the 1890s.

32. F. E. Korsh, "Iz vospominanii o T. N. Granovskom," *Golos minuvshego*, no. 7 (July 1913), p. 169.

33. Like Tretiakov, Soldatenkov collected chiefly Russian art; his collection went to the Rumiantsev Museum in Moscow after his death. The series of scholarly works published by Soldatenkov (known as the Shchepkin Library) included mostly Russian translations of European works, such as Gibbon's *Decline and Fall of the Roman Empire* and the works of Mommsen. In addition, in 1859–1862 he published the collected works of V. G. Belinskii, the proceeds from which went to the support of Belinskii's widow. Soldatenkov's publishing activities gave employment to numerous intellectuals as translators and editors. N. G. Chernyshevskii worked for Soldatenkov while he was in exile in Siberia, his income from his translations being his sole means of support for many years. "Nekrologi. Soldatenkov, K. T.," pp. 378–79; Lukin, "Moskovskie pis'ma," *Novosti*, 7 July 1890; Moskvich, "Kupecheskaia Moskva," *Novoe vremia*, 11 June 1903.

34. *Vospominaniia P. I. Shchukin*, 3: 23; Ziloti, p. 258.

35. *Shchukinskii sbornik*, 10: 148ff.

36. Ibid., 10: 245–71.

37. *Iz zapisnoi knizhki A. P. Bakhrushina. Kto chto sobiraet* (Moscow, 1916), pp. 35–36.

38. Shchukin published the *Shchukinskii sbornik*, a ten-volume collection of documents relating to Russian history. In addition, he brought out a two-volume collection of documents pertaining to Russia at the time of the Napoleonic invasion of 1812.

39. *Shchukinskii sbornik*, 10: 166–67.

40. E. F. Korsh, *Petr Ivanovich Shchukin* (Moscow, 1913), p. 7.

41. Buryshkin, pp. 141, 143.

42. Volkova, pp. 4, 16; Vishniakov, 3: 36. Volkova's father was I. P. Vishniakov, the practical joker mentioned by N. P. Vishniakov. Volkova was almost the same age as N. P. Vishniakov, who was her uncle.

43. Volkova, pp. x, 18.

44. Ibid., pp. xii–xiii, xv.

45. E. Shchepkina, "Vospominaniia i dnevniki russkikh zhenshchin," *Istoricheskii vestnik* 137 (Aug. 1914): 554.

46. Volkova, pp. 84–85.

47. See also N. I. Astrov, *Vospominaniia* (Paris, 1941), p. 203, concerning the strains imposed on individuals who sought to raise themselves above the traditional merchant milieu.

48. E. Shchepkina, p. 554.

49. A. N. Tikhonov [Aleksandr Serebrov], *Vremia i liudi. Vospominaniia 1898–1905* (Moscow, 1955), p. 180.

50. "Botkiny. Iz pis'ma P. I. Shchukina k izdateliu 'Russkogo arkhiva,'" *Russkii arkhiv*, no. 7 (1910), pp. 458–59; A. Fet, *Moi vospominaniia 1848–1889*, 2 vols. (Moscow, 1890), 1: 187–88; Aleksandra Vladimirovna Shchepkina, *Vospominaniia* (Moscow, 1915), pp. 148–49; N. A. Belogolovyi, "Iz moikh vospominanii o Sergee Petroviche Botkine," *Russkie vedomosti*, 19 Jan. 1897; Chulkov, p. 495; Buryshkin, pp. 160–66.

51. *Vsia Rossiia. Russkaia kniga promyshlennosti, torgovli, sel'skogo khoziaistva i administratsii; torgovo-promyshlennyi adres-kalendar' rossiiskoi imperii* (n.p., 1895), p. 676.

52. *Moskovskie vedomosti*, 9 Jan. 1900.

53. Many intellectuals were coming to believe that some form of public

control ought to be exercised in order to prevent the wasting of huge sums donated by private philanthropists on essentially frivolous purposes and to direct this money into undertakings which would be most beneficial to the public interest. One liberal newspaper noted that "it is time, finally, to get away from the view that the fate of tens of millions [of rubles] appointed for socially beneficial goals should not be subjected to public control" (*Russkie vedomosti*, 1 Nov. 1903). Even Buryshkin noted that many "philanthropical" undertakings were extremely arbitrary and capricious, such as the case of the Moscow industrialist who left a huge sum for the purchase of church bells. "And," Buryshkin commented, "it was impossible to do anything about such peculiar philanthropy." Buryshkin, p. 104.

54. Rakshanin, "Iz Moskvy," *Novosti*, 17 Dec. 1894.

55. See P. S., "Moskva," *Novoe vremia*, 25 Sept. 1893.

56. *Istoriia Moskvy*, 4: 818.

57. Quoted in V. D.-ii, "Zemetki ob obshchestvennom prizrenii," *Russkie vedomosti*, 27 June 1893.

58. See Giliarovskii, *Sochineniia*, 3: 63.

59. "Nekrolog. (A. K. Medvednikova)," *Promyshlennyi mir*, no. 4 (1 Dec. 1899), p. 86.

60. Buryshkin, p. 224.

61. Ivan Belousov, *Ushedshaia Moskva. Zapiski po lichnym vospominaniiam s nachala 1870 godov* (Moscow, n.d.), pp. 57–58.

62. Liashchenko, 2: 463.

63. V. N. Storozhev, *Voina i moskovskoe kupechestvo* (Moscow, 1914), p. 98.

64. *Moskovskie vedomosti*, 29 Jan. 1904.

65. Vishniakov, 3: 110.

66. *Manufaktur-sovetnik Prokhorov*, pp. 11, 13.

67. *Materialy k istorii prokhorovskoi manufaktury*, pp. 109–10.

68. Ibid., p. 108.

69. Quoted in ibid., p. 85.

70. Ibid., p. 108.

71. Ibid.

72. *Gorodskie uchrezhdeniia Moskvy, osnovannye na pozhertvovaniia, i kapitaly, pozhertvovannye moskovskomu gorodskomu obshchestvennomu upravleniiu v techenie 1863–1904 g.* (Moscow, 1906), pp. 71–72.

73. Quoted in Lukin, "Moskovskie pis'ma," *Novosti*, 23 June 1890.

74. *Gorodskie uchrezhdeniia Moskvy*, p. 72.

75. *Moskovskie vedomosti*, 20 May 1904.

76. *Gorodskie uchrezhdeniia Moskvy*, p. 72.

77. *Gorodskie uchrezhdeniia Moskvy*, passim. The Bakhrushins were especially famed in Moscow for their philanthropy and were known to Muscovites as "professional philanthropists." Each year they automatically set aside a certain percentage of their profits for charitable purposes. As a result of their philanthropy, the Bakhrushin brothers were made honorary citizens of Moscow, an extremely rare honor, and they were also honorary citizens of their native town of Zaraisk because of their charitable activities there. Buryshkin, p. 128.

Between 1880 and 1904, the Bakhrushin family contributed a total of 2,791,265 rubles to the town of Moscow for philanthropical purposes (*Gorodskie uchrezhdeniia Moskvy*, pp. 446–47). The total sum spent for charity by the family in these years was considerably greater than this, as they also contributed to or created a variety of institutions not under municipal control (including a home for the blind and a home for aged actors). One can also assume that, like most families of the business elite, the Bakhrushins handed out considerable sums in the form of private grants to needy individuals. See B. A. Shchetinin, "Petr Petrovich Botkin," *Istoricheskii vestnik* 109 (Aug. 1907): 549–51, for a description of the innumerable private requests for aid which were received by all reputed philanthropists and of their method of dealing with them.

78. Shchepkin, *Soslovnoe khoziaistvo*, p. 29.
79. See Ianzhul, *Mezhdu delom*, pp. 188–91.
80. See D. Tsertelev, "Mysli i fakty. Altruizm i zemstvo," *Moskovskie vedomosti*, 14 Jan. 1900.
81. Botkina, pp. 295–96; Storozhev, *Istoriia Moskovskogo Kupecheskogo Obshchestva*, vol. 5, part 2, supp., pp. 234–39.
82. *Torgovoe i promyshlennoe delo Riabushinskikh*, p. 53.
83. Rakshanin, "Iz Moskvy," *Novosti*, 26 June 1899.
84. *Vospominaniia I. I. Ianzhula o perezhitom i vidennom v 1864–1909 gg.*, 2 vols. (St. Petersburg, 1910–1911), 2: 183–84.
85. Quoted in Botkina, pp. 238–41. In 1860, only four years after he began collecting paintings, Tretiakov made out a will in which he left his collection to the town of Moscow. Thus, from the earliest days of his collecting activity he intended his collection to be not merely a personal pleasure and achievement but a gift to Moscow and all Russia. Botkina, p. 8.
86. Riabushinskii, p. 173.
87. Naidenov, 2: 169.
88. Ibid., 2: 4, 12ff.
89. Grover, pp. xix, 365–66.
90. Quoted in Bill, p. 130.
91. Grover, p. 366.
92. S. I. Mamontov to V. D. Polenov, 4 Dec. 1897, in E. V. Sakharova, *Vasilii Dmitrievich Polenov. Elena Dmitrievna Polenova. Khronika sem'i khudozhnikov* (Moscow, 1964), p. 575.
93. Polenova, p. 20.
94. Ibid., p. 46.
95. D. Kogan, *Mamontovskii kruzhok* (Moscow, 1970), p. 60.
96. Polenova, p. 46.
97. *Iz zapisnoi knizhki A. P. Bakhrushina*, pp. 22–23, 42–43.
98. E. F. Korsh, p. 6.
99. Quoted in Buryshkin, p. 142.
100. Sergei Sharapov, *Tri sbornika 1900 goda*, 2nd ed. (Moscow, 1901), p. 97.
101. Mark Basanin, "Torgovyi dom Bakhvalova synov'ia. Roman iz kupecheskoi zhizni," *Istoricheskii vestnik* 144 (1916): 309.
102. Aleksandr V'iurkov, *Rasskazy o staroi Moskve*, 3rd ed. (Moscow, 1960), p. 200.
103. Their great concern for the well-being of their workers is a theme running through most of the histories of Moscow business families. See *Materialy k istorii prokhorovskoi manufaktury*, pp. 249, 263; Chetverikov, pp. 13–15; *Piatidesiatiletie fabriki Khludovykh*, pp. 19, 22–23, 26–27; *Tovarishchestvo manufaktur Ivana Konovalova*, pp. 32, 40; *Kratkii obzor Tovarishchestva Konovalova*, passim.
104. Vishniakov, 3: 115.
105. Grover, pp. 42–43, 365.
106. Quoted in ibid., p. 42.
107. Golitsyn, p. 152.
108. Old Gentleman, "Moskva, Tipy i kartinki," *Novoe vremia*, 13 March 1893.
109. Alekseev's assassin was a former inmate of a St. Petersburg mental

hospital who habitually tried to interest influential persons in his peculiar writings, dealing with subjects such as "the influence of magnetism and electricity on psychological and social phenomena." He had recently sent Alekseev a work entitled "A Psychological Introduction to Influenza" and having received no reply, he evidently determined to assassinate the mayor as a way of drawing attention to his neglected genius. "Ubiistvo moskovskogo gorodskogo golovy N. A. Alekseeva," *Birzhevye vedomosti*, 12 March 1893; see also N. T., "Pamiati N. A. Alekseeva," *Russkoe obozrenie* 20 (April 1893): 994–1002.

110. Storozhev, *Istoriia Moskovskogo Kupecheskogo Obshchestva*, vol. 5, part 2, supp., pp. 235–36, 239.

111. Ibid., vol. 5, part 3, p. 807.

112. *Moskovskie vedomosti*, 10 Jan. 1900.

113. See V. S. Mamontov, *Vospominaniia o russkikh khudozhnikakh (Abramtsevskii khudozhestvennyi kruzhok)* (Moscow, 1950).

114. Ziloti, pp. 147–48, 207–44; Botkina, pp. 197, 199; *Vospominaniia P. I. Shchukin*, 3: 23–24.

115. Ziloti, pp. 19–20, 106, 263; S. K. Av'erino, "Zabytyi (Pamiati N. G. Rubinshteina)," *Vozrozhdenie*, no. 1 (Jan. 1949), p. 163.

116. S. K. Av'erino, "Zabytyi," p. 157; N. Av'erino, "Moi vospominaniia o P. I. Chaikovskom," *Vozrozhdenie*, no. 16 (July–Aug. 1951), p. 99.

117. Buryshkin, pp. 121–22; S. P. Mel'gunov, *Vospominaniia i dnevniki* (Paris, 1964), pp. 101–3. Varvara Morozova (born a Khludov) was the widow of Abram Abramovich Morozov, who, in a final burst of domestic despotism, provided in his will that his wife should be deprived of her inheritance from him if she ever married again. Morozov was no doubt concerned to keep the family holdings entirely in Morozov hands, but the effect of his final disposition of his wife's fate was to force her to establish an irregular relationship with Sobolevskii. Though the two never married, and maintained separate residences, their relationship was well known and produced two children who bore the Morozov name.

118. *K stoletiiu firmy "V. Perlov"*, p. 102.

119. B. A. Shchetinin, "Revnitel' prosveshcheniia (Pamiati P. G. Shelaputina)," *Istoricheskii vestnik* 137 (July 1914): 236.

120. Botkina, p. 248.

121. Ziloti, p. 19.

122. Nemirovitch-Dantchenko, pp. 127–29. By contrast, Stanislavsky, the other founder of the Art Theater and himself a scion of the Moscow *kupechestvo*, showered these same patrons with unreserved praise. Stanislavsky, p. 12.

123. Mel'gunov, pp. 102–3; Nemirovitch-Dantchenko, pp. 114–15.

124. Paul Miliukov, *Political Memoirs 1905–1917*, ed. Arthur P. Mendel, trans. Carl Goldberg (Ann Arbor, 1967), pp. 15–16. The "Portuguese castle" was the Morozov home on Prechistenka, built in the style of the Portuguese Renaissance. It is the present House of International Friendship on Kalinin Boulevard.

125. See Fiodor Chaliapine, *Pages de ma vie* (Paris, 1927), pp. 223–39; S. K. Av'erino, "Russkii samorodok—S. I. Mamontov," *Vozrozhdenie*, no. 9 (May–June 1950), pp. 102–5; Stanislavsky, pp. 13–14; Mamontov, pp. 55–71.

126. Sakharova, pp. 626–39.

127. Grover, pp. 351–57. Grover, who believed that Mamontov's reputation as a patron had a substantial effect on the outcome of the trial, noted the public support expressed for Mamontov by his artist-friends and concluded that "in the face of such support, it was difficult for the jurors not to have sympathy for Mamontov. They were also aware of his support for Russian music, and of his

NOTES TO PAGES 106–113 · 239

private opera. Mamontov was accused of appropriating money from the rail-road to use for support of his opera. It is possible that the jurors held in the patron's favor, and decided with Gorky that Mamontov had been carried away by his love of beauty" (p. 357). It should be emphasized, however, that what-ever factors most influenced the thinking of the jury, it seems apparent from reading the detailed accounts of the trial which appeared in the Moscow press that the government failed to prove in court its main contention: that Mamon-tov, through his various financial manipulations, intentionally and knowingly caused financial harm to his railroad company. The prosecutors showed that Mamontov was undoubtedly guilty of negligence and mismanagement; but they could not prove intent to do harm, and it was on this point that their whole case rested.

128. Rakshanin, "Iz Moskvy," *Novosti*, 12 Dec. 1898.

129. See Naidenov, 2: 14, 38, 41–44, for a humorous description of the *ordenomaniia* of V. M. Bostandzhoglo, and Golitsyn, pp. 129–32, for confirma-tion of the existence of a similar malady among the nobility. Although it was regarded as great sport to poke fun at *kuptsy* avid for medals, the avidity was hardly restricted to the *kupechestvo*. However, respect for orders and medals in particular seemed to be declining in all the upper social strata toward the end of the century. (See E.P. Karnovich, "Sluzhebnye, dolzhnostnye i soslovnye znaki otlichii v Rossii," *Istoricheskii vestnik* 22 [Nov. 1885]: 238.) Respect for official ranks may also have been on the wane: *Novoe vremia* noted that "the abolition of ranks would hardly be noticed in society." (Quoted in "Dnevnik pechati," *Moskovskie vedomosti*, 31 Oct. 1896.) But whatever the attitude of the upper levels of society, the love of orders, medals, and ranks was still very much alive among Moscow's more modest *kuptsy*. Polunin tells how his father's longing for medals led him into the clutches of a charlatan who made a profes-sion of selling "foreign orders" to small merchants. When his father finally received the diploma conferring his long-awaited foreign order, his son, who could read French, heartily congratulated him on his new title: Active Member of the French Fire Brigade. Polunin, pp. 190–91.

130. Donald Mackenzie Wallace, *Russia*, 2 vols., 6th ed. (London, 1877), 1: 272–73.

131. *Vospominaniia P. I. Shchukin*, 3: 56; Botkina, pp. 242–43; Vishnia-kov, 2: 206.

132. In his letters, Mamontov frequently expressed, somewhat senten-tiously, if sincerely, his love for art. When he was in prison awaiting trial and translating the libretto of Mozart's *Don Giovanni* into Russian, he wrote to Polenov: "Never have I felt so deeply the great significance of art as now. I always sincerely loved it and in these difficult days it saves my soul." S. I. Mamontov to V. D. Polenov, 21 Sept. 1899, in Sakharova, pp. 626–27; see also S. I. Mamontov to V. D. Polenov, 4 Dec. 1897, in ibid., p. 575.

133. *Iz zapisnoi knizhki A.P. Bakhrushina*, pp. 27–28.

CHAPTER 4

1. M. P. Shchepkin, *Obshchestvennoe khoziaistvo goroda Moskvy v 1863–1887 godakh. Istorichesko-statisticheskoe opisanie* (Moscow, 1888), part 1, sec. 1, pp. 41–63; Naidenov, 2: 5–7.

2. Naidenov, 2: 6–9; Vishniakov, 3: 92–94.

3. Vishniakov, 3: 94n.

4. Ibid., 3: 92–93.

5. *Tovarishchestvo manufaktur Ivana Konovalova*, p. 20.

6. See Shchepkin, *Obshchestvennoe khoziaistvo goroda Moskvy*, pp. 67–87.

7. Golitsyn, p. 137ff.; Naidenov, 2: 12ff.

8. *Istoriia Moskvy*, 4: 478–81.

9. Ibid., 4: 498–99; Naidenov, 2: 30, 33.

10. Naidenov, 2: 34, 130–33; E. I. Kozlinina, *Za polveka, 1862–1912. Vospominaniia, ocherki i kharakteristiki* (Moscow, 1913), pp. 221–40.

11. *Istoriia Moskvy*, 4: 494–98, 512–13.

12. Whereas the duma of 1873–1876 had contained 86 nobles and officials and 81 merchants (with the remaining 13 seats going to representatives of the *meshchane* and artisans), the duma which sat from 1877 to 1880 included 143 merchants and honorable citizens and only 26 nobles. The *kupechestvo* thus had 80 percent of the duma seats. This stunning majority was somewhat reduced in later years; for instance, in the duma elected in 1893, there were only 86 merchants and honorable citizens, comprising 61.9 percent of the duma membership. Ibid., 4: 498, 514.

13. Golitsyn, p. 147; Pokrovskii, "Ocherki Moskvy," *Istoricheskii vestnik* 57 (Sept. 1894): 741–44; Lukin, "Moskovskie pis'ma," *Novosti*, 8 Aug. 1892.

14. Golitsyn, pp. 154–55; B. N. Chicherin, *Vospominaniia Borisa Nikolaevicha Chicherina. Zemstvo i moskovskaia duma* (Moscow, 1934), p. 166ff.

15. See P. V. Sytin, *Kommunal'noe khoziaistvo. Blagoustroistvo Moskvy v sravnenii s blagoustroistvom drugikh bol'shikh gorodov* (Moscow, 1926).

16. Lukin, "Moskovskie pis'ma," *Novosti*, 4 Jan. 1892.

17. P. S., "Moskva," *Novoe vremia*, 18 Sept. 1893.

18. See Lukin, "Moskovskie pis'ma," *Novosti*, 16 May 1892, and 18 April 1893.

19. Golitsyn, pp. 153–54.

20. See Dilettant, "Vchera, segodnia, zavtra," *Birzhevye vedomosti*, 12 March 1893.

21. See Rakshanin, "Iz Moskvy," *Novosti*, 26 July 1894.

22. M. P. Shchepkin, *Obshchestvennoe khoziaistvo goroda Moskvy. Narodnoe obrazovanie v 1863–1898 godakh. Istorichesko-statisticheskoe opisanie* (Moscow, 1901), part 4, sec. 1, pp. 306–7.

23. Astrov, pp. 248–50.

24. See *Stenograficheskie otchety o sobraniiakh moskovskoi gorodskoi dumy* (Moscow, 1889–1905).

25. Ibid.

26. Astrov, pp. 255, 270–271; *Istoriia Moskvy*, 4: 505.

27. See N. Bogolepov, "Rol' gorodov v predstoiashchei reform," *Promyshlennyi mir*, no. 25 (3 July 1905), pp. 499–500.

28. Rakshanin, "Iz Moskvy," *Novosti*, 30 Sept. 1895.

29. N. Karzhanskii, *Kak izbiralas' i rabotala moskovskaia gorodskaia duma*, 2nd ed. (Moscow, 1950), pp. 16–19.

30. Astrov, p. 269.

31. Ibid., pp. 254–58.

32. Ibid., p. 267.

33. Rakshanin, "Iz Moskvy," *Novosti*, 29 Aug. 1898.

34. N. I. Fal'kovskii, *Moskva v istorii tekhniki* (Moscow, 1950), p. 497.

35. Sytin, *Kommunal'noe khoziaistvo*, pp. 34, 225.

36. *Russkie vedomosti*, 22 Oct. 1904.

37. Ibid., 17 Dec. 1900; Rakshanin, "Iz Moskvy," *Novosti*, 2 Nov. 1896. Also *Novosti*, 21 Dec. 1896 and 9 Dec. 1900.

38. *Russkie vedomosti*, 23 Nov. 1904.

39. Skromnyi nabliudatel', "Nabliudeniia i zametki," ibid., 19 Nov. 1900.

40. See ibid., 5 Jan. 1897 and 25 March 1897. The conservative *Moskovskie vedomosti*, by contrast, simply dismissed the municipal administration by wishing a plague on the heads of both the *kuptsy* and the members of the "so-called intelligentsia" in the duma and arguing that Moscow would be far better off if all its affairs were handled by the state bureaucracy. See "Tsirkuliar po gorodskomu upravleniiu," *Moskovskie vedomosti*, 10 Nov. 1896; N. Znamenskii, "Malen'kie zemetki. K voprosu o demokratizatsii gorodskogo upravleniia," ibid., 19 May 1900.

41. Hanchett, pp. 110–14.

42. *Moskovskaia gorodskaia duma 1897–1900* (n.p., n.d.).

43. Astrov, pp. 272–73, 279.

44. V. Ia. Laverychev, "Russkie kapitalisty i periodicheskaia pechat' vtoroi polovine XIX v.," *Istoriia SSSR*, no. 1 (Jan.–Feb. 1972), p. 47; and *Krupnaia burzhuaziia v poreformennoi Rossii, 1861–1900* (Moscow, 1974), p. 231.

45. Buryshkin, p. 247.

46. See Alfred J. Rieber, "The Moscow Entrepreneurial Group: The Emergence of a New Form in Autocratic Politics," *Jahrbücher für Geschichte Osteuropas* 25 (1977): 1–20, 174–99; Owen, *Capitalism and Politics*, pp. 29–45. Rieber's and Owen's views on the significance of the alliance between Slavophiles and businessmen largely differ from those presented here. See also Laverychev, *Krupnaia burzhuaziia*, pp. 111–15.

47. Michael Ginsburg, "Art Collectors of Old Russia. The Morosovs and the Shchukins," *Apollo*, n.s. 98, no. 142 (Dec. 1973): 483–84.

48. Ibid., p. 477.

49. Boborykin, in *Kitai-gorod*, vividly portrayed the mixing of Russian and European cultures within Moscow's business elite. Particularly memorable is his description of the home of commercial councillor Evlampii Grigor'evich Netov, built by a strong-willed architect, who paid no attention to the preferences of the owner, in the fashionable neo-Russian style. The inside of the house Boborykin described as "a museum of Muscovite-Byzantine rococo," noting that some of the "Muscovite-Byzantine" furnishings had come from France and Germany. Boborykin, pp. 147–54.

50. Ginsburg, pp. 481–82.

51. [N. A. Naidenov, ed.], *Materialy dlia istorii moskovskogo kupechestva*, 9 vols. (Moscow, 1883–89).

52. Naidenov, 2: 11–12.

53. *Trudy Torgovo-promyshlennogo s"ezda 1896 g. v Nizhnem-Novgorode*, 8 vols. (St. Petersburg, 1897), vol. 6, sec. 11: 107–19; sec. 5:11.

54. Hanchett, pp. 496–501.

55. L. T. Senchakova, " 'Sviashchennaia druzhina' i ee sostav," *Vestnik Moskovskogo Universiteta*, ser. 9, no. 2 (1967): 62–83. See Owen, *Capitalism and Politics*, p. 102, for a differing view.

56. Hanchett, p. 176.

57. Lensen, p. 6.

58. Vishniakov, 2: 82, 102–3, 115.

59. Ginsburg, p. 475.

60. Vishniakov, 3: 94–107; Hanchett, pp. 283–309.

61. Nikolai Naidenov to K. P. Pobedonostsev, 16 Oct. 1882, in *K. P. Pobedonostsev i ego korrespondenty. Pis'ma i zapiski*, vol. 1 (Moscow-Petrograd, 1923), p. 295.

62. Ianzhul, *Iz vospominanii*, p. 70.

63. *Dnevnik A. S. Suvorina* (Moscow-Petrograd, 1923), p. 30.

64. Vishniakov, 3: 3–4.

65. Ibid., 3: 88.
66. Ibid., 3: 74.
67. Ibid., 3: 99–100.
68. Vasilii Kokorev, "Vospominaniia davnoproshedshego," *Russkii arkhiv*, no. 3 (1885), pp. 263–72; Z. A. Popel'nitskii, "Zapreshchennyi po vysoch. poveleniiu banket v Moskve 19 fevralia 1858 g.," *Golos minuvshego*, no. 2 (Feb. 1914), pp. 202–12; "Moskovskii obed 28-go dekabria 1857 goda," *Russkie vedomosti*, 19 Feb. 1898.
69. Chicherin, pp. 259–60.
70. Ibid., pp. 248–56.
71. *Moskovskie vedomosti*, 6 Aug. 1905.
72. S. Iu. Witte, *Vospominaniia. Tsarstvovanie Nikolaia II*, vol. 2, 2nd ed. (Berlin, 1922), p. 146.
73. Gor'kii, *Literaturnye portrety*, pp. 305–6.
74. Owen, *Capitalism and Politics*, pp. 38, 239n.; Naidenov, 2: 71.
75. Naidenov, 2: 63ff.
76. There has been considerable debate among Russian Marxist writers as to whether the Russian "bourgeoisie" possessed actual power, or only influence, in the tsarist government. Menshevik writers generally argued that businessmen, particularly after 1905, had the power to force the government to accede to their wishes, rather than just having mere influence. See P. A. Berlin, *Russkaia burzhuaziia v staroe i novoe vremia* (Moscow, 1922), pp. 127, 164, 167; A. Gushka [A. Ermanskii], "K kharakteristike rossiiskoi krupnoi burzhuazii (Po povodu novogo fakticheskogo materiala ob organizatsiiakh kapital v Rossii)," *Nasha zaria*, nos. 1–2 (1912), pp. 47–59; and "Krupnaia burzhuaziia do 1905 goda," in L. Martov, P. Maslov, and A. Potresov, eds., *Obshchestvennoe dvizhenie v Rossii v nachale XX-go veka*, vol. 1, *Predvestniki i osnovnye prichiny dvizheniia* (The Hague, 1968), pp. 313–48. V. I. Lenin took issue with the Menshevik position, arguing that they overemphasized the degree of actual power wielded by businessmen. See V. I. Lenin, "Anketa ob organizatsiiakh krupnogo kapital," *Sochineniia*, 38 vols., 4th ed. rev. (Moscow, 1941–1950), 18: 39–55.

Although over the decades there have been some waverings in Soviet historiography on this question, for the most part, conclusions of Soviet scholars have been in line with those of Lenin and have stressed the relative political impotence of big business. See Livshin, p. 116; E. D. Chermenskii, *Burzhuaziia i tsarizm v pervoi russkoi revoliutsii*, 2nd ed. (Moscow, 1970), pp. 3–17; P. G. Ryndziunskii, "Rossiiskoe samoderzhavie i ego klassovye osnovy," *Istoriia SSSR*, no. 2 (March–April 1977), pp. 34–52. One recent exception to the general trend in Soviet scholarship was Semeniuk's dissertation, the abstract of which has been previously cited. Semeniuk tried to strike a position midway between Lenin and Engels, who wrote in 1894 that "the young Russian bourgeoisie holds the government completely in its hands. In all important economic questions it forces it to submit to its wishes." But Semeniuk was rather more with Engels than with Lenin. It seems unquestionable that the conclusions of Lenin's followers are much closer to the truth than those of the Mensheviks, of Engels, or of Semeniuk.
77. A. F. Vovchik, *Politika tsarizma po rabochemu voprosu v predrevoliutsionnyi period (1895–1904)* (Lvov, 1964), pp. 218–19.
78. Ibid., pp. 123–24, 134–42.
79. Berlin, pp. 165–66.
80. See Gindin, "Russkaia burzhuaziia," no. 2, pp. 72–73; Berlin, pp. 175–

82; V. Ia. Laverychev, *Po tu storonu barrikad (Iz istorii bor'by moskovskoi burzhua-zii s revoliutsiei)* (Moscow, 1967), pp. 16–17.
81. Gindin, "Moskovskie banki," pp. 66–68.
82. Laverychev, *Po tu storonu barrikad,* p. 17; Gindin, "Russkaia burzhua-ziia," no. 2, pp. 73, 77.
83. S. Gvozdev, *Zapiski fabrichnogo inspektora (iz nabliudenii i praktiki v period 1894–1908 gg.)* (Moscow, 1911), pp. 208–12; I. Kh. Ozerov, *Politika po rabochemu voprosu v Rossii za poslednie gody (Po neizdannym dokumentam)* (Moscow, 1906), pp. 23–26.
84. Litvinov-Falinskii, pp. 112–13, 307–10; "Ekonomicheskie zametki," *Russkoe obozrenie* 20 (April 1893): 1086–114.
85. Ianzuhl, *Iz vospominanii,* pp. 118–20; *Novoe vremia,* 26 Jan. 1899.
86. Buryshkin, pp. 245–46.
87. Naidenov, 2: 49.
88. Rakshanin, "Iz Moskvy," *Novosti,* 4 Nov. 1895. Also *Novosti,* 24 Feb. 1896, 30 March 1896, and 19 Oct. 1896.
89. "Zaiavlenii kupechestva i rechi ministra finansov," *Birzhevye vedomosti,* 15 Aug. 1893; "Prebyvanie ministra finansov v Nizhnem-Novgorode," *Novosti,* 17 Aug. 1893; "Khodataistvo moskovskogo kupechestva," ibid., 22 Sept. 1893; Lukin, "Moskovskie pis'ma," ibid., 29 Jan. 1894; Rakshanin, "Po russkim fabrikam," ibid., 31 March 1894.
90. Ianzhul, *Iz vospominanii,* pp. 118–20, 150–62; "Dokladnaia zapiska nizhe-gorodskogo iarmarochnogo kupechestva, podannaia g. ministru finansov," *Birzhevye vedomosti,* 18 Aug. 1893 and 20 Aug. 1893.
91. Iu B. Solov'ev, "Protivorechiia v praviashchem lagere Rossii po voprosu ob inostrannykh kapitalakh v gody pervogo promyshlennogo pod"ema," in *Iz istorii imperializma v Rossii* (Moscow-Leningrad, 1959), pp. 282–83; *Novoe vremia,* 26 Jan. 1899.
92. The text of this petition may be found in S. B. Ippo, *Moskva i London. Istoricheskie, obshchestvennye i ekonomicheskie ocherki i issledovaniia* (Moscow, 1888), pp. 248–54.
93. Rakshanin, "Iz Moskvy," *Novosti,* 13 Aug. 1894.
94. See L. N. Voronov, "Ekonomicheskoe obozrenie," *Russkoe obozrenie* 2 (April 1890): 890–908, for a discussion of some of the factors that discouraged Moscow industrialists from seeking foreign markets. Also see Laverychev, *Krupnaia burzhuaziia,* pp. 194–206.
95. Rakshanin, "Iz Moskvy," *Novosti,* 13 Aug. 1894.
96. Berlin, p. 305.
97. The journalist Lukin noted the changeable character of Moscow manufacturers' views on the Jewish question, their stance at any particular moment depending on their evaluation of how one or another government policy might affect trade. Lukin wrote of a report presented by S. I. Prokhorov at a meeting of Moscow businessmen in which Prokhorov stated that the demand for cotton textiles in Central Asia was increasing: "It would have increased still more had it not been for the expectation of expulsion of the Jews from our Asiatic possessions. Mr. Prokhorov is against this measure. Of course, like a true Muscovite, he in truth is not opposed to letting the Jews stew in their own juice. . . . But once the profit of the 'calico king' depends on the inviolability of the Jews, his view on the Jewish question changes, and Mr. Prokhorov finds that it is impossible to expel the Jews from Central Asia, since all the trade in manufactured goods there is concentrated in their hands." Lukin, "Moskovskie pis'ma," *Novosti,* 29 Jan. 1894.

98. George Edward Snow, "The Kokovtsov Commission. An Abortive Attempt at Labor Reform in Russia in 1905," *Slavic Review* 40, no. 4 (Dec. 1972): 795.

99. Solov'ev, p. 385.

100. Rakshanin, "Iz Moskvy," *Novosti*, 19 Oct. 1896.

101. "Rech' S. Iu. Witte o samodeiatel'nosti torgovo-promyshlennogo klassa," *Promyshlennyi mir*, no. 47 (23 Nov. 1903), p. 1050.

102. Quoted in Rakshanin, "Nizhegorodskaia iarmarka," *Novosti*, 16 Aug. 1895.

103. Laverychev, "Russkie kapitalisty i periodicheskaia pechat'," pp. 32–35, 42, 44–45; and *Krupnaia burzhuaziia*, pp. 111–35.

104. Buryshkin, p. 120.

105. Laverychev, "Russkie kapitalisty i periodicheskaia pechat'," pp. 32, 35–36.

106. K. Krasil'nikov, "Ekonomicheskie zametki," *Russkoe obozrenie* 22 (July 1893): 461–79.

107. Naidenov, 2: 78.

108. On one occasion, Moscow industrialists directly expressed their contempt for public, as opposed to government, opinion. When, in 1902, during a private meeting with Moscow businessmen, Zubatov noted that few people were aware of the good things that Moscow employers had done for their workers in the form of schools and hospitals, the Moscow employers replied, in a petition protesting against the Zubatov experiment, that the only people who needed to know of these things did know, i.e., the government officials. Morskoi, pp. 99–100.

109. See Buryshkin, p. 262; also Naidenov, 1: 110.

110. See *Ukazatel' g. Moskvy* (Moscow, 1866), p. 149; Gindin, "Russkaia burzhuaziia," no. 2, p. 63.

111. Rakshanin, "S nizhegorodskoi iarmarki," *Novosti*, 18 Aug. 1893; V. Iuch, "Iarmarochnie pis'ma," ibid., 23 July 1900; W., "S nizhegorodskoi iarmarki," *Russkie vedomosti*, 25 Aug. 1898, and 10 July 1900.

112. Lukin, "Moskovskie pis'ma," *Novosti*, 11 Nov. 1889.

113. Naidenov, 2: 37; Rakshanin, "Iz Moskvy," *Novosti*, 9 Dec. 1900.

114. Rakshanin, "Iz Moskvy," *Novosti*, 5 April 1897.

115. See Laverychev, *Po tu storonu barrikad*, p. 26; Gindin, "Sotsial'no-ekonomicheskie itogi," pp. 75–79; Berlin, pp. 140–41, 147–48, 150–51.

CHAPTER 5

1. There were altogether nine Riabushinskii brothers in this generation (P. M. Riabushinskii also fathered thirteen daughters). Of the nine brothers, Boris died in childhood, and, of those surviving, only Sergei appears to have been unremarkable in any field. *Torgovoe i promyshlennoe delo Riabushinskikh*, pp. 41–43.

2. Buryshkin, pp. 189, 288–90; V. N. Seletskii, "Obrazovanie partii progressistov (K voprosu o politicheskoi konsolidatsii russkoi burzhuazii)," *Vestnik Moskovskogo Universiteta*, ser. 9, no. 5 (Sept.–Oct. 1970): 36, 39–41; V. S. Diakin, *Russkaia burzhuaziia i tsarizm v gody pervoi mirovoi voiny 1914–1917* (Leningrad, 1967).

3. Buryshkin, p. 193; P. Kovalevskii, "Russkie uchenye za rubezhom," *Vozrozhdenie*, no. 44 (Aug. 1955), pp. 6, 10.

4. *Torgovoe i promyshlennoe delo Riabushinskikh*, pp. 79–80.
5. Buryshkin, p. 192.
6. Ibid., pp. 104, 192.
7. Ibid., pp. 191–92; N. Istselennov, "Pamiati Vladimira Pavlovicha Ria-bushinskogo," *Vozrozhdenie*, no. 47 (Nov. 1955), pp. 105–6.
8. Buryshkin, p. 192; E. A. Borisova and T. P. Kazhdan, *Russkaia arkhitek-tura kontsa XIX—nachala XX veka* (Moscow, 1971), pp. 90, 94–97, 100. Actually, S. P. Riabushinskii's home, also in "decadent" style, was equally exotic—pictures of the interior give the impression of a movie set designed as a compromise between the tastes of Fritz Lang and Walt Disney. Like many of the Riabushinskii buildings, it was designed by F. O. Shekhtel, perhaps Moscow's most outstanding architect at the turn of the century.
9. Stanislavsky, p. 12.
10. Ziloti, passim.
11. Stanislavsky, pp. 23, 32.
12. Ibid., pp. 24–25.
13. Ibid., pp. 39–54; Ziloti, p. 194.
14. Botkina, p. 289.
15. Increasing recognition of the need for education, which was spreading not only among the business elite but in the lower levels of the Moscow *kupe-chestvo* as well, was the subject of frequent laudatory comment in the press. For instance, one columnist, basically hostile to the *kupechestvo*, admitted that "the more intelligent and educated layer of merchant Moscow has in recent times begun to expand quickly. The Moscow *kupechestvo*, to do it justice, has understood the need for education, and with every year the number of educated *kuptsy* who have graduated from higher educational institutions is increasing." It might be added that, like other commentators, this writer did not believe that education was having what he would consider a desirable effect on the *kupechestvo*. Educated sons of business families, he wrote, "very quickly adapt to the factory and warehouse atmosphere and in their practicality and tenacity go far beyond the preceding generation." Education, he believed, may have made them better businessmen (this, in Russia, was not necessarily a compliment), but it failed to instill in them "any broad social ideals." Moskvich, "Kupecheskaia Moskva," *Novoe vremia*, 11 June 1903.
16. See Stanislavsky, pp. 55–56.
17. *Biografii chlenov vremennogo pravitel'stva, ispol'nitel'nogo komiteta gosud. dumy i chlenov ispol'nitel'nogo komiteta soveta rabochikh i soldatskikh deputatov* (n.p., n.d.), p. 5.
18. Gor'kii, *Literaturnye portrety*, p. 299.
19. Ziloti, p. 162; Lensen, p. xi.
20. Lensen, pp. x and vii.
21. A. M. Shampan'er, ed., *Deiateli Rossii* (St. Petersburg, 1906), sec. 4, p. 38.
22. Bill, p. 26; Sakharova, p. 819.
23. Abrikosov served as one of Lenin's embalmers and later was occasionally called in on medical consultations when Stalin was ill. Lensen, pp. x–xi.
24. V. Unkovskii, "A. M. Remizovu—80 let," *Vozrozhdenie*, no. 66 (June 1957), pp. 52–57. Remizov was one of the few scions of the Moscow business elite to become involved in radical political activities. Arrested during a student demonstration, he was expelled from the university and spent six years (1897–1903) in exile. Almost the only other examples of involvement in radical political activity were two grandsons of Vikula Morozov whose mother, a Moro-

zova, had married a well-known furniture manufacturer by the name of Schmidt. One of the Schmidt brothers was arrested for his participation in the Moscow uprising in December 1905 and died in prison. Buryshkin, p. 119.

25. Sakharova, p. 816.

26. "Nekrologi. Guchkov, F. I.," *Istoricheskii vestnik* 131 (Feb. 1913): 725–27.

27. Shampan'er, sec. 2, p. 14; P. N. Miliukov, *Vospominaniia (1859–1917)*, vol. 1 (New York, 1955), pp. 116–17.

28. Lensen, pp. 68, 131–33.

29. Ziloti, pp. 101, 125–26, 242.

30. Naumov, 1: 171–72. Naumov, a Samara landowner and minister of agriculture for a brief period during World War I, married A. K. Ushkova. Interestingly enough, his predecessor at the Ministry of Agriculture, A. V. Krivoshein, was related by marriage to Sergei Morozov, who had married a Krivoshein (Bill, p. 26). These two marriages were among the very few which united members of the Moscow business elite with higher noble and official circles.

31. Ziloti, p. 78.

32. Sakharova, pp. 533, 813.

33. N. V. Nekrasov, "M. V. Iakunchikova (Po povodu posmertnoi vystavki eia proizvedenii)," *Russkie vedomosti*, 26 March 1905; Sakharova, pp. 41–42. Iakunchikova was related by marriage to the painter V. D. Polenov, who had married her sister—one of the fairly numerous marriages between members of the Moscow business elite and representatives of the artistic intelligentsia.

34. Lukin, "Moskovskie pis'ma," *Novosti*, 21 May 1894. In the same article, this journalist noted the growing tendency of Moscow's leading *kuptsy* to try their own hand at art or literature, rather than supporting the activities of others. He viewed this trend with extreme disapproval, making clear his conviction that *kuptsy* should stay in their warehouses and not venture into the world of art and scholarship, which had no need of them. His views confirmed Buryshkin's assertion that "the opinion that occupation with abstract sciences [and, he might have added, art and literature] was not the business of the *kupechestvo* was long preserved in Russia." Buryshkin, p. 33.

35. Nemirovitch-Dantchenko, p. 133; Stanislavsky, pp. 385–89.

36. Sakharova, p. 819; *Moskovskie vedomosti*, 18 Jan. 1900; *Promyshlennyi mir*, no. 51 (16 Dec. 1901), p. 1127. Sergei Morozov, like his brother Savva, was one of the few "repentant" industrialists of his generation. Rakshanin interviewed Morozov in 1900 in regard to his efforts to revive *kustar* industries and found that "his basic point of view comes down to the idea that the impoverishment of the Russian *muzhik* is the direct result of the much praised successes of factory industry and its victory over popular industry—*kustar* industry." Morozov believed that "it is he, the Russian peasant, in reality, who encourages all-Russian industry—he has created it, he nourishes it, he maintains it." Such a burden, said Morozov, was simply too great for the peasant to bear and thus the development of industry involved "great injustice." Morozov had no illusions about the ability of peasant industries to compete with mechanized industry, but he believed that in certain cases *kustar* industry was still viable and was a necessary source of income for the peasantry. What Rakshanin called Morozov's "fanatical conviction" on this subject led Morozov to contribute considerable sums of money, in part through the Moscow provincial zemstvo, for the revival of *kustar* industries. Rakshanin, "Iz Moskvy," *Novosti*, 22 Jan. 1900.

37. Ibid., 27 Sept. 1903. Actually, the most notable collector of the younger

generation was probably I. A. Morozov, who, like S. I. Shchukin, concentrated on French impressionist paintings rather than Russian art. Buryshkin, p. 141.

38. Stanislavsky, p. 387.

39. Ibid., p. 386.

40. One visitor to the Konovalov factory, a man well-acquainted with Russian factory conditions, had been so impressed by A.P. Konovalov (the grandfather of Aleksandr Ivanovich) and his policy toward his workers that after his visit he wrote that he had seen here nothing less than the "dawning of new human relations" (I. Kolyshko, *Ocherki sovremennoi Rossii* [St. Petersburg, 1887], p. 375). The Konovalovs' reputation as good employers was perhaps one reason why, as Buryshkin noted, they were practically the only family of the Moscow business elite ever to receive favorable mention in Russian literature (in P.I. Mel'nikov-Pecherskii's novel *V lesakh*). Buryshkin, pp. 30–31.

A. I. Konovalov also preached what he practiced. He was a staunch advocate of achieving harmonious relations between employers and workers by means of concessions on the part of the former. After 1905 his was perhaps the most progressive voice in industrial circles on the subject of labor relations. Diakin, p. 34.

41. *Kratkii obzor uchrezhdenii Konovalova*, pp. 4–23; *Tovarishchestvo manufaktur Ivana Konovalova*, pp. 40, 43–44, 50; Ioksimovich, sec. 1, pp. 95–107. Pictures of the buildings in which Konovalov housed his philanthropical undertakings at the factory show them to have been grandiose edifices, with marble columns, more along the lines of the Bolshoi Theater than what one would expect of factory schools or hospitals. The buildings themselves were undoubtedly intended to constitute a striking advertisement for the beneficence of Russia's enlightened employers, while at the same time attracting the attention of and providing models for Russia's not-so-enlightened employers.

42. Moskvich, "Kupecheskaia Moskva," *Novoe vremia*, 11 June 1903.

43. Stanislavsky, pp. 76–77.

44. Rakshanin, "Iz Moskvy," *Novosti*, 20 April 1902.

45. Moskvich, "Kupecheskaia Moskva," *Novoe vremia*, 11 June 1903.

46. Lensen, pp. 13–14.

47. Ibid., pp. 24–26.

48. Stanislavsky, p. 20.

49. Buryshkin, p. 276.

50. Nemirovitch-Dantchenko, p. 293.

51. Ibid., p. 131.

52. Ibid., pp. 129, 132.

53. Gor'kii, *Literaturnye portrety*, p. 322.

54. Nemirovitch-Dantchenko, p. 149.

55. Moskvich, "Kupecheskaia Moskva," *Novoe vremia*, 11 June 1903.

56. M. A. Morozov [Mikhail Iu'rev], *Spornye voprosy zapadno-evropeiskoi istoricheskoi nauki* (Moscow, 1894), and *Karl Piatyi i ego vremia* (Moscow, 1894).

57. Morozov wrote of his own generation: "In Moscow, among the *kupechestvo*, the sons are worse than their fathers. The 'fathers,' whom Ostrovskii depicted, were illiterate and wore long beards, but all the same they understood that there are professions higher than brokerage 'in cotton and tea,' that happiness does not consist only of a three-million dividend from the factory." M. A. Morozov [Mikhail Iu'rev], *Moi pis'ma (4-go dekabria 1893 goda–15 maia 1894 goda)* (Moscow, 1895), pp. 239–40.

58. *Russkie vedomosti*, 19 July 1898 and 14 Oct. 1903.

59. Lensen, pp. 51–52.

60. Stanislavsky, p. 296.

61. Lensen, p. 4; see also Blackwell, pp. 260–61.

62. A detailed Prokhorov genealogy may be found in *Materialy k istorii prokhorovskoi manufaktury*, pp. 441–50; see also Appendix.

63. Buryshkin, 147–48; Pokrovskii, "Ocherki Moskvy," *Istoricheskii vestnik* 52 (May 1893): 297–98.

64. In the case of the Konovalovs, A. I. Konovalov evidently forced his father, representative of the third generation of the family, into an early retirement, gave him a pension, and sent him off to Kharkov. His father, I. A. Konovalov, seems to have been notable only for his debauchery, his physical resemblance to Peter the Great, and his failure to keep his factory technically up-to-date. Buryshkin, p. 185.

CHAPTER 6

1. As will become apparent to the reader in the course of this chapter, I am for the most part omitting the Guchkov brothers from my discussion of the political activities of Moscow's leading businessmen. The reason for this is that I do not regard the Guchkovs, and most especially Aleksandr Guchkov, as typical representatives of the Moscow business elite in the political arena. Indeed, it seems questionable that Aleksandr Guchkov was in any sense at all a representative of Moscow businessmen in politics, either typical or atypical. Buryshkin was extremely insistent on the point that Guchkov did not represent the Moscow *kupechestvo*, and I am inclined to agree with him. He wrote that even though Guchkov was a scion of the Moscow industrial milieu, he had entirely left that milieu. Further: "In spite of the fact that he came from the genuine Moscow *kupechestvo*, he was not considered their own man, but a 'politician.' He had genuine commercial and industrial qualifications; for example, he was a director of the insurance company 'Russia,' but he did not represent the Moscow *kupechestvo*. . . . And the Octobrist Party, which he founded and led, also was not considered a 'trade industrial' party." Buryshkin, pp. 177–78, 285.

There was little in Guchkov's background that would have prepared him to serve as a political representative of the business world. He took almost no part in the family business, and his official positions in several banks, an insurance company, and a steamship company did not entail any consistent involvement in the operation of those businesses. Before 1905, instead of entering the family business, Guchkov's "career"—and it was one of the strangest careers pursued by any member of the Moscow business elite—was essentially that of a professional adventurer. Between 1894 and 1905, Guchkov's wanderlust took him to Anatolia to watch Turks massacring Armenians; to Manchuria as the captain of a detachment providing protection for work on the Trans-Siberian Railroad; to Mongolia and the Gobi Desert; to Central Asia; to South Africa as a volunteer fighting with the Boers against the British; to China as an observer of the Boxer Rebellion; to the Balkans as a witness to the Macedonian insurrection; to Manchuria again, as a representative of the Red Cross during the Russo-Japanese War (Menashe, pp. 68–70). These early experiences undoubtedly help to explain the preoccupation with military matters which marked Guchkov's entire political career—a preoccupation which most definitely was not shared by Moscow businessmen.

My views on Guchkov remain unchanged even after reading Menashe's interesting dissertation. Menashe has "posited Guchkov and the Guchkov family as a kind of analytical 'specimen' illustrating the political direction in which the Russian bourgeoisie was heading in the course of development as a modern entrepreneurial class" (Menashe, p. vi). But if Guchkov was in some sense representative of an emerging Russian bourgeoisie, as a politician he simply did not represent the interests of the Moscow business elite. While Guchkov as a politician was concerned chiefly with military affairs, and secondarily with "efficient administration," and was a principled nationalist, to Moscow and other Russian businessmen the primary concerns were labor policy, the tariff, measures for the encouragement of trade and industry—concerns in which Guchkov consistently showed little interest.

2. Stanislavsky, pp. 379–80.
3. Tikhonov, p. 115.
4. Miliukov, *Political Memoirs*, pp. 23–25.
5. Lensen, p. 6.
6. Terence Emmons, "The Beseda Circle, 1899–1905," *Slavic Review* 32, no. 3 (Sept. 1893): 466, 468n., 469n.
7. "Probuzhdenie kupechestva," *Promyshlennyi mir*, no. 47 (21 Nov. 1904), p. 895.
8. Maxim Gorky, *Foma Gordyeeff*, trans. Isabel F. Hapgood (New York, 1901), pp. 150–51.
9. Gor'kii, *Literaturnye portrety*, pp. 270, 300–301. Views somewhat similar to those of Maiakin had been expressed in Moscow as early as the 1880s by N. P. Lanin, a manufacturer of soft drinks and publisher of the newspaper *Russkii kur'er*. In 1887, for example, his newspaper noted that "the bourgeoisie is a more progressive class than the nobility; it is an all-class element, alien to traditions and class prejudices." (Quoted in Ruth Amende Roosa, "The Association of Industry and Trade, 1906–1914: An Examination of the Economic Views of Organized Industrialists in Prerevolutionary Russia" [Ph.D. diss., Columbia University, 1967], pp. xiii–xiv.) Lanin, however, was neither a member of the Moscow business elite nor particularly representative of the views of the older generation of the Moscow *kupechestvo* as a whole. He was somewhat ahead of his time, giving voice to ideas which would be expressed even more strongly by P. P. Riabushinskii's *Utro Rossii* after 1905.
10. Quoted in "Iz obshchestvennoi khroniki," *Vestnik Evropy* 355, no. 9 (Sept. 1896), pp. 408.
11. Quoted in "Rech' S. T. Morozova," *Moskovskie vedomosti*, 16 Aug. 1893.
12. I. K. Krestovnikov to N. K. Krestovnikov, 17 Feb. 1898, in *Semeinaia khronika Krestovnikovykh*, 3: 115.
13. See Rakshanin's conversation with an unidentified Moscow cotton textile manufacturer who saw in the textile industry the foundation "for the rise of popular well-being," in "Iz Moskvy," *Novosti*, 19 Oct. 1896. Buryshkin also expressed a similar view in his memoirs, arguing that factory industry in Russia was a powerful force for promoting desirable social and cultural change. Buryshkin, p. 99.
14. K. K. Krestovnikov to N. K. Krestovnikov, 29 Jan. 1899, in *Semeinaia khronika Krestovnikovykh*, 3: 125.
15. K. K. Krestovnikov to N. K. Krestovnikov, 24 Oct. 1899, in ibid., 3: 126.
16. Buryshkin, p. 312.
17. *Promyshlennyi mir*, no. 44 (17 Sept. 1900), pp. 1022–23; Aleksandr Morokin, "Torgovaia zametka," *Moskovskie vedomosti*, 12 Dec. 1900.

18. "Ispoved' nabolevshego serdtsa," *Promyshlennyi mir*, no. 46 (1 Oct. 1900), p. 1071.

19. Kokorev, "Ekonomicheskie provaly," no. 5, bk. 2, p. 133. "Financiers" is Kokorev's term for officials of the Ministry of Finance.

20. Ibid., no. 2, bk. 1, pp. 258–59.

21. Ibid., no. 7, bk. 3, pp. 413–15.

22. A. Morokin and K. K., "Oblastnoi otdel. Iz Vichugi," *Russkoe obozrenie* 20 (March 1893): 504; K. S., "Ekonomicheskie zametki," ibid., p. 516; K. Krasil'nikov, "Ekonomicheskie zametki," ibid., 22 (July 1893): 461–62.

23. K. K.-v, "Sovremennaia letopis'. Vnutrennee obozrenie," ibid., 23 (Oct. 1893): 1042.

24. K. S., "Ekonomicheskie zametki," ibid., 20 (March 1893): 522.

25. K. K., ibid., 21 (May 1893): 435.

26. V. N. Semenkovich, ibid., 20 (April 1893): 1115–22.

27. *Promyshlennyi mir*, no. 46 (1 Oct. 1900), p. 1071.

28. "Vliianie kupechestva (Pis'mo v redaktsiiu)," ibid., no. 58 (24 Dec. 1900), pp. 1377–78.

29. Ianzhul, *Iz vospominanii*, pp. 35–36, 94.

30. See ibid., p. 69.

31. "Ekonomicheskie zametki," *Russkoe obozrenie* 20 (April 1893): 1090–91; see also Litvinov-Falinskii, pp. 307–10.

32. There is a considerable literature on tsarist factory legislation. The works used in preparation of this study include those by Ozerov, Litvinov-Falinskii, Vovchik, and Ianzhul, all previously cited, as well as two articles by Theodore H. Von Laue: "Tsarist Labor Policy, 1895–1903," *Journal of Modern History* 34, no. 2 (June 1962): 135–45; and "Factory Inspection under the 'Witte System': 1892–1903," *American Slavic and East European Review* 19, no. 3 (Oct. 1960): 347–62.

33. See Vovchik, pp. 170–72, 218–23; L. N. Voronov, "Ekonomicheskoe obozrenie," *Russkoe obozrenie* 3 (June 1890): 879–80.

34. Vovchik, pp. 178–83.

35. See Kyril Tidmarsh, "The Zubatov Idea," *American Slavic and East European Review* 19, no. 3 (Oct. 1960): 337–39; N. M. Ezhov, "Russkie metamorfozy," *Istoricheskii vestnik* 119 (Feb. 1910): 590–602. The most complete account of the *zubatovshchina* may be found in Jeremiah Schneiderman, *Sergei Zubatov and Revolutionary Marxism: The Struggle for the Working Class in Tsarist Russia* (Ithaca, N.Y., 1976).

36. The industrialists' note was reproduced in Morskoi, pp. 98–105. The summary of the note that appears in the text was taken from this source.

37. Aleksandr Morokin, "Iz Vichugi," *Russkoe obozrenie* 21 (May 1893): 424–28; -ova, "Ekonomicheskie zametki," ibid., 25 (Jan. 1894): 469.

38. *Promyshlennyi mir*, no. 11 (14 March 1904), p. 241; no. 36 (5 Sept. 1904), p. 709.

39. See ibid., no. 6 (7 Feb. 1904), p. 134; A. Z., "'Na chashku chaia,'" ibid., no. 20 (16 May 1904), pp. 411–21; M. S. M., "Torgovyi obzor," ibid., no. 21 (23 May 1904), p. 437.

40. Luigi Villari, *Russia Under the Great Shadow* (London, 1905), pp. 59, 61, 253, 263, 301.

41. Chermenskii, p. 28.

42. Laverychev, *Po tu storonu barrikad*, p. 26.

43. V. Ia. Laverychev, "Moskovskie promyshlenniki v gody pervoi russkoi revoliutsii," *Vestnik Moskovskogo Universiteta*, ser. 9, no. 3 (May–June 1964): 39.

44. D. Iu. El'kina, "Moskovskaia burzhuaziia i rabochii vopros v gody pervoi

russkoi revoliutsii (1905–1907)," *Uchenye zapiski kafedra istorii SSSR (Moskovskii gosudarstvennyi pedagogicheskii institut im. V. I. Lenina)* 35 (1946): 119; Laverychev, *Po tu storonu barrikad*, pp. 30–31.

45. Laverychev, *Po tu storonu barrikad*, pp. 36, 39–40.

46. El'kina, p. 118; Chermenskii, pp. 67, 73–74.

47. Laverychev, *Po tu storonu barrikad*, pp. 37–39; Chermenskii, pp. 84–88.

48. Quoted in El'kina, p. 124.

49. Laverychev, *Po tu storonu barrikad*, p. 55; Livshin, p. 110.

50. See Buryshkin, pp. 77–78, 266–67. The basic divergency of views between the Moscow *molodye* and their apolitical colleagues in St. Petersburg culminated in 1917 in the formation of a second national association of industry and trade as a rival to the existing association, dominated by Petersburg interests. The new group was called the All-Russian Union of Trade and Industry, and its first (and only) president was P. P. Riabushinskii. This new grouping was primarily political rather than "professional" in its goals. Laverychev, *Po tu storonu barrikad*, p. 182ff.

51. Laverychev, *Po tu storonu barrikad*, p. 30.

52. "Zapiska gruppy fabrikantov i zavodchikov tsentral'nogo raiona," *Izvestiia Obshchestva dlia sodeistviia uluchsheniiu i razvitiiu manufakturnoi promyshlennosti* 9, no. 2 (1905): 77–78. The January note may be found in "Zapiska moskovskikh fabrikantov," *Russkie vedomosti*, 28 Jan. 1905. The summary of the content of these notes in the text is derived from these two sources. All quotations are from the February note except where otherwise indicated in the text.

53. Vishniakov, 3: 96; *Vospominaniia I. I. Ianzhula*, 1: 175.

54. El'kina, pp. 126–27.

55. "Kommissiia po rabochemu voprosu pri moskovskom birzhevom komitete," *Russkie vedomosti*, 6 April 1905.

56. El'kina assumed that the Moscow industrialists were planning to create "yellow unions"—an assumption which seems entirely justified. El'kina, p. 127.

57. Laverychev, *Po tu storonu barrikad*, p. 29. In fact, they were in many cases forced to make concessions. The average monthly wage at the Prokhorov factory, for instance, rose gradually from 14 rubles in May 1905 to 19 rubles and 54 kopeks in November. El'kina, p. 126.

58. "Zapiska gruppy fabrikantov," p. 76.

59. *Promyshlennyi mir*, no. 17 (8 May 1905), p. 360.

60. El'kina, pp. 132–33.

61. *Russkie vedomosti*, 14 May 1905.

62. Quoted in *Promyshlennyi mir*, no. 19 (22 May 1905), p. 404.

63. Quoted in ibid.

64. When the Moscow duma, under the prodding of P. P. Riabushinskii and other young businessmen, passed a resolution in January calling for legalization of strikes and unions, Naidenov sent a note to the Ministry of Finance declaring that the views expressed in the duma resolution "cannot be accepted as the opinion of the industrial *soslovie*." (Quoted in Chermenskii, p. 83.) There is no evidence that Naidenov ever changed his mind on this question.

65. The various resolutions and petitions emanating from Russian industrialists in 1905 nearly unanimously endorsed the views of the Moscow *molodye* on the labor question—their unanimity testifying to an emerging consensus on this question among Russia's business elite. See K. Pazhitnov, "Ocherk razvitiia burzhuazii v Rossii," *Obrazovanie* 16, no. 3 (1907): 65–67.

From a generational standpoint, it is worth noting that G. A. Krestovnikov, S. I. Chetverikov, and N. A. Alekseev—the three most progressive members of the older generation of the 1890s—were all born in the 1850s. They were thus among the youngest members of their own generation and were better able to find some common ground with the younger generation. In a sense, they may be seen as a bridge between the older and younger generations, being not quite so conservative as most members of the older generation while still not quite as liberal as the leading spokesmen for the younger generation. Krestovnikov's election as president of the Exchange Committee after Naidenov's death at the end of 1905 can be explained in part by the fact that he occupied a middle ground between the two generations and was therefore perhaps the only candidate acceptable to both factions within the elite.

The reason for the more progressive views of these three men was partly that they felt the impact of the intellectual ferment of the 1860s and 1870s at a more malleable age than did most members of their generation. Chetverikov noted that he had been "born in 1850, and, consequently, brought up entirely during the period of enthusiasm and enlightenment in Russian society in the 1860s, which was reflected in the whole structure of our family life." Thoroughly imbued with enlightened ideas by the time he graduated from the gymnasium in 1869, Chetverikov, now sent off to the family factory to learn the business, reacted with horror to the conditions that he found there. "I was shaken to the depths of my young soul," he later wrote, "by the whole structure and all the conditions of life at the Gorodishchenskaia factory" (Chetverikov, p. 8). His willingness to accept changes in the factory order and, later, political reform no doubt stemmed largely from these early experiences.

66. For instance, *Russkie vedomosti*, until late in the year a consistent supporter of working-class demands, was finally provoked by the economic chaos of the final months of 1905 to criticize the workers' movement. The paper blamed the current economic instability primarily on incessant strikes, during which the workers put forth impossible demands. "Even the complete abolition of profits for the employer," it commented, "will still not create the possibility of immediately fulfilling everything that the workers demand." The paper argued that the demand for immediate introduction of the eight-hour day was unrealistic and further defended industrialists who had shut down their factories, stating that they had no intention of acting as "provocateurs" but were forced to take this step by the economic chaos created largely by the workers themselves. *Russkie vedomosti*, 20 Nov. 1905.

67. Leopold Haimson, "The Problem of Social Stability in Urban Russia, 1905–1917," in Michael Cherniavsky, ed., *The Structure of Russian History: Interpretive Essays* (New York, 1970), p. 348.

68. Rakshanin, "Po russkim fabrikam," *Novosti*, 20 Feb. 1894.

69. Tikhonov, p. 192.

70. Ibid., pp. 202–6.

71. Chetverikov, p. 18.

72. *Materialy k istorii prokhorovskoi manufaktury*, pp. 286–87; *Tovarishchestvo manufaktur Ivana Konovalova*, p. 50.

73. T. Von Laue, "Russian Peasants in the Factory, 1892–1904," *Journal of Economic History* 21, no. 1 (March 1961): 71–80.

74. *Morozovskaia stachka 1885–1935 g. Sbornik statei, dokumentov i vospominanii* (Moscow, 1935), p. 63.

BIBLIOGRAPHY

NEWSPAPERS AND JOURNALS

Birzhevye vedomosti. 1893.
*Izvestiia Obshchestva dlia sodeistviia uluchsheniiu i razvitiiu manufakturnoi pro-
myshlennosti.* 1905.
Moskovskie vedomosti. 1893, 1896, 1900, 1904, 1905.
Novoe vremia. 1893, 1896, 1899, 1900, 1903, 1904.
Novosti i birzhevye vedomosti. 1889–1904.
Promyshlennyi mir. 1899–1905.
Russkie vedomosti. 1893, 1898, 1900, 1903, 1904, 1905.
Russkoe obozrenie. 1890–1894.
S.-Peterburgskie vedomosti. 1892.

PRIMARY MATERIALS

Astrov, N. I. *Vospominaniia.* Paris, 1941.
Atava, Sergei. "Oskudenie (Ocherki, zemetki i razmyshleniia tambov-
skogo pomeshchika)." *Otechestvennye zapiski* 249 (1880): 207–26.
Av'erino, N. "Moi vospominaniia o P. I. Chaikovskom." *Vozrozhdenie*, no.
16 (1951), pp. 97–106.
Belousov, Ivan. *Ushedshaia Moskva. Zapiski po lichnym vospominaniiam s na-
chala 1870 godov.* Moscow, n.d.
Botkina, A. P. *Pavel Mikhailovich Tret'iakov v zhizni i iskusstve.* Moscow,
1951.
Briusov, Valerii. *Iz moei zhizni. Moia iunost'. Pamiati.* Moscow, 1927.
Buryshkin, P. A. *Moskva kupecheskaia.* New York, 1954.

Chaliapine, Fiodor. *Pages de ma vie.* Translated by H. Pernot. Paris, 1927.
Chetverikov, S. I. *Bezvozvratno ushedshaia Rossiia. Neskol'ko stranits iz knigi moei zhizni.* Berlin, n.d.
———. *Istoriia vozniknoveniia i razvitiia gorodishchenskoi sukonnoi fabriki.* Moscow, 1918.
Chicherin, B. N. *Vospominaniia Borisa Nikolaevicha Chicherina. Zemstvo i moskovskaia duma.* Moscow, 1934.
Dnevnik A. S. Suvorina. Moscow, 1923.
Fet, A. *Moi vospominaniia 1848–1889.* 2 vols. Moscow, 1890.
Golitsyn, V. "Moskva v semidesiatykh godakh." *Golos minuvshego,* nos. 5–12 (1919), pp. 111–62.
Gor'kii, M. *Literaturnye portrety.* Moscow, 1959.
Gvozdev, S. *Zapiski fabrichnogo inspektora (iz nabliudenii i praktiki v period 1894–1908 gg.).* Moscow, 1911.
Ianzhul, I. I. *Iz vospominanii i perepiski fabrichnogo inspektora pervogo prizyva. Materialy dlia istorii russkogo rabochego voprosa i fabrichnogo zakonodatel'stva.* St. Petersburg, 1907.
———. *Vospominaniia I. I. Ianzhula o perezhitom i vidennom v 1864–1909 gg.* 2 vols. St. Petersburg, 1910–1911.
Iz zapisnoi knizhki A. P. Bakhrushina. Kto chto sobiraet. Moscow, 1916.
Kizevetter, A. A. *Na rubezhe dvukh stoletii (Vospominaniia 1881–1914).* Prague, 1929.
Kokorev. V. A. "Ekonomicheskie provaly po vospominaniiam s 1837 goda." *Russkii arkhiv,* no. 2 (1887), bk. 1, pp. 245–79; no. 3 (1887), bk. 1, pp. 369–82; no. 4 (1887), bk. 2, pp. 503–14; no. 5 (1887), bk. 2, pp. 130–44; no. 6 (1887), bk. 2, pp. 263–72; no. 7 (1887), bk. 3, pp. 394–416.
———. "Vospominaniia davnoproshedshego." *Russkii arkhiv,* no. 9 (1885), bk. 3, pp. 154–57; no. 10 (1887), bk. 3, pp. 263–72.
Korsh, F. E. "Iz vospominanii o T. N. Granovskom." *Golos minuvshego,* no. 7 (1913), pp. 160–73.
Kozlinina, E. I. *Za polveka, 1862–1912. Vospominaniia, ocherki i kharakteristiki.* Moscow, 1913.
K. P. Pobedonostsev i ego korrespondenty. Pis'ma i zapiski. Vol 1. Moscow, 1923.
Kratkii obzor uchrezhdenii kul'turno-prosvetitel'nykh i po okhrane zdorov'ia rabochikh i sluzhashchikh pri fabrikakh Tovarishchestva manufaktur Ivana Konovalova s synom. Moscow, 1913.
Kratkoe opisanie bumagopriadil'noi i tkatskoi fabriki prinadlezhashchei Tovarishchestvu egor'evskoi bumagopriadil'noi fabriki brat'ev A. i G. Khludovykh. Moscow, 1900.
K stoletiiu chainoi firmy "V. Perlov s synov'iami" (1787 g.–1887 g.). Istoriko-statisticheskii ocherk. Moscow, 1897.

Lensen, George Alexander, ed. *Revelations of a Russian Diplomat: The Memoirs of Dmitrii I. Abrikossow*. Seattle, 1964.

Mamontov, V. S. *Vospominaniia o russkikh khudozhnikakh (Abramtsevskii khudozhestvennyi kruzhok)*. Moscow, 1950.

Materialy k istorii prokhorovskoi trekhgornoi manufaktury i torgovo-promyshlennoi deiatel'nosti sem'i Prokhorovykh gody 1799–1915. Moscow, n.d.

Mel'gunov, S. P. *Vospominaniia i dnevniki*. Vol. 1. Paris, 1964.

Miliukov, Paul. *Political Memoirs, 1905–1917*. Edited by Arthur P. Mendel. Translated by Carl Goldberg. Ann Arbor, 1967.

———. *Vospominaniia (1859–1917)*. Vol. 1. New York, 1955.

Morozov, M. A. [Mikhail Iu'rev]. *Karl Piatyi i ego vremia*. Moscow, 1894.

———. *Moi pis'ma (4-go dekabria 1893 goda—15 maia 1894 goda)*. Moscow, 1895.

———. *Spornye voprosy zapadno-evropeiskoi istoricheskoi nauki*. Moscow, 1894.

Naidenov, Nikolai. *Vospominaniia o vidennom, slyshannom i ispytannom*. 2 vols. Moscow, 1903–1905.

Naumov, A. N. *Iz utselevshikh vospominanii 1868–1917*. 2 vols. New York, 1954–1955.

Nemirovitch-Dantchenko, Vladimir. *My Life in the Russian Theatre*. Translated by John Cournos. Boston, 1936.

Obzor sel'sko-khoziaistvennoi fermy Tovarishchestvo manufaktur Anny Krasil'shchikovoi s synov'iami v s. Rodnikakh, kostromskoi gub. Shuia, 1913.

Pavlov, F. *Za desiat' let praktiki (Otryvki vospominanii, vpechatlenii i nabliudenii iz fabrichnoi zhizni)*. Moscow, 1901.

Piatidesiatiletie bumago-priadil'noi fabriki, nyne prinadlezhashchei vysochaishe utverzhdennomu Tovarishchestvu egor'evskoi bumago-priadil'noi fabriki brat'ev A. i G. Khludovykh. Moscow, 1895.

Polenova, N. V. *Abramtsevo. Vospominaniia*. Moscow, 1922.

Polunin, Vladimir. *Three Generations: Family Life in Russia, 1845–1902*. Translated by A. F. Birch-Jones. London, 1957.

Prokhorovskaia trekhgornaia manufaktura v Moskve, 1799–1899. Istoriko-statisticheskii ocherk. Moscow, 1900.

Promyshlennoe i torgovoe tovarishchestvo br. A. i N. Mamontovykh v Moskve 1854–1909. Moscow, n.d.

Rabenek, L. "Moskva i eia 'khoziaeva' (Vremeni do pervoi mirovoi voiny 1914 g.)." *Vozrozhdenie*, no. 105 (1960), pp. 101–4.

———. "Moskva vremeni do pervoi mirovoi voiny." *Vozrozhdenie*, no. 107 (1960), pp. 101–12.

Riabushinskii, Vladimir. "Kupechestvo moskovskoe." *Den' russkogo rabenek* 18 (April 1951):168–89.

Rybnikova, M. A. *Gorbovskaia khronika po arkhivu sem'i Shchukinykh*. Moscow, 1919.

Semeinaia khronika Krestovnikovykh. 3 vols. Moscow, 1903–1904.

Shchepkina, Aleksandra Vladimirovna. *Vospominaniia.* Moscow, 1915.

Shcherbatov, S. A. "Moskovskie metsenaty. Iz vospominanii." *Sovremennye zapiski* 67 (1938):158–71.

Shchukinskii sbornik. Vol. 10. Moscow, 1912.

Slonov, I. A. *Iz zhizni torgovoi Moskvy (Polveka nazad).* Moscow, 1914.

Stanislavsky, Constantin. *My Life in Art.* Translated by J. J. Robbins. Boston, 1935.

Stenograficheskie otchety o sobraniiakh moskovskoi gorodskoi dumy. 17 vols. Moscow, 1889–1905.

Tikhonov, A. N. [Serebrov, Aleksandr]. *Vremia i liudi. Vospominaniia, 1898–1905.* Moscow, 1955.

Torgovoe i promyshlennoe delo Riabushinskikh. Moscow, 1913.

Torgovo-promyshlennaia deiatel'nost' firmy Ivana Aleksandrovicha Konovalova, 1812–1896 g. (Istoriko-statisticheskii ocherk). Moscow, 1896.

Tovarishchestvo manufaktur Ivana Konovalova s synom, 1812–1912 g. Kratkii istoricheskii ocherk. Moscow, n.d.

Trubetskoi, Evgenii. *Iz proshlogo.* Vienna, n.d.

———. *Vospominaniia.* Sofia, 1922.

Trudy Torgovo-promyshlennogo s"ezda 1896 g. v Nizhnem-Novgorode. 8 vols. St. Petersburg, 1897.

Vospominaniia D. Nikiforova. Moskva v tsarstvovanie Imperatora Aleksandra II. Moscow, 1904.

Vospominaniia P. I. Shchukin. Vols. 3 and 4. Moscow, 1912.

Vishniakov, N. *Svedeniia o kupcheskom rode Vishniakovykh (s 1848–1854 g.).* 3 vols. Moscow, 1903–1911.

Witte, S. Iu. *Vospominaniia. Tsarstvovanie Nikolaia II.* Vol. 2. 2nd. ed. Berlin, 1922.

Volkova, Anna Ivanovna. *Vospominaniia, dnevnik i stat'i.* Edited by Ch. Vetrinskii. Nizhnii Novgorod, 1913.

Ziloti, V. P. *V dome Tret'iakova.* New York, 1954.

SECONDARY MATERIALS

Books and Dissertations

Akademiia Nauk SSSR. Institut Istorii. *Istoriia Moskvy.* Vol. 4: *Period promyshlennogo kapitalizma.* Vol. 5: *Period imperializma i burzhuazno-demokraticheskikh revoliutsii.* Moscow, 1945–1955.

Beliajeff, Anton Serge. "The Rise of the Old Orthodox Merchants of Moscow, 1771–1894." Ph.D. dissertation, Syracuse University, 1975.

Bendix, Reinhard. *Work and Authority in Industry: Ideologies of Management in the Course of Industrialization.* New York, 1963.

Berlin, P. A. *Russkaia burzhuaziia v staroe i novoe vremia*. Moscow, 1922.

Bill, Valentine T. *The Forgotten Class: The Russian Bourgeoisie from the Earliest Beginnings to 1900*. New York, 1959.

Blackwell, William L. *The Beginnings of Russian Industrialization, 1800–1860*. Princeton, 1968.

Borisova, E. A., and Kazhdan, T. P. *Russkaia arkhitetktura kontsa XIX— nachala XX veka*. Moscow, 1971.

Chermenskii, E. D. *Burzhuaziia i tsarizm v pervoi russkoi revoliutsii*. 2nd ed. Moscow, 1970.

Diakin, V. S. *Russkaia burzhuaziia i tsarizm v gody pervoi mirovoi voiny (1914–1917)*. Leningrad, 1967.

Dukes, Paul. *Catherine the Great and the Russian Nobility: A Study Based on the Materials of the Legislative Commission of 1767*. Cambridge, Eng., 1967.

Elishev, A. I. *Dvorianskoe delo. Sbornik statei*. Moscow, 1898.

Fal'kovskii, N. I. *Moskva v istorii tekhniki*. Moscow, 1950.

Gately, Michael Owen. "The Development of the Russian Cotton Textile Industry in the Pre-Revolutionary Years, 1861–1913." Ph.D. dissertation, University of Kansas, 1968.

Gerschenkron, Alexander. *Europe in the Russian Mirror: Four Lectures in Economic History*. Cambridge, Eng., 1970.

Giliarovskii, V. A. *Moskva i moskvichi*. Moscow, 1968.

———. *Sochineniia*. 4 vols. Moscow, 1967.

Grover, Stuart R. "Savva Mamontov and the Mamontov Circle, 1870–1905: Art Patronage and the Rise of Nationalism in Russian Art." Ph.D. dissertation, University of Wisconsin, 1971.

Hanchett, Walter S. "Moscow in the Late Nineteenth Century: A Study in Municipal Self-Government." Ph.D. dissertation, University of Chicago, 1964.

Häusler, Eugen. *Der Kaufmann in der russichen Literatur*. Königsberg, 1935.

Haxthausen, August von. *Studies on the Interior of Russia*. Edited by S. Frederick Starr. Translated by Eleanore L. M. Schmidt. Chicago, 1972.

Ianzhul, I. I. *Mezhdu delom. Ocherki po voprosam narodnogo obrazovaniia, ekonomicheskoi politiki i obshchestvennoi zhizni*. St. Petersburg, 1904.

Ippo, S. B. *Moskva i London. Istoricheskie, obshchestvennye i ekonomicheskie ocherki i issledovaniia*. Moscow, 1888.

Karzhanskii, N. *Kak izbiralas' i rabotala moskovskaia gorodskaia duma*. 2nd ed. Moscow, 1950.

Kliuchevskii, V. O. *Istoriia soslovii v Rossii*. Hattiesburg, Miss., 1969.

Kocharovskii, K. *Sotsial'nyi stroi Rossii*. Prague, 1926.

Kogan, D. *Mamontovskii kruzhok*. Moscow, 1970.

Kolyshko, I. *Ocherki sovremennoi Rossii*. St. Petersburg, 1887.

Korsh, E. F. *Petr Ivanovich Shchukin.* Moscow, 1913.

Kovalewsky, Maxime. *La Crise Russe. Notes et impressions d'un Témoin.* Paris, 1906.

Laverychev, V. Ia. *Krupnaia burzhuaziia v poreformennoi Rossii, 1861–1900.* Moscow, 1974.

———. *Po tu storonu barrikad (Iz istorii bor'by moskovskoi burzhuazii s revoliutsiei).* Moscow, 1967.

———. *Tsarizm i rabochii vopros v Rossii (1861–1917 gg.).* Moscow, 1972.

Leikina-Svirskaia, V. R. *Intelligentsiia v Rossii vo vtoroi polovine XIX veka.* Moscow, 1971.

Lenin, V. I. *Sochineniia.* 38 vols. 4th rev. ed. Moscow, 1941–1950.

Leroy-Beaulieu, Anatole. *L'Empire des Tsars et les Russes* Vol. 1: *Le Pays et les Habitants.* 3rd ed. Paris, 1890.

Liashchenko, P. I. *Istoriia narodnogo khoziaistva SSSR.* Vol. 2: *Kapitalizm.* 3rd ed. Moscow, 1952.

Litvinov-Falinskii, V. P. *Fabrichnoe zakonodatel'stvo i fabrichnaia inspektsiia v Rossii.* 2nd ed. St. Petersburg, 1904.

McKay, John P. *Pioneers for Profit: Foreign Entrepreneurship and Russian Industrialization, 1885–1913.* Chicago, 1970.

Manufaktur-sovetnik, moskovskii kupets Timofei Vasil'evich Prokhorov. N.p., n.d.

Mel'nikov, A. P. *Stoletie nizhegorodskoi iarmarki.* N.p., 1917.

Menashe, Louis. "Alexander Guchkov and the Origins of the Octobrist Party: The Russian Bourgeoisie in Politics, 1905." Ph.D. dissertation, New York University, 1966.

Morozovskaia stachka 1885–1935 g. Sbornik statei, dokumentov i vospominanii. Moscow, 1935.

Morskoi, A. *Zubatovshchina. Stranichka iz istorii rabochego voprosa v Rossii.* Moscow, 1913.

Nifontov, A. S. *Moskva vo vtoroi polovine XIX stoletiia.* Moscow, 1947.

Ocherk torgovoi i obshchestvennoi deiatel'nosti manufaktur sovetnika pochetnogo grazhdanina i kavalera byvshego moskovskogo gorodskogo golovy E. F. Guchkova. St. Petersburg, 1867.

Owen, Thomas C. *Capitalism and Politics in Russia: A Social History of the Moscow Merchants, 1855–1905.* New York, 1981.

Ozerov, I. Kh. *Politika po rabochemu voprosu v Rossii za poslednie gody (Po neizdannym dokumentam).* Moscow, 1906.

Pazhitnov, K. A. *Ocherki istorii tekstil'noi promyshlennosti dorevolutsionnoi Rossii. Khlopchatobumazhnaia, l'no-pen'kovaia i shelkovaia promyshlennost'.* Moscow, 1958.

Raeff, Marc, ed. *Catherine the Great: A Profile.* New York, 1972.

Rieber, Alfred J. *Merchants and Entrepreneurs in Imperial Russia.* Chapel Hill, N.C., 1982.

Roosa, Ruth Amende. "The Association of Industry and Trade, 1906–1914: An Examination of the Economic Views of Organized Industrialists in Prerevolutionary Russia." Ph.D. dissertation, Columbia University, 1967.

Sakharova, E. V. *Vasilii Dmitrievich Polenov. Elena Dmitrievna Polenova. Khronika sem'i khudozhnikov.* Moscow, 1964.

Schneiderman, Jeremiah. *Sergei Zubatov and Revolutionary Marxism: The Struggle for the Working Class in Tsarist Russia.* Ithaca, N.Y., 1976.

Sef, S. *Burzhauziia v 1905 godu. Po neizdannym arkhivnym materialam.* Moscow, 1926.

Sharapov, Sergei. *Sochineniia.* Vol 1: *Moi dnevnik.* Moscow, 1900.

———. *Tri sbornika 1900 goda.* 2nd ed. Moscow, 1901.

Shchepkin, M. P. *Obshchestvennoe khoziaistvo goroda Moskvy. Narodnoe obrazovanie v 1863–1898 godakh. Istorichesko-statisticheskoe opisanie.* Moscow, 1901.

———. *Obshchestvennoe khoziaistvo goroda Moskvy v 1863–1887 godakh. Istorichesko-statisticheskoe opisanie.* Moscow, 1888.

———. *Soslovnoe khoziaistvo moskovskogo kupechestva. Istoriko-statisticheskii ocherk.* Moscow, 1872.

Shestakov, P. M. *Rabochie na manufakture T-va "Emil' Tsindel' " v Moskve.* Moscow, 1900.

Sliozberg, G. B. *Dorevoliutsionnyi stroi Rossii.* Paris, 1933.

Storozhev, V. N. *Voina i moskovskoe kupechestvo.* Moscow, 1914.

Sytin, P. V. *Iz istorii moskovskikh ulits (Ocherki).* 2nd ed. Moscow, 1952.

———. *Kommunal'noe khoziaistvo. Blagoustroistvo Moskvy v sravnenii s blagoustroistvom drugikh bol'shikh gorodov.* Moscow, 1926.

Szamuely, Tibor. *The Russian Tradition.* Edited by Robert Conquest. New York, 1974.

Tugan-Baranovsky, Mikhail I. *The Russian Factory in the 19th Century.* Translated by Arthur Levin and Claora S. Levin. Homewood, Ill., 1970.

Villari, Luigi. *Russia under the Great Shadow.* London, 1905.

V'iurkov, Aleksandr. *Rasskazy o staroi Moskve.* 3rd ed. Moscow, 1960.

Von Laue, Theodore H. *Sergei Witte and the Industrialization of Russia.* New York, 1969.

Vovchik, A. F. *Politika tsarizma po rabochemu voprosu v predrevoliutsionnyi period (1895–1904).* Lvov, 1964.

Wallace, Donald Mackenzie. *Russia.* 2 vols. 6th ed. London, 1877.

Articles

Amburger, Erik. "Behördendienst und sozialer Aufstieg in Russland um 1900." *Jahrbücher für Geschichte Osteuropas,* n. f. 18 (1970):127–34.

Annenskii, N. "Vserossiiskii torgovo-promyshlennyi s"ezd." *Russkoe bogatstvo*, no. 9 (1896), pp. 141–62.

Av'erino, S. K. "Russkii samorodok—S. I. Mamontov." *Vozrozhdenie*, no. 9 (1950), pp. 102–5.

———. "Zabytyi (Pamiati N. G. Rubinshteina)." *Vozrozhdenie*, no. 1 (1949), pp. 156–63.

Baltalon, Ts. P. "Tronulos'-li vpered temnoe tsarstvo?" *Artist*, no. 36 (1894), pp. 183–201.

Besançon, Alain. "La Russie et 'L'esprit du capitalisme.' " *Cahiers du monde russe et soviétique* 8 (1967):509–27.

"Botkiny. Iz pis'ma P. I. Shchukina k izdateliu 'Russkogo arkhiva.' " *Russkii arkhiv*, no. 7 (1910), pp. 458–59.

Chulkov, N. P. "Moskovskoe kupechestvo XVIII i XIX vekov." *Russkii arkhiv*, no. 12 (1907), pp. 489–502.

El'kina, D. Iu. "Moskovskaia burzhuaziia i rabochii vopros v gody pervoi russkoi revoliutsii (1905–1907)." *Uchenye zapiski kafedra istorii SSSR (Moskovskii gosudarstvennyi pedagogicheskii institut im. V. I. Lenina)* 35 (1946):111–34.

Feldmesser, Robert A. "Social Classes and Political Structure." In *The Transformation of Russian Society: Aspects of Social Change since 1861*. Edited by Cyril E. Black, pp. 338–50. Cambridge, Mass., 1960.

Gindin, I. F. "Moskovskie banki v period imperializma (1900–1917 gg.)." *Istoricheskie zapiski* 58 (1956):38–106.

———. "Russkaia burzhuaziia v period kapitalizma, ee razvitie i osobennosti." *Istoriia SSSR*, no. 2 (1963), pp. 57–80; no. 3, (1963), pp. 37–60.

———. "Sotsial'no-ekonomicheskie itogi razvitiia rossiiskogo kapitalizma i predposylki revoliutsii v nashei strane." In *Sverzhenie samoderzhaviia* pp. 39–88. Moscow, 1970.

Ginsburg, Michael. "Art Collectors of Old Russia. The Morosovs and the Shchukins." *Apollo*, n.s. 98, no. 142 (1973):470–85.

Gushka. A. [Ermanskii, A.]. "K kharakteristike rossiiskoi krupnoi burzhuazii (Po povodu novogo fakticheskogo materiala ob organizatsiiakh kapitala v Rossii)." *Nasha zaria*, nos. 1–2 (1912), pp. 47–59; no. 3, (1912), pp. 21–31.

———. "Krupnaia burzhuazii do 1905 goda." In *Obshchestvennoe dvizhenie v Rossii v nachale XX-go veka*. Edited by L. Martov, P. Maslov, and A. Potresov. Vol. 1: *Predvestniki i osnovyne prichiny dvizheniia*, pp. 313–48. The Hague, 1968.

Haimson, Leopold. "The Problem of Social Stability in Urban Russia, 1905–1917." In *The Structure of Russian History: Interpretive Essays*. Edited by Michael Cherniavsky, pp. 341–80. New York, 1970.

Inkeles, Alex. "Summary and Review: Social Stratification in the Modernization of Russia." In *The Transformation of Russian Society: Aspects of*

Social Change since 1861. Edited by Cyril E. Black, pp. 338–50. Cambridge, Mass., 1960.

Istselennov, N. "Pamiati Vladimira Pavlovicha Riabushinskogo." *Vozrozhdenie,* no. 47 (1955), pp. 105–6.

Karnovich, E. P. "Sluzhebnye, dolzhnostnye i soslovnye znaki otlichii v Rossii." *Istoricheskii vestnik* 22 (1885):235–57.

Kovalevskii, P. "Russkie uchenye za rubezhom." *Vozrozhdenie,* no. 44 (1955), pp. 5–30.

Laverychev, V. Ia. "K voprosu ob osobennostiakh eksporta tkanei iz Rossii v kontse XIX—nachale XX veka." *Vestnik Moskovskogo Universiteta,* ser. 9, no. 6 (1965):58–69.

———. "Moskovskie fabrikanty i sredneaziatskii khlopok." *Vestnik Moskovskogo Universiteta,* ser. 9, no. 1 (1970):53–72.

———. "Moskovskie promyshlenniki v gody pervoi russkoi revoliutsii." *Vestnik Moskovskogo Universiteta,* ser. 9, no. 3 (1964):37–53.

———. "Nekotorye osobennosti razvitiia monopolii v Rossii (1900–1914 gg.)." *Istoriia SSSR,* no. 3 (1969), pp. 80–97.

———. "Russkie kapitalisty i periodicheskaia pechat' vtoroi poloviny XIX v." *Istoriia SSSR,* no. 1 (1972), pp. 26–47.

Livshin, Ia. I. " 'Predstavitel'nye' organizatsii krupnoi burzhuazii v Rossii v kontse XIX—nachale XX vv." *Istoriia SSSR,* no. 2 (1959), pp. 95–117.

"Nekrologi. Guchkov, F. I." *Istoricheskii vestnik* 131 (1913):725–27.

"Nekrologi. Soldatenkov, K. T." *Istoricheskii vestnik* 85 (1901):378–79.

Nevzorov, A. S. "Russkie birzhi. Otchet po komandirovke vo vnutrennie gubernii Rossii na letnie mesiatsy 1896 goda." *Uchenye zapiski Imperatorskogo Iurevskogo Universiteta,* no. 3 (supp.) (1897), pp. 1–48; no. 4 (supp.) (1897), pp. 49–144.

O'Boyle, Lenore. "The Middle Class in Western Europe, 1815–1848." *American Historical Review* 71 (1966):826–45.

Oreshnikov, A. "P. I. Shchukin." *Golos minuvshego,* no. 1 (1913), pp. 279–81.

Owen, Thomas C. "The Moscow Merchants and the Public Press, 1858–1868." *Jahrbücher für Geschichte Osteuropas* 23 (1975):26–38.

Pazhitnov, K. "Ocherk razvitiia burzhuazii v Rossii." *Obrazovanie* 16, no. 2a (1907): sec. 2, 1–23; no. 3, sec. 2, 59–88.

Pokrovskii, D. "Ocherki Moskvy." *Istoricheskii vestnik* 51 (1893):451–80, 778–95; 52 (1893):116–32, 389–411, 746–62; 53 (1893):112–41, 403–30; 58 (1894):713–45.

Popel'nitskii, A. Z. "Zapreshchennyi po vysoch. poveleniiu banket v Moskve 19 fevralia 1858 g." *Golos minuvshego,* no. 2 (1914), pp. 202–12.

Portal, Roger. "Aux origines d'une bourgeoisie industrielle en Russie." *Revue d'histoire moderne et contemporaine* 8 (1961):35–60.

———. "Du servage à la bourgeoisie: La famille Konovalov," *Revue des études slaves* 38 (1961):143–50.

———. "Industriels moscovites: Le secteur cotonnier (1861–1914)." *Cahiers du monde russe et soviétique* 4, nos. 1–2 (1963):5–46.

Protopopov, D. "O burzhuaznosti." *Zhizn'*, bk. 2 (1899):17–29.

Raeff, Marc. "Some Reflections on Russian Liberalism." *Russian Review* 18 (1959):218–30.

Rieber, Alfred J. "The Moscow Entrepreneurial Group: The Emergence of a New Form in Autocratic Politics." *Jahrbücher für Geschichte Osteuropas* 25 (1977):1–20, 174–99.

Roosa, Ruth Amende. "Russian Industrialists Look to the Future: Thoughts on Econonic Development, 1906–17." In *Essays in Russian and Soviet History in Honor of Geroid Tanquary Robinson*. Edited by John Shelton Curtiss, pp. 198–218. New York, 1963.

Rosovsky, Henry. "The Serf Entrepreneur in Russia," In *Explorations in Enterprise*. Edited by Hugh G. J. Aitken, pp. 341–70. Cambridge, Mass., 1965.

Ryndziunskii, P. G. "Rossiiskoe samoderzhavie i ego klassovye osnovy." *Istoriia SSSR*, no. 2 (1977), pp. 34–52.

Seletskii, V. N. "Obrazovanie partii progressistov (K voprosu o politicheskoi konsolidatsii russkoi burzhuazii)." *Vestnik Moskovskogo Universiteta*, ser. 9, no. 5 (1970):32–48.

Senchakova, L. T. " 'Sviashchennaia druzhina' i ee sostav," *Vestnik Moskovskogo Universiteta*, ser. 9, no. 2 (1967):62–83.

Shchepkina, E. "Vospominaniia i dnevniki russkikh zhenshchin." *Istoricheskii vestnik* 137 (1914):536–55.

Shchetinin, B. A. "Petr Petrovich Botkin." *Istoricheskii vestnik* 109 (1907):547–54.

———. "Revnitel' prosveshcheniia (Pamiati P. G. Shelaputina)." *Istoricheskii vestnik* 137 (1914):230–37.

Snow, George Edward. "The Kokovstov Commission. An Abortive Attempt at Labor Reform in Russia in 1905." *Slavic Review* 40 (1972):780–96.

Solov'ev, Iu. B. "Protivorechiia v praviashchem lagere Rossii po voprosu ob inostrannykh kapitalakh v gody pervogo promyshlennogo pod"ema." In *Iz istorii imperializma v Rossii*, pp. 371–88. Moscow, 1959.

Tidmarsh, Kyril. "The Zubatov Idea." *American Slavic and East European Review* 19 (1960):335–46.

Unkovskii, V. "A. M. Remizovu—80 let." *Vozrozhdenie*, no. 66 (1957), pp. 52–57.

Vigdorchik, N. "Golos kapitalistov v rabochem voprose." *Obrazovanie* 16, no. 2a (1907): sec. 3, 1–10.

Von Laue, Theodore H. "Factory Inspection under the 'Witte System': 1892–1903." *American Slavic and East European Review* 19 (1960):347–62.

———. "Russian Peasants in the Factory, 1892–1904." *Journal of Economic History* 21 (1961):61–80.

―――. "Tsarist Labor Policy, 1895–1903." *Journal of Modern History* 34 (1962):135–45.
Zhuravlev, N. "Iz rospisi lichnykh raskhodov fabrikanta M. A. Morozova." *Krasnyi arkhiv* 83 (1937):224–27.

FICTION

Basanin, Mark. "Torgovyi dom Bakhvalova synov'ia. Roman iz kupecheskoi zhizni." *Istoricheskii vestnik*, 143 (1916):1–34, 321–53, 625–53; 144 (1916):1–31, 305–39, 577–612; 145 (1916):1–42.
Boborykin, Petr. *Kitai-gorod.* 2 vols. St. Petersburg, 1883.
―――. "Pereval." *Vestnik Evropy,* 339 (1894):45–120, 529–614; 340 (1894):5–98, 508–610; 341 (1894):44–131, 458–537.
Chekhov, Anton. *Tales of Chekhov.* 4 vols. Translated by Constance Garnett. New York, 1917.
Gorky, Maxim. *Foma Gordyeeff.* Translated by Isabel F. Hapgood. New York, 1901.
Nemirovich-Danchenko, V. I. *Tsari birzhi.* St. Petersburg, 1893.
Noyes, George Rapall, ed. *Plays by Alexander Ostrovsky.* New York, 1969.
Ostrovskii, A. N. *Izbrannye proizvedeniia.* Moscow, 1965.
Sumbatov, A. I. *Polnye sobranye sochineniia.* Vol. 3. 2nd. ed. Moscow, 1910.

REFERENCE WORKS

Biografii chlenov vremennogo pravitel'stva, ispolnitel'nogo komiteta gosud. dumy i chlenov ispolnitel'nogo komiteta soveta rabochikh i soldatskikh deputatov. N.p., n.d.
Budagov, S. G., and Orlov, P. A., eds. *Ukazatel' fabriki i zavodov evropeiskoi Rossii. Materialy dlia fabrichno-zavodskoi statistiki.* 3rd ed. St. Petersburg, 1894.
Entsiklopedicheskii slovar'. St. Petersburg, 1890–1904.
Golubev, A. K., ed. *Russkie banki. Spravochnye i statisticheskie svedeniia o vsekh deistvuiushchikh v Rossii gosudarstvennykh, chastnykh i obshchestvennykh kreditnykh uchrezhdeniiakh.* St. Petersburg, 1899.
Gorodskie uchrezhdeniia Moskvy, osnovannye na pozhertvovaniia, i kapitaly, pozhertvovannye moskovskomu gorodskomu obshchestvennomu upravleniiu v techenie 1863–1904 g. Moscow, 1906.
Ioksimovich, Ch. M. *Manufakturnaia promyshlennost' v proshlom i nastoiashchem.* Moscow, 1915.
Moskovskaia gorodskaia duma 1897–1900. N.p., n.d.
Moskovskoe Kupecheskoe Sobranie. Istoricheskii ocherk. Moscow, 1911.
[Naidenov, N. A., ed.]. *Materialy dlia istorii moskovskogo kupechestva.* 9 vols. Moscow, 1883–1889.

Perepis' Moskvy 1882 goda. Vol. 2: *Naselenie i zaniatiia.* Moscow, 1885.

Pros'bin, S. A. *Torgovo-promyshlennyi sbornik (Svod deistvuiushchikh uzakonenii po chasti promyshlennosti i torgovli).* St. Petersburg, 1904.

Russkii biograficheskii slovar'. St. Petersburg, 1896–1918.

Shampan'er, A. M., ed. *Deiateli Rossii.* St. Petersburg, 1906.

Shershenevich, G. F. *Uchebnik torogovogo prava.* 3rd ed. St. Petersburg, 1907.

Storozhev, V. N., ed. *Istoriia Moskovskogo Kupecheskogo Obshchestva, 1863–1913.* 5 vols. N.p., n.d.

Ukazatel' g. Moskvy. Moscow, 1866.

Vsia Rossiia. Russkaia kniga promyshlennosti, torgovli, sel'skogo khoziaistva i administratsii; torgovo-promyshlennyi adres-kalendar' rossiiskoi imperii. N.p., 1895.

INDEX OF PERSONAL NAMES

SUBJECT INDEX

-